ROMANTICISM, WRITING, AND
SEXUAL DIFFERENCE

ROMANTICISM
WRITING
═══ AND ═══
SEXUAL
DIFFERENCE

Essays on *The Prelude*

MARY JACOBUS

CLARENDON PRESS · OXFORD
1989

Oxford University Press, Walton Street, Oxford OX2 6DP
Oxford New York Toronto
Delhi Bombay Calcutta Madras Karachi
Petaling Jaya Singapore Hong Kong Tokyo
Nairobi Dar es Salaam Cape Town
Melbourne Auckland
and associated companies in
Berlin Ibadan

Oxford is a trade mark of Oxford University Press

Published in the United States
by Oxford University Press, New York

© Mary Jacobus 1989

British Library Cataloguing in Publication Data
Jacobus, Mary
Romanticism, writing and sexual difference: essays
on The Prelude.
1. Poetry in English. Wordsworth, William, 1770–1850.
Prelude, The—Critical studies
821'.7
ISBN 0–19–812969–6

Library of Congress Cataloging in Publication Data
Jacobus, Mary.
Romanticism writing and sexual difference: essays on the Prelude/
Mary Jacobus.
p. cm.   Bibliography: p.   Includes index.
1. Wordsworth, William, 1770–1850. Prelude. 2. Sex role in
literature. 3. Romanticism—England. I. Title.
PR5864.J27 1989   89–8528
821'.7—dc20   CIP
ISBN 0–19–812969–6

Typeset by Cambrian Typesetters, Frimley, Surrey
Printed and bound in Great Britain by
Biddles Ltd,
Guildford and King's Lynn

For Reeve

Preface and Acknowledgements

THIS book collects together essays on *The Prelude* written, and in some cases published, during the past decade. It therefore represents the work of differing phases in my thinking about Wordsworth, as well as evolving critical approaches to its central concerns. These can be roughly summarized under the three headings of its title: Romanticism, writing, and sexual difference; inevitably, a preoccupation with autobiography runs throughout the entire book. Although the divisions are at times both arbitrary and overlapping, I have found it useful, and hope that the reader may also find it so, to divide the book into three sections. Beginning with Romantic autobiography, theatre, and history, the book moves by way of Romantic attitudes to language and style to considering the role of gender in Romantic self-representation and Romantic pedagogy. The opening chapter and the closing 'Afterword' deal especially with metaphors of inscription and with the status of metaphor in *The Prelude*; focusing respectively on the crossing of the Alps in Book VI and the climbing of Snowdon in Book XIII, they are intended to frame the book as a whole.

The first section attempts to read Romanticism from three different perspectives. The introductory chapter sketches a version of Romantic autobiography predicated on the impossibility—the unreadability—of the entire autobiographical project; it is followed by a chapter on the connection between anxieties about theatricality, representation, and the French Revolution; while a third chapter traces the repressed relation between the emergence of the Romantic individual and the slave-trade in order to raise questions about Romantic history. The chapters in Part II deal with matters of influence, intertextuality, language, and voice as they surface in *The Prelude* and elsewhere in Romantic prose. The first chapter explores the linguistic strands in *The Prelude* which lead towards Wordsworth's larger anxiety about literary priority; the second moves outwards from *The Prelude* to examine attitudes to literacy and self-representation in the writing of Hazlitt, Lamb, and De Quincey; the third uses the privileged figure of Romantic poetry, apostrophe, as a stalking-horse for Wordsworth's conception of lyric voice in *The Prelude*. The final part of the book invokes

questions involving sexual difference in order to argue that the
gender of the poet bears on the figures of, and in, his poem; the first
chapter reads the Vaudracour and Julia episode in terms of the
intersection of genre and gender in *The Prelude*, the second chapter
explores the figure of the prostitute in Wordsworth's and De
Quincey's writing in order to throw light on the notoriously
denigrated figure of Romantic personification, while the last
chapter in Part III compares representations of sexual difference in
Wordsworth and Rousseau, arguing that Romantic teaching has
persistently excluded women from its assumptions. The final
chapter posits 'Romantic analogy' as Wordsworth's attempt to halt
the tropological movement of *The Prelude* and install his poem in
the domain of the readable, where its future reception is assured.

These three divisions are linked as much by their common
approach to aspects of Wordsworth's poetry and issues in
Wordsworthian Romanticism which have continued to intrigue me
as by their overarching argument, whether about *The Prelude* or
about Romanticism in general. Although I would now identify
some of these aspects and issues differently, I have let the earlier
chapters stand much as first written; in some cases, there is a
submerged dialogue between early and later chapters. Each takes
The Prelude as its starting-point for considering the relation
between Romantic autobiography and signification—Romantic
attitudes to reading, writing, representation, language, and figuration. All work closely from a particular passage or episode in *The
Prelude*, some make excursions into other Romantic literature.
Each contains a discrete argument which also bears on larger
arguments—about literary influence or genre theory, about anti-
theatrical prejudice or differing versions of new Historicism, or
about the gender-related aspects of high Romantic criticism. The
actual writing of these chapters occurred in transition—sometimes,
it felt, in limbo—between the scholarly and critical locations
designated as 'Oxford' and 'Cornell', as well as alongside work in
feminist criticism and theory which has gradually come to inform
my reading of Romanticism; as a result, some readers may find my
practice insufficiently historical, while for others it will be insufficiently theoretical—for some too textually enclosed, for others too
eclectic. But, for me at least, it has involved a process of continuous
exploration and rereading that has been energized by contemporary
literary theory. In particular, post-structuralism and psychoanalysis

(latterly, feminist theory) have provided the enabling basis for this rereading. Deconstructive approaches to rhetoric and figuration have also been a continuing stimulus to my thinking about the ideological as well as formal stakes of critical analysis, while matters of history and politics—whether sexual politics or the politics of literary theory—are also often at issue.

The text used throughout—that of 1805 unless otherwise specified—is quoted from the Norton edition of *The Prelude*, edited by Jonathan Wordsworth, M. H. Abrams, and Stephen Gill, to which I am greatly indebted for textual guidance about the complex evolution of Wordsworth's poem as well as for the information contained in its notes and appendices; I am grateful for permission to quote one of these as an appendix here. I am also grateful for permission to reprint material that originally appeared elsewhere—Chapter 2 in *SiR* 22 (1983), Chapter 4 in *ELH* 44 (1979), Chapter 5 in *Romanticism and Language*, ed. Arden Reed (Ithaca, NY, 1984), a shortened version of Chapter 6 in *Lyric Poetry: Beyond New Criticism*, ed. Chaviva Hosek and Patricia Parker (Ithaca, NY, 1985), and Chapter 7 in *Diacritics*, 14 (Winter 1984).

Since this book has been some time in the making, it is difficult to do justice to the many strands of which it is made up and to the different people to whom I am indebted. Among those who have contributed in identifiable ways to its thinking and writing, however, I owe special debts to the stimulus and discussion provided over the years by Cynthia Chase, Neil Hertz, and Reeve Parker, as well as to numerous graduate participants in seminars on Wordsworth, Romantic prose, and Romantic autobiography at Cornell. Jonathan Arac, James Chandler, Jerome Christensen, Paul Hamilton, Alan Liu, Patricia Parker, and Jon Stallworthy have all taken time to comment generously on particular chapters at different times. As the person who long ago taught me to know *The Prelude* and to pay attention to its different versions, Jonathan Wordsworth deserves special mention. I am also grateful for encouragement at various stages by Geoffrey Hartman, whose work initiated a new phase of Wordsworth criticism for my generation of Wordsworthians. At Cornell M. H. Abrams and Stephen Parrish, editor of the Cornell Wordsworth, have both been unfailingly generous. I hope that other intellectual debts are sufficiently recorded in my notes. I am especially grateful to Sabrina

Barton, from whom I have received invaluable practical help in preparing and checking the MS, and to Anne Brinton and Phillis Mollock, who put in long hours at the word-processor. Finally, Frances and Josiah (whose arrival complicated the final stages of this book) have been mostly understanding of the time it has taken away from them.

M. J.

Ithaca

Contents

List of Figures

List of Abbreviations

BNYPL	*Bulletin of the New York Public Library*
ELH	*English Literary History*
EY	*The Letters of William and Dorothy Wordsworth*, ed. E. de Selincourt, 2nd edn., *The Early Years*, rev. C. L. Shaver (Oxford, 1967)
Howe	*The Complete Works of William Hazlitt*, ed. P. P. Howe (21 vols.; London, 1930–4)
Lucas	*The Works of Charles and Mary Lamb*, ed. E. V. Lucas (5 vols.; London, 1903–4)
Masson	*The Collected Writings of Thomas De Quincey*, ed. D. Masson (14 vols.; Edinburgh, 1889–90)
MLN	*Modern Language Notes*
MLQ	*Modern Language Quarterly*
NLH	*New Literary History*
OED	*Oxford English Dictionary*
PMLA	*Publications of the Modern Language Society of America*
PQ	*Philological Quarterly*
Prel.	*The Prelude 1799, 1805, 1850*, ed. J. Wordsworth, M. H. Abrams, and S. Gill (New York and London, 1979)
Prose Works	*The Prose Works of William Wordsworth*, ed. W. J. B. Owen and J. W. Smyser (3 vols.; Oxford, 1974)
PW	*The Poetical Works of William Wordsworth*, ed. E. de Selincourt and H. Darbishire (5 vols.; Oxford, 1940–9)
SEL	*Studies in English Literature*
SiR	*Studies in Romanticism*
YFS	*Yale French Studies*

I
ROMANTICISM

THE WRITING ON THE WALL
Autobiography and Self-Inscription
in *The Prelude*

LAMB'S essay on contemporary painting, 'Barrenness of the Imaginative Faculty in the Productions of Modern Art' (1833), offers as its chief example of the decline in modern art John Martin's painting, *Belshazzar's Feast*. Lamb illustrates his critique with an anecdote about the Prince Regent entertaining at the Brighton Pavilion:

The court historians of the day record, that at the first dinner given by the late King (then Prince Regent) at the Pavilion, the following characteristic frolic was played off. The guests were select and admiring; the banquet profuse and admirable; the lights lustrous and oriental; the eye was perfectly dazzled with the display of plate, among which the great gold salt-cellar, brought from the regalia in the Tower for this especial purpose, itself a tower! stood conspicuous for its magnitude. And now the Rev. * * * *, the then admired court Chaplain, was proceeding with the grace, when, at a signal given, the lights were suddenly overcast, and a huge transparency was discovered, in which glittered in golden letters—

'BRIGHTON—EARTHQUAKE—SWALLOW-UP-ALIVE!'

Imagine the confusion of the guests; the Georges and garters, jewels, bracelets, moulted upon the occasion! The fans dropt, and picked up the next morning by the sly court pages! Mrs. Fitz-what's-her-name fainting, and the Countess of * * * * holding the smelling bottle, till the good-humoured Prince caused harmony to be restored by calling in fresh candles, and declaring that the whole was nothing but a pantomime *hoax*, got up by the ingenious Mr. Farley, of Covent Garden, from hints which his Royal Highness himself had furnished! Then imagine the infinite applause that followed, the mutual rallyings, the declarations that 'they were not much frightened', of the assembled galaxy.[1]

Prinny's pantomime hoax parodies the mysterious writing on the wall in Daniel 5: 24 (MENE, MENE, TEKEL, and PARSIN), not least by its tabloid legibility. In Martin's painting, Lamb complains,

---

[1] Lucas, ii. 228–9.

'stupendous architectural designs' form the backdrop to a similar
scene of mass consternation; the panic-struck dinner-guests read
their doom in a flash. By contrast, the biblical Belshazzar must
summon Daniel to interpret the cryptic writing—a message of
doom which (so Lamb insists) should be visible to him alone, even
if its import is for his entire kingdom.[2]

Lamb invokes the solitary consciousness of Belshazzar as a type
of the consciousness of the artist, to whom a story must be revealed
in a way simultaneously apocalyptic and cryptic: at once demanding
interpretation and baffling it. His objection is to the very legibility
of Martin's painting: 'Not all that is optically possible to be seen, is
to be shown in every picture', he insists.[3] What we look for in visual
narrative, according to Lamb, is a moment of resistance to seeing, a
resistance which here becomes the resistance of writing to being
read. By contrast to the fiery letters of Martin's painting we are to
imagine what Lamb calls 'the plain text' of Daniel 5: 5:

In the same hour came forth fingers of a man's hand, and wrote over
against the candlestick upon the plaster of the wall of the king's palace; and
the *king* saw the part of the hand that wrote. Then the *king's* countenance
was changed, and his thoughts troubled him, so that the joints of his loins
were loosened, and his knees smote one against another.[4]

The 'plain' text turns out to be not so much a clearly legible
warning as a mysterious representation of inscription—'fingers of a
man's hand' engaged in the act of writing. In this disembodied hand,
we might suspect, Lamb saw not only the painter at work but
himself, the writer. Belshazzar's private seeing becomes a representation of Lamb's own stance as both reader and writer; the hand
that writes and the eye that reads belong to the same doubled and
self-reflexive consciousness, that of 'writer reading', or rather,
'writer reading himself'. In this reading, self-presence is always
perplexed by the 'two consciousnesses' (consciousness of past and
present) which characterize Romantic autobiographies such as
Wordsworth's. Lamb, in fact, complains about the absence, in the
productions of modern art, of the readerly introspection and the
'double Time' which he locates, by contrast, in Titian's *Bacchus*

---

[2] Commentaries suggest that the meaning of the message, written in Aramaic and
involving words connected with weights and division, is a prophecy that the Neo-
Babylonian kingdom is to be conquered and divided by the Medo-Persians. Perhaps
Lamb intended a similar message for the Prince Regent.

[3] Lucas, ii. 230.   [4] Ibid. 229.

and Ariadne: 'from the depth of the imaginative spirit Titian has recalled past time, and laid it contributory with the present to one simultaneous effect.'[5] Structured by individual consciousness and temporality, such a moment is analogous to the reflexive *différence* and temporal deferral involved not only in reading, but in autobiography. What is at stake in such moments, which paradoxically make reading possible, is the absence of self-identity—the perplexity attending any inscription of (or as) self-presence.

But there is another way to conceive of unreadability. Because it represents an apocalyptic moment, the biblical revelation rendered by Martin's painting is also coterminous with the Sublime; specifically with the extinction of consciousness intimated by the Sublime, which Lamb associates both with unreadability and with the threat of imminent death. 'Suppose', Lamb continues, the swallowing up in an earthquake, not of Brighton, but Pompeii:

There they were to be seen—houses, columns, architectural proportions, differences of public and private buildings, men and women at their standing occupations, the diversified thousand postures, attitudes, dresses, in some confusion truly, but physically they were visible. But what eye saw them at that eclipsing moment, which reduces confusion to a kind of unity, and when the senses are upturned from their proprieties, when sight and hearing are a feeling only?[6]

In that final 'eclipsing moment', when sight is extinguished and confusion reduced to unity, seeing gives way to blindness and hearing becomes 'a feeling only'. Along with the near-extinction of consciousness and perception goes a suspension of the temporal order. Simultaneity renders the spectacle unreadable. Belshazzar's feast, similarly, ought to be a blur, its message as obscure to the viewer as the writing on the wall is to Belshazzar himself. Our reading of the picture ought therefore to mime the Pompeian earthquake that throws the entire visual and legible order into disarray—and with it, the viewing subject. Thomas Weiskel has identified the Wordsworthian imagination specifically with 'a resistance to reading itself as opposed to seeing', a resistance to the recognition of the signifier as such; in his terms, the representative moment of the Sublime, which is also that of the Wordsworthian 'spot of time', occurs when signifier overwhelms signified to produce what he calls 'a saving resistance to the passage from

---

[5] Ibid. 226.   [6] Ibid. 230–1.

image to symbol'—a kind of word-blindness.[7] In such moments of blockage or impasse, the arbitrariness of linguistic signs becomes literally visible, producing the crisis or negation of meaning which Weiskel associates not only with the Wordsworthian imagination but with the Romantic Sublime. The crossing of the Alps and its aftermath, in Book VI of *The Prelude*, constitute in Weiskel's reading just such a hermeneutic crisis, a 'defile of the Word' or deprivation of sense. There lurks in the Simplon Pass passage, he writes, 'perplexity which seems to resist the light of interpretation'.[8] For some theorists of both autobiography and the Sublime, the type of this interpretive perplexity in *The Prelude* is to be found in the confrontation between the Blind London Beggar with his label and the blinded eye of the self-seeing autobiographer in Book VII.[9] I want, however, to propose the 'characters of the great apocalypse' in the Vale of Gondo passage from Book VI as an alternative site for the surfacing of the question of autobiography in the very landscape of the Sublime.

Alpine terror, by threatening the extinction of individual consciousness, risks throwing into disarray the entire autobiographical project. The inscription of the Sublime—indeed, the figuring of the Sublime *as* (unreadable) inscription—makes literal the collapse of autobiography in the face of the too great visibility that constitutes Weiskel's readerly or negative Sublime. The crossing of the Alps and the descent into the Vale of Gondo could be read as a symbolic representation of another crossing—that of an autobiographical poem's turning on itself at its midpoint to reflect on the peculiar status of autobiographical inscription, and, in so doing, on the impossibility of autobiographical self-encounter. At the centre of *The Prelude* is a missed meeting, a missed meaning—a *rite de passage* that encounters a road-block or moment of blockage.[10] This failed encounter, or blockage before a

---

[7] *The Romantic Sublime: Studies in the Structure and Psychology of Transcendence* (Baltimore and London, 1976), 175, 185.   [8] Ibid. 195.

[9] See e.g. L. Renza, 'The Veto of the Imagination: A Theory of Autobiography', in J. Olney (ed.), *Autobiography* (Princeton, 1980), 268–95, esp. p. 295; N. Hertz, in 'The Notion of Blockage in the Literature of the Sublime', *The End of the Line* (New York, 1985), 40–60, esp. pp. 59–60; G. Hartman, *The Unremarkable Wordsworth* (Minneapolis, 1987), 321–33, esp. pp. 331–3; and, most recently, J. D. Kneale, 'Wordsworth's Images of Language: Voice and Letter in *The Prelude*', *PMLA* 101 (1986), 351–61.

[10] See A. Warminski, 'Missed Crossings: Wordsworth's Apocalypses', *MLN* 99 (1984), 983–1006, for a rhetorical reading of this and other Romantic 'crossings' relevant to the Simplon Pass episode.

meaning that cannot be read (like the writing on the wall at Belshazzar's feast), ultimately spells death to the subject. Reconstructing the original sequence in Book VI as Wordsworth first wrote it reveals that the crossing of the Alps involved a moment of failed revelation for which death-dealing inscription became the figure. After the anticlimax of crossing the Alps unawares, and before the great compensatory invocation of the imagination ('Imagination!—lifting up itself | Before the eye and progress of my song . . .', vi. 525–6), Wordsworth initially inserted a meditation on the difference between the saving blindness of vision and the deathly fixity of the written page. Illustrated by a simile which eventually found its way into Book VIII, that of the Cave of Yordas, the reconstructed sequence suggests that we should read the apocalyptic descent into the Vale of Gondo as a willed attempt to overcome anticlimax, rather than (as Weiskel would argue) the scene of profound imaginative trauma.[11] Here as elsewhere in *The Prelude*, inscription is associated with mortality. Unless both face and writing can be redefined as transcendental, inscription undoes the autobiographer's imagined presence in the text to leave only dead letters. Book VI of *The Prelude* simultaneously makes visible and attempts to evade the limits and condition of autobiography by putting a divine face on landscape, thereby erasing the mark of the autobiographer's death, that is, his writing. Because inscription—any inscription—spells the death of the writer, the Vale of Gondo must substitute divine writing for Wordsworth's own, and a world without end for the mortality intimated by the Alpine Sublime.

Crossing the Alpine Impasse

But first, a question. Why is Wordsworth's 'Imagination!—lifting up itself | Before the eye and progress of [his] song', in the passage with which he chose to interrupt his narrative in the final version of Book VI, specifically *'unfathered'* ('Like an unfathered vapour', vi. 525–7)? The crossing of the Alps is narrated as a moment of temporary dejection retrospectively overcome in the time present of composition with a compensatory insight—a hymn of praise to the

---

[11] See *The Romantic Sublime*, p. 200: 'the remembered disappointment—*"that we had crossed the Alps"*—is in fact a screen memory drastically inflated (if not created) in order to block the emergence of the deeper, more terrifying and traumatic memory of Gondo Gorge.'

mind's ability to surpass the limits of the material world: 'our home, | Is with infinitude—and only there' (vi. 538–9). The Alpine landscape functions traditionally both as a trope for nature's embodiment of the apocalyptic or divine imagination, and as the privileged site of the life-threatening Sublime. Wordsworth's own story is that the Alps obliterate their own materiality with the traces of divine inscription in the same way that the imagination, confronted by something vaster and more dangerous than it can comprehend, yet finds its own apotheosis in loss of bounds or limits. At once overwhelmed by the spectacle of the Alps and yet adequate to it, the imagination sees in alpine grandeur the simultaneous sign and guarantee of its own sublimity—a consoling mirror of its limitlessness. But as Shelley was later to insist, mountains are symbols of the mind's own symbol-making capacity. As such they both console and disturb; 'what if . . . ?' (Shelley's question) is a question about the imposition and limits of meaning. What if mountains really refuse the subjectivity that so powerfully projects its own apotheosis on to them? Where does the imperialism of the mind meet its Waterloo?[12] This is where the unfathered vapour comes in. For Weiskel, the vapour without origin or reference is like a signifier without a determinate signified, representing, furthermore, a moment of 'extreme consciousness of self mounting in dialectical recoil from the extinguishing of the self which an imminent identification with the symbolic order enjoins'.[13] To identify oneself with the symbolic order would be analogous, in Lacanian terms at least, to a resolution of the Oedipus complex and to the saving passage from the Imaginary to the Symbolic. In Weiskel's reading, any scenario involving the Sublime is also necessarily an Oedipal scenario; the claim of the imagination to be unfathered therefore becomes a rejection of the Oedipus complex— hence, a claim to found the self, and with it the fiction of originality (the author as father of his works).

But even without the specifically psychoanalytic frame of reference which informs Weiskel's influential reading, Book VI of *The Prelude* might be thought to invoke a literary father, that of *Paradise Lost* (at once Milton and God himself). How should we

---

[12] For a reading of the Simplon Pass episode in the light of Napoleonic history, see A. Liu, 'Wordsworth: The History in "Imagination" ', *ELH* 51 (1984), 505–48, repr. in *Wordsworth: The Sense of History* (Stanford, 1989), 3–31.

[13] *The Romantic Sublime*, pp. 202–3.

view Wordsworth's invocation to this prior imagination? Surely, as a ruse that attempts to contain inscription under the heading of literary priority or the anxiety of influence, limiting the workings of textuality to a traffic among discrete autobiographical texts named 'Milton' and 'Wordsworth'. Read as Wordsworth's negotiation of the strait of literary influence, the crossing of the Alps yields up the consoling fiction of sublime *agon* between two great poets. I want to remark this reading of *The Prelude* in order to contest it. When Wordsworth goes on to rewrite the landscape of the Sublime by way of the Vale of Gondo (descent, or sublime bathos), he concludes his highly wrought account of apocalyptic unity-in-difference with a line used to describe God the Father in *Paradise Lost*, Book V: 'Of first, and last, and midst, and without end' (vi. 572). The context in Milton's poem is the hymn of adoration in which Adam and Eve call upon creation 'to extol | Him first, him last, him midst, and without end' (*Paradise Lost*, v. 164–5). After enumerating the stars, the sun, moon, planets, and elements, they invoke 'Ye mists and exhalations that now rise | From hill or steaming lake, dusky or grey', exhorting them: 'In honour to the world's great author rise' (*Paradise Lost*, v. 185–8). A sign of the reciprocal interdependence of the elements, mists symbolize the possibility that one (material) element might transform itself into another (immaterial, or clouds) in Milton's Ciceronian natural economy, guaranteeing the stable continuance of the universe. But in Wordsworth's 'unfathered' system, mists destabilize the universe. 'Lost as in a cloud, | Halted without a struggle to break through' (vi. 529–30), the traveller temporarily falters before the mind's powers of resistance to the finite world; the recovery that transforms mist back into water is a metaphoric carry-over 'Which hides it like the overflowing Nile' (vi. 548). Here the (arguably always Oedipal) question about literary origins—is Milton the father of the Wordsworthian Sublime?—gets rephrased as a question about whether the mind's relation to the visible world is ever anything but arbitrary. This is Wordsworth's own question, and metaphor allows him to settle it both ways, giving him access to the symbolic realm (and so resolving the Oedipus complex, in Weiskel's terms), while at the same time appearing to claim that he is self-authored (and so refusing the Oedipus complex). The double movement at once accommodates Miltonic sublimity as the father or guide of a (literary) imagination and stakes a claim for independence. In a narrative that speaks of ascent, descent, and a place of perplexity, the path points both ways.

A Miltonic (self-)comparison necessarily shadows this entire section of *The Prelude*. The aftermath of the crossing of the Alps compounds the allusion to *Paradise Lost* by attempting to arrest its ambiguous double movement with an ameliorated version of poetic continuity, or path regained. When Wordsworth moves on to greet the pastoral landscapes of Lakes Locarno and Como, he invokes his own earlier poetry in *Descriptive Sketches* (1793) in the context of an explicit (if silent) prayer of thanks;[14] in doing so, he puts himself in Adam's place in *Paradise Lost* as he commands winds, trees, and waters to join him in praising God ('His praise ye winds . . . Breathe soft or loud; and wave your tops, ye pines . . . Fountains and ye, that warble, as ye flow, | Melodious murmurs, warbling tune his praise', *Paradise Lost*, v. 192–6):

> While yet a youth undisciplined in verse,
> Through fond ambition of my heart I told
> Your praises, nor can I approach you now
> Ungreeted by a more melodious song,
> Where tones of learned art and Nature mixed
> May frame enduring language.
>
> (*Prel.* vi. 600–5)

'A youth undisciplined in verse', the spontaneous Wordsworth of the first Alpine tour had warbled his praises like Milton's melodious streams; now, in the retrospect of *The Prelude*'s composition, his 'more melodious song' approximates not to nature's but to that of *Paradise Lost*—to Milton's art rather than Adam's artlessness, or to poetry made enduring by the addition of 'learned art' to 'Nature'. The maker of an earlier song of praise, Milton figures as the literary father to whom an Adamic Wordsworth must submit if he is to father poetry himself. This has all the signs of a face-saving compromise. The crossing of the Alps had actually been marked by a more threatening pre-inscription—a writing traced in the very landscape of the Sublime, always prior to Wordsworth's own, and hence disallowing any claim to self-authored subjectivity, but (rightly construed) also providing the occasion for the saving resistance which Weiskel identifies with the

---

[14] See *Descriptive Sketches*, ed. E. Birdsall (Ithaca, NY, and London, 1984), 1793: ll. 80–161.

Wordsworthian imagination. Although it may be tempting to view resistance to reading as resistance to a Miltonic pre-text, to do so is to ignore the deeper threat posed by this writing on the wall.

Undoing the very notion of subjectivity implied by the scheme in which Milton is to Wordsworth as father is to son, (prior) writing not only constitutes the subject, but necessarily constitutes it as unreadable, fracturing the line of literary inheritance and linear continuity. Adam, the Miltonic child, may father the Wordsworthian man, but only at the price of censoring the discontinuity latent in a sublime impasse—its annihilation of individual consciousness, and its threat to subjective coherence. The aftermath of the Italian lakes therefore proposes a spurious resolution to the Oedipal scenario by denying its central component, the threat of destruction. To take the 'unfathered vapour' as a cue for the successful transformation of Milton's power into Wordsworth's not only suggests too stable an economy of poetic elements, but also masks a more dangerous transaction. At the turning or crossing-point of Wordsworth's autobiographical poem, the poet is undone, like Belshazzar, by writing that means or signifies him but whose meaning he cannot grasp, since he is not it, even if his is the hand that writes. Milton is merely a name that makes manageable what textuality unfolds as confuting all claims to literary identity (or, for that matter, paternity). Although a successfully resolved passage of literary influence may be the strait ostensibly negotiated by the crossing of the Alps, the Vale of Gondo marks a disturbance pointing beyond literary selves or identity (the humanistic drama which continues to shadow readings of *The Prelude*, even post-structuralist readings such as Weiskel's) to the identity-dissolving action of inscription.[15] The halting sequences of Book VI—its movements of anti-climax (vi. 491–524), compensation (vi. 525–48), apocalypse (vi. 549–72), and amelioration (vi. 573–616)—enact a narrative faltering or stammering which is both unwilled and (since we know Wordsworth removed one crucial passage from the sequence) deliberately intensified. Like the tumultuous instability of the Vale of Gondo, this faltering suggests a loss of bearings that is beyond self-loss, beyond any account of literary or symbolic relations—

[15] See J. Christensen, 'The Sublime and the Romance of the Other', *Diacritics*, 8 (Summer 1978), 10–23, for an analysis of Weiskel's book which places it, finally, 'within the idealist tradition as a considered, authentic, broken winding in the path charted by M. H. Abrams in *Natural Supernaturalism*' (p. 18).

beyond what an earlier generation of psychoanalytic critics of
Wordsworth would call 'the character of the poet'.[16] Rather, such a
disarticulating movement enacts the perplexity which turns, not on
the adequacy or otherwise of landscape to imagination, but on the
always displaced and displacing relation between 'character' and
the characters that inscribe it.

The 'Characters of the great apocalypse' constitute for Weiskel
the more terrifying and traumatic memory which the anticlimactic
crossing of the Alps serves to block. Before re-entering a paradise
seen again as pastoral (a site of reassuring continuity for the
Adamic self), the journeying imagination of *Prelude*, Book VI, must
confront this terror-inducing landscape and the apocalyptic face
which it discloses:

> The immeasurable height
> Of woods decaying, never to be decayed,
> The stationary blasts of waterfalls,
> And everywhere along the hollow rent
> Winds thwarting winds, bewildered and forlorn,
> The torrents shooting from the clear blue sky,
> The rocks that muttered close upon our ears—
> Black drizzling crags that spake by the wayside
> As if a voice were in them—the sick sight
> And giddy prospect of the raving stream,
> The unfettered clouds and region of the heavens,
> Tumult and peace, the darkness and the light,
> Were all like workings of one mind, the features
> Of the same face . . .

> (*Prel.* vi. 556–69)

What price an organicism ('blossoms upon one tree', vi. 569) so
denatured that woods forever decay, waterfalls stand still, winds
thwart winds, and stony crags have voices, while poets—by
implication at least—fall silent? Is this a landscape of self-presence,
or of death? Just such questions assault the bewildered onlooker in
London, where the Blind London Beggar with his cryptic label
stands as an emblem of their unanswerability, as well as of the
incommensurability of a subject figured as both blind and self-
inscribed ('the utmost that we know | Both of ourselves and of the
universe', vii. 619–20). Or, to put it in terms of Wordsworth's
writing of *The Prelude*, a moment of self-reflexivity holds up the

[16] See R. Onorato, *The Character of the Poet* (Princeton, 1971).

text as the mirror for the hand that writes, then posits that writing as blindingly unreadable; the guarantee of meaning—a subject who reads—is placed in jeopardy. In the Vale of Gondo passage we are similarly moved to ask: what constitutes the subject here, and what prevents its fragmentation in the face of such a (blinding) face? Is the agency that produces the inscription 'Nature' (i.e. the hand of a subject named Wordsworth, or Adam's and Eve's artless hymn of praise), or is it rather 'learned art'—all that has been written before (and that does not just mean *Paradise Lost*)? If the latter, then the writing on the wall inscribes the death sentence of an imagination which the crossing of the Alps had attempted to preserve by way of the incommensurability between visible world and the mind's sublimity. There is only writing after all.

The 'narrow chasm' of the Vale of Gondo can be read as a strait in which autobiography struggles with the conditions of self-inscription. In the passage from the book of Daniel quoted by Lamb, the unsettled and unsettling 'countenance' is that of Belshazzar himself; the writing on the wall unloosens his joints ('Then the *king's* countenance was changed, and his thoughts troubled him, so that the joints of his loins were loosened, and his knees smote one against another').[17] The mystic characters unknit Belshazzar, change his face. They not only warn the king of his imminent undoing but perform it—leaving him without a settled or intelligible expression; as the prophecy is written, so he must be (undone). The disarticulating landscape of the Vale of Gondo contains a similar message for the journeying Wordsworth. For de Man, theorizing the nature of autobiography as a reading effect, death-by-letter is the danger inherent in autobiographical acts. Autobiography paradoxically involves defacement or loss of the face that must be posited in every autobiographical instance, as a specular reflection of the reader's own face. In de Man's words, the reading subject and the autobiographical subject (blinded poet and blind beggar) 'depend on a substitutive exchange that constitutes the subject', an alignment involving both difference and similarity, or what Neil Hertz has redefined as a structure of minimal difference.[18] In this light, the Vale of Gondo might be read as a

---

[17] Lucas, ii. 229.
[18] See P. de Man, 'Autobiography as De-Facement', in *The Rhetoric of Romanticism* (New York, 1984), 70, and Hertz, *The End of the Line* (New York, 1985), pp. 59–60, 233–7.

sublime landscape in which the face of God stands in phantasmally for the endangered autobiographical self, his voice muttering from the crags ('that spake . . . As if a voice were in them', vi. 563–4)—constituting a saving presence rather than the destructive absence glimpsed in Shelley's 'Mont Blanc'. We know that the figure of a face ('the features | Of the same face, blossoms upon one tree', vi. 568–9) overlies the earlier figure which Wordsworth himself had excised and repositioned elsewhere, in Book VIII.[19] In the immediate aftermath of the anticlimactic crossing of the Alps, Book VI had initially invoked a book or written text. This passage, with its simile of the cave as book, unmasks the hidden terror of the Vale of Gondo, not as that of the Alpine Sublime, but rather as that of the letter or 'character' itself. Read like this, the apocalyptic landscape of the Vale of Gondo compensates for the threat to the self inherent in writing, offering, as a privileged instance of writing, *apocalyptic* writing. Lamb's criticism of the too legible painting, the too legible inscription—Prinny's tabloid prank—actually points to what is wrong (from the point of view of revelation) with *all* writing, *any* inscription. What the Prince Regent's glittering golden letters reveal is the fact that apocalyptic writing, however unreadable, is still just more writing in the end.

In the narrative aftermath of the crossing of the Alps, Wordsworth had originally addressed the problem by way of the extended simile later moved to Book VIII, that of the Cave of Yordas. 'As when a traveller hath from open day | With torches passed into some vault of earth',

> He looks and sees the cavern spread and grow,
> Widening itself on all sides, sees, or thinks
> He sees, erelong, the roof above his head,
> Which instantly unsettles and recedes—
> Substance and shadow, light and darkness, all
> Commingled, making up a canopy
> Of shapes, and forms, and tendencies to shape,
> That shift and vanish, change and interchange
> Like spectres—ferment quiet and sublime,
> Which, after a short space, works less and less
> Till, every effort, every motion gone,
> The scene before him lies in perfect view
> Exposed, and lifeless as a written book.
>
> (*Prel.* viii. 711–12, 715–27)

[19] See *Prel.*, p. 304 n.

Transposed to Book VIII, the Cave of Yordas becomes a simile for the way in which London, while alive to the inner eye, is dead (or deathly) to the viewer—yet always contains the potential for imaginatively revivified spectacle. In its original context in Book VI, the passage comments similarly on the 'effort, and expectation, and desire' associated in anticipation with the crossing of the Alps, and on the bathos of experience announced by the peasant to the two travellers who (he tells them) have 'crossed the Alps'. Here the Alps are unmasked as a literary experience, bookish at best—a dead text when crossed in all its literalness. The Vale of Gondo thus reverses, in a compensatory fashion, the trajectory of this earlier passage, so that we are left with ferment ('tumult and peace') instead of a scene 'Exposed, and lifeless as a written book' (viii. 727). Writing comes in aid of writing, reanimating the dead page with intimations of a meaning that always exceeds it, making the definite indefinite and indeterminate. In other words, the Vale of Gondo might be seen as an attempt to cancel the initial experience of the negative Sublime (excess on the level of the signifier) with what Weiskel sees as the poet's Sublime (excess on the level of meaning). This excess stands as the final guarantee of the existence of a meaning-making autobiographical subject beyond or above the text.

In this reading, the Vale of Gondo itself becomes the blocking 'memory' (the screen memory) for the more profound anticlimax that resides in discovering that one's very imagination, or at any rate its sublime aspect, is not only textual but textually produced. Death by writing, the lack of life in a written book, is the defile which so traumatically confronts Wordsworth in the failure of the Sublime to inscribe itself beyond textuality, which is also the failure of the subject to reside 'with infinitude, and only there'. In Book VI, 'The types and symbols of eternity' come to his rescue wishfully, rather than annihilatingly. Because they are unreadable, because they insist on a face rather than a book, they reassure the autobiographer that he has a countenance and a meaning—a shape, a form, a tendency to shape—that is spectral, immaterial, sublime, beyond inscription; the autobiographer can now claim for his mind an interior 'ferment quiet and sublime' resembling that of the dark and ever-widening cave before it quiets. The passage returns us to Lamb's essay, and to Lamb's implied fear that too legible writing signifies 'Barrenness of the Imaginative Faculty'. Textuality, in this sense, stills the imaginary ferment of the Sublime unless it is

rendered as unreadable or transcendental. Weiskel may be right
that resistance to reading is constitutive of the Wordsworthian
imagination, but if one reads beyond Weiskel's own powerfully
suggestive reading to the interpretive issues involved in autobiography, then the humanistic self which still lurks in Weiskel's post-
structuralist, Lacanian scheme becomes visible as a legacy of the
Romanticism-as-(self-)consciousness school of criticism of which
Geoffrey Hartman's *Wordsworth's Poetry 1787–1814* (1964) remains the great monument. Beyond 'the fiction of originality [which]
founds a poet'[20] is the more troubling fiction of Weiskel's own
reading, that of a self (a face) which is—I would argue—necessarily
at risk in writing. Belshazzar's joints, loosened by the writing on the
wall, become an emblem of the lifelessness glimpsed not only in the
Brighton Pavilion, but in the Simplon Pass and the Vale of Gondo.
The Cave of Yordas had to be excised because it too nakedly
revealed the condition of *The Prelude* as the lifelessness of a written
book, and the fiction of an autobiographical self as that specular
phantasm, the features of a divine face—the Romantic humanism
which has continued to haunt post-Romantic readings and theories
of autobiography since Wordsworth's time.[21]

The Characters of Danger or Desire

Elsewhere in Wordsworth's poetry, 'Characters of the great
apocalypse', or writing writ large in landscape, link autobiography
to elegiac inscription. Wordsworth's fascination with epitaphs is in
part a fascination with monumental writing: 'It need scarcely be
said, that an Epitaph presupposes a Monument, upon which it is to
be engraven';[22] thus the opening sentence of his first 'Essay upon
Epitaphs' (1810). Wordsworth attributes to the earliest form of
the epitaph—'rude stones placed near the graves, or . . . mounds of
earth raised over them'—the twofold desire to prevent the violation
of human remains and to preserve their memory. With the advent
of letters, the epitaphs inscribed on funeral monuments fulfil more
surely this underlying desire to assert 'the consciousness of a
principle of immortality in the human soul'.[23] Or, epitaphs attempt

---

[20] *The Romantic Sublime*, p. 203.
[21] For a critique of this Romantic legacy, see C. Lang, 'Autobiography in the
Aftermath of Romanticism', *Diacritics*, 12 (Winter 1982), 2–16.
[22] *Prose Works*, ii. 49.   [23] Ibid. 50.

to defend against the very death they inscribe. They mark a grave, yet (in the fiction of linguistic presence) they 'speak' everlasting life. Wordsworth's account of primitive epitaphs—typically, rude stones and mounds of earth—and their subsequent inscription once nations had learned the use of letters, suggests by analogy the two forms, early and revised, of the 'spot of time' involving a gibbet in Book XI of *The Prelude*. Here, an initially unmarked grave later reappears marked by monumental writing. In the earlier two-part *Prelude* of 1798–9, the scared child, 'disjoined' from his comforting companion and guide, stumbles on a spot

> where in former times
> A man, the murderer of his wife, was hung
> In irons. Mouldered was the gibbet-mast;
> The bones were gone, the iron and the wood;
> Only a long green ridge of turf remained
> Whose shape was like a grave.
>
> (1799: *Prel.* i. 308–13)[24]

The grave mound lacks an epitaph or inscription; its effect on the man remembering the child is also to deprive him of words for the 'visionary dreariness' which afterwards invests the visible scene ('I should need | Colours and words that are unknown to man' (1799: *Prel.* i. 320–1). The absence of writing and the impossibility of representing the child's state of mind both seem to mark the site of a repression. What is buried is at once an affect and a story (guilt, fear of death, the elements in a landscape which constitute Wordsworth's metonymic or displaced narrative). The sign of this repression is a grave.

In the revised version worked up for Book XI of *The Prelude*, the primitive imagination has learned its letters:

> The gibbet-mast was mouldered down, the bones
> And iron case were gone, but on the turf
> Hard by, soon after that fell deed was wrought,
> Some unknown hand had carved the murderer's name.
> The monumental writing was engraven
> In times long past, and still from year to year

---

[24] See R. Young, ' "For Thou Wert There": History, Erasure, and Superscription in *The Prelude*', in *Demarcating the Disciplines* (Glyph Textual Studies, NS 1; Minneapolis, 1986), 123–6, for a discussion of the relation between epitaph, superscription, superstition, and history in this passage.

By superstition of the neighbourhood
The grass is cleared away; and to this hour
The letters are all fresh and visible.
Faltering, and ignorant where I was, at length
I chanced to espy those characters inscribed
On the green sod . . .

(*Prel.* xi. 290–301)

Wordsworth identifies the writing hand as 'unknown', but it is, after all, his own hand that has added the inscription, cleared away the grass, and converted the original site of repression into a sign of memory or immortality rather than forgetfulness or death—a sign that is crucial to the unfolding argument of his own poem. Seeing 'those characters inscribed | On the green sod' enables the faltering child to find his bearings; just so, in a book entitled 'Imagination. How Impaired and Restored', the 'spots of time' passages function in their new setting as a mnemonic for recoverable imaginative loss ('The days gone by | Come back upon me', xi. 333–4), even in a context that is suffused with elegy: 'I see by glimpses now, when age comes on | May scarcely see at all' (xi. 337–8). The 'spot of time' allows the reinscription of an epitaph whose 'tendency' or purpose is now to immortalize—to 'enshrine'—rather than mark the death of the poet: 'I would enshrine the spirit of the past | For future restoration' (xi. 341–2). Wordsworth, in effect, carves his own name in place of the murderer's, so that it may live for ever. But the price of that immortality is empirical death. What we call 'Wordsworth' comes into being by way of the relation between the terrified child and the murderous sign or shape like a grave which uncannily means him; the written story covering that past burial constitutes the secondary revision which a Freudian reading would identify with yet another layer of repression, this time in the form of denial. Or, in the meta-narrative represented by his revisions to the passage, Wordsworth seems to be telling us that inscription—contrary to his own argument in the *Essay upon Epitaphs*—always attempts to reverse the meaning of the sign on which it is inscribed, that of an un(re)marked or forgotten grave. Writing, by a double movement, simultaneously remarks and recovers (displays and conceals) an originating, cryptic, undecipherable death.

These 'characters', then—what Wordsworth elsewhere calls 'the characters | Of danger or desire' (i. 497–8), characters typically inscribed on the landscape of *The Prelude* ('On caves and trees, upon the woods and hills')—are monitory 'Presences' (or rather absences) that at once mask and announce, epitaphically, the blankness and death encrypted in signs. But they do so by doing work, by 'working', as a face might do, in the register of affect or feeling. In the third *Essay upon Epitaphs*, Wordsworth alludes to a more elaborated form of the epitaph as 'an epitomized biography' which he associates particularly with 'a kind of commiseration' (Wordsworth is citing Weever's *Ancient Funerall Monuments* of 1631) combined with 'a concern on the part of the dead for the well-being of the living made known by exhortation and admonition':

> let this commiseration and concern pervade and brood over the whole so that what was peculiar to the individual shall still be subordinate to a sense of what he had in common with the species—our notion of a perfect Epitaph would then be realized . . .[25]

The epitomized biography becomes a direct address from the dead, an admonition or exhortation as well as a commiseration, and thus not only biographical but autobiographical—an inscription which enables the dead to speak from the grave with a voice restored by secondary revision; 'brooding' ('let this commiseration and concern pervade and brood over the whole'), of course, always in Wordsworth an act of verbal repetition associated with the creative imagination.[26] De Man identifies the master-trope of the *Essay upon Epitaphs* (the very one which Wordsworth prohibits) as prosopopoeia, the giving of speech to what is properly inanimate or dead, and hence—by extension—the elevation of prosopopoeia to the defining or constitutive trope of autobiography by which 'one's name . . . is made as intelligible and memorable as a face'.[27] What speaks in autobiography is a dead man; the master-trope or 'figure' of autobiography both gives and takes away (undoes or obliterates) a face. The commiseration in Wordsworth's epitaphic autobiography is self-commiseration ('I see by glimpses now'), the subject of his elegy the unwritten, no longer writing, poetic identity which spells poetic death as well as immortality. If, therefore, the murderer's name engaved on the turf stands in for an absent face, that face is

[25] *Prose Works*, ii. 89.
[26] As in 'Over his own sweet voice the Stock-dove *broods*'; see 1815 'Preface' for 'the manner in which the bird reiterates and prolongs her soft note' (*Prose Works*, iii. 32).
[27] *The Rhetoric of Romanticism*, p. 76.

surely Wordsworth's own, by a primitive displacement or substitution of the dead man for the child who fears death, and who (like
Belshazzar) is undone by it. But, since any face is better than none
at all, it could be said that the murderer whose name is thus kept
alive allows the child to find his own face in that of a dead man; to
find, in short, his own imaginary identity as a speaking and desiring
subject, even at the cost of identifying with and assuming the guilt
and sorrow that properly belongs to another, 'works' the features
of another's face. In the same displaced manner, 'the *characters* | Of
danger and desire' make 'The surface of the universal earth. . . .
Work like a sea' (i. 497–501; my italics); the surface of the earth
works like a face, as the child's face 'works' with emotions (fear or
desire). We are back with Book VI and the Vale of Gondo, where
the tumultuous elements of the scene 'Were all like *workings* of one
mind, the features | Of the same face . . . Characters of the great
apocalypse' (vi. 568–70; my italics). The face of nature and the
inscription of the Sublime (nature denatured by apocalypse) is also
the face of the autobiographer, apocalyptically inscribed in the very
signs of its undoing, its 'working' at the scene of imagined death. By
a sleight of hand, what undoes a face becomes what makes it
'work', both affectively, and as a figure for death. When we speak,
then, of the powerful 'workings' of the text—of the characters of
danger and desire—it is the affect in our own reading, our
identification with the displaced epitaph, that constitutes or 'works'
the text of a brooding autobiographical subject, whose face the text
puts on in the image of ours. We read our own autobiographies
(our own affect) in the epitaph or epitomized biography—the
monumental writing—which constitutes *The Prelude*.

The Prelude reminds us that central to all autobiography is the
longing for invulnerability to death. The child is father to the man
in order to guarantee his continued life. Thus, in Book VII of *The
Prelude*, Wordsworth imagines 'the lovely boy' of Drury Lane

> Among the wretched and the falsely gay,
> Like one of those who walked with hair unsinged
> Amid the fiery furnace.
>
> (*Prel.* vii. 397–9)

Here the reference is once more to the book of Daniel, where
Daniel's companions, Shadrach, Meshach, and Abednego, survive
the fiery furnace into which they are cast by Belshazzar's father, King

Nebuchadnezzar, when they refuse to worship his golden image.
An account of exile, the book of Daniel can be viewed as a success
story in which the aliens at Nebuchadnezzar's court win influence
by sticking to their own values and enlisting divine intervention.
But Daniel is also a book of, and about, interpretation. Daniel rises
to his position of eminence by explaining Nebuchadnezzar's
dreams and, later, the writing on the wall which appears during
Belshazzar's feast. By implication too (so contemporary commentators argue), the book of Daniel suggests a theological trend in
which the mediation of a privileged interpreter increasingly stands
between man and his visions, whose meaning may remain hidden
even then.[28] The book of signs, Book VII of *The Prelude* contains a
parodically illuminated inscription like the one that glitters at the
Prince Regent's Brighton frolic. The actor who 'dons his coat of
darkness, on the stage' achieves his wonders by a similar hoax:
'How is it wrought?—his garb is black, the word | INVISIBLE flames
forth upon his chest (vii. 309–10). If the audience was literate, as
this implies, it was also literal; or else, like Wordsworth and the
lovely boy, capable of surviving this fall into, or fall of, the word as
spectacle—as lie, or writing that covers an absence. A type of
innocence, the unsinged boy becomes an emblem for the poet's own
unharmed immersion in the world of all too legible writing figured
by the theatre. Given that epitaphic autobiography involves a
sleight of hand whereby the poet substitutes a working face for a
name, the image of the lovely boy smokes out a necessary,
compensatory fantasy—that of immunity to the death-dealing
power of inscription. I want to end by pursuing this fantasy in De
Quincey's self-immolating autobiography, *Confessions of an English
Opium-Eater* (1822) and Freud's dream of a burning child in *The
Interpretation of Dreams* (1900). At stake in both, I will argue—
and therefore able to throw light on the interconnection between
writing, epitaph, and autobiography in *The Prelude*—is the status
of the letter itself. Where does the letter engrave itself on the reality
of the subject? Or, to what does it refer?

In his 1856 preface to the enlarged *Confessions*, De Quincey
claims that he had reserved for the final pages of the volume a
sequence of opium dreams, some of which had been consumed 'in a
sudden conflagration which arose from the spark of a candle falling

---

[28] See S. Talmon, 'Daniel', in R. Alter and F. Kermode (eds.), *The Literary Guide
to the Bible* (Cambridge, Mass., 1987), 350–3.

unobserved amongst a very large pile of papers in a bedroom, when [he] was alone and reading'.[29] De Quincey goes on to imagine the fire among his papers rapidly engulfing bedhangings, ceiling, and the entire house, had it not been extinguished with the help of a large cloak. In the 'real' of solitary reading, another reality obtrudes on the text, 'a sudden light upon [his] book', with a materiality only prevented from extensive and fatal consequences at the price of at least some literal extinction of meaning (the loss of a portion of his papers). This sounds like a convenient fiction—the self-consuming artefact as an excuse for non-productivity. But it also resonates interestingly with the 1844 letter to Miss Mitford in which De Quincey writes of the difficulty of deciphering the horror of his opium addiction ('what I cannot make intelligible for myself, the undecipherable horror that night and day broods over my nervous system') and of its relation to his inability to conclude the writing in which he is engaged:

One effect of this is—to cause at uncertain intervals such whirlwinds of impatience as precipitate me violently, whether I will or not, into acts that would seem insanities, but are not such in fact, as my understanding is never under any delusion. Whatever I may be writing becomes suddenly overspread with a dark frenzy of horror. I am using words perhaps, that are tautologic. But it is because no language can give expression to the sudden storm of frightful revelations opening upon me from some abyss of eternity, an eternity not coming but past and irrevocable. Whatever I may have been writing is suddenly wrapt as it were in one sheet of consuming fire: the very paper is poisoned to my eyes: I cannot endure to look at it: and I sweep it away into vast piles of unfinished letters or inchoate pages begun and interrupted under circumstances the same in kind, though differing unaccountably in degree. I am always alone in my study so nobody witnesses these paroxysms: nor if they did, would my outward appearance testify to the dreadful transports within.[30]

This is the negative version of the Vale of Gondo in Book VI of *The Prelude*. Here the face gives no sign of 'the dreadful transports within'. Not being able to write, or a writer's block, is figured as a conflagration which consumes both paper and writing. 'I cannot endure to look at it'—blinding aversion or horror—rationalizes the figurative 'wrapt as it were in one sheet of consuming fire'. Side by side, these two passages interrogate one another. Is the fire among

[29] Masson, iii. 221.
[30] Quoted by H. A. Eaton, *Thomas De Quincey* (New York, 1936), 417–18.

De Quincey's papers a literalization of the metaphoric conflagration which 'no language' can express? Is it a fatal destruction which letters ('figures and words that are unknown to man') can only bury in the grave of the unwritten, or the space of repression? In the letter to Miss Mitford, the conjunction of what is undecipherable and what is on fire—the impossibility of explaining the horror of opium addiction and the impossibility of bringing an autobiography to its completion, however much one 'broods'—suggests that De Quincey is figuring the impossibility of autobiography itself. An unintelligible and ultimately interminable project, De Quincey's autobiography wishfully provokes a conflagration of signs, or the darkness visible of Milton's demonic Sublime, as the figure for its own impasse.

Freud's *Interpretation of Dreams* contains a peculiarly affecting dream similarly involving a conflagration, and one that is also ambiguously dreamed while simultaneously occurring in the material realm. The puzzle lies in determining the relation between these realms. At once metaphorical and literal, the dream is read by Freud himself in terms of the dreamer's paradoxical wish to remain asleep, even though the dream serves to wake him to the reality of an actual fire. This 'model' dream opens the seventh and final chapter of *The Interpretation of Dreams*, seeming to occupy an especially significant position in relation to Freud's culminating discussion of 'The Psychology of the Dream-Processes'. Freud narrates it without elaboration:

A father had been watching beside his child's sickbed for days and nights on end. After the child had died, he went into the next room to lie down, but left the door open so that he could see from his bedroom into the room in which his child's body was laid out, with tall candles standing round it. An old man had been engaged to keep watch over it, and sat beside the body murmuring prayers. After a few hours' sleep, the father had a dream that *his child was standing beside his bed, caught him by the arm and whispererd to him reproachfully: 'Father, don't you see I'm burning?'* He woke up, noticed a bright glare of light from the next room, hurried into it and found that the old watchman had dropped off to sleep and that the wrappings and one of the arms of his beloved child's dead body had been burned by a lighted candle that had fallen on them.[31]

Freud's interpretation does not take issue with the common-sense

[31] *The Standard Edition of the Complete Psychological Works of Sigmund Freud*, trans. and ed. J. Strachey (24 vols.; London, 1953–74), v. 509.

explanation for the dream, namely, that the glare of the overturned candle had shone into the sleeping father's eyes and led him to conclude in his sleep that something was on fire. Instead, he asks; why did he dream at all, instead of instantly awakening? The answer he gives is that, in dreaming that his child is on fire, the bereaved father prolongs for an instant the illusion that he is still alive; the wish that the dream thus fulfils—the wish to remain asleep, refusing to recognize the reality of his child's death—is reinforced by the father's actual need for sleep. The meaning of the dream becomes both deferral and satisfaction; it operates simultaneously in the register of desire (the wish that the child should not be dead), and in the register of need or satisfaction (the need for sleep).

What part does this 'model' dream play in Freud's own unfolding narrative, his interpretation of dreams? Standing on its own as a preface to Freud's final chapter, it dispenses with interpretation in order to pose other questions. Positioned at the point of resistance, when interpretation has seemingly exhausted itself, the dream marks the moment at which explanation fails: 'Hitherto, unless I am greatly mistaken, all the paths along which we have travelled have led us towards the light—towards elucidation and fuller understanding.'[32] Like the awakened father, Freud is drawn to the light. But there remains a central core of darkness; will Freud, as Wordsworth had done during his Alpine crossing, miss the way at this place of perplexity? Freud continues: 'But as soon as we endeavour to penetrate more deeply into the mental process involved in dreaming, every path will end in darkness. There is no possibility of *explaining* dreams as a psychical process, since to explain a thing means to trace it back to something already known . . .'[33] Origins hold no mystery, then, but only what is already known; even death is a pre-text. What remain unknown are the mental processes or structures involved in the dreaming mind, 'the structure of the apparatus of the mind and . . . the play of forces operating in it'. If (as Lacan would have it) the structure of the unconscious is the structure of language—a system of displacements and substitutions—the mystery lies in the uncanny coincidence of the dreamed events and the actual events to which the dreamer awakens, but to which the dream can never, literally, 'refer'. Although the child really is on fire, this is not the meaning of the dream. Seemingly anchored in reality, the dream has all the 'meant'

[32] Strachey (ed.), *Standard Edition . . . Sigmund Freud*, 511.   [33] Ibid.

quality of the supernatural—like the writing on the wall—commonly subsumed under the heading of coincidence, an apparently over-determined meaning in which arbitrariness is rerouted by way of supernatural management or agency. In other words: why *this* dream to *this* dreamer at *this* particular moment in time? How can the coincidence of the waking fire and the dreamed fire be explained when dreams, according to Freud's own theory, are neither warnings, nor intimations of things to come, nor reflections of the waking world? The arbitrary relation between waking and dreaming scenarios, which neither common sense nor theoretical explanations seem able to account for, suggests an unexplored path connecting the dream, not so much to the darkness of the dreamer's unconscious, as to what remains obscure in Freud's own theory—the unconscious of his interpretation of dreams, a place where meaning is missing or missed; a place which Lacan seems to identify with the real, foreclosed as it is from the domain of both textuality and psychoanalysis as an always resistant residue, and ultimately associated with the impossibility of encountering (one's own) death.

Lacan insists apropos of this dream that 'what we have in the discovery of psycho-analysis is an encounter, an essential encounter—an appointment to which we are always called with a real that eludes us'.[34] This missed encounter with an elusive 'real' lies beyond what he calls 'the *automaton*, the return, the coming back, the insistence of the signs'. Everything that is repeated occurs '*as if by chance*'; something has been forgotten, a trauma unveiled in the very fact of repetition: 'How can the dream, the bearer of the subject's desire, produce that which makes the trauma emerge repeatedly—if not its very face, at least the screen that shows us that it is still there behind?'[35] In language coincidentally recalling that of Wordsworth's invocation to the imagination ('Effort, and expectation, and desire, | And something evermore about to be', vi. 541–2), Lacan defines these encounters as taking place in the realm of a *souffrance* that is marked both by suffering and by suspense (as in *en souffrance*—both 'on sufferance' and 'in suspense', 'in abeyance', 'pending').[36] This is the realm of primary process, which Lacan locates 'between perception and consciousness, in that non-

[34] J. Lacan, *The Four Fundamental Concepts of Psycho–Analysis*, ed. J.-A. Miller, trans. A. Sheridan (New York, 1978), 53.
[35] Ibid. 53–5.   [36] Ibid. 56 and n.

temporal locus . . . which forces us to posit what Freud calls . . . the idea of another locality, another space, another scene, *the between perception and consciousness*'. In other words, the non-temporal scene of the unconscious, where the real is endlessly produced as an effect of repetition. Lacan compares Freud's model dream with one of his own, in which he is 'knocked up' from sleep by a knocking at his door before the moment of actual awakening. What am I, he asks, 'at the moment, so immediately before and so separate, which is that in which I began to dream under the effect of the knocking which is, to all appearances, what woke me'?[37] What am I in the space between perception and consciousness, when the subject is unconscious—what or where am I *really*?

Acknowledging that the father's dream of his burning child appears to function anomalously, not simply as the realization of a desire, but also in relation to his need to prolong the very sleep it seems to interrupt, Lacan suggests that Freud positions it where he does as an apparent confirmation of his thesis about dreams precisely because it produces another reality besides that of the overturned candle: namely, the child's whispered message ('*Father, don't you see I'm burning?*'), which Lacan suggests may have been words actually addressed by the dying child to his father in his fatal illness. 'Is not the missed reality that caused the death of the child expressed in these words?' asks Lacan. Is the dream not essentially, he goes on,

an act of homage to the missed reality—the reality that can no longer produce itself except by repeating itself endlessly, in some never attained awakening? What encounter can there be henceforth with that forever inert being—even now being devoured by the flames—if not the encounter that occurs precisely at the moment when, by accident, as if by chance, the flames come to meet him? Where is the reality in this accident, if not that it repeats something actually more fatal *by means of* reality, a reality in which the person who was supposed to be watching over the body still remains asleep, even when the father reemerges after having woken up?

Thus the encounter, forever missed, has occurred between dream and awakening, between the person who is still asleep and whose dream we will not know and the person who has dreamt merely in order not to wake up.[38]

'The terrible vision of the dead son taking the father by the arm', Lacan concludes, 'designates a beyond that makes itself heard in the

---

[37] Lacan, *Four Fundamental Concepts . . .*, 56.   [38] Ibid. 58–9.

dream' (the 'beyond' that lies between perception and consciousness, in the never-to-be-recovered 'real' that forms the umbilical cord of the symbolic realm through which alone it may be approached). What we 'hear' are burning words, words of reproach: '*Father, don't you see I'm burning?*' As Lacan writes, 'this sentence is itself a firebrand—of itself it brings fire where it falls—and one cannot see what is burning, for the flames blind us to the fact that the fire bears on the *Unterlegt*, on the *Untertragen*, on the real'. These words from the grief-stricken father's dream, branding it on his consciousness in letters of fire, also blind him to its foreclosed meaning—to the always resistant reality of his child's (and his own) death, the impossible residue of symbolic articulation. As Lacan points out, the unfortunate accident 'in reality' is the fire set by this voice, heard when everybody is asleep—the father who wished to take a little rest, the old man who fell asleep during his vigil over the body, and the dead child himself, 'the person of whom some well intentioned individual, standing at his bedside, must have said, *He looks just as if he is asleep*'.[39] Prinny's letters hoax his captive guests with the intimation of their mortality: the burning child utters in words of flame the repeated, traumatic intuition of a missed encounter which lies beyond reproach or even mourning, alike for the sleeping watchman and the awakened father.

'*The Word INVISIBLE Flames Forth*'

Shoshana Felman, writing about madness and psychoanalysis, alludes to Lacan's metaphor, elsewhere, of the fire of the Freudian truth which burns its way along—like Lacan's own—by metaphors which consume their own logical stages. Translating Lacan's question ('Where is *the reality* in this accident?') as a question about the reality of the desire that governs us (is it 'of the order of the "fire" of our sleep, or of the order of the fire to which we awaken?') she asks a question which she defines as the literary, textual, or rhetorical question implicit in the relations (or difference) between the discourse of philosophy and the discourse of literature, discourses which she calls, respectively, those of meaning and of madness:

Which is the *real fire*: the one burning the living person in the dream, or the one burning, by metonymic repetition, the corpse in the next room . . . ?

[39] Ibid. 59.

The rhetoricity of the Lacanian 'fire,' but also the rhetorical 'burning' involved in every text, occurs precisely at the level of just such a missed encounter, of an *unarticulated* but dynamically metonymic, encounter between sleep and waking.[40]

Because this question is ultimately undecidable ('since the fire is of course burning in *both* rooms, in sleep and in waking life alike'), its meaning can never be located in philosophical discourse, but only in a literary one such as Lacan's—in the 'blindness' or rhetoricity of the literary text, or the way in which (for instance) 'the word | INVISIBLE flames forth' upon the actor's chest. Lacan's own remark about the Freudian truth 'burning all about us' comes from his seminal essay, 'The Agency of the Letter in the Unconscious'. Starting from the 'science' of Saussurian linguistics, Lacan arrives at 'the Freudian truth . . . burning all about us' by way of his famous discussion of metonymy and metaphor. It is metaphor that (in Lacan's own metaphor) initiates 'the creative spark' which 'flashes' between two signifiers, one of which replaces the other in the signifying chain. Lacan illustrates this process with a line from Hugo's poem, 'Booz endormi': '*His sheaf was neither miserly nor spiteful* . . .'[41] Booz, obliterated by the natural bounty of the sheaf, is simultaneously reduced to '*less than nothing*' by its munificence and transformed into the figure of burgeoning fecundity implied by the promise of his accession to paternity; the poetic spark is produced (metaphorically) between 'the signifier in the form of the proper name of a man and the signifier that metaphorically abolishes him'.[42] This poetic spark also reproduces the 'mythical event' of identification with the father (who, unlike the mother, is always uncertain), by which the speaking subject installs himself in the symbolic realm of language. Access to paternity, or resolution of the Oedipal scene, involves just such a 'spark', an apprehension of metaphoric relations, in which the name of the Father (the proper name of a man) reconstitutes the subject in the symbolic realm, albeit at the price of a natural death. The letter that kills also 'fathers'—gives symbolic life. Lacan's instance of how to read the letter of the unconscious is, of course, Freud's own reading of the letter of the dream-as-rebus in *The Interpretation of Dreams*, where 'the value of the image as signifier has nothing whatever to do with

[40] S. Felman, *Writing and Madness*, trans. M. N. Evans and the author (Ithaca, NY, 1985), 138–9.
[41] J. Lacan, *Écrits*, trans. A. Sheridan (London, 1977), 156.   [42] Ibid. 158.

its signification'. Like Egyptian hieroglyphics, the signifier is undecipherable, resistant to any symbolism derived from natural analogy. Denaturing the signifier, Lacan reminds us that our home is with signification, and only there. This too is the ultimate assertion of Wordsworth's *Prelude*, when the Alpine Sublime comes athwart him in the form of an unfathered vapour.

For Lacan, Hamlet's question is the place of the subject in the Freudian universe, that is, as subject of the signified.[43] Is Wordsworth (to paraphrase Lacan) the same as that of which he speaks? We might rephrase the question and ask: where is the subject of *The Prelude* located? One answer might be that the name 'Wordsworth' is at once abolished and rendered symbolically alive, 'fathered', by the poem's metaphorical discourse, like that of Booz. Another answer might be that 'Wordsworth' is constituted by way of the relation—that is, the gap—between the figure of a child and the figure of a grave, or the non-equivalence of the self-reading subject and his self-inscription. Lacan's own adaptation of the Freudian imperative ('Where id was, there ego shall be') runs 'I think where I am not, therefore I am where I do not think'.[44] The autobiographical subject of *The Prelude* is to be found in the poem's unconscious, which we might call its textuality. By definition, the subject can only endlessly repeat itself in this in-between space, the space 'beyond', which is not an ideal space, but rather the space where reality makes itself felt. The 'unfathered vapour' of Book VI, the imagination which comes athwart the poet as he recollects his missed encounter, turns out to be an encounter with death by metaphor, or the symbolic death which allows his reconstitution as an autobiographical subject. Like Freud's model dream, and like the fire that is dreamed and the conflagration set by a candle, it is at once coincidental and no coincidence at all that Wordsworth's missed encounter should occur in the landscape of the Sublime which Weiskel has identified with the passage through the Oedipus complex. The danger to the subject, the death that is involved in symbolic accession to the Name of the Father, is the triumphant, compensatory apocalypse figured by 'The types and symbols of eternity, | Of first, and last, and midst, and without end' (vi. 571–2). The writing on the wall in Book VI of *The Prelude*

[43] 'Is the place that I occupy as the subject of a signifier concentric or excentric, in relation to the place I occupy as subject of the signified?—that is the question' (ibid. 165).　　[44] Ibid. 166.

announces the death by writing that constitutes at once the impossibility and the possibility of the subject and of autobiography.

The metaphoricity of the Wordsworthian subject (his accession to the symbolic, but at the price of natural death) is precisely a matter of the 'coincidence' of the real and the symbolic, or the literal and the metaphorical realm, which Wordsworth's narrative of the crossing of the Alps reproduces in its own pedestrian fashion. As Wordsworth tells it, the experience is one of anticlimactic 'dejection', a term associated, by way of Coleridge, with devastating failure of the creative imagination. The work of *The Prelude* narrative is to transform this failure in, and of, the literal into a light that never fails (the invocation to the Imagination). Wordsworth insists on the coincidence of the reality of the Simplon Pass with the interior reality of his metaphoric crossing in order to repress the very gap between the two which renders him (like the Wordsworthian Imagination) a product of signification rather than—as *The Prelude* appears to argue—a product of nature. The visible track leads uphill; 'chance', the chance meeting with an informative peasant, reveals that the true path had lain in 'the place which had perplexed [them] first', there, where the road and the channel of the stream had coincided. Further questioning produces, not an answer, but a baffling moment of resistance to the literal import of the man's words:

> Hard of belief, we questioned him again,
> And all the answers which the man returned
> To our inquiries, in their sense and substance
> Translated by the feelings which we had,
> Ended in this—that we had crossed the Alps.
>
> (*Prel.* vi. 520–4)

To these affectively 'translated' answers, which are no answer at all, there succeeds a moment when the wish for a sublime crossing so powerfully negates literalness with the manifestation of metaphor that the dreamwork of 'Imagination' takes over altogether, 'lifting up itself | Before the eye and progress of my song | Like an unfathered vapour' (vi. 525–7). With Freud's 'model' dream in mind, we may now be in a position to reread the question of the father and his place in autobiography. The unfathered vapour occupies the same structural position as the child's burning words, serving as they do to set light to a metaphorical conflagration that coincides with (but is not) 'real'. The vapour sprung free is a sign of the absence of one-to-one causal or referential relations between actuality and dream; this is the meaning sparked by Wordsworth's metaphor.

As we see from the passage or pass—the missed road—that leads up to this central invocation in *The Prelude*, Wordsworth has all along been stalking the figurative aspect of his Alpine crossing, preparing us for the moment when the paths of anticlimax and affirmation will part ways by pretending that it is possible to talk about literalness without necessarily talking about metaphor. Or, the missed reality of the Alpine crossing is that there is no way to distinguish a literal crossing from a metaphorical crossing; all crossings are metaphorical, 'translated by the feeling which we [have]'. The writing on the wall in the Vale of Gondo passage— 'Characters of the great apocalypse, | The types and symbols of eternity' (vi. 570–1)—unveils a face that exists in the realm of dreaming, which is also that of reading, or the realm which for Felman corresponds to the rhetoricity of the literary text; the realm where Wordsworth finds (misses) himself 'translated'. He must necessarily miss this encounter with himself, with death, and with the Alps, since it can only take place in the coincidental world of correspondences sketched by his autobiographical journey. What M. H. Abrams, elaborating the trajectory of Romantic autobiography, has characterized as the long journey home, Lacan redefines as the missed encounter—an encounter that *The Prelude* relocates in the impassable or perplexing passages of Romantic autobiography. These are the passages where 'Imagination' is necessarily inscribed in the apocalyptic characters that spell its own death; passages in which interpretation has to turn from the Romantic self as origin to the always missed encounter, not simply with the meaning of Romantic autobiography, but with the meaning—the reality—of its metaphors. The spark that ignites both De Quincey's page and Freud's dream of the burning child (Wordsworth's 'light of sense' that 'Goes out in flashes', vi. 534–5) is the light that for Lamb should illuminate Belshazzar's feast—that is, the light of textuality, of the unconscious, of non-equivalence between signs and (what we usually mean by) ourselves. If there is a real-life autobiography, all that autobiography can provide access to is the repetition of the real in the symbolic realm of its writing. Wordsworth's *Prelude*, like Freud's *Interpretation of Dreams*, can be read as a sustained meditation on the moments of perplexity— the limits of interpretation—which punctuate its feat of self-representation and self-reading. Like Wordsworth himself, we end by asking, 'How is it wrought?' only to answer, as he does, with a riddlingly unreadable inscription that parodies, in its own way, the fiery writing on the wall at Belshazzar's feast: 'the word | INVISIBLE flames forth upon his chest' (vii. 309–10).

CHAPTER 2

'THAT GREAT STAGE WHERE SENATORS PERFORM'

Macbeth and the Politics of Romantic Theatre

'PASS we', writes Wordsworth in the 1805 *Prelude*, from the theatrical spectacles of late eighteenth-century London to 'that great stage | Where senators, tongue-favored men, perform . . .' (vii. 522–3). The casual passage from 'tragic sufferings'—in the 1850 *Prelude*, specifically Shakespearean tragedy—to parliamentary eloquence subsumes orators, along with lawyers and preachers, under the general heading of popular entertainment; compare Boswell's verdict on the most famous parliamentary speaker of his age, Burke: 'It was like the exhibition of a favourite Actor.'[1] Wordsworth's London is above all a city of performance and play-acting, viewed with the 'quick and curious eye' of half-seduced satire (vii. 581). There is even a touch of Zeal-of-the-Land-Busy in his condemnation: 'Extravagance in gesture, mien and dress . . . Lies to the ear, and lies to every sense' (vii. 573–5). Given the Romantic predilection for closet drama, his anti-theatrical prejudice is not in itself remarkable. But where later critics like Lamb complain about the unactability of Shakespearean tragedy, Wordsworth is more concerned with the power of the stage to seduce and betray. When the all too solid boards parody *Macbeth* by 'Prat[ing] somewhat loudly of the whereabout' of the tragic actor (vii. 461), prosaic reality becomes the assassin of illusion. The *Prelude* account of the London theatre reveals not so much Wordsworth's indifference as the reverse—his fear of being too much moved, and not (as he suggests) insufficiently so. His very sobs and tears 'When, wrought upon by tragic sufferings, | The heart was full' become suspect; 'the imaginative power . . . slept,' he insists, 'though I was most passionately moved' (vii. 499–504). We glimpse here less

---

[1] See *Boswell for the Defense, 1769–1774*, ed. W. K. Wimsatt and F. A. Pottle (New York, 1959), 162.

dissatisfaction with the tawdriness of the stage than unease at
the theatricality of the imagination. It is this unease that I want
to pursue. What are the politics of Romantic theatre and how do
they impinge on another theatre altogether—that of the French
Revolution?

In Book VII, Wordsworth's humorous condescension gives way
to 'More lofty themes' at the point where what he calls the 'gross
realities' of the contemporary stage are displaced by the ideality of
the poet's world, 'called forth, | With that distinctness which a
contrast gives' (vii. 511–12). Recognizing 'As by a glimpse, the
things which I had shaped | And yet not shaped, had seen and
scarcely seen' (vii. 514–15), Wordsworth recognizes his own
imagination. From such half-shapings come the 'Presences' and
'Powers' of his poetry. It is in this moment of Wordsworthian
hesitation between the half-perceived and the created world that
the supernatural characteristically emerges. Hazlitt's Macbeth is
recreated in the same image when, poet-like, he 'stands in doubt
between the world of reality and the world of fancy' and lives 'in a
waking dream'.[2] Macbeth (like the stage-struck Wordsworth of
The Prelude, Book VII) can be seen above all as the type of an
imagination self-seduced and self-betrayed. As with Wordsworth,
what is in question is the source of his 'shapings'—within or
without? Are they real, or hallucinatory and fantastic? Considering
the same question, Lamb later asserts of the Shakespearean
supernatural: 'It is the solitary taper and the book that generates a
faith in these terrors.'[3] The 1850 version of the passage quoted
above emphasizes more clearly such solitary after-effects, 'When,
having closed the mighty Shakespear's page, | I mused, and
thought, and felt, in solitude' (1850: vii. 484–5; my italics), taking
the argument a step further. Solitude, it seems, allows one's mind to
work upon the text: the theatre, by contrast, works upon the mind
of the spectator ('wrought upon by tragic sufferings'). The theatre
becomes most profoundly unsettling at the uncanny moment when
the imagination finds its own shapings realized—represented back
to it in satisfaction of hitherto unconscious desires, like the
shapings of Macbeth's ambition. By a train of submerged
Shakespearean allusion, Wordsworth's half-glimpsed poetic

---

[2] 'Macbeth', *Characters of Shakespeare's Plays* (1817), Howe, iv. 193.
[3] 'On the Tragedies of Shakespeare Considered with Reference to their Fitness for
Stage-Representation' (1811), Lucas, i. 109.

world brings to mind the guilt by association of Macbeth himself.

The source of Wordsworth's playful allusion to the 'prating' boards of the London stage is the burst of self-analytic perplexity prompted by Macbeth's sighting of the dagger. Hallucinatory or not ('There's no such thing'), the dagger beckons Macbeth in a direction which threatens to make the 'very stones prate of [his] whereabout' (II. i. 58). It is appropriate that the dagger speech should particularly have troubled Yvor Winters as licensing not only 'imitation' but 'hamming', since what troubles the speech itself is precisely representation:

> Art thou not, fatal vision, sensible
> To feeling, as to sight? Or art thou but
> A dagger of the mind, a false creation,
> Proceeding from the heat-oppressed brain?
> I see thee yet, in form as palpable
> As this which now I draw.
> Thou marshall'st me the way that I was going;
> And such an instrument I was to use.
> Mine eyes are made the fools o' th'other senses,
> Or else worth all the rest . . .
>
> (*Macbeth*, II. i. 36–45)[4]

The vision here is 'fatal' not simply because it foretells Duncan's murder, but because the representation of desire will cause it to be realized. Macbeth's equivocation (are his eyes 'the fools o' th'other senses' or 'worth all the rest'?) is like Wordsworthian hesitation, permitting the supernatural to emerge—here as an objectified image of repressed desire. Such seeing not only creates the illusion that the world is a theatre for one's desires; it breeds murderous action. A dagger in the air will later cause one to be wielded, 'in form as palpable | As this which now I draw'. It is as if the image, or representation, becomes murderous itself. One might say that while language brings desire home to the desirer, such representation keeps it dangerously at arm's length. If by speaking one's desires one is put in possession of them, desire disowned and estranged, or made 'weird', like the Weird Sisters, assumes the aspect of the supernatural for Macbeth; instead of possessing murderous thoughts, murderous thoughts seem to possess him. Macbeth's self-alienation, the spectator role which he assumes in the face of his own crimes, is

---

[4] See J. Barish, 'Yvor Winters and the Antimimetic Bias', *The Anti-Theatrical Prejudice* (Berkeley, 1981), 440–2.

often noted by critics. But his peculiar disturbance might be said to be an epistemological one, lying in the confused hinterland between imagining and doing: 'Strange things I have in head, that will to hand, | Which must be acted, ere they may be scann'd' (III. iv. 138–9). 'In doubt between the world of reality and the world of fancy' (Hazlitt's diagnosis), Macbeth can only know what he has in mind by proposing the dangerously progressive equation: 'head-hand-scanned'.

Acting, or acting out, becomes the heady substitute for knowledge in *Macbeth*, making performance an estranged version of self-scanning. Too much imagination (so it seems), like too much violence on television, can give rise to a vision that is 'fatal' because it blurs the distinction between spectator and actor. To paraphrase *The Prelude* with *Macbeth*, when the imaginative power goes to sleep in the theatre ('the imaginative power . . . slept . . . amid my sobs and tears | It slept', vii. 499–503), it risks being usurped by 'a false creation' | Proceeding from the heat-oppressed brain'. It is, of course, usurpation—the prerogative of Wordsworthian imagination—which marks the point of intersection between anxieties about representation and anxieties about regicide.[5] *Macbeth* becomes doubly charged for writers of this period—whether revolutionary sympathizers or not—since it at once makes representation problematic (does the dagger merely figure future action, or conjure it into being?) and, as a regicide play, provides a touchstone for 'reflections' on the French Revolution such as Wordsworth's and Burke's. Late eighteenth-century interpretations of Macbeth as a man of feeling—for Hazlitt, a man of conscience, even—make him a man of his troubled times.[6] A philosopher in thought and word as well as a tyrant in deed, Macbeth unsettles moral, social, and natural hierarchies by murdering Duncan. He becomes the victim of fatal confusions between turbulent inner and outer worlds; as Hazlitt writes, 'All is tumult and disorder within and without his mind.'[7] This contemporized Macbeth finds himself in the midst of a revolution which Wordsworth, writing of his own experiences in the troubled post-revolutionary period, called a 'turn of sentiment' (*Prel*. x. 236) and Burke, one of 'sentiments, manners,

[5] Cf. Wordsworth's invocation to imagination—'In such strength | Of usurpation, in such visitings | Of awful promise . . . doth greatness make abode' (*Prel*. vi. 532–6).

[6] See J. Donoghue, *Dramatic Character in the English Romantic Age* (Princeton, 1970), 253–69.

[7] Howe, iv. 193.

and moral opinions'.[8] Though Macbeth is no Godwinian intellectual, the problem for Wordsworth himself was precisely that of testing the relation between theory and practice, between 'the light of circumstances, flashed | Upon an independent intellect' (*Prel.* x. 828–9) and the realities of political action in an age of tumultuous revolutionary upheaval. As Mazzini wrote, 'A Revolution is the passage of an idea from *theory* to *practice*';[9] from head to hand.

Despite the fact that it was among the most celebrated of all Shakespeare's tragedies to be performed at this period, with Garrick, Kean, Kemble, and Mrs Siddons in the leading parts, *Macbeth* became the most demonic, inward, and unactable to Romantic critics of Shakespeare.[10] For De Quincey and Lamb 'the too close pressing semblance of reality' gave murder 'the painful sense of presence';[11] it had to be relegated to a hell within. Closet dramatists and closet revolutionaries alike had difficulty in confronting an undisguised act of regicide; even in Shakespeare's play, and for whatever reasons, the murder itself takes place off-stage, while in De Quincey's reading of *Macbeth* it is translated on to a different plane of reality altogether. But there were other reasons for writers like Wordsworth to fear being 'wrought upon by tragic sufferings' during the aftermath of 1789. For radicals, the notoriety of Burke's *Reflections on the Revolution in France* (1790) lay partly in being suspected of having unleashed the very horrors it prophesied. It is as if the conjunction of theatrical and political concerns in the French Revolution (concerns figured also in the disordered hierarchies of *Macbeth*) became for Romantic writers a paradigm of their own unease about the power of the imagination. Could poetry make something happen, after all? What we witness in Romantic responses to *Macbeth* is not so much anti-theatrical prejudice in yet another of its historical manifestations, as the difficulty of confronting the inherent theatricality of the imagination itself. The relation between Wordsworth, Burke, and the politics of Romantic theatre offers one way of illuminating the nature of this difficulty, as does the banishing of Macbeth's regicide from the stage by Romantic critics of Shakespeare—thereby consigning

---

[8] E. Burke, *Reflections on the Revolution in France*, ed. C. C. O'Brien (Harmondsworth, 1968), 175.

[9] J. Mazzini, *The Duties of Man and Other Essays* (London, 1907), 266.

[10] See D. Bartholomeusz, *Macbeth and the Players* (London, 1979), 98–153, and Donoghue, *Dramatic Character in the English Romantic Age*, pp. 233–69, 333–43.

[11] Lucas, i. 106.

Macbeth to the inner theatre or textual world of Romantic poetry, and effecting a palace revolution from which the reader emerges as the leading actor and the author's only legitimate usurper.

'Genius of Burke!'

'Genius of Burke! forgive the pen seduced | By specious wonders . . .' (1850: vii. 512–13): Wordsworth's 1850 invocation to a tongue-favoured senator not named in the 1805 version of *The Prelude* makes amends for his earlier satire on parliamentary long-windedness ('like a hero in romance | He winds away his never-ending horn', vii. 538–9).[12] Burke becomes both the representative of eloquence in an age as famous for its political oratory as for its political upheavals, and the spokesman for tradition—proclaiming 'the majesty . . . | Of Institutes and Laws, hallowed by time' (1850: vii. 525–6). Wordsworth's famous tribute to Burke revises at a stroke his text, his politics, and his account of the French Revolution in Book X. Such interruptions to chronology from the imaginary present of the poem's composition signal, as critics have recognized, an overflow of temporal, spatial, and literal boundaries under the pressure of affect or imagination.[13] In this case the vision is literally a revision or afterthought. But its concern to rehabilitate eloquence makes it as much a self-reflexive moment as those other interruptions which take the form of invocations elsewhere in *The Prelude* ('Imagination! lifting up itself | Before the eye and progress of my song', vi. 525–6). Now a spokesman for tradition himself, Wordsworth could be seen as making a take-over bid for 'the weight of classic eloquence' (1850: vii. 542) by which he claims to have been inspired in his youth. Burke's tongue is silenced, adroitly, in the very act of invoking it ('thy most eloquent tongue— | Now mute, for ever mute in the cold grave', 1850: vii. 517–18), and the

---

[12] The lines do not make their way into *The Prelude* until 1832, but go back to a pre-1820 period of revision (see *The Prelude*, ed. E. de Selincourt, rev. H. Darbishire [2nd ed., Oxford, 1959], 250 app. crit. and 565); cf. the sentiments expressed elsewhere in Wordsworth's 1818 *Addresses to the Freeholders of Westmoreland*. See J. K. Chandler, *Wordsworth's Second Nature: A Study of the Poetry and Politics* (Chicago, 1984), 26–61, for a reading of this passage in the context of Wordsworth's changing relations to Burke; Chandler, however, argues that Wordsworth was at all stages closer to Burke than I would see him as having been, and that *The Prelude* was from its inception Burkian in spirit.

[13] As Geoffrey Hartman has argued; see *Wordsworth's Poetry 1787–1814* (New Haven, 1964), p. 46.

image of an oak, 'old, but vigorous in age', seems to invite Oedipal rivalry as well as awe from 'the younger brethren of the grove' (1850: vii. 519–22). Though Wordsworth's own conservatism of the 1820s and 1830s is speaking here, the invocation is surely more than a retrospective attempt to make Burke the prophet of Wordsworthian counter-revolution. Rather, we might hear in it a reminder that there had always been in *The Prelude* and in Wordsworth himself an ambitiously public and political voice, as well as the voice of private self-communion.

Historically, the years to which the 1850 revision alludes are those immediately following Burke's *Reflections on the Revolution in France*—the period also of Wordsworth's unpublished *Letter to the Bishop of Llandaff* (1793). The 'froward multitude' of the 1850 *Prelude* murmur Wordsworth's own former discontent 'As the winds fret within the Æolian cave, | Galled by their monarch's chain' (1850: vii. 531–4). The fretting republican of the 1790s would have felt free to use the word 'Liberty'. Influenced by Paine, his letter constitutes another of the many 'replies' directed at Burke; it complains about 'the idle cry of modish lamentation which has resounded from the court to the cottage' in response to 'the personal sufferings of the royal martyr', alluding caustically to the *Reflections* as 'a philosophic lamentation over the extinction of Chivalry'.[14] Written in the months immediately following Louis's execution, Wordsworth's *Letter* not only contains the defence of regicide which is strikingly absent from *The Prelude* itself, but provides unmistakable evidence of his ambition to add another voice to the debate: his own. If not exactly regicidal, it includes a none too embarrassed apology for revolutionary violence: Liberty, for instance, is 'often obliged to borrow the very arms of despotism' to overthrow a despot, 'and in order to reign in peace must establish herself by violence'.[15] Clearly, Wordsworth had once believed that the end might justify the means; his later account of the French Revolution must take some of its distressful colour from the earlier views which he had disowned. He himself came tantalizingly close to witnessing 'the personal sufferings of the royal martyr', if not the martyrdom itself, as he returned to Paris at the very moment (September 1792) when Louis was imprisoned in

---

[14] *Prose Works*, i. 32, 35; for the date of the *Letter*, see ibid. 19–21.
[15] Ibid. 33. But cf. his changed position in June 1794: 'I am a determined enemy to every species of violence'; see *EY* 124.

the Temple. Having just missed the storming of the Tuileries and
the September Massacres, Wordsworth found himself a mere
sightseer—a tourist rather than a revolutionary, and with nothing
to be seen of the momentous events themselves ('I crossed . . . The
square of the Carousel, few weeks back | Heaped up with dead and
dying', *Prel.* x. 46–8). But by the double movement characteristic
of *The Prelude*, anticlimactic incomprehension or blindness is
succeeded by a resurgence of visionary eloquence which returns his
own voice to him as that of another: Macbeth's.

  Wordsworth had written that tragic sufferings 'Passed not
beyond the suburbs of the mind' (*Prel.* vii. 507); in the theatre, the
mind is a city resistant to besieging passion. Writing of Paris, he
turns the city into a book, and himself into a baffled reader:

> looking as doth a man
> Upon a volume whose contents he knows
> Are memorable but from him locked up,
> Being written in a tongue he cannot read,
> So that he questions the mute leaves with pain,
> And half upbraids their silence.
>
>   (*Prel.* x. 49–54)

Unmarked by recent bloodshed, Paris becomes not so much
foreign, not so much a closed book, as mute—voiceless. Wordsworth
seems to want to engage in that peculiar midway stage between
reading and acting, reading aloud. Re-enactment is what the
historical imagination seeks above all, as a means to regain control
over the lost past. In Wordsworth's account, the rehearsal of the
last few weeks' events—also foretelling future cycles of violence—
comes later that night: 'With unextinguished taper I kept watch, |
Reading at intervals' (*Prel.* x. 61–2). Here too, 'It is the solitary
taper and the book that generates a faith in these terrors.'
Wordsworth's apprehension of the revolutionary Sublime mingles
tragedy and history with apocalyptic prophecy. The implication is
that he is not so much 'wrought upon by tragic sufferings' as
wrought upon by himself, and it is the chilling proof of his success
that makes him, if not exactly an accessory after the crime, at least
the victim of his own theatrical imaginings:

> The fear gone by
> Pressed on me almost like a fear to come.
> I thought of those September massacres,
> Divided from me by a little month,

And felt and touched them, a substantial dread
(The rest was conjured up from tragic fictions,
And mournful calendars of true history,
Remembrances and dim admonishments):
'The horse is taught his manage, and the wind
Of heaven wheels round and treads in his own steps;
Year follows year, the tide returns again,
Day follows day, all things have second birth;
The earthquake is not satisfied at once'—
And in such way I wrought upon myself,
Until I seemed to hear a voice that cried
To the whole city, 'Sleep no more!'

(*Prel.* x. 62–77).

The voice is that of Macbeth's overwrought imagination ('Methought, I heard a voice cry, "Sleep no more! | Macbeth does murther sleep" ', II. ii. 34–5). Wordsworth's aural hallucination seems as much the result of reading too late as of revolutionary disquiet. Though his apocalyptic dread was retrospectively well founded (as he would obviously have known by the time of writing), the transfer of power from what threatens him to elevated blank verse utterance installs him in an essentially rhetorical relationship to the Revolution—perhaps, in the last resort, the only relationship open to him.[16]

The transfer of power from threat to poetry might be seen as a means to distance a too close pressing reality. Burke had written, 'terror is a passion which always produces delight when it does not press too close':[17] here, 'The fear gone by | Pressed on me almost like a fear to come.' One remarkable aspect of the *Prelude* account is the lack of reference to the execution of Louis XVI, then only a few months away. The *Macbeth* allusion is the nearest we come to a sense of Wordsworth's complicity—if only the complicity of sympathy—in that regicide. With fear sublimated and guilt repressed, the way lies open to assimilate revolution into the astronomical and natural cycles which make up the traditional connotations of the word.[18] The effect is to naturalize revolution,

[16] Neil Hertz has written of this transfer in the context of Longinus; see 'A Reading of Longinus', *The End of the Line*, pp. 1–20.

[17] E. Burke, *A Philosophical Enquiry into the Origin of Our Ideas of the Sublime and Beautiful*, ed. J. T. Boulton (London, 1958), 46.

[18] See E. Sewell, 'Coleridge on Revolution', *SiR* 2 (1972), 342–59, for some of the ways in which Coleridge (and presumably Wordsworth) conceptualized the term 'revolution'.

transforming an unintelligible cataclysm into a recognizable pattern of repetition, and even into a means of restoring order. Tragedy provides another pattern, and one with special attractions for a Girondist. Wordsworth was a typical moderate in turning to 'tragic fictions' as a way to make sense of frightening reality when a predominantly republican and humanitarian commitment to the revolutionary cause found itself faced by the bewildering ferocity of revolutionary practice. The appropriation of tragedy by the troubled consciences of men like Wordsworth gave them a potent language in which to describe their own powerlessness, or what J. P. Farrell calls 'the struggle between conscience and consciousness' precipitated by revolution: 'While revolution seemed to the men in the middle a bizarre alloy of the ineffable and the unspeakable, tragedy seemed, conversely, a loosening of the tongue.'[19] *Macbeth* not only dramatizes this struggle between conscience and consciousness in a highly recognizable form—it loosens the tongue of a book whose leaves had been mute, and Wordsworth's tongue with it. But this is not all. Though Wordsworth's closet revolution may be an attempt to confine bloody events to the safety of the page ('mournful calendars of true history'), or make the September Massacres trouble Macbeth's conscience rather than his own, the repressed and disowned violence of revolution finds a way to return with redoubled and hallucinatory power: 'I seemed to hear a voice that cried, | *To the whole city . . .*'(my italics).

From his vantage-point in the chronological future of the *Prelude* narrative, Wordsworth might well have been able to claim: 'Strange things I have in head, that will to hand, | Which must be acted, ere they may be scanned' (*Macbeth*, III. iv. 138–9). Hindsight imagined as foresight creates the illusion of terrifying omniscience or guilty prior knowledge. This is in contrast to Wordsworth's actual inability to affect the course of history. By his own account, he would have liked to have played a part in the tragedy:

> An insignificant stranger and obscure,
> Mean as I was, and little graced with powers
> Of eloquence even in my native speech,
> And all unfit for tumult and intrigue,
> Yet would I willingly have taken up
> A service at this time for cause so great . . .
>
> (*Prel.* x. 130–5)

---

[19] J. P. Farrell, *Revolution as Tragedy: The Dilemma of the Moderate from Scott to Arnold* (Ithaca, NY, 1980), 21, 36.

Not yet tongue favoured himself (or, at any rate, an as yet unpublished poet and apologist for revolution), he 'could almost | Have prayed that throughout earth upon all souls . . . The gift of tongues might fall' (*Prel.* x. 117–21). Believing that 'one paramount mind' might have redeemed the Revolution and set it in the right track ('Creed which ten shameful years have not anulled', *Prel.* x. 178–9), he experienced instead the helplessness of a spectator. Another actor, Louvet, is depicted as taking his station in the Tribune to declare (since Wordsworth himself could not): 'I, Robespierre, accuse thee!' (*Prel.* x. 100).[20] This is the 'text' of the *Prelude* account. Revolutionary violence is cast out with Robespierre, chief organizer of the September Massacres and enemy of the Girondists with whom Wordsworth identified politically. In the eyes of a Wordsworth ultimately committed to 'just government . . . according to example given | By ancient lawgivers' (*Prel.* x. 185–8), Robespierre becomes Macbeth, the murderous architect of the Terror. *The Prelude* largely internalizes the later course of the French Revolution as a period of personal crisis and self-division (a 'turn of sentiment—that might be named | A revolution', x. 236–7) from which Wordsworth is only delivered by the death of Robespierre. On the one hand, England was at war with France, dividing the loyalties of a republican patriot, and on the other, France had entered into the violent phase of the Revolution which coincided with Robespierre's regime: 'Domestic carnage now filled all the year | With feast-days', 'Head after head, and never heads enough | For those who bade them fall' (*Prel.* x. 329–30, 335–6). The cosmic wind of revolution ('the wind | Of heaven wheels round . . .') becomes a child with a toy windmill who 'runs amain | To make it whirl the faster' (*Prel.* x. 344–5). Worse still, eloquence itself becomes breath ill spent. Wordsworth's nightmares take the form of 'long orations which in dreams I pleaded | Before unjust tribunals, with a voice | Labouring . . .' (*Prel.* x. 376–8). The failure of his revolutionary optimism makes eloquence futile; threat, taking back its power from poetry, leaves him speechless.

[20] Louvet's *Narrative of the Dangers to which I have been Exposed* (1795) was one of the books Wordsworth read while working on *The Borderers*: see *EY* 166 and n. David Erdman has argued that Wordsworth anticipates the future course of the French Revolution by compressing it into his account of the Paris visit: see 'Wordsworth as Heartsworth; or, Was Regicide the Prophetic Ground of Those "Moral Questions"?', in D. Reiman, M. Jaye, and B. Bennett (eds.), *The Evidence of the Imagination* (New York, 1978), 29.

Wordsworth's image for the worst excesses of the French Revolution is of 'a reservoir of guilt . . . That could no longer hold its loathsome charge, | But burst and spread in deluge through the land' (*Prel.* x. 436–9). The deluge symbolically abates with the news of Robespierre's death: 'the great sea . . . Was at safe distance, far retired' (*Prel.* x. 528–9). The episode announcing, Miltonically, 'That this foul tribe of Moloch was o'erthrown, | And their chief regent levelled with the dust'—'In the familiar language of the day . . . *Robespierre was dead*'—(*Prel.* x. 468–9, 534–5) involves a number of significant repetitions. Returning to the Lake District and his childhood, Wordsworth revisits the grave of his former schoolmaster, whom he imagines as endorsing his own poetic career; the scene is set by one of those empyrean cloudscapes with which Wordsworth customarily celebrates being a chosen son. Structurally, too, the episode marks a return or repetition of another kind—a recollection of childhood, the exultant moment in Book II when with childhood jubilation 'We beat with thundering hoofs the level sand' (*Prel.* x. 566; cf. *Prel.* ii. 144). The same line concludes both early and later episodes, and in the 1850 version of *The Prelude* Wordsworth immediately began a new book with the optimistic note of his next lines ('From this time forth in France, as is well known, | Authority put on a milder face', x. 567–8). The effect is to place the bloodier portions of Wordsworth's account in a kind of parenthesis, consigning them to the same nightmare world as his disturbed dreams. The demonic, irrational, and violent sides of revolution are given the status of the unconscious, in the interests of asserting the continuity of the post-revolutionary adult with his unfallen childhood self. The psychological dislocation is that of Macbeth's 'To know my deed, 'twere best not know myself' (ii. ii. 72); either the deed or the self must be disowned if the fiction of a continuous and coherent identity is to be maintained.

Wordsworth's disavowal—like his invocation to Burke—is not simply a question of wishing to suppress the earlier revolutionary sympathies of his *Letter to the Bishop of Llandaff*, or a case of republican turned conservative. Rather, it is autobiography itself that *The Prelude* conserves with this episode. As Leo Bersani writes, 'finding patterns, analogies, themes (in short, repetitions) in the history of our imagination, we are naturally led to view that history as the display of a coherent character'.[21] A stable self is the

[21] L. Bersani, *A Future for Astyanax: Character and Desire in Literature* (Boston, Mass., and Toronto, 1969), 271.

necessary, saving pretext for *The Prelude*'s existence, like a unifying voice. When Coleridge called it 'An unpublished Poem on the Growth and Revolutions of an Individual Mind',[22] he tacitly conceded the unending work of forming and reforming the 'mind' or Wordsworthian self. Other voices constantly interrupt—Macbeth's, for instance—to divide or multiply the author and turn him into an actor, shifting, discontinuous, lacking identity of his own; now Robespierre, now Burke. Perhaps Robespierre threatens Wordsworth most in wounding the illusion of integrity on which *The Prelude* depends. This is the murderous attraction of the theatre itself—a scene that Bersani calls 'the privileged esthetic space for structurally unassimilable desires'.[23] Wordsworth was, as it were, constitutionally unable to give full utterance to 'the struggle between conscience and consciousness' in other than dramatic form. His tragedy of disillusion, *The Borderers*, occupies the same privileged aesthetic space as *Macbeth* and the French Revolution itself; only in his play can Wordsworth act out the self-division which *The Prelude* must heal in order to conform to its redemptive pattern. The post-revolutionary Book XI is called: 'Imagination, How Impaired and Restored'; after revolution and regicide comes the Restoration of an anti-theatrical imagination.

The Revolutionary Sublime

Attempting to salvage a kind of pleasure in the region of pain or danger on which the Sublime depends, Burke cites Homer's description of a fugitive successfully evading pursuit:

> As when a wretch, who conscious of his crime,
> Pursued for murder from his native clime,.
> Just gains some frontier, breathless, pale, amaz'd;
> All gaze, all wonder! [24]

The sublime moment is at once an escape and a spectacle that 'affects the spectators': 'This striking appearance of the man whom Homer supposes to have just escaped an imminent danger, the sort

[22] *The Friend*, ed. B. Rooke (2 vols.; London, 1969), i. 368.
[23] *A Future for Astyanax*, p. 272. Cf. Barish, *The Antitheatrical Prejudice*, p. 349: 'On the one hand we wish to license the fullest mimetic exploration of our own condition—for self-understanding, delight, and self-mastery. But to do so through the medium of other human beings like ourselves means licensing the liberation of much that we wish ultimately to control.'
[24] *Enquiry into . . . the Sublime*, p. 34 (Pope's *Iliad*, xxiv. 590–3; misquoted by Burke).

of mixt passion of terror and surprize, with which he affects the spectators, paints very strongly the manner in which we find ourselves affected upon occasions any way similar.'[25] Onlookers too become actors in the face of the Sublime, like Wordsworth in the Paris of 1792. The narrow escape of the fugitive images the narrow escape of the audience from participating directly in his drama. Pursuit of sublime effects is essentially a spectator sport; but we might also speculate about the nature of the crime committed by the fleeing man in whom the sense of the sublime moment, or escape, originates. Thomas Weiskel's Freudian reading of Burke's *Philosophical Enquiry into the Origin of our Ideas of the Sublime and the Beautiful* (1757) traces the Homeric simile back to its original context, the scene in which the aged Priam breaks in on Achilles to sue for the body of his son, Hector, and succeeds in making Achilles (a son himself) honour the memory of his own father. For Weiskel, it is a scene of parricide averted; an Oedipal situation has been healthily resolved. Such a reading illuminates Burke's persistently theatrical analogy for the Sublime of revolution by pointing to the unconscious fantasy of parricide to which we are at once exposed and from which we are then released in the sublime moment. Wonder, Burke's 'sense of awe', is the psychic equivalent of a positive identification with the father 'which both presupposes the renunciation of parricidal aggression and facilitates an escape from the imagined consequences of a murder'.[26] One is reminded that, even in the Terror, Wordsworth himself found 'Something to glory in . . . | And in the order of sublimest laws' (*Prel.* x. 412–13). Was he, perhaps, unconsciously savouring his escape from being either a parricide, a regicide, or a Robespierre?

It would be tempting to see the figure of Burke in the 1850 *Prelude* as a kind of Priam to Wordsworth's Achilles, the angry young man of the 1790s. But Burke himself had found something to wonder at in the events of 1789:

As to us here our thoughts of every thing at home are suspended, by our astonishment at the wonderful Spectacle which is exhibited in a Neighbouring and rival Country—what Spectators, and what actors! England gazing with astonishment at a French struggle for Liberty, and not

[25] *Enquiry into . . . the Sublime*, pp. 34–5.
[26] See *The Romantic Sublime*, pp. 88–92; compare Burke: 'The authority of a father, so useful to our well-being, and so venerable upon all accounts, hinders us from having that entire love for him that we have for our mothers', *Enquiry into . . . the Sublime*, p. 111.

knowing whether to blame or to applaud! The thing indeed . . . has still
something in it Paradoxical and Mysterious. The spirit it is impossible not
to admire; but the old Parisian ferocity has broken out in a shocking
manner.[27]

Here England is like Priam's audience ('All gaze, all wonder!');
the astonished spectators are uncertain 'whether to blame or
to applaud'. The uncertainty ('something . . . Paradoxical and
Mysterious') which Burke identifies in his own reaction to the
spectacle of revolutionary France is that of audience response to
tragedy. On the execution of Louis XVI in January 1793, Burke
wrote, almost with satisfaction, 'the Catastrophe of the Tragedy of
France has been compleated. It was the necessary result of all the
preceding parts of that monstrous Drama.'[28] His *Reflections* had
denounced the Revolution Society, and Price's sermon in particular,
for their failure to register appropriate emotions in the face of
Louis's humiliation in October 1789; their exultation, he wrote,
inaugurated 'a revolution in sentiments, manners, and moral
opinions'.[29] Republican audiences are bad audiences in this
historical theatre. Burke's answer to his own question, 'Why do I
feel so differently from the Reverend Dr Price?' ('because it is
natural I should'), lies in the aesthetic realm of tragedy; the work
that Wordsworth dismissed as 'a philosophic lamentation over the
extinction of Chivalry'[30] is at least as much about 'Taste' in the
broad sense in which Burke had used the term as the point of
departure for his *Enquiry into . . . the Sublime*. It was this
aestheticizing of the French Revolution which so outraged Burke's
opponents, who rightly detected in the élitism of tragedy (the fall of
great men from high estate) an element opposed to the levelling
impulse of revolution. 'Misery, to reach your heart, I perceive, must
have its cap and bells; your tears are reserved . . . for the
declamation of the theatre, or for the downfall of queens', wrote
Mary Wollstonecraft in *A Vindication of the Rights of Men*
(1790).[31] Tragedy becomes the literary manifestation of the *ancien
régime*—the genre of tradition or queen of genres.

[27] 9 Aug. 1789, in *The Correspondence of Edmund Burke*, ed. A. Cobban and
R. A. Smith (9 vols.; Cambridge, 1967), vi. 10.

[28] 27 Jan. 1793, ibid. vii. 344.

[29] *Reflections on the Revolution in France*, p. 175.   [30] *Prose Works*, i. 35.

[31] M. Wollstonecraft, *A Vindication of the Rights of Men* (2nd edn., London,
1790), 26. Cf. Tom Paine: 'His hero or his heroine must be a tragedy-victim expiring
in show, and not the real prisoner of misery, sliding into death in the silence of a
dungeon', *The Rights of Man*, ed. H. Collins (Harmondsworth, 1969), 73.

Amplifying his answer ('because it is *natural*'), Burke lays out the ideological basis of his tragic analogy. for any leveller to see; 'because', he continues,

we are so made as to be affected at such spectacles with melancholy sentiments upon the unstable condition of mortal prosperity, and the tremendous uncertainty of human greatness; because in those natural feelings we learn great lessons; because in events like these our passions instruct our reason; because when kings are hurl'd from their thrones by the Supreme Director of this great drama, and become the objects of insult to the base, and of pity to the good, we behold such disasters in the moral, as we should behold a miracle in the physical order of things. We are alarmed into reflexion; our minds (as it has long since been observed) are purified by terror and pity; our weak unthinking pride is humbled, under the dispensations of a mysterious wisdom.—Some tears might be drawn from me, if such a spectacle were exhibited on the stage. I should be truely ashamed of finding in myself that superficial, theatric sense of painted distress, whilst I could exult over it in real life. With such a perverted mind, I could never venture to shew myself at a tragedy. People would think the tears that Garrick formerly, or that Siddons not long since, have extorted from me, were the tears of hypocrisy; I should know them to be tears of folly.[32]

In a human condition perceived as fundamentally unstable, all change has a melancholy aspect, and great change, the aspect of Mrs Siddons as Tragedy. The vanity of human wishes teaches Johnsonian humility in the face of a status quo presided over by God, 'the Supreme Director of this great drama'. Once change has been moralized and the existing social order equated with a natural, God-given order, the way lies clear to represent the French Revolution as a tragic spectacle designed to purge its audience by terror and pity. Even revolution, it seems, can be represented as part of the edifying display that Bagehot called 'the *theatrical show* of society'—that special visibility of courts and aristocracies which, ideologically deployed, permits them to rule the multitude.[33] At first uncertain 'whether to blame or to applaud', Burke comes down finally on the side of socially stabilizing catharsis. The danger

---

[32] *Reflections on the Revolution in France*, pp. 175–6.

[33] 'Courts and aristocracies have the great quality which rules the multitude, though philosophers can see nothing in it—visibility', W. Bagehot, *The English Constitution*, ed. Lord Balfour (London, 1949), 236; quoted by N. Wood, 'The Aesthetic Dimension of Burke's Political Thought', *Journal of British Studies*, 4 (1964), 62–3.

in this is of seeming to forget that in France the tragic actors were for real. Hence, presumably, his emphatic disclaimer: 'I should be truely ashamed of finding in myself that superficial, theatric sense of painted distress, whilst I could exult over it in real life.' The touch of paranoia ('I could never venture to shew myself at a tragedy'), and the self-accusation ('I should know them to be tears of folly'), suggest a writer intent on disarming the suspicion that he might himself exult at being a spectator in the theatre of history.

Instead of making tragedy the paradigm of revolution, Burke makes revolution the paradigm of tragedy. His tactic of casting himself as 'the Supreme Director of this great drama' was shrewdly detected by Paine in *The Rights of Man* (1791):

As to the tragic paintings by which Mr Burke has outraged his own imagination, and seeks to work upon that of his readers, they are very well calculated for theatrical representation, where facts are manufactured for the sake of show, and accommodated to produce, through the weakness of sympathy, a weeping effect. But Mr Burke should recollect that he is writing History, and not Plays; and that his readers will expect truth, and not the spouting rant of high-toned exclamation.[34]

'He degenerates into a composition of art, and the genuine soul of nature forsakes him', Paine concludes. Analysing the politics of Burke's aesthetics, Paine sees in it a deliberate self-delusion ('Mr Burke has outraged his own imagination') calculated to manipulate political realities. But it would be possible to argue that Burke is self-deluding in a different way: that the aesthetics of his politics provide the means by which Burke himself can assume the historical role in relation to the French Revolution which Wordsworth had also wished for. Like Paine, who was unable to view the *Reflections* in 'any other light' than a dramatic performance', James Mackintosh in his introduction to *Vindiciae Gallicae* (1791) endowed him with the genius, pathos, and sneering of a tragic villain—almost, a rabble-rousing Macbeth: 'Absolved from the laws of vulgar method, he can advocate a groupe of magnificant horrors to make a breach in our hearts, through which the most indisciplined rabble of arguments may enter in triumph.'[35] Even the phrasing recalls Macbeth's gilded words as he lays the guilt of

[34] *The Rights of Man*, pp. 71–2.
[35] 'The superiority of a man of genius over common men is infinite . . . He can sap the most impregnable conviction by pathos, and put to flight a host of syllogisms with a sneer', Sir James Mackintosh, *Vindiciae Gallicae* (London, 1791), pp. vi–vii.

Duncan's murder on the grooms ('his gash'd stabs look'd like a breach in nature . . . their daggers | Unmannerly breach'd with gore', II. iii. 113–16). The scary suspicion lurking behind such language is not that Burke's eloquence is impotent, but that it might prove altogether too powerful—that representation itself might change the course of history. This is the anxiety underlying Joel Barlow's denunciation of Burke in *The Conspiracy* (1793):

Giving himself up to the frenzy of an unbridled imagination, he conceives himself writing tragedy, without being confined to the obvious laws of fiction . . . he paints ideal murders, that they may be avenged by the reality of a widely extended slaughter . . . the war of Mr. Burke was let loose, with all the horrors he intended to excite. And what is the language proper to be used in describing the character of a man, who, in his situation, at his time of life, and for a pension of only fifteen hundred pounds a year, could sit down deliberately in his closet and call upon the powers of earth and hell to inflict such a weight of misery on the human race?[36]

Though Barlow ostensibly accuses Burke of having been paid by the British Government to whip up anti-French feeling, the fear that writing could lead to the proliferation of war heightens his language into saying something else—not just that painting 'ideal murders' provides a justification for a real revenge, but that 'the frenzy of an unbridled imagination' puts the writer in league with the powers of hell. Such a mode of influencing events yet to come threatens to undo our entire sense of history.[37]

Burke's writing shatters for us the illusion of historical objectivity. He unwittingly unveils the technique of the *Reflections* when he laments without irony the loss of 'the decent drapery of life', 'the super-added ideas, furnished from the wardrobe of a moral imagination', without which 'the defects of our naked shivering nature' are exposed. These are 'the pleasing illusions' of ideology itself, making 'power gentle' (disguising despotism) and 'obedience liberal' (oppression voluntarily borne). With a movement that is not exactly Swiftian in its savagery, yet whose civilized indignation half-recalls that deluded mouthpiece for '*a perpetual Possession of*

---

[36] See *Edmund Burke*, ed. I. Kramnick (Englewood Cliffs, 1974), 127–8; quoted by P. Hughes, 'Originality and Allusion in the Writings of Edmund Burke', *Centrum*, 4 (1976), 33.

[37] Peter Hughes urges just this; not only that Burke 'becomes the chief actor in a drama that he has also staged and written', but that he 'does intend to force action upon his audience'; see *Centrum*, 4 (1976), 41.

being well Deceived', the author of *A Tale of a Tub*,[38] Burke exposes the nakedness of a social order unfurnished by the decent drapery of an ideological wardrobe:

On this scheme of things, a king is but a man; a queen is but a woman; a woman is but an animal; and an animal not of the highest order. All homage paid to the sex in general as such, and without distinct views, is to be regarded as romance and folly. Regicide, and parricide, and sacrilege, are but fictions of superstition, corrupting jurisprudence by destroying its simplicity. The murder of a king, or a queen, or a bishop, or a father, are only common homicide; and if the people are by any chance, or in any way gainers by it, a sort of homicide much the most pardonable and into which we ought not to make too severe a scrutiny.[39]

The revolution for Burke is not just one of 'sentiment'; it would turn his own account into unreadable old-speak. Like tragedy, it depends on a literary tradition in which the values of the past and touchstones of humanism are permanently enshrined. Ronald Paulson suggests, plausibly enough, that for a writer like Burke one 'solution to the confrontation with this unthinkable phenomenon, the French Revolution . . . was to fit it into the framework of aesthetic categories'[40] which were already in place. The French Revolution, Paulson argues, was assimilated to what people knew. But did it prove more recalcitrant than he allows, if only in its excesses? Paris in September 1792 had after all exceeded the bounds of legibility for Wordsworth. Burke too, falling back into the confusion of his initial reaction, invokes the disorders of *Macbeth* ('Everything seems out of nature') to denounce a demonic tragi-comic chaos:

Every thing seems out of nature in this strange chaos of levity and ferocity, and of all sorts of crimes jumbled up together with all sorts of follies. In viewing this monstrous tragi-comic scene, the most opposite passions necessarily succeed, and sometimes mix with each other in the mind; alternate contempt and indignation; alternate laughter and tears; alternate scorn and horror.[41]

This is a vision of the world in which 'Regicide, and parricide, and

[38] See J. Swift, *A Tale of a Tub*, ed. A. C. Guthkelch and D. N. Smith (2nd edn., Oxford, 1958), 171.

[39] *Reflections on the Revolution in France*, p. 171.

[40] R. Paulson, *Representations of Revolution 1789–1820* (New Haven, 1983), 68.

[41] *Reflections on the Revolution in France*, pp. 92–3.

sacrilege, are but fictions of superstition'. The indecorum, the
indeterminacy, the ambivalence of the onlooker's reaction, all point
to an unresolved aspect of Burke's own relationship with revolution,
with authority, and (Paulson suggests) with the Oedipal father
himself.[42] But the slippage of sacred categories gestures beyond
Oedipal anxiety to another fear—that the incomprehensibility of
revolution might confound all literary attempts to contain it.

Burke's 'monstrous tragi-comic scene' sounds for all the world
like Wordsworth's 'Parliament of Monsters', Bartholomew Fair
('all freaks of Nature, all Promethean thoughts | Of man . . . All
jumbled up together', *Prel.* vii. 689–91). The London of Book VII
of *The Prelude* is a city of representation, an open air theatre in
which Promethean art usurps on nature with the 'blank confusion'
of indecipherability. 'Differences | That have no law' (vii. 704–5)—
like those between regicide, parricide, and sacrilege when viewed as
superstitious fictions—create an unreadable urban text. This is the
demonic or negative Sublime which Burke invokes when he cites
Book II of *Paradise Lost* to illustrate ideas 'not presentable but by
language'.[43] The common literary source for Burke's revolutionary
chaos and Wordsworth's urban anarchy, Milton's Hell, provides
ready-made images of demonic revolt and bloodshed. Already in
Paradise Lost itself the fallen Satan had been compared to an
eclipsed sun that 'with fear of change | Perplexes monarchs'
(i. 598–9), in a phrase glossed by Burke himself as 'the revolutions
of kingdoms',[44] while Wordsworth celebrates the fall of Robespierre
with a reference to 'Moloch, horrid king besmeared with blood'
(*Paradise Lost*, i. 392; *Prel.* x. 468–9). But in a speech of 1794,
Burke claimed that Milton would have recoiled from describing the
French hell, believing 'his design revolting to the most unlimited
imagination, and his colouring overcharged beyond all allowance
for the license even of poetical painting'.[45] An imagination in revolt

---

[42] *Representations of Revolution 1789–1820*, pp. 70–1. Cf. also I. Kramnick,
The Rage of Edmund Burke: Portrait of an Ambivalent Conservative (New York,
1977), 109.

[43] 'O'er many a dark and dreary vale | They pass'd, and many a region dolorous;
| O'er many a frozen, many a fiery alp; | Rocks, caves, lakes, fens, bogs, dens and
shades of death, | A universe of death' (*Paradise Lost*, ii. 618–22). Burke points out
how much would be lost of the sublime effect without the phrase, 'A universe of
death', *Enquiry into . . . the Sublime*, pp. 174–5.

[44] Ibid. 62.

[45] *Speeches of the Right Honourable Edmund Burke* (4 vols.; London, 1816), iv.
164–5; quoted by Paulson, *Representations of Revolution 1789–1820*, p. 66.

against limitlessness and licence is one resistant to the demands of the Sublime. The mode against which the imagination revolts is that of excess. Yet in the context of his discussion of Milton's Hell, Burke writes revealingly:

> The truth is, all verbal description, merely as naked description, though never so exact, conveys so poor and insufficient an idea of the thing described, that it could scarcely have the smallest effect, if the speaker did not call to his aid those modes of speech that mark a strong and lively feeling in himself. Then, by the contagion of our passions, we catch a fire already kindled in another, which probably might never have been struck out by the object described.[46]

'Then . . . we catch a fire already kindled'; then we are in hell. The incendiary force of language is here already a mode of excess. Burke comes close to admitting that no such thing as 'naked description' exists, and therefore that no colouring can ever be 'overchanged'— no limits set. Where representation is concerned, there can be no crossing from nature to art, since there is no realm but art.

Burke's tragi-comic scene and Wordsworth's Bartholomew Fair are alike in marking risky moments; they uncover the Promethean excesses that both authors must conceal if their respective fictions of history and nature are to be maintained. Burke needs history because, despite the anti-mimetic bias of his remarks on language, it provides the basis for his theory of tragedy. Since art imitates reality, the *Enquiry* argues, the highest form of art is reality, and the highest form of tragedy, history:

> The prosperity of no empire, nor the grandeur of no king, can so agreeably affect in the reading, as the ruin of the state of Macedon, and the distress of its unhappy prince. Such a catastrophe touches us in history as much as the destruction of Troy does in fable . . . there is no spectacle we so eagerly pursue, as that of some uncommon and grievous calamity; so that whether the misfortune is before our eyes, or whether they are turned back to it in history, it always touches with delight. This is not an unmixed delight, but blended with no small uneasiness . . . we shall be much mistaken if we attribute any considerable part of our satisfaction in tragedy to a consideration that tragedy is a deceit, and its representations no realities. The nearer it approaches the reality, and the further it removes us from all idea of fiction, the more perfect is its power. *But be its power of what kind it will, it never approaches to what it represents.*[47]

---

[46] *Enquiry into . . . the Sublime*, pp. 175–6.
[47] Ibid. 45–7; my italics.

Burke argues against the Aristotelian commonplace that what pleases in tragedy would shock in real life by pointing out how fast the theatre empties, whatever the tragedy, at the news 'that a state criminal of high rank is on the point of being executed in the adjoining square'. The Sublime may require the 'no small uneasiness' of actual danger, crime, or punishment; but if Burke is not to put his own neck or someone else's at risk—if he is not to be either the state criminal or his executioner—he has to engage in a thoroughly Macbeth-like piece of equivocation: 'we do not sufficiently distinguish what we would by no means chuse to do, from what we should be eager enough to see if it was once done.'[48] Letting 'I dare not' wait upon 'I would' (*Macbeth*, I. vii. 44), Burke comes close to saying that while he would not choose to send Louis XVI to the guillotine, he would leave the theatre to watch the sight. He also installs the *Reflections* on the same equivocal border as the fleeing criminal of Homer's simile, suspended between the real perils of history and the uneasy delights of tragedy. Burke hesitates between seeing 'Priam dragged to the altar's foot, and there murdered'[49] (failing to gain the frontier safely), and the 'Ambition' which his *Enquiry* described as 'that glorying and sense of inward greatness, that always fills the reader of such passages in poets and orators as are sublime'.[50] He hesitates, in other words, between the excesses of revolution and the excesses of his own rhetoric, uncertain whether he prefers the rhetorical to the revolutionary Sublime; the threat to the poetry. That uncertainty is the common point of instability on which his discussion of the theatre and his representation of revolution both rest.

De Quincey's 'Awful Parenthesis'

Coleridge's Macbeth is 'a commanding genius', one who possesses 'an imagination of just that degree of vividness which disquiets and impels the soul to try to realize its images'.[51] This allies him to the dramatist—if not to the revolutionary, as defined by Coleridge's

---

[48] *Enquiry into . . . the Sublime*, p. 47.

[49] 'A picture of Priam dragged to the altar's foot, and there murdered, if it were well executed would undoubtedly be very moving; but there are very aggravating circumstances which it could never represent', ibid. 174.

[50] Ibid. 51.

[51] *Coleridge's Shakespeare Criticism*, ed. T. M. Raysor (2 vols.; London, 1960), i. 73, 52.

Biographia Literaria distinction between commanding genius and the 'absolute' genius of poet-philosophers, those who 'rest content between thought and reality, as it were in an intermundium'. Commanding geniuses, by contrast, 'must impress their preconception on the world without, in order to present them back to their own view with the satisfying degree of clearness, distinctness, and individuality'. Impresarios of representation, they can be either benign despots like Kubla Khan or the revolutionary destroyers of more recent times:

These in tranquil times are formed to exhibit a perfect poem in palace or temple or landscape-garden; or a tale of romance in canals that join sea with sea, or in walls of rock, which shouldering back the billows imitate the power, and supply the benevolence of nature to sheltered navies; or in aqueducts that arching the wide vale from mountain to mountain give a Palmyra to the desert. But alas! in times of tumult they are the men destined to come forth as the shaping spirit of Ruin, to destroy the wisdom of ages in order to substitute the fancies of a day, and to change kings and kingdoms, as the wind shifts and shapes the clouds.[52]

Given the context (the 'Supposed irritability of men of Genius'), one might suspect that Coleridge has a special investment in the fantasy of omnipotent thought, or 'a real sense of inward power', which insulates the absolute genius from the irritations attending 'an intense desire to possess the reputation of poetic genius'.[53] The apologia of a compulsive underachiever, *Biographia Literaria* uses its contrast between dreamer and man of action to vindicate 'conceptions of the mind . . . so vivid and adequate, as to preclude [the] impulse to the realizing of them'.[54] To this end, Coleridge draws together anti-theatrical prejudice in its most generalized form and a conservative prejudice against revolution.

Representation, Coleridge seems to imply, is itself a kind of usurpation. The doubling whereby mimesis usurps what it represents—the doubling that enables something to present itself—is for him the activity of an insufficiently strong imagination in search of evidences of its strength. The metaphysics of presence

---

[52] *Biographia Literaria*, ed. J. Engell and W. J. Bate (2 vols.; Princeton and London, 1983), i. 32–3. Coleridge footnotes Wordsworth's poem, 'Rob Roy's Grave' ('Kingdoms shall shift about, like clouds, | Obedient to my breath', ll. 91–2); Rob Roy becomes the type of the social dreamer turned man of action about whose contemporary manifestations Wordsworth speculates.

[53] *Biographia Literaria*, i. 38.   [54] Ibid. i. 31.

might be said to constitute a distinct element in Romantic prejudice against the theatre. As the unveiling of a hidden truth, or prior text, dramatic representation must always lack self-sufficiency, like commanding genius. The more the poet is credited with a self-sufficing inner world, the more this will tend to be the case. Not surprisingly, then, Romantic criticism of Shakespeare—the type of the myriad-minded, negatively capable, and God-like creator—tends to subordinate stage to page and actors to text. The price of stressing Shakespearean integrity and inwardness of imagination will be a corresponding denigration of the theatre. The metaphysical pressure to maintain the priority of what is represented over its representation helps to retire Shakespeare into the closet; and if not Shakespeare, then at least action, acting, and actors. Hence the Romantic appropriation of Shakespeare as above all a soliloquist, and the emergence of the monodrama as the characteristic form of high Romantic theatre—a verse form never intended for the stage. De Quincey offers his brief *tour de force* of dramatic criticism, 'On the Knocking at the Gate in *MacBeth*' (1823), as a 'specimen of psychological criticism' designed for those 'who are accustomed to reflect on what they *read*'.[55] This is psychological criticism not only in its appeal to reader response and to the 'perspective' of imagination, but in its concern to illuminate the inner world in which Macbeth's crime originates. The taboo'd consciousness of the murderer moves to the centre of the play, at the price, however, of relegating his crime to an 'awful parenthesis'. The proof of Shakespearean 'design and self-supporting arrangement', of an art which belongs to the same order as nature, 'like the sun and the sea, the stars and the flowers',[56] may lie for De Quincey in a spectacular series of murders in which the same incident (a thunderous knocking at the door) punctuates the crime;[57] but the effect of his argument is simultaneously to uncover and to repress—to suspend, as it were—the murder itself.

For De Quincey, 'Murder, in ordinary cases, where the sympathy is wholly directed to the case of the murdered person, is an incident of coarse and vulgar horror'; it appeals merely to the instinct for self-preservation common to all living creatures, and thereby

---

[55] *De Quincey as Critic*, ed. J. E. Jordan (London and Boston, Mass., 1973), 224; my italics.   [56] Ibid. 244.

[57] See ibid. 241, and cf. De Quincey's 1854 postscript to 'On Murder Considered as one of the Fine Arts', Masson, xiii. 70–124.

annihilates significant distinctions between them. The poet, by contrast, 'must throw the interest on the murderer: our sympathy must be with *him*'; 'in the murderer, such a murderer as a poet will condescend to, there must be raging some great storm of passion . . . which will create a hell within him; and into this hell we are to look.'[58] The demonic Sublime resembles the effect of perspective which the man in the street, or ordinary reader, is unable to reproduce: 'he does not know that he has seen . . . that which he *has* seen every day of his life.' Forgotten or repressed, the familiar becomes strange, even satanic; 'the human heart' gives way to 'the fiendish heart'.[59] Macbeth's crime thus occupies the inner stage of Bersani's theatre of unassimilable desires. De Quincey's *Macbeth* becomes a play within a play. The knocking at the gate is for him the device by which Shakespeare achieves this effect of recession:

In order that a new world may step in, this world must for a time disappear. The murderers and the murder must be insulated—cut off by an immeasurable gulf from the ordinary tide and succession of human affairs—locked up and sequestered in some deep recess: we must be made sensible that the world of ordinary life is suddenly arrested—laid asleep—tranced—racked into dread armistice: time must be annihilated; relation to things without abolished; and all must pass self-withdrawn into a deep syncope and suspension of earthly passion.[60]

Paradoxically, the 'new world' of realized desires—of images made 'palpable' (De Quincey's term) like Macbeth's dagger—must be 'self-withdrawn into a deep syncope and suspension of earthly passion'. *Syncope* brings with it, as well as its evident meaning (a pause or sudden cessation, an interruption), an unexpectedly apt pathological sense: that of 'failure of the heart's action, resulting in loss of consciousness, and sometimes in death' (*OED*). Not content with transferring sympathy from victim to murderer, De Quincey transfers the victim's death to the temporal aspect of drama. Time stops, not Duncan's heart. The act of murder is, as it were, undone. *Suspension* works to reinforce this condition of arrest since as well as meaning a temporary cessation or intermission, it can also involve 'the action of keeping any mental action in suspense or abeyance . . . hesitation or caution in decision, refraining from decisive action' (*OED*). A temporal pause becomes the means of

---

[58] *De Quincey as Critic*, p. 242.   [59] Ibid. 241, 243.   [60] Ibid. 243.

denying that a murder took place at all. By this means also, De Quincey not only vindicates Macbeth, but justifies his own sympathetic identification with a hesitant regicide.

De Quincey's 'awful parenthesis' involves at once denial and containment; 'the entrance of the fiendish heart' can only take place in a deep recess where time is annihilated. In his 'Theory of Greek Tragedy' (1840), De Quincey argues for the entire removal of action from the Greek stage, relocating it literally between the acts. As he reminds us, 'the very meaning of an *act* is, that in the intervals, the suspension of the acts, any possible time may elapse, and any possible action may go on'; 'No action of *any kind*', he insists, 'proceeds legitimately on that stage.'[61] De Quincey's peculiar conflating of murder and drama, regicide and suspended action, makes him compare the 'life within a life' of Greek tragedy to Shakespeare's play within a play in *Hamlet*. Shakespeare's problem, he writes, 'was—so to differentiate a drama that it might stand within a drama, precisely as a painter places a picture within a picture'; the secondary or inner drama had to be 'non-realized' so as to throw by contrast 'a reflex colouring of reality upon the principal drama'.[62] Hamlet's play, one might note in passing, is not only regicidal and fratricidal, but, given the Oedipal content of the principal drama, very likely parricidal as well. Claudius, moreover, is 'struck to the soul' by watching it—self-betrayed through recognizing the representation of his own desires. Despite its theatrical 'stilting'—compared by De Quincey to the stylization of Greek tragedy—Hamlet's play crosses the perilous border between actor and spectator. When is a play an act? What distinguishes representation from reality? De Quincey can only tolerate the murderous potentialities of drama by framing mimesis with yet more mimesis:

Sometimes the same thing takes place in painting. We see a chamber, suppose, exhibited by the artist, on the walls of which (as a customary piece of furniture), hangs a picture. And as this picture again might represent a room furnished with pictures, in the mere logical possibility of the case we might imagine this descent into a life below a life going on *ad infinitum*.[63]

In his management of this 'retrocession', the artist must create the illusion of a series of graduated or subordinated orders of reality, each less 'real' than the preceding one; which is itself always 'a mimic—an unreal life'.[64] The term 'introvolution', coined by De Quincey for the common recessive structure which he identifies in *Macbeth*, *Hamlet*, and Greek tragedy, points to another kind of management. It constitutes a defence against 'revolution'—the cyclical return, or sublime turn, which threatens to overwhelm the spectator with a too pressing reality. 'Introvolution' maintains hierarchy, suspending the illegitimate aspect of representation.

De Quincey's 'bagatelle', 'On Murder Considered as One of the Fine Arts' (1827 and 1839), admiringly compares the assassination of the king of Sweden in the midst of a battle to 'Hamlet's subtle device of a tragedy within a tragedy'. In this 'little parenthesis on a vast stage of public battle-carnage', regicide masquerades as legalized slaughter.[65] One might ask what constitutes the covert design of this elaborate *jeu d'esprit* on the aesthetics and psychology of violence. According to De Quincey, 'the final purpose of murder, considered as a fine art, is precisely the same as that of tragedy . . . viz, "to cleanse the heart by means of pity and terror" '.[66] Like Williams, the murderer who provides him with his 'solution' to the unaccountable effect of the knocking at the gate in *Macbeth*, De Quincey performs in the dress of an artist.[67] For his 'morbidly virtuous' *alter ego*, this makes him an accessory to the crime. Citing Lactantius' Christian denunciation of the brutalities of the Roman amphitheatre, the 'Advertisement of a Man Morbidly Virtuous' solemnly provides its readers with a classic statement of anti-theatrical prejudice—but one which draws them into uneasy proximity with real murders instead of feigned ones:

'What is so dreadful,' says Lactantius, 'what so dismal and revolting, as the murder of a human creature? Therefore it is, that life for us is protected by laws the most rigorous: therefore it is, that wars are objects of execration. And yet the traditional usage of Rome has devised a mode of authorizing murder apart from war, and in defiance of law; and the demands of taste (voluptas) are now become the same as those of abandoned guilt. . . . Now, if merely to be present at a murder fastens on a man the character of an accomplice; if barely to be a spectator involves us in one common guilt

[64] Ibid. 178.
[65] 'On Murder Considered as One of the Fine Arts', Masson, xiii. 23.
[66] Ibid. 47.
[67] 'In his second great performance, it was particularly noticed . . . that Mr. Williams wore a long blue frock, of the very finest cloth, and richly lined with silk', ibid. 79.

with the perpetrator, it follows, of necessity, that, in these murders of the amphitheatre, the hand which inflicts the fatal blow is not more deeply embrued in blood than his who passively looks on; neither can *he* be clear of blood who has countenanced its shedding; nor that man seem other than a participator in murder, who gives his applause to the murderer, and calls for prizes on his behalf.'[68]

Where does this leave De Quincey, celebrating the gratuitous violence of Williams's diabolically executed and apparently unmotivated murders? One answer would be: on the side of excess, with Burke. Though the purpose of his 'bagatelle' is 'to graze the brink of horror', the comic Sublime keeps him from tumbling in: 'The very excess of the extravagance, in fact, by suggesting to the reader continually the mere aeriality of the entire speculation, furnishes the surest means of disenchanting him from the horror which might else gather upon his feelings.' Excessive extravagance undoes the enchantments of horror—or rather, licenses them. If the first murderer was an artist ('As the inventor of murder, and the father of the art, Cain must have been a man of first-rate genius'), those who improved on his fratricide are artists of excess; Milton, for instance, who, as Richardson notices in his *Explanatory Notes . . . on 'Paradise Lost'*, embellished the Genesis account with a large bloody wound, adding 'a warm, sanguinary colouring' to the primitive school; or Shakespeare, the professional, with his gilded description of the murdered Duncan.[69] This makes Macbeth himself a notable practitioner of the art of verbal assassination: 'Here lay Duncan, | His silver skin lac'd with his golden blood . . .' (*Macbeth*, II. iii. 111–12). Installing himself in a long line of improvers on the murderer's art, De Quincey aligns himself not only with Milton's picturesque embellishments, but with Macbeth's. Art becomes a performance that doubles, conceals, and denies; correspondingly, the writer becomes a kind of Williams in disguise.

It is this doubling which creates anxiety, since it presents the possibility of a self that might at once murder and give it 'a warm, sanguinary colouring'. The discontinuity of acts and words becomes a dangerous split, or 'breach in nature' ('And his gash'd stabs look'd like a breach in nature', *Macbeth*, II. iii. 113). Lamb's peculiar fascination with actors and acting lies in this unnatural breach, since it constitutes for him the protective gap between an empirical self and his alias, Elia. Yet his essay 'On the Tragedies of

[68] 'On Murder . . .', Masson, xiii. 11.   [69] Ibid. 70–1, 17–18.

Shakespeare Considered with Reference to their Fitness for Stage-Representation' (1811) denounces not bardolatry, but the idolizing of Shakespeare's players. A recent statue of Garrick had scandalized him by introducing 'theatrical airs and gestures' into Westminster Abbey. According to the epitaph inscribed beneath, Garrick was no mere actor, but an improver in his own right: 'Though sunk in death the forms the Poet drew, | The Actor's genius bade them breathe anew.' Putting Shakespeare and Garrick on the same level confounds for Lamb 'the power of originating poetical images and conceptions with the faculty of being able to read or recite the same when put into words'.[70] To blur the identity of a great dramatic poet and a mere player risks the loss of 'that absolute mastery over the heart and soul of man' which is the author's prerogative; it risks losing, in fact, his authority over the text. Hence Lamb's reference to 'that affecting sonnet of Shakespeare which alludes to his profession as a player' ('almost thence my nature is subdued | To what it works in, like the dyer's hand').[71] The attempt to keep Garrick and Shakespeare apart is a way of preventing the disappearance of the playwright into his plays, and thus of maintaining an imaginary poetic integrity. In this context it is illuminating to come on an unwitting display of antitheatrical prejudice by Jonas Barish himself, at the conclusion of his chapter on Lamb:

So long as we seek to render the quality of our existence in voice, gesture, and color, the simple integrity to which we all at heart aspire will continue to haunt us. To this integrity the antitheatrical prejudice will continue to pay its wry tribute, preserving our awareness of the corruption we risk in the very act of attempting to express and subdue it.[72]

The fantasy which seems to haunt Barish here is not just that of integrity of self, but that of corruption through multiplicity. Lamb's anti-theatrical prejudice manifests nothing less than his wish to save the author from the multiplicity of the dramatic text in performance, thereby preserving 'the very idea of *what an author is*'.[73]

One way to guard against the subduing of an author's nature to what it works in is by reducing his plays to soliloquy; for Lamb, '*speaking*' is only a medium 'for putting the reader or spectator into possession of . . . the inner structure and workings of mind in a

[70] Lucas, i. 97.
[72] *The Antitheatrical Prejudice*, p. 349.
[71] Ibid. 104.
[73] Lucas, i. 98.

character'.[74] Speech itself becomes redundant in *Hamlet*, the soliloquist's play ('nine parts in ten of what Hamlet does, are transactions between himself and his moral sense'). If Hamlet's solitary musings are only 'reduced to *words* for the sake of the reader', how much more redundant must acting be: 'These profound sorrows, these light-and-noise-abhorring ruminations, which the tongue scarce dares utter to deaf walls and chambers, how can they be represented by a gesticulating actor . . .?'[75] As the gesticulating actor murders the illusion of privacy, so action itself—especially the criminal actions of a character like Macbeth—usurps motive. When we read, 'the impulses, the inner mind in all its perverted greatness, solely seems real and is exclusively attended to' while 'the crime is comparatively nothing'. With representation, by contrast, 'the acts . . . are comparatively everything, their impulses nothing'. Lamb chooses to illustrate his argument with the dagger scene from *Macbeth*—an odd choice, on the face of it, since in it we see Macbeth meditating rather than performing a murder:

> The state of sublime emotion into which we are elevated by those images of night and horror which Macbeth is made to utter, that solemn prelude with which he entertains the time till the bell shall strike which is to call him to murder Duncan—when we no longer read it in a book, when we have given up that vantage ground of abstraction which reading possesses over seeing, and come to see a man in bodily shape before our eyes actually preparing to commit a murder, if the acting be true and impressive, as I have witnessed it in Mr. K[ean]'s performance of that part, the painful anxiety about the act, the natural longing to prevent it while it yet seems unperpetrated, the too close pressing semblance of reality, give a pain and an uneasiness which totally destroy all the delight which the words in the book convey, where the deed doing never presses upon us with the painful sense of presence: it seems rather to belong to history—to something past and inevitable if it has anything to do with time at all.[76]

What presses too closely upon us is less the semblance of reality, or the painful sense of presence, than the imminence of action. 'The painful anxiety about the act, the natural longing to prevent it' suggests in Lamb that dangerous pull towards identification which merges audience and actor, making them feel capable of the murderer's forbidden acts as well as longing to prevent them. Reading thus becomes the source of sublime emotion for Lamb, since—being always a form of re-enactment—it allows one, like

[74] Lucas, i. 99.   [75] Ibid. 100.   [76] Ibid. 106.

historical writing, to master action rather than be mastered by it. That, perhaps, is why Mrs Siddons's Lady Macbeth comes to personify Tragedy for Romantic critics of Shakespeare like Hazlitt.[77] With her eyes open and her senses shut, she is the image of someone not acting, but imaginatively re-enacting—the image of a reader, in fact. Providing as it does an 'intermundium' between thought and reality, reading offers Romantic critics access to something akin to Coleridge's 'absolute' genius.

'A Tale Told by an Idiot'

Arguing for the abstracting and neutralizing effect of antiquity in Greek tragic drama, De Quincey cites the unpopularity of 'the Charles I. of Banks' (an untraceable play), not on the score of its modernity simply, but on the score of its too urgent contemporary and political relevance:

The objection to it is, that a parliamentary war is too intensely political: and political, moreover, in a way which doubly defeated its otherwise tragic power; first, because questions too *notorious* and too domineering of law and civil polity were then at issue; the very same which came to a final hearing and settlement in 1688–9. Our very form of government, at this day, is the result of the struggle then going on,—a fact which eclipses and dwarfs any separate or private interest of an individual prince, though otherwise and by his personal character, in the very highest degree, an object of tragic sympathy. Secondly, because the political interest afloat at that era (1649) was too complex and intricate; it wanted the simplicity of a poetic interest. That is the objection to Charles I. as a tragedy! not because modern, but because too domineeringly political; and because the casuistic features of the situation were too many and too intricate.[78]

[77] 'In speaking of the character of Lady Macbeth, we ought not to pass over Mrs. Siddons's manner of acting that part. We can conceive of nothing grander. It was something above nature. It seemed almost as if a being of a superior order had dropped from a higher sphere to awe the world with the majesty of her appearance. Power was seated on her brow, passion emanated from her breast as from a shrine; she was tragedy personifed. In coming on in her sleep-walking scene, her eyes were open, but her senses shut', Howe, iv. 189–90.

[78] *De Quincey as Critic*, pp. 185–6; cf. Hume's *Of Tragedy* (1757) for the observation that Clarendon omits from his *History of the Rebellion* (1702–4) any account of Charles I's actual execution: 'He considers it as too horrid a scene to be contemplated with any satisfaction, or even without the utmost pain and aversion. He himself, as well as the readers of that age, were too deeply concerned in the events, and felt pain from subjects which an historian and a reader of another age would regard as the most pathetic and most interesting', D. Hume, *Of the Standard of Taste and Other Essays*, ed. J. W. Lenz (Indianapolis, 1965), 35–6.

This comes close to saying that a regicide which forms the foundation of 'our very form of government, at this day' (the result of the Settlement of 1688–9) must at all costs be repressed. The unconstitutionality of the constitution would otherwise be too evident, especially to a conservative like De Quincey. His argument that political issues at once too notorious and too complex militate against tragedy offers a sidelight on Wordsworth's abstraction of the revolutionary dilemma in his own historical tragedy, *The Borderers*. Completed in early 1797, *The Borderers* was written, according to Wordsworth himself, with the recent course of the French Revolution fresh in his memory. His contemporary 'Preface' to the play, he wrote later, was particularly intended 'to preserve in my distinct remembrance what I had observed of transition in character & the reflections I had been led to make during the time I was a witness of the changes through which the French Revolution passed'.[79] David Erdman has argued persuasively for a greater degree of topical reference and political specificity than that often accorded to *The Borderers*, seeing in it at once a record of the events of 1792–3 and a dramatized version of Wordsworth's painful reappraisals of 1795–6.[80] But perhaps the most interesting aspect of Erdman's argument is that whereas the *Prelude* account tends to stress the reasons for assassinating a revolutionary turned tyrant, like Robespierre, the case for regicide which would have surrounded Wordsworth in the Paris of 1792 is displaced on to *The Borderers*.[81] A parricide play, it literally relegates to the dramatic space or 'awful parenthesis' material which Wordsworth was unable to assimilate into *The Prelude* except in terms of the familiar paradigm of post-revolutionary disillusion.

The Borderers is dramatically divided—flawed, some would say—between the remorse of a hero tricked into letting an old man

---

[79] *The Borderers*, ed. R. Osborn (Ithaca, NY, and London, 1982), 815; subsequent references are to the reading text of the early version. For the composition of *The Borderers* and its 'Preface', see M. L. Reed, *Wordsworth: The Chronology of the Early Years 1770–1799* (Cambridge, Mass, 1967), 329–30.

[80] D. Erdman, 'Wordsworth as Heartsworth; or, Was Regicide the Prophetic Ground of Those "Moral Questions"?', in Reiman, Jaye, and Bennett (eds.), *The Evidence of the Imagination*, pp. 31–2.

[81] Ibid. 27. Erdman points out that the theme of tyrannicide appears in Book IX of *The Prelude* in connection with Wordsworth's mentor, Beaupuy, who is compared to Dion, Plato's pupil in 'philosophic war' and destined for the overthrow of a tyrant; see Reimen, Jaye, and Bennett (eds.), *The Evidence of the Imagination*, p. 40 n. 27, and cf. *Prel*. ix. 414–23.

die and the metaphysical villainy of the man who tricks him. The play's divided consciousness images the terror of self-betrayal, a split between the imagining and the doing of a parricidal crime ('in the after vacancy | We wonder at ourselves like men betray'd').[82] It asks the price of continuity between the innocent and the criminal self, offering two answers—one, its villain's self-professed emancipation from traditional morality (he too has been responsible for the death of an innocent man); the other, its hero's self-imposed expiation through solitary wandering, at the end of the play, for his creed-induced crime against humanity. Like the Girondins as described by Louvet, he was too virtuous to credit crimes, until the day he fell victim to them.[83] What stands out from the implausible intricacy of Wordsworth's gothic plot is the seductive power of the argument for homicide—rather as if Wordsworth had transposed Burke's irony ('Regicide, and parricide, and sacrilege, are but fictions of superstition') into the special form of temptation appropriate for a Girondist sympathizer:

> Murder! What, of whom?
> Of whom—or what? we kill a toad, a newt,
> A rat—I do believe if they who first
> Baptised the deed had called it murder, we
> Had quaked to think of it.[84]

Or, as the 1842 text has it, 'Hew down a withered tree, | And none look grave but dotards'. Urging the superfluousness of circumstantial evidence, Wordsworth's villain-hero—renamed Oswald in the revised, later version—perhaps recalls the English Jacobin, 'Colonel' Oswald, who suggested to the Convention of 1793 the 'Loi des Suspects' calling for the death of every suspected man in France; among the first of the Girondists to go was Gorsas, whose execution Wordsworth later claimed to have witnessed.[85] Such extremes of revolutionary zeal may have suggested to Wordsworth

---

[82] *The Borderers*, III. v. 62–3.

[83] 'All their faults were the faults of virtue . . . they originated from the extreme goodness of their hearts. They were too virtuous to credit crimes, till the very day they fell victims to them', J.-B. Louvet, *Narrative of the Dangers to which I have been Exposed* (London, 1795), pp. v–vi.

[84] *The Borderers*, II. iii. 230–4.

[85] See Erdman in Reiman, Jaye, and Bennett (eds.), *The Evidence of the Imagination*, pp. 39–40 n. 25. The possibility that Wordsworth returned to France at the time of Gorsas's execution is discussed both by Erdman (pp. 28–9) and Reed, *Wordsworth: The Chronology of the Early Years*, p. 147.

(in the language of his later commentary) that there are 'no limits to the hardening of the heart, and the perversion of the understanding to which they may carry their slaves'.[86] If there are no limits in Oswald, there may be no limits in his virtuous *alter ego* either. The two characters are aspects of the same fear: the ease with which what De Quincey calls 'the retiring of the human heart and the entrance of the fiendish heart' may take place.

That fear of uncontrollable inner division surely lies behind much anti-theatrical prejudice—behind the ethical anxieties of a Lactantius or De Quincey himself, or the ethical ambiguities diagnosed by Barish as troubling us 'so long also as in life "all doers are actors" '.[87] Liberating what we wish rather to control brings with it the perils of not being able to stop there. This is the gist of Wordsworth's prefatory essay to *The Borderers*, which sets out to analyse his revolutionary villain-hero: 'The period in which he lives teems with great events, which he feels he cannot controul.' Rationalism becomes a mode of attempted mastery over 'a dark and tempestuous age'.[88] It tries to retrieve from history the sense of omnipotence which the original moment of criminal choice had induced ('in a course of criminal conduct every fresh step that we make ... seems to bring back again the moment of liberty and choice'). Repetition itself becomes a kind of denial, or rewriting of the past: 'Every time we plan a fresh accumulation of our guilt, we have restored to us something like that original state of mind, that perturbed pleasure, which first made the crime attractive.'[89] It perpetuates the moment of temptation or self-seduction before the crime (like Macbeth's dagger speech); the moment which might be said to constitute the extended dramatic action of *The Borderers*. In effect, this is also the moment before theory becomes practice, or desire sets action in motion. Coleridge later praised Burke for his 'prejudice against all abstract grounds, against all deduction of practice from theory' ('Against all systems built on abstract rights ... Exploding upstart Theory', in the language of Wordsworth's invocation to Burke; 1850 *Prel*. vii. 524–9). These are the terms in which Wordsworth analyses his villain-hero:

[86] *The Borderers*, p. 813. [87] *The Antitheatrical Prejudice*, p. 349.
[88] *Prose Works*, i. 78.
[89] Ibid. 79. W. J. B. Owen, '*The Borderers* and the Aesthetics of Drama', *The Wordsworth Circle*, 6 (1975), 227–39, has pointed to parallels between Wordsworth's analysis and the analysis of Macbeth by W. Richardson in *Essays on Some of Shakespeare's Dramatic Characters* (5th edn., London, 1798).

'dallying with moral calculations, he becomes an empiric . . . assuming the character of a speculator in morals, and one who has the hardihood to realize his speculations'.[90] Travestying Godwin, Oswald is a rationalist prompted by unacknowledged desires, propounding 'the immediate law | Flashed from the light of circumstances | Upon an independent intellect'.[91] *The Prelude* characterizes Wordsworth's self-seduction in the same way. Social freedom was to be founded 'on its only basis: | The freedom of the individual mind' (x. 824–5), a flattering dream of intellectual power. Another name for this 'self-knowledge and self-rule', this 'resolute mastery' (x. 819–21), would be commanding genius—that cast of mind that impels one to impress one's preconceptions on the world without.

Coleridge's distinction between absolute and commanding genius proves to have the same structure as the relation between 'theory' and 'practice', between the theatre of desire and the political arena, or the Shakespearean page and the stage. The problem with this distinction lies in maintaining a sufficiently clear-cut border between the absolutely autonomous imagination and one that usurps commandingly on reality. My mind to me a kingdom is— but what if I should want someone else's crown, or even head? The theatre presents the same difficulty of distinguishing identification from guilt, or meditated acts from real ones. Unlike the book which 'never presses upon us with the painful sense of presence', the stage constantly threatens to come too close, blurring that clear-cut border. Paradoxically, Wordsworth's actual powerlessness to be anything other than a spectator of the French Revolution resulted in a play. If, as Farrell argues, tragedy gave the moderate a language in which to 'give utterance to the very conditions that deprived him of action',[92] it is ironic that it should also have confronted him with the dangerous theatricality of the imagination. While a political view of the relation between tragedy and revolution, such as Farrell's, would suggest that the function of tragedy is to contain, a psychoanalytic view of the theatre, such as Bersani's, suggests otherwise—that its function is to liberate. This tension between

[90] *Prose Works*, i. 78.
[91] *The Borderers*, III. v. 31–3; cf. *Prel.* x. 828–9.
[92] *Revolution as Tragedy*, p. 36. See also R. Parker, 'Reading Wordsworth's Power: Narrative and Usurpation in *The Borderers*', *ELH* 54 (1987), 299–331, for Wordsworth's relation to political theatre, and the theatre of politics, in revolutionary France.

control and excess, limitation and the limitlessness of the Sublime, conforms to the tension between constitutionality and revolution. But perhaps underlying the oppositions which structure both anti-theatrical prejudice and the representation of revolution in Romantic writing there is an unuttered, radically contradictory anxiety: not that the mind (or, if not the mind, the reader) might cease to be self-sufficingly absolute; not that to watch a regicide play or to sympathize with the arguments for regicide is as good as being a party to it—but that, as for Macbeth, reality itself could come to seem no more than mere representation. The fear of 'signifying nothing' is what finally haunts Macbeth, making him a tongue-favoured spokesman for Romantic theatre as it troubles the texts of Wordsworth, Burke, De Quincey, and Lamb in the aftermath of the French Revolution:

> Life's but a walking shadow; a poor player,
> That struts and frets his hour upon the stage,
> And then is heard no more: it is a tale
> Told by an idiot, full of sound and fury;
> Signifying nothing.
>
> (*Macbeth*, v. v. 24–8).

CHAPTER 3

GEOMETRIC SCIENCE AND ROMANTIC HISTORY

or Wordsworth, Newton, and the Slave-Trade

The invisible is the darkness, the blinded eye of the theoretical problematic's self-reflection when it scans its non-objects, its non-problems without seeing them, *in order not to look at them.*

The text of history is not a text in which a voice (the Logos) speaks, but the inaudible and illegible notation of the effects of a structure of structures.

(Althusser, *Reading Capital*)[1]

WHAT three-way connection can plausibly exist between *The Prelude*, Newtonian science, and 'the traffickers in Negro blood' (*Prel.* x. 206) invoked in Book X? I want to argue that the very invisibility of the relation between Wordsworth's autobiographical poem, Isaac Newton, and the slave-trade at once marks the site of a historical absence and identifies the entire *Prelude* as a site of historical repression; indeed, the repression of this crucial chapter of eighteenth-century economic history may even be symptomatic of the mission of high Romanticism, as defined by Wordsworth himself in resonant terms at the close of his poem ('Prophets of Nature, we to [men] will speak | A lasting inspiration . . . Instruct them how the mind of man becomes | A thousand times more beautiful than the earth | On which he dwells . . .', xiii. 442–8). My argument therefore engages with recent new historicist accounts of the ideological functioning of Romantic poetry such as that of Jerome McGann; I have in mind his view of Wordsworth as exemplary of the tendency of Romantic poems 'to develop different sorts of artistic means with which to occlude and disguise their own involvement in a certain nexus of historical relations'. Character-

---

[1] L. Althusser and É. Balibar, *Reading Capital*, trans. B. Brewster (London, 1970), 26, 17.

istically, McGann suggests, Wordsworth relegates history to a region 'too deep for tears'—a move with which (until recently) Romantic criticism has been complicit.[2] I differ from McGann, however, in viewing an institution such as the slave-trade not simply as a historical context which needs to be reconstructed in order to show what has been omitted from *The Prelude*, by what process, for what gains, and at what cost; nor, on the other hand, do I view it entirely as a ghostly, immanent topicality surfacing with uncanny persistence where least expected. History, in this sense, is neither the true referent of *The Prelude*—that to which it allegorically refers—nor its political unconscious. Rather, *The Prelude* is itself the text of history, in which we can trace the 'inaudible and illegible notation' (Althusser) of effects which include both its history of privileged individual poetic subjectivity ('The Growth of a Poet's Mind'), and the characteristic autobiographical mode of that history. I want, then, to read the slave-trade as an economic instance—one structure among others—of which *The Prelude* is an effect, but which the poem itself must erase from its vision as a condition of its very legibility.

The Prelude was completed in 1805: the abolition of the British slave-trade finally took place in 1807. The historical moment when 'Wordsworth' comes into being as the author of *The Prelude*, the ideologue of Romantic humanism, and (with hindsight) the major exponent of Romantic autobiography, coincided both with the numerical peaking of the British slave-trade and with the most vigorous period of Abolitionist agitation. During the 1790s, nearly half a million slaves (approximately 448,000) were shipped by Britain from Africa to the West Indies and America at an average annual rate of 45,000 per year.[3] At the same time, Abolitionist legislation was introduced into Parliament almost annually during the late 1780s and early 1790s. In Revolutionary France, mulatto agitation and slave revolts on the island of Saint Domingue had intensified Abolitionist debate as well as producing the specific acts

[2] See J. J. McGann, *The Romantic Ideology: A Critical Investigation* (Chicago and London, 1983), 82–3, 90–2. For a somewhat different attempt to put the ghost of history back into Imagination, see A. Liu, 'Wordsworth: The History in "Imagination" ', *ELH* 51 (1984), 505–48, repr. in Liu, *Wordsworth: The Sense of History*, pp. 3–31, which also contains a running dialogue about the relation of Liu's own new Formalist work to new Historicism.

[3] See J. A. Rawley, *The Transatlantic Slave Trade: A History* (New York and London, 1981), 165, Table 7.1.

of legislation by which, in 1792, the Gironde-dominated Legislative Assembly upheld the rights of citizenship granted to free-born people of colour in 1791.[4] One might have expected Wordsworth to be caught up in the Abolitionist movement during his stay in France in the early 1790s when the issues were being debated by Brissot and others; Thomas Clarkson himself (Wordsworth's senior at St John's College, Cambridge, by only a few years), had already visited Revolutionary Paris in the summer of 1789 in order to make contact with the Societé des amis des noirs, of which Condorcet and Brissot were members.[5] Yet Wordsworth's single explicit allusion to the Abolition movement occurs in the context of his account in Book X of returning from Revolutionary France to England in 1792, to find 'the air yet busy with the stir | Of a contention which had been raised up | Against the traffickers in Negro blood' (*Prel.* x. 204–6). At this point he perceived the Abolitionist cause as just another 'caravan . . . travel[ling] forward towards Liberty'; a cause, moreover, which 'had ne'er | Fastened on [his] affections', and one whose failure did not 'much excite | [His] sorrow' since he believed, in Utopian fashion, that the slave-trade would wither away automatically once the Revolution in France succeeded ('this most rotten branch of human shame . . . Would fall together with its parent tree', x. 216–26).

The radical Wordsworth of the early 1790s may well have been reacting against Abolitionist anxiousness to dissociate the cause of

---

[4] Wordsworth's introduction to the National Assembly (possibly by Brissot) took place in December 1791 when it was preoccupied with events in Saint Domingue; see N. Roe, *Wordsworth and Coleridge: The Radical Years* (Oxford, 1988), 43. For a history of these events, see D. P. Geggus, *Slavery, War, and Revolution: The British Occupation of Saint Domingue 1793–1798* (Oxford, 1982). Briefly, after the decree granting citizenship to free-born people of colour, the black slaves of Saint Domingue (Haiti) rose in revolt and were joined by the free-born mulattos, who together outnumbered the French colonial planters; as a result of the ensuing civil unrest, the latter successfully petitioned the French Government to repeal the decree, although the government commissioners sent to Saint Domingue ended by taking the part of the black slaves and mulattos and a decree of 1792 re-established the equality of mulattos and whites. Slavery itself was not abolished in the French colonies until 1794.

[5] William Wilberforce (also a graduate of St John's College, Cambridge) had originally intended to visit Paris, but was dissuaded for political reasons, and Clarkson went in his stead; see R. Furneaux, *William Wilberforce* (London, 1974), 90–2. Absorbed into the Cercle social in 1791, the Societé des amis des noirs resembled it in campaigning only for the civil rights of free persons of colour; see G. Kates, *The Cercle Social, the Girondins, and the French Revolution* (Princeton, 1985).

anti-slavery from Jacobin politics;[6] wide political support for the movement was thought to depend on its perception as a primarily humanitarian issue. But Wordsworth's detachment in the time present of *The Prelude*'s composition is harder to explain. By then he had become the close friend of Coleridge, whose active involvement as an Abolitionist speaker is well documented, and spills over into his poetry during the 1790s.[7] The occasion of Wordsworth's well-known sonnet 'To Toussaint L'Ouverture', the symbolic leader and spokesman for the slave Revolution of Saint Domingue, was Toussaint's arrest in 1802 after resisting Napoleon's edict re-establishing slavery.[8] By 1804, Clarkson himself had become a Lake District friend and neighbour, and the two families were in regular correspondence as the pressure for Abolition mounted once more.[9] In 1807, Wordsworth's sonnet 'To Thomas Clarkson, on the Final Passing of the Bill for the Abolition of the Slave Trade' hails him as the leader of 'that enterprise sublime'. In other words, we know where Wordsworth and his friends stood on the issue of slavery—firmly with freedom—yet *The Prelude* seems to have nothing to say about it.[10] Why not? What follows attempts

[6] See K. R. Johnston, 'Philanthropy or Treason? Wordsworth as "Active Partisan" ', *SiR* 25 (1986), 371–409, for the suggestion that Wordsworth's political sympathies may have led him dangerously far into opposition journalism during the mid-1790s.

[7] See Coleridge's 1795 'Lecture on the Slave-trade', reprinted as an essay in 1796 in *The Watchman*, for Coleridge's familiarity with contemporary Abolitionist writing: *Lectures 1795 on Politics and Religion*, ed. L. Patton and P. Mann (Princeton, 1971), 232–51. For the importance of the lecture form in the Abolitionist movement, see J. Walvin, 'The Propaganda of Anti-Slavery', in J. Walvin (ed), *Slavery and British Society 1776–1846* (Baton Rouge, 1982), 49–68. Cf. also the many references to the slave-trade in Coleridge's poems, for instance *Religious Musings*, ll. 139–41, *The Destiny of Nations*, ll. 442–7, 'Ode to the Departing Year', ll. 88–9, and 'Fears in Solitude', ll. 49–53—all of which Wordsworth would have known by the time he wrote *The Prelude*. For Coleridge's own account of his involvement in the Abolitionist cause in a letter to Clarkson of 1808, see *Collected Letters of Samuel Taylor Coleridge*, ed. E. L. Griggs (6 vols.; Oxford, 1956–71), iii. 78.

[8] 1803 saw the formal restoration of slavery and colour lines in the French colonies; cf. also Wordsworth's companion sonnet, 'September 1, 1802', when the rights of citizenship extended across racial boundaries by the French Convention in 1794 were rescinded and blacks expelled from France (see *PW* iii. 113).

[9] See the correspondence between the Wordsworths and the Clarksons between 1802 and 1805, *EY passim*. The Abolition movement languished during the decade from 1794 until its active revival in 1804, when the time again seemed ripe for further attempts at Abolitionist legislation.

[10] In 1801, when Wordsworth sent Wilberforce (along with James Fox) a copy of the 2nd edn. of *Lyrical Ballads* (1800), he writes of himself as a 'Fellow-labourer . . .

to answer the question, and to sketch the implication of *The Prelude* in its own historical moment, not as its mirror, but rather as an aspect of the writing of that very history. In short, I want to propose a symptomatic reading which uncovers the text of slavery as at once a necessary absence in *The Prelude* and what its very lacunae—its inaudible and illegible notations—paradoxically inscribe.

The ideology of transcendence articulated by *The Prelude* demands a corresponding silence about the material conditions on which Wordsworth's society, his poetry, and his autobiographical self-representation were ultimately founded. The characteristic expression of this ideology in *The Prelude* is providential narrative, or the singling out of the individual mind as the privileged subject, not so much of, as outside of, history, both past and present. An instance of the repression of history in the interests of philosophic autobiography occurs in Book IV of *The Prelude* where Wordsworth's humanitarian concern with the pathetic detritus of Britain's West Indian campaign in the 1790s produces the figure of the Discharged Soldier. Although the episode was composed in early 1798, the meeting is located a decade earlier, during Wordsworth's first long vacation at Hawkshead.[11] By removing the

in the same Vineyard', see *EY* 685. The history of Wordsworth's relations towards the slave-trade is complicated by the fact that he numbered among his friends the sons of prominent Bristol sugar merchants and wealthy Nevis plantation owners such as John Pinney and James Tobin; Bristol was at this point Britain's second largest slaving port as well as closely tied by its mercantile economy to the sugar-producing West Indian colonies. John Pinney, Jr., who arranged for Wordsworth's lease of Racedown, inherited the Nevis estate in 1794 on his 21st birthday: see *EY* 148 n. James Tobin (the 'dear brother Jem' of 'We are Seven') spent the end of his life superintending his father's plantation on Nevis and working for the abolition of slavery: see ibid. 210 n. James Tobin, Sr., by contrast, gave evidence to the House of Commons in favour of continuing the slave-trade (see Rawley, *The Transatlantic Slave Trade*, p. 173) and he had earlier been involved in a famous pamphlet debate with the Revd James Ramsay, formerly a minister on the West Indian island of St Christopher, over the conditions of slaves in the plantations: see J. Tobin, *Cursory Remarks upon the Reverend Mr Ramsay's Essay on the Treatment and Conversion of African Slaves in the Sugar Colonies* (Bristol, 1785) and *A Short Rejoinder to the Reverend Mr Ramsay's Reply with a Word or Two on some other publications of the same tendency* (Bristol, 1787). Clarkson's *Essay on the Slavery and Commerce of the Human Species* (London, 1786) singles out Tobin's name as one 'which I feel myself obliged to hand down with detestation' (p. xviii).

[11] If *The Prelude*'s own chronology is to be believed, the encounter with the Discharged Soldier took place in 1788 or 1789; see Reed, *Wordsworth: The Chronology of the Early Years, 1770–1799*, pp. 30–1, 88 and n., 95, 215. While the episode has a Hawkshead setting, it incorporates details belonging to the Alfoxden

Discharged Soldier from his contemporary context, Wordsworth obliterates the passage of colonial history to which he properly belongs. The West Indian campaigns of which the soldier is a veteran are never named, nor is their purpose; after the slave revolution in Saint Domingue, Britain had sided with the colonial French against both free blacks and slaves—in effect maintaining the institution of slavery via British occupation—in order to harass Revolutionary France and further Britain's own colonial interests in the West Indies.[12] The Discharged Soldier, a spectral shape iconographically related to Milton's Death, is seen by Wordsworth (and frequently so read by his critics) as an ambiguous representation of a troubling Romantic quietism, solipsism, or solitude, whose ultimate referent is the poet himself.[13] Here the 'history' that Wordsworth makes visible for us is assimilated to the interiorized poetic history voiced in parodic form by the fever-wasted soldier when he explains that 'My trust is in the God of Heaven, | And in the eye of him that passes me' (*Prel.* iv. 494–5). The Discharged Soldier thus comes to us, transfigured, as an instance of sublimely self-negligent faith in providence, rather than as the waste product of an ultimately imperial enterprise.

Slavery as such, colonialism as such, must be excluded from *The Prelude* if it is to maintain its fictive representation of the providentially self-shaped mind, preserved by election from the distorting forces of its own time. But despite the overarching providential design of *The Prelude*, a counter-movement within it points to a different, more troubling reading of the history on which the poem is actually predicated. The very process which made the Romantic individual its typical (and typically autobiographical) hero also, arguably, brought about the abolition of the slave-trade. Like other social reform movements in the 1790s, the Abolitionist cause fed on the prosperity which the economic

period, and the major epidemics of yellow fever of which the Discharged Soldier is presumably a survivor took place during the 1790s: see Geggus, *Slavery, War, and Revolution: The British Occupation of Saint Domingue 1793–1798*, pp. 347–72.

[12] For the history of British involvement in Saint Domingue during the 1790s, see ibid. The British response to the events in Saint Domingue had been to send troops to help the French colonial planters, fighting against both the black insurgents and the French Revolutionary troops, and eventually to set up its own occupied zone, which lasted until 1797. See also R. Blackburn, *The Overthrow of Colonial Slavery, 1776–1848* (London, 1988), pp. 213–64.

[13] See *Paradise Lost*, ii. 666–73, and cf. also the spectral poet of Wordsworth's schoolboy exercise in gothicism, *The Vale of Esthwaite*, ll. 325–59 (*PW* i. 277–8).

arrangements of a mercantile and imperialist society had helped to create. The history in, and of, *The Prelude* is among other things the history of an enlightenment which Wordsworth (along with the Abolitionists) might call a triumph of Reason, but which also took the form of an ideological contradiction so intolerable that it had either to be hidden from sight, or else legislated out of existence. The coherence of *The Prelude* depends on its refusal to 'see' the contradiction. I want to indicate some of the effects of this oversight, most notably as they appear in two passages of textual disturbance which mark the very moment when its blindness to the slave-trade (what Althusser would call 'the blinded eye of [*The Prelude*'s] self-reflection when it scans its non-objects . . . *in order not to look at them*') comes closest to a form of seeing. The first passage, which involves a form of narrative displacement or metonymy, occurs in Book IV, where Isaac Newton, the revolutionary scientist, meets John Newton, the Evangelical ex-captain of a slave ship. The second passage, characterized by all the violence and condensation of metaphor, occurs in Book XII; slavery and the origins of modern astronomy are again brought into strange conjunction, this time in the Druidic past of Salisbury Plain. Finally, I will suggest that Wordsworth's remarking of the signs of the past gestures towards the Romantic reading of history itself—history as literary history, the history of *The Prelude*'s own writing; in other words, that the poem's glimpse of its self-reflection also constitutes a significant moment of self-reading.

'*Mighty is the charm of those abstractions . . .*'

I want to begin by putting forward the seemingly bizarre suggestion that Isaac Newton, the scientific thinker who dominated Wordsworth's formal Cambridge education, is at once a figure for philosophic transcendence in *The Prelude*, a means of obliterating contemporary institutions such as the slave-trade, and, paradoxically, the figure by which that censorship is at least partially overcome. On the face of it, Newton is yet another of the symbolic solitaries in *The Prelude* who serves as a refraction for Wordsworth himself. But while Newtonian science enters the poem as an intellectual abstraction—or rather, as a symbol for abstract thought ('Mighty is the charm | Of those abstractions', vi. 178–9)—its contemporary application to sea-going commerce and colonial activity during the

eighteenth century, of which the slave-trade is an aspect, remains
unwritable. 'Newton with his prism and silent face' (iii. 59)
becomes an emblem of unworldliness; in the famous later revision
to *The Prelude*, 'Voyaging through strange seas of Thought, alone'
(1850: iii. 63), rather than eighteenth-century entrepreneurial
activity. In Wordsworth's revision, Newton's voyage is 'just'
a metaphor; we know nothing of his cargo, his destination,
or his instruments of navigation. Elsewhere, when Newton's
'physiognomy' figures in London (along with that of 'Boyle,
Shakespear ... or the attractive head | Of some quack-doctor,
famous in his day', vii. 182–3), it does so, not as a token of his
contribution to the commercial world of the city, but rather as a
symptom of its jumbled semiotics and debased cultural inscriptions.
But precisely because the institutionalization of Newtonian science
at Cambridge led Wordsworth to regard it in the light of
intellectual, even religious, abstraction, rather than in relation to
eighteenth-century technology and commerce, Newton offers a
point of entry into the scandal of the slave-trade, allowing it,
paradoxically, to surface by way of its metaphoric freight—the very
metaphor of exploration which Wordsworth later deploys in the
1850 *Prelude*.

When Wordsworth lists the formidable intellectual acquisitions
of the infant prodigy in Book V of *The Prelude*, he turns out to be a
budding imperialist, precociously equipped to navigate a voyage of
exploration:

> The ensigns of the empire which he holds—
> The globe and sceptre of his royalties—
> Are telescopes, and crucibles, and maps.
> Ships he can guide across the pathless sea
> And tell you all their cunning . . .
>
> (*Prel.* v. 328–32)[14]

The boy prodigy's learning includes the use of the very instruments

---

[14] Wordsworth's target seems also to be Evangelical education—'the moral part |
Is perfect', v. 318–19. Because many of the early Newton-influenced thinkers had
been forced to leave the universities for religious reasons, they became clustered
within the dissenting academies; Isaac Watts, the hymn writer, himself educated at a
dissenting academy, published *the knowledge of the heavens and the earth made
easy, or the first principles of astronomy and geography explain'd by the use of
globes and maps* (London, 1726) which may well have been required reading for the
boy prodigy.

—telescopes, nautical quadrants, maps—symbolic of Britain's mercantile success during the eighteenth century. These instruments represented the technological application of Newtonian theory in the century that precedes the writing of *The Prelude*. In 1714, Parliament had offered a reward of £20,000 to anyone who could discover a practicable means of finding the longitude at sea. As E. G. R. Taylor writes about the mathematicians of Hanoverian England,

It was held as a matter of course ... at this period that the country's prosperity depended upon trade, and that the safety and expansion of shipping on the trans-oceanic routes was therefore all-important. The preoccupation of men of science with the problem of establishing position at sea is consequently understandable, and this applied particularly to the astronomers.[15]

Even if it made up only a small percentage of British income— perhaps half of one per cent—the slave-trade was still a crucial ingredient in England's so-called 'triangular' sea trade, the export of industrial manufactured goods to African markets, the shipping of slaves to the colonies, and the reimportation of raw materials from the West Indies for processing in England.[16] By the 1790s, Britain alone was responsible for over half the entire African trade. Nor should we forget that the early voyages of exploration were in themselves an aspect of European colonial expansion; Columbus's voyage of discovery could even be said to have opened up the Atlantic slave-routes.[17]

The late eighteenth-century Cambridge where Wordsworth studied was an educational institution transformed—unlike Oxford at the same period—by the legacy of Newtonian physics and

[15] E. G. R. Taylor, *The Mathematical Practitioners of Hanoverian England 1714–1840* (Cambridge, 1966), 16. See also M. Strong, *An Essay on the Usefulness of Mathematical Learning* (2nd edn., Oxford, 1721), which credits 'The grand secret of the whole Machine' to 'the incomparable Mr Newton' (p. 9), for an explicit identification of astronomy and geometry with navigation—'so noble an Art, that upon this single account those excellent Sciences [i.e astronomy and geometry] deserve most of all to be study'd, and merit the greatest encouragement from a Nation, that owes to it both its Riches and Security' (ibid. 27). Strong's essay is a powerful argument for the importance of applied mathematics to all aspects of maritime technology.

[16] For the economics of the slave-trade, both theoretical and actual, see Rawley, *The Transatlantic Slave Trade*, pp. 247–81; Rawley argues that both 'triangular' and 'direct trade' coexisted during the 18th cent. (see ibid. 260–1).

[17] See ibid. 3.

astronomy.[18] Along with *Principia Mathematica* (1687), Euclid's *Elements* had pride of place. Newton had established the privileged status of Euclid in Cambridge mathematics for the entire eighteenth century by choosing to present his system in terms of classical geometry. But Newtonianism went far beyond the mathematical tripos in which Wordsworth, coming from a school distinguished for its mathematical training and arriving at Cambridge already a year ahead of his contemporaries, would have been expected to excel.[19] Besides ensuring a place in the syllabus for works of philosophy designed to assimilate Christianity to post-Newtonian thought, the Newtonian spirit was also associated with the spirit of philosophic enquiry, of which the boy prodigy's scepticism may be an instance ('He sifts, he weighs, | Takes nothing upon trust . . . All things are put to question', *Prel.* v. 337–8, 341), but which also helped to make Cambridge a school for political radicalism and religious dissent.[20] Clarkson himself singles out the adoption in 1786 of William Paley's *Moral Philosophy* (1785) as part of the official Cambridge syllabus for the 'extensive effect' its condemnation of slavery had on the minds of students like himself (and why not Wordsworth?).[21] His own famous prize-winning Latin *Essay on the Slavery and Commerce of the Human Species* (1786) had been written for an undergraduate competition set by the Vice-Chancellor, Dr Peckard, himself a vocal opponent of the slave-trade. But the Newtonian spirit figures in Wordsworth's own account of his Cambridge education chiefly as a sublime consolation; he writes of finding in 'the elements | Of geometric science . . . Enough to exalt, to chear [him] and compose', despite the fact that, as an amateur, he 'had stepped | In these inquiries . . . | No farther

[18] For a detailed account of Cambridge mathematics, the impact of Newton, and the mathematical tripos, see W. W. R. Ball, *A History of the Study of Mathematics at Cambridge* (Cambridge, 1889), esp. pp. 97–116.

[19] See C. Wordsworth, *Memoirs of Wordsworth* (2 vols.; London, 1851), i. 14, and see also B. R. Schneider, *Wordsworth's Cambridge Education* (Cambridge, 1957), 4–5. In the event, Wordsworth, as Dorothy puts it in a letter of 1791, 'lost the chance . . . of a fellowship', and 'gave way to his natural dislike of studies so dry as many parts of the mathematics, consequently could not succeed at Cambridge' (*EY* 52).

[20] See Schneider, *Wordsworth's Cambridge Education*, pp. 112–63, for a general account of the radical and 'philosophic' spirit fostered by late 18th-cent. Cambridge; for Wordsworth's academic reading, see ibid. 263–4.

[21] See ibid. 180–1 and n., and Clarkson's *History of the Rise, Progress, and Accomplishment of the Abolition of the African Slave-Trade* (2 vols.; London, 1808), i. 91–4.

than the threshold' (*Prel.* vi. 136–41). As he meditates with 'Indian awe and wonder' on the geometrical sublime ('the alliance of those simple, pure | Proportions and relations, with the frame | And laws of Nature', vi. 142–6), we witness not only the power of science to provide an abstract model of the natural world, but the evaporation of history. Or rather, we glimpse the way in which the alliance of Newtonian geometry and the 'laws of Nature' subsumes the temporal into the transcendent realm which Wordsworth, like Newton, associates with a Christian deity:

> Yet from this source more frequently I drew
> A pleasure calm and deeper, a still sense
> Of permanent and universal sway
> And paramount endowment in the mind,
> An image not unworthy of the one
> Surpassing life, which—out of space and time,
> Nor touched by welterings of passion—is,
> And hath the name of, God.
>
> (*Prel.* vi. 150–7)

In this realm, the historically unmoored subject, buffeted by events beyond its comprehension or control, can take comfort from the Newtonian scheme of overarching order and proportion: 'Transcendent peace | And silence did await upon these thoughts' (vi. 157–8).[22]

Newtonian physics is a powerful tool in the service of the governing myth of *The Prelude*, that of a subjectivity immune even to the Cambridge education which had set him intellectually adrift. But the analogy Wordsworth goes on to offer—between himself and a castaway who mitigates his isolation and despair with a geometrical treatise—brings in its train quite different associations. From Isaac Newton, voyaging through strange seas of thought, we shift to an actual eighteenth-century voyager, a namesake who exposes the commercial and economic underside of the institution of Newtonian science at Cambridge. Wordsworth's account of his castaway is well known to be based on an episode from John Newton's *Authentic Narrative* (1764), which Dorothy Wordsworth had copied into a notebook sometime between 1799 and 1880:

Though destitute of food and clothing, depressed to a degree beyond common wretchedness, I could sometimes collect my mind to mathematical

---

[22] Wordsworth's theological revisions to this difficult passage, vi. 154–7, begin as early as 1807; see *Prel.*, p. 193 n.

studies. I had bought *Barrow's Euclid* at *Plymouth*; it was the only volume
I brought on shore; it was always with me, and I used to take it to remote
corners of the island by the sea-side, and drew my *diagrams* with a long
stick upon the sand. Thus I often beguiled my sorrows, and almost forgot
my feeling—and thus, without any other assistance, I made myself, in a
good measure, master of the first six books of *Euclid*.[23]

Mastery of the first six books of Euclid would have resonated for
Wordsworth with the Cambridge syllabus for advanced students.
The verbal parallels in *The Prelude* are so close that he must have
had the excerpt in front of him as he wrote—must, in fact, have
been aware of the strikingly incongruous context from which he
had drawn this analogy for his own undergraduate lack of
direction:

> as I have read of one by shipwreck thrown
> With fellow sufferers whom the waves had spared
> Upon a region uninhabited,
> An island of the deep, who having brought
> To land a single volume and no more—
> A treatise of geometry—was used,
> Although of food and clothing destitute,
> And beyond common wretchedness depressed,
> To part from company and take this book,
> Then first a self-taught pupil in those truths,
> To spots remote and corners of the isle
> By the seaside, and draw his diagrams
> With a long stick upon the sand, and thus
> Did oft beguile his sorrow, and almost
> Forget his feeling . . .
>
> (*Prel.* vi. 160–74)

[23] J. Newton, *An Authentic Narrative of Some Remarkable and Interesting
Particulars in the Life of . . .* (6th edn., London, 1786), 63. James Tobin, Jr., whom
Wordsworth had asked in Mar. 1798 to 'collect for [him] any books of travels' he
could find (*EY* 212), seems the likeliest source for Wordsworth's acquisition of
Newton's *Authentic Narrative*; Newton's account of the power of geometry to
preserve the mind despite solitude and hardship finds its way into *The Pedlar*, which
was being composed at this time. Tobin had also supplied Wordsworth with the
political tragedy, *Gustavus Vasa* (1739)—which, by another nominal coincidence,
brings to mind the much reprinted *Interesting Narrative of the Life of Olaudah
Equiano, or Gustavus Vassa the African, written by himself* (1789); Equiano
(Gustavus Vasa or Vassa—named after the Swedish hero by his first master) was
an articulate veteran of the Middle Passage and the West Indian colonies whose
autobiography made him a spokesman for anti-slavery during the 1790s (see *EY*
210 n.).

John Newton—Evangelical preacher, writer, curate of Olney, friend of Cowper, minister of St Mary Wolnoth and confidante of the Abolitionist Wilberforce—was not only (as he himself remarks in the context of his own attempts to while away the *longueurs* of the notorious Middle Passage with mathematical studies) Isaac Newton's namesake, but a former captain in the slave-trade.[24] Later to testify publicly about the evils of the trade, Newton was initially best known for a conversion narrative which predates his Abolitionist stance. Why should the figure of a retired slave-trader turned Evangelical minister and Abolitionist spokesman have surfaced at this point in *The Prelude*?

One answer may lie not only in the accident of a name, not only in the subtext of slavery which the institution of Newtonian science brought in its train, but in the relationship of John Newton's spiritual autobiography to Wordsworth's own. Following the conventional form of the Evangelical conversion narrative, Newton represents himself as a spectacular reprobate, saved only in the nick of time, and warned many times over by the fate of less fortunate friends and shipmates. During his unwilling sojourn on the African coast, the young Newton was doubly a castaway—a slave-trader himself virtually enslaved to the local slaver he worked for, and in addition a spiritual castaway. Newton hints at one specifically colonial aspect of his degradation, the fact that, although white, he grew (in the phrase then current in Africa) 'black'—'went native', in a more recent colonial idiom. Wordsworth's 'So was it with me then' (vi. 177) therefore sketches an unlikely parallel between himself as an undergraduate adrift in late eighteenth-century Cambridge and a Kurtz-like castaway beguiling his sorrows with Euclid. Unless, that is, the nautical metaphor holds, and Wordsworth is suggesting that he too would have been all at sea without 'that clear synthesis built up aloft | So gracefully'—without some cosmic scheme from which a solipsistic 'mind beset | With images, and

---

[24] See J. Newton, *Letters to a Wife* (Edinburgh, 1808), 90: 'I am pleased with the mathematics, because there is truth and certainty in them, which are seldom found in other branches of learning. Yet even in these I am discouraged; for the more I advance, the more clearly I perceive, that the greatest human knowledge amounts but to a more pompous proof of our ignorance, by showing us how little we know of any thing . . . when, possibly before I have been an hour within the vail, I shall know more intuitively, than my namesake, Sir Isaac, had ever a glimpse of.' For conditions during the Middle Passage, as well as attempts to counter the high mortality rates among both human cargo and crew, see Rawley, *The Transatlantic Slave Trade*, pp. 283–306.

haunted by itself' (vi. 179–83) might take its bearings. Wordsworth, one might speculate, found in the *Authentic Narrative* (where God personally oversees the redemption of a single sinner) a debased version of the providential scheme of *The Prelude*—and indeed of Isaac Newton's *Principia*, in which God oversees the entire universe. What is *The Prelude* itself, after all, if not just such another narrative in which the growth of a chosen son is overseen by the design of providence?

Newton's *Authentic Narrative* risks exposing the Wordsworthian fiction of special election as an Evangelical commonplace. But the castaway's geometrical diagrams also gesture towards the larger historical instance of the slave-trade and its repression in *The Prelude*. Originally involved in it by accident, Newton stuck to the slave-trade as his profession, and by the time of his marriage had made a respectable career for himself as a captain in the Liverpool-based Atlantic trade. With hindsight, the scandal of the *Authentic Narrative* is its blindness to, and silence about, the institution of slavery which structured Newton's entire sea-going experience. Newton himself later testified that even after his Evangelical conversion, although he disliked his work, he did not think it wrong ('I never had a scruple upon this head, at the time').[25] Only after his later awakening to the Abolitionist cause, when he came to write his pamphlet *Thoughts upon the African Slave-trade* (1788)—which he termed 'a public confession'—did he acknowledge that 'many things which I saw, heard and felt, upon the Coast of Africa, are so deeply engraven in my memory, that I can hardly forget, or greatly mistake them, while I am capable of remembering any thing'.[26] Listing the evils of the trade, he includes among its ill effects a 'tendency to efface the moral sense'.[27] The image of things deeply and unforgettably engraved on the memory (branded, so to speak) suggests that we might read Newton's self-preoccupied account of drawing Euclidean diagrams on the sand as a cover-up—as an effacement: a figure for repression itself. Wordsworth's 1807 sonnet to Clarkson hails Abolition with the words 'The blood-stained Writing is for ever torn' (l. 11). Here the history of slavery is figured as a text written in the blood, and on the bodies, of those who could not themselves write, like the routine branding of slaves with the initials of the trading company which shipped

[25] J. Newton, *Thoughts upon the African Slave-trade* (London, 1788), 3–4.
[26] Ibid. 40.   [27] Ibid. 14.

them 'out of Africa' (a phrase whose connection with the African diaspora has been effaced by a more recent colonial romance). We could go further and suggest that Newton's geometrical diagrams were themselves a form, not only of cosmic writing, but also of cosmic imperialism—the inscription of intellectual mastery effected by Newtonian science over the physical and material world during the eighteenth century. Not for nothing did Blake make Newton, Western civilization's most commanding symbol for the power of the mind to chart the *terra incognita* of the cosmos, a figure of rational bounding, limitation, and, ultimately, of political tyranny. This doubly Newtonian episode in Book VI allows us to read the repressed connection between the branding of slaves and Euclidean geometry; between the economics of the slave-trade and the Newtonian education offered by Cambridge at the end of the eighteenth century. But because writing simultaneously functions as effacement and as a trace of the multiple inscriptions of the text of history in *The Prelude*, we can also say that—like the figure of Newton—inscription serves to bring to light what it hides from view.

'Things that may be Viewed . . . in the Obscurities of Time'

I want to turn now to the other passage in *The Prelude* where slavery and astronomy are brought into disturbing conjunction. Writing of Charlotte Brontë's *Jane Eyre*, Gayatri Spivak suggests that Bertha Mason sets fire to Thornfields 'so that Jane Eyre can become the feminist individualist heroine of British fiction'. She goes on to read the conflagration as 'an allegory of the general epistemic violence of imperialism, the construction of a self-immolating colonial subject for the glorification of the social mission of the colonizer'.[28] Spivak's argument—that the construction, or rather destruction, of the self-immolating colonial subject guarantees the survival of the colonizer—might well be applied to Wordsworth's double vision of barbaric human sacrifice and proto-humanist astronomy in Book XII of *The Prelude*. In the *Salisbury Plain* poems of the mid-1790s, barbaric immolation had already functioned as Wordsworth's own allegory for the consuming violence of Britain's war-mongering imperialism. Seeing the past

[28] 'Three Women's Texts and a Critique of Imperialism', *Critical Inquiry*, 12 (1985), 251.

meant seeing the present by its lurid light, hearing the voices of present suffering in the groans of imagined sacrificial victims.[29] But by the time of *The Prelude*, the Salisbury Plain episode is overlaid by a process analogous to the birth of the feminist individualist heroine; that is, the emergence of the prophetic poet-visionary whose growth is Wordsworth's announced subject. Book XII describes this process in humbly self-aggrandizing terms ('I, the meanest of this band', xii. 306) as Wordsworth's claim to be counted among those poets 'Connected in a mighty scheme of truth' and dowered with the ability 'to perceive | Something unseen before' (xii. 302–5); located specifically at the period when the Salisbury Plain episode actually took place is Wordsworth's hope that 'in some sort [he] possessed | A privilege'—that 'a work of [his] ... might become | A power like one of Nature's' (xii. 308–12).[30] Seeing 'Something unseen before', however, turns out to mean not seeing; in his antiquarian reverie ('I had a reverie and saw the past', xii. 320), Wordsworth both calls upon the darkness to blind him and perceives the darkness visible of a literary fiction that is also a (his) literary history:

> I called upon the darkness, and it took—
> A midnight darkness seemed to come and take—
> All objects from my sight; and lo, again
> The desart visible by dismal flames!
> It is the sacrifical altar, fed
> With living men—how deep the groans!—the voice
> Of those in the gigantic wicker thrills
> Throughout the region far and near, pervades
> The monumental hillocks, and the pomp
> Is for both worlds, the living and the dead.
>
> (*Prel.* xii. 327–36)

This moment of imagined blindness to the phenomenal world

[29] See *The Salisbury Plain Poems of William Wordsworth*, ed. S. Gill (Ithaca, NY, 1975), 1793, ll. 424–32: 'Though from huge wickers paled with circling fire | No longer horrid shrieks and dying cries | To ears of Daemon-Gods in peals aspire, | To Daemon-Gods a human sacrifice ... What does it more than while the tempests rise, | With starless glooms and sounds of loud dismay, | Reveal with still-born glimpse the terrors of our way?'

[30] Cf. Coleridge's well-known praise, on the basis of his early reading of *Salisbury Plain*, for Wordsworth's 'original gift of spreading the tone, the *atmosphere*, and with it the depth and height of the ideal world around forms, incidents, and situations, of which, for the common view, custom had bedimmed all the lustre, had dried up the sparkle and the dew-drops', *Biographia Literaria*, i. 80.

allows Wordsworth to read the past by the light of *Paradise Lost* and eighteenth-century antiquarianism. To be specific, he reads on to the landscape the bloody practices commonly (but mistakenly) associated with one version of the Druid myth in his sources.[31] Or, to put it another way, his vision in blindness unveils the human sacrifice that feeds an entire literary culture.

In the light of Spivak's allegory, we might say that Wordsworth's narrative of the attainment of vision in *The Prelude* sets in motion an economy of consumption; living men burn so that Wordsworth himself may join the elect band of poet-visionaries. Aylett Sammes, in his *Britannia Antiqua Illustrata* (1676) tells us that 'the gigantic wicker' was 'a Statue or Image of a MAN in vast proportion, whose limbs consisted of Twigs, weaved together in the nature of Basket-ware: These they fill'd with live men . . .'[32] Romantic humanism, whose preferred icon is also the 'image of a MAN in vast proportion', arguably rests on this base of human sacrifice. But in a sequence which ostensibly enacts the gentling of the violence of the imagination by a compensatory humanity, the prehistoric conflagration gives way to the 'charm' of what Wordsworth calls 'an antiquarian's dream' (xii. 348)—a timeless, Romanticized image of the past, represented by cosmic nature and its accompanying Newtonian abstraction. Now Druidic priests reappear in the guise of pre-Newtonian astronomers; natural teachers, they point 'to the starry sky, | Alternately, and plain below', where 'Lines, circles, mounts, a mystery of shapes' inscribe the 'infant science' of astronomy on the landscape with 'imitative forms' which 'imaged forth | The constellations' (xii. 340–51). Although these priestly astronomers had already been present in the earliest version of *Salisbury Plain* ('Long bearded forms with wands uplifted . . . trace with awe their various files | All figured on the mystic plain below',

---

[31] For the tradition of the Druids as practitioners of human sacrifice on which Wordsworth draws both in *The Prelude* and in the earlier *Salisbury Plain*, see A. L. Owen, *The Famous Druids* (Oxford, 1962), 20–1, 154–68; for antiquarian interest in the archaeological traces of Druid 'temples', and the astronomical calendars speculatively associated with them, see ibid. 101–37. The most pervasive account of Druids as scholar–priests especially associated with astronomy and mathematics would have been Caesar's *Gallic Wars*. For Wordsworth's own scholarly bibliography of classical sources dealing with the Druids, see *The Salisbury Plain Poems of William Wordsworth*, p. 35 n. Liu, *Wordsworth: The Sense of History*, pp. 190–201, offers a detailed account of Wordsworth's Druidic sources as well as a persuasive alternative reading of the Salisbury Plain episode as an allegory of the French Revolution.   [32] See *Prel.* 454 n.

ll. 191, 195–6), nothing there had specifically associated them
with Wordsworth.[33] In Book XII of *The Prelude*, however, they are
summoned up as prototypes of the poet-humanist ('he [who] hath
stood | By Nature's side among the men of old', xii. 296–7) at the
very moment when Wordsworth installs himself and his poem in
the ahistorical, timeless scheme of the Newtonian cosmos. The
politics of visibility surface in the Salisbury Plain passage to show
us the self-reflection of Wordsworth's 'blinded eye'—the way in
which his recently acquired ability 'to have sight | Of a new world'
(xii. 370–1) demands his oversight of the most striking contemporary
instance of the barbarism which he had originally associated with
Stonehenge and which now takes its place in what Althusser calls
'the *inner darkness of exclusion*'.[34]

In the light of the earlier *Salisbury Plain*, we might be tempted to
read this passage from Book XII of *The Prelude* as an optimistic narrative about the historical triumph of enlightenment Reason (symbolized by early mathematics and astronomy) over Superstition.[35]
But the juxtaposition of human sacrifice and pre-Newtonian
astronomy also suggests a darker reading. 'Enlightenment' itself—
the very spirit of humanistic and scientific inquiry represented by
Clarkson's anti-slave-trade investigations—may depend on the
ideological climate of a society whose prosperity was bound up
with the commercial system to which slavery had been integral, but
in which free-labour systems were also strikingly successful. One
such argument has recently been advanced for the eventual success
of the Abolition movement, superseding earlier accounts represented
on the one hand by Wordsworth's contemporary, Thomas
Clarkson, and on the other, by classic twentieth-century Marxist
analyses. In the *History of the Rise, Progress, and Accomplishment
of the Abolition of the African Slave-Trade* (1808), Clarkson saw
the success of the Abolitionist cause as the triumph of moral
enlightenment over historical error; this is the so-called 'intellectual

---

[33] In a later revision to Book III, Wordsworth writes of himself at Cambridge as
'A youthful Druid taught in shady groves | Primeval mysteries, a Bard elect . . .'; see
The Prelude, ed. de Selincourt, rev. Darbishire, pp. 75–6 app. crit.

[34] See *Reading Capital*, p. 26.

[35] Cf. the closing stanza of *Salisbury Plain*, where 'the herculean mace | Of
Reason' ousts Error, 'till not a trace | Be left on earth of Superstition's reign, | Save
that eternal pile which frowns on Sarum's plain' (ll. 547–9). Martin Strong, in *An
Essay on the Usefulness of Mathematical Learning*, lists among the general
advantages of mathematical study those of freeing the mind 'from prejudice,
credulity and superstition' (pp. 2–3).

diffusionist' argument. The counter-argument, that of economic and material self-interest, finds its classic expression in Eric Williams's *Capitalism and Slavery* (1944); Abolition ultimately succeeded because the slave-trade had ceased to be profitable and revenues from the plantations had declined—an explanation with which economic historians since Williams have taken issue on its own terms.[36] Recently, however, more complex cultural arguments have tended to suggest that a consumer society's image of and discourse about itself had evolved by the end of the eighteenth century to the point where the slave-trade—imperialism's most visible form of human consumption—was no longer tolerable.[37] Such a reading of the passage from Book XII of *The Prelude* turns it, not simply into an allegory of the economy of consumption on which Wordsworthian election depends, or by which the Enlightenment itself was secretly nourished, but into a more complex allegory of the way in which that Enlightenment must erase from its consciousness, or at least from its legal discourse (the codified expression of ideology), the barbarism of modern human sacrifice. History—'the obscurities of time'—becomes the depository for what is unthinkable in the present.

But there is more to be said, and once more it turns on a moment of reading associated with this attempted erasure; or rather, a moment of self-reading. We might be justified in seeing the

[36] For a brief critique of these two differing explanations for the success of the Abolition movement, see H. Temperley, 'The Ideology of Anti-Slavery', in D. Eltis and J. Walvin (eds.), *The Abolition of the Atlantic Slave Trade* (Madison, 1981), 21–35, and 'Capitalism, Slavery, and Ideology', *Past and Present*, 75 (1977), 94–118. Notable contestations of Williams's thesis on economic grounds include S. Drescher, *Econocide: British Slavery in the Era of Abolition* (Pittsburgh, 1977), and B. L. Solow and S. L. Engerman (eds.), *British Capitalism and Caribbean Slavery* (Cambridge, 1987). For an extended discussion of the political, religious, and ideological climate in which Abolition finally took place, see also D. B. Davis, *The Problem of Slavery in the Age of Revolution* (Ithaca, NY, 1975), 343–468.

[37] See e.g. Temperley, in Eltis and Walvin (eds.), *The Abolition of the Atlantic Slave Trade*, pp. 21–35: 'the attack on slavery can be seen as an attempt by a dominant metropolitan ideology to impose its values on the societies of the economic periphery . . . this attack was the product of a widening ideological gap occasioned by the extraordinary success, not least in material terms, of those societies which practiced a free-labor system, among which Britain and the northern United States were outstanding examples' (ibid. 29–30). The issue is also argued at length by D. Eltis, *Economic Growth and the Ending of the Transatlantic Slave Trade* (Oxford, 1987), and S. Drescher, *Capitalism and Antislavery: British Mobilization in Comparative Perspective* (Oxford, 1988).

mysterious shapes inscribed on Salisbury Plain, 'With intricate profusion figuring o'er | The untilled ground' (xii. 342–3), as an allusion to the layering of texts in Book XII; traces of the *Salisbury Plain* poems which underlie this episode of *The Prelude* disrupt the surface of 'a work . . . like one of Nature's' to show us the past of Wordsworth's own poetry. Where nature seems to be, there was once *The Prelude*'s textual history. Such moments of temporal and textual overdetermination have the further implication that we might be hard put to distinguish between the erasure of history and the erasure of a precursor poem, whether Wordsworth's or another's. Wordsworth's confrontation with the text of history is in any case necessarily a moment of imaginative projection or construction, a reading from and of the present of *The Prelude* ('This for the past, and things that may be viewed, | *Or fancied*, in the obscurities of time', xii. 354–5; my italics). Eighteenth-century antiquarianism shapes the form of the past, whether primitivistic or proto-humanist. Recuperating history into the Newtonian scheme traced on the landscape of Salisbury Plain has the effect of recasting it in the providential mould which underpins the entire autobiographical enterprise of *The Prelude*. In so doing, it also provides an image—a figure—for Romantic reading of the past. The 'infant science' that is 'covertly expressed' here is not astronomy but what astronomy stands for elsewhere in Wordsworth's writing, namely, 'the telescope of Art' which in his *Reply to 'Mathetes'* (1809–10) 'call[s] the invisible Stars out of their hiding-places' and reveals to the self-enquirer 'the system of his Being'.[38] Astronomy, in other words, is synonymous with the introspective self-reading performed by autobiography. Romantic history necessarily involves a reading of its own history.

What did the text of history mean for Wordsworth himself? His *Reply to 'Mathetes'*, published in *The Friend* during late 1809 and early 1810, deals explicitly with what I have called the ideology of transcendence, or the argument of *The Prelude* that the seductions of the present can be overcome by a return to timeless nature. 'Mathetes' (the discipular John Wilson and Alexander Blair) idealistically poses the present as a degenerate age. How then avoid an unwarranted admiration for the past? To which Wordsworth replies: progress is not self-evident (but the ultimate end of what he

[38] *Prose Works*, ii. 18. Cf. 'the optic tube of thought' in Wordsworth's MS Y drafts for Book VIII of *The Prelude*: see *Prel.*, p. 503, ll. 148–58.

calls 'the economy of Providence' may be progressive—more like a river than a Roman road) and education is really self-education ('The Growth of a Poet's Mind'): the disciple should look not to Wordsworth as a teacher, but, by implication, to his recipe for self-education in *The Prelude*. My particular concern here, however, is with Wordsworth's 'remarks' about 'the assumed inferiority of the present Age in moral dignity and intellectual power, to those which have preceded it'.[39] His answer to the problem of modern degeneration turns out to be something like a defence of modern poetry—and hence, of his own. At once self-diagnosis and self-justification, Wordsworth's *Reply to 'Mathetes'* suggests that the Romantic past is not only a projection of present concerns but (at least in his own case) specifically a literary past; the past in which *The Prelude* takes its place as part of an imaginary continuum of great works speaking essentially the same language.

Wordsworth alludes at the start of his *Reply* to 'two errors, in which we easily slip when thinking of past times', the first of which

lies in forgetting, in the excellence of what remains, the large overbalance of worthlessness that has been swept away. Ranging over the wide tracts of Antiquity, the situation of the Mind may be likened to that of a Traveller in some unpeopled part of America, who is attracted to the burial place of one of the primitive Inhabitants. It is conspicuous upon an eminence, 'a mount upon a mount!' He digs into it, and finds that it contains the bones of a Man of mighty stature: and he is tempted to give way to a belief, that as there were Giants in those days, so that all Men were Giants. But a second and wiser thought may suggest to him, that this Tomb would never have forced itself upon his notice, if it had not contained a Body that was distinguished from others, that of a Man who had been selected as a Chieftain or Ruler for the very reason that he surpassed the rest of his Tribe in stature, and who now lies thus conspicuously inhumed upon the mountain-top, while the bones of his Followers are laid unobtrusively together in their burrows upon the Plain below.[40]

As Wordsworth reads the landscape of an imagined terrain, 'some unpeopled part of America', what comes to mind first is the skeleton of a giant past, then an individual singled out from others by his stature. Although, ostensibly, 'the question is not of the

[39] *Prose Works*, ii. 8.
[40] Ibid. 9–10. Wordsworth's source is T. Ashe, *Travels, in America, Performed in 1806* (1808). For the 18th-cent. assimilation of Druids and Ancient Britons to contemporary accounts of American Indians, see S. Piggot, *The Druids* (London, 1968), 127–33.

power or worth of individual Minds, but of the . . . merits of an Age',[41] his argument is unwittingly informed by the same traveller's error that colours his double vision of the Druids—that of allowing 'the bearded teachers' to erase the traces of their vast, forgotten audiences, or even of the groaning victims consumed on the sacrifical altar depicted in his first glimpse of the druidic past. Oblivion is the fate of lesser men, whether poets, or those further down the socio-economic pile. Only the exceptional individual (the 'Man of mighty stature') survives, by way of his conspicuously eminent memorial. In place of the doctrine of universal giantism, we find Wordsworth elaborating an élitist theory of literary stature that says: only those who were greater than the rest leave their marks on the landscape. Wordsworth's antiquarian sources may have told him about the vast wicker 'MAN'; but did he himself forget the massive immolation—the huge forgetting—which provides the basis for his own poem, and hence his literary stature?

The second error involves a theory of literature in which the past and the present are contrasted—'in this comparison of Age we divide time merely into past and present, and place them in the balance to be weighed against each other'—instead of

considering that the present is in our estimation not more than a period of thirty years, or half a century at most, and that the past is a mighty accumulation of many such periods, perhaps the whole of recorded time, or at least the whole of that portion of it in which our own Country has been distinguished. We may illustrate this by the familiar use of the words Ancient and Modern, when applied to Poetry—what can be more inconsiderate or unjust than to compare a few existing Writers with the whole succession of their Progenitors?[42]

Wordsworth's construction of literary history involves something like an ahistorical moment, or the synchronous 'One great society alone on earth: | The noble living and the noble dead' (x. 968–9) celebrated in *The Prelude*. One function of the discourse of high Romanticism represented by *The Prelude* is to create the illusion of a unified and continuous literary community, immune to the accidents, repressions, and discontinuities of history, from which all casualties—though not, of course, all martyrs—have been excised. In his *Reply to 'Mathetes'*, Wordsworth makes a timeless continuum link present and past, and in particular the great poets

---

[41] *Prose Works*, ii. 11.   [42] Ibid. 10.

of the present and the past, thereby preventing the injustice of comparing 'a few existing Writers with the whole succession of their Progenitors'; the risk posed by the jejune contrast between Ancients and Moderns is that the past will dwarf the poets of the present (presumably Wordsworth among them) as a few giant figures proliferate into a threatening horde. Assimilating himself to the band of 'poets, even as prophets, each with each | Connected in a mighty scheme of truth' (*Prel.* xii. 301–2) not only allows Wordsworth to claim as his own a 'peculiar dower' which is transhistorical, but prevents him being measured and found wanting in relation to the precursor poets of the past. To obliterate history (and with it, the present as a distinct moment in time) is thus to defend oneself against literary oblivion—at worst, against not being read.

To say that the literary motive which ultimately fuels Wordsworth's repression of history is the familiar one of anxiety about literary priority or pre-eminence risks dwarfing the very issues raised by attempting to read the historical phenomenon of slavery back into the text of *The Prelude*. At the same time, it serves to suggest that the text of history and the text of *The Prelude* are one and the same—that its reading of history is necessarily a self-reading; and that the poem's place in an intertext of literary-historical notations is both its meaning and its history. It goes without saying that this intertext is no less imaginary than the antiquarian dream of Druid astronomy. What structures it, however, is a similar effect—the cultural possibility into which the individual Romantic poet called Wordsworth is inserted (the 'Wordsworth' effect). In other words, *The Prelude* necessarily inscribes not just 'The Growth of a Poet's Mind', but the growth—ideological, cultural, economic—which permitted this particular autobiographical trope to emerge when and as it did. Read like this, the story finally told by the invisibility of the slave-trade in *The Prelude* is not simply an accusatory one relating to Wordsworth's fiction of himself as a chosen poet—the price paid (in Spivak's terms) by the self-immolating colonial subject for the creation of the Romantic individual(ist). Rather, it is a story that installs the poem itself in the discursive context where the massive legislative reform of Abolition finally took place. An expression of the Romantic humanism to which this context also gave rise, *The Prelude* contains its own reading of the erased inscription of institutions as apparently unrelated as Newtonian science and the slave-trade. If, as I have argued, the condition of *The Prelude*'s legibility is what it has rendered illegible, the two episodes from Books VI and XII none the less make fleetingly visible what the poem cannot see but must blindly read, even as it looks away.

As a coda to the issue of slavery in *The Prelude* I want finally to notice an unexpected equivalence in Wordsworth's writing between the slave and the poet. His *Reply to 'Mathetes'* goes on to offer a fable involving 'the WORLD, a female figure approaching at the head of a train of willing or giddy followers' as opposed to 'INTELLECTUAL PROWESS, with a pale cheek and severe brow, leading in chains Truth, her beautiful and modest Captive'.[43] The choice is between 'a discourse of ease, pleasure, freedom, and domestic tranquility' on the one hand, and on the other 'the impediments of disappointments, the ignorance and prejudice which her Followers will have to encounter . . . a scheme of solitary and unremitting labour'. What are we to make of this (gendered) drama of the choice between giddy freedom and solitary, unremitting labour? And what has the chained female slave—a figure of eroticized pathos in the literature and representations of Abolitionist protest—to do with the Wordsworthian education advocated both here and in *The Prelude*? Wordsworth's *Reply to 'Mathetes'* concludes with a quotation from his own 'Ode to Duty':

> Give unto me, made lowly wise,
> The spirit of self-sacrifice;
> *The confidence of reason give:*
> *And in the light of truth thy Bondsman let me live!*
>
> (ll. 61–4)[44]

Here the poet becomes the slave of duty, the sacrificial victim in a scenario involving submission to a higher power; bondage is sublimated as the voluntary obedience which Milton defines as the essence of Liberty. In this economy, the rewards of Intellectual Prowess are represented by the chained captive, Truth. Just as the slave's lack of legal rights, of which the most obvious is the

[43] *Prose Works*, ii. 15. The source of Wordsworth's fable is Xenophon's *Memorabilia*, II. i. 21–33; see *Prose Works*, ii. 37.

[44] Ibid. 25; the italics are Wordsworth's. 'Why fix on me for sacrifice?', Wordsworth had demanded of his Druid persecutors in *The Vale of Esthwaite*, l. 34 (*PW* i. 270).

absence of the right to profit by his or her own work, becomes an image of unworldliness in Wordsworth's fable, so the image of human sacrifice in the 'Ode to Duty' becomes the basis for a new doctrine, that of self-sacrifice; the Romantic self gives up its unbounded freedom ('Me this unchartered freedom tires', l. 37) and instead submits to the 'Stern Lawgiver!' (l. 49) of a post-revolutionary era, in a process analogous to the subject's free acceptance of his or her subjection to the absolutes (Duty, God) which correspond in ideology to the invisible authority of social formations. Wordsworth's 'Ode to Duty', although composed in 1804, was published in 1807, the same year that the Abolition of the slave-trade became law. Could it be that with the increasing strength of the Abolition movement and the eventual outlawing of the slave-trade, slavery became capable of functioning as its opposite, a metaphor for freedom? If the Newtonian scheme surfaces in *The Prelude* at moments where contradictions or disorders in the system threaten to disrupt the visible order of things, one might argue that the figure of the slave surfaces in Wordsworth's educational fable at a corresponding moment—the moment when the poet-subject risks appearing as what he is; namely, the subject of, as well as in, history, a slave to the text in which both he and *The Prelude* are necessarily inscribed.

II
WRITING

CHAPTER 4

WORDSWORTH AND THE LANGUAGE OF THE DREAM

THE strange figure at the start of *The Prelude*, Book V—'This arab phantom . . . This semi-Quixote', 'from the world of sleep' (v. 140–2)—is at once the most dreamlike and the most literary of all Wordsworth's solitaries. Lodged between the phantasmal and the bookish, he occupies the same hinterland as those 'old men, | Old humourists' of Wordsworth's childhood who 'have into phantoms passed | Of texture midway betwixt life and books' (iii. 609–13). The intermediacy here (what kind of texture might this be?) is one that Wordsworth elsewhere emphasizes in its own right with his account of the imagination at work on stone and sea-beast to produce an 'intermediate image', that of the semi-supernatural Leech Gatherer.[1] One might point to Cervantes himself as the most important source for such indeterminacy; Don Quixote both figures and—in his own perceptions—exemplifies the processes of this imaginative hinterland. Similar shocks of indeterminacy unsettle many of the climactic moments of arrest and recognition in *The Prelude*, when the limits of comprehension and of language are reached together, and the invisible world is disclosed. The tumultuous rhetoric of the Vale of Gondo passage ('Characters of the great apocalypse, | The types and symbols of eternity', vi. 570–1) gestures towards a ghostly revelation beyond the scope of writing; if the face of nature could itself become an intelligible text, there would be no need of representation, and no need of nature either. Wordsworth's prototypically Romantic nostalgia for an original or apocalyptic plenitude in language (the word made Logos) hardly needs dwelling on. What does seem worth exploring is the troubling status of both looks and writing—of textuality itself—in a poem which enlists them to 'enshrine the spirit of the past | For future restoration'; 'I would give', Wordsworth yearns in

---

[1] 1815 'Preface', *Prose Works*, iii. 33. Cf. Wordsworth's letter of 14 June 1802 on the 'feeling of spirituality or supernaturalness' aroused by the Leech Gatherer (*EY* 366).

Book XI, '*as far as words can give*, | A substance and a life to what I feel' (xi. 338–42; my italics). One might go further and ask why it is that a dream, the dream of the Arab Quixote, should become the means of confronting this anxiety about the representability of a self that is always by definition 'Of texture midway betwixt life and books'. Though it seems reasonable enough to lament the perishability of books ('shrines so frail'), it is an odd tack to start a Book on books with a dream that turns them, rather ludicrously, into a stone and a shell clutched by a crazed quester—unless the point is precisely the opacity of texts, a difficulty in making sense of the relation between the textual world and the empirical world.

Wordsworth is engagingly eager to claim the Maniac's anxiousness as his own:

> I methinks
> Could share that maniac's anxiousness, could go
> Upon like errand.
>
> (*Prel.* v. 159–61)

And the Arab Quixote, 'crazed | By love, and feeling, and internal thought' (v. 144–5), is an extreme type of the poet himself, at work on his backward-looking, recuperative task, his endless rereading. Enlisting in the quest, he becomes a kind of Sancho Panza converted to the fantasies of his master. There is certainly an air of quirkiness in the 'disquietude' shrewdly noted by Wordsworth's 'friend' ('in plain truth | 'Twas going far to seek disquietude', v. 51–2); as if Wordsworth were indulging in a far-fetched line of thought under the auspices of Romance. How different from the unmediated prophetic note of his culminating invocation to words—the instrument of salvation, but only 'as far as words *can*' save—at the end of Book V. Eloquent and elusive, even windily so (inspired by inspiration), the lines not only raise questions about the nature of that 'texture midway betwixt life and books', but constitute a strange moment in themselves. Well known as it is, the passage is worth another look:

> Visionary power
> Attends upon the motions of the winds
> Embodied in the mystery of words;
> There darkness makes abode, and all the host
> Of shadowy things do work their changes there
> As in a mansion like their proper home.
> Even forms and substances are circumfused

By that transparent veil with light divine,
And through the turnings intricate of verse
Present themselves as objects recognised
In flashes, and with a glory scarce their own.

(Prel. v. 619–29)

I used the word 'look' deliberately. Wordsworth writes like a man trying to net the wind in the 'turnings intricate' of his own blank verse; for all its insubstantiality, his meaning can only be glimpsed if we actually *look* at the lines (and at the spaces between them) rather than read them. We have, so to speak, to *see*, not *feel*, how beautiful they are. The deadening of a text already slowed by its solemn rhythms allows us, paradoxically, to endow it with a living spirit—lodged in the interstices of the web, behind the veil, as a ghostly and unrepresentable presence. As always, Wordsworth's straining of language to its limits has its own fullness; if the motions of winds can never be embodied, if the mystery of words must remain ineffable, still, the veil of poetry irradiates and makes strange the objects it obscures (the rhetoric is infectious). The gap between word and thing, once opened, typically proves Wordsworth's richest source of meaning ('all the host | Of shadowy things do work their changes there') and by a sleight of hand it is enshrined in the intertext rather than the text: in 'a mansion like their proper home' that 'Tintern Abbey' helps us to gloss as the mind ('thy mind | Shall be a mansion for all lovely forms', ll. 139–40); not a memorial shrine for the dead, but a spacious and sanctified dwelling—less a pleasure dome than a sacred edifice.

The precariousness of this edifice gives *The Prelude* both its characteristic plangency about poetic vision ('I see by glimpses now, when age comes on | May scarcely see at all . . .', xi. 337–8) and its moments of triumphant recoil on what cannot be seen ('an obscure sense | Of possible sublimity', ii. 336–7). It is just this precariousness, this anxious relation between representation and vision, writing and salvation, that I want to pursue as a way of approaching the dream of the Arab Quixote in terms other than those proposed by Wordsworth himself (who was, of course, bound to misinterpret his own—his 'friend's'—dream).[2] It is nothing new to say that the deepest imaginative experiences

---

[2] The 'dream'—long since identified as Descartes's—was attributed to Wordsworth himself in MS versions from 1839 onwards; see J. W. Smyser, 'Wordsworth's Dream of Poetry and Science: *The Prelude*, V': *PMLA* 71 (1956), 269–75.

recorded in *The Prelude* are bound up with anxiety of one sort or another. Readings of the spots of time passages in Books I and XI have amply shown the threats to a stable sense of self and reality which they narrate. But it may be that the spots of time indirectly articulate other anxieties that are as much to do with language as with the self or the unconscious. In particular, the relation between writing and anxiety remains obscure, as does the relation between 'Books' and 'Imagination'. I want, however, to suggest that both the anxiousness and the bookishness—the literariness—of *The Prelude* are, like the anxiousness of the Old Cumberland Beggar, 'vital': vital in the sense of energizing, impelling Wordsworth ever onwards in his time- and text-defying quest.

I have already touched on the dual power of language to estrange and transfigure, on the flight that is also a salvage (one could reverse the order in each case, in the interests of a darker psychic reading), and the same duality is present in the coexistence of urgency and prolixity in *The Prelude*; Blake, after all, had done with it in a single aphorism ('Eternity is in love with the productions of time'). Writing about it and about it allows Wordsworth himself, while looking back over his shoulder at the fleet waters of the drowning world, to exit on a loud prophetic blast of harmony from what has been in many ways a profoundly elegiac poem ('I see by glimpses now . . .'). Writing as deferral postpones the promised End; it also defends against non-being by textualizing it. But, as we all know, the self is not to be written out so easily, remaining obstinately lodged in the intertext, midway between life and books. What results is less a web of meaning than an enmeshing of absences—those shadowy objects glimpsed 'through the turnings intricate of verse'. I want to follow one of the strands of the net, not so much in the hope that it will wind to the centre of the labyrinth and back (where should such a centre lie?) as in the hope of tracing the process by which meaning is at once generated and unsettled in *The Prelude*. After what has been said by way of introduction, it will not be surprising that my chosen thread, a semantic one, leads from *anxiety* itself to *motion*, from *motion* to *spectre*, from there to *spectacle*, and finally back to *dream*. Whether visionary or nightmarish, this progression uncovers some of the problems of representation which must trouble with peculiar intensity a poem whose autobiographical project is to represent the growth of a poet's mind, or the self that writes.

Anxious Motions

Wordsworth himself tells us that his friend's dream is the product of reading ('perusing . . . The famous history of the errant knight') and of thought ('On poetry and geometric truth . . . he mused'). To put it another way, Romance has been crossed with Philosophy, Cervantes with Descartes. Already within the dream itself, interpretation has begun:

> the arab told him that the stone—
> *To give it in the language of the dream*—
> Was *Euclid's Elements*. 'And this', said he,
> 'This other', pointing to the shell, 'this book
> Is something of more worth.' 'And, at the word,
> The stranger', said my friend continuing,
> 'Stretched forth the shell towards me, with command
> That I should hold it to my ear. I did so
> And heard that instant in an unknown tongue,
> Which yet I understood, articulate sounds,
> A loud prophetic blast of harmony,
> An ode in passion uttered, which foretold
> Destruction to the children of the earth
> By deluge now at hand.
>
>   (*Prel.* v. 86–99; my italics)

'What is a poet if not a translator, a decipherer?', asks Baudelaire. To interpret further is to risk introducing yet another substitution in an endlessly proliferating series.[3] But suppose one skews the passage sideways to look at 'the language of the dream' in another way. It is worth noticing, for instance, that Wordsworth gives only one line to the stone, but spends six on the shell—that utterance concerns him more than order. The disordering blast or destructive ode restores originary speech to poetry in an apocalyptic logocentricity which destroys the need of texts. Is this something to hold on to?—that *Dream*, lodged at the line-ending with *stone*, may be working to trump the stony certainties of Euclid with its own

---

[3] Baudelaire's remark is quoted by W. H. Auden in *The Enchafed Flood or the Romantic Iconography of the Sea* (New York, 1950), 62—itself one of the most extended 'interpretations' of the dream of the Arab Quixote. See also J. H. Miller, 'The Stone and the Shell: The Problem of Poetic Form in Wordsworth's Dream of the Arab', in *Mouvements premiers: études critiques offertes à Georges Poulet* (Paris, 1972), 125–47. For a recent essay dealing with the Arab dream and with issues of language and figuration, see R. Woodman, '*The Prelude* and the Fate of Madness', *SiR* 27 (1988), 3–29.

irrefutable logic. Pairing ('rhyming') *book* and *word* and setting
them in the same way against another, later pair, *tongue* and
sounds, produces a similarly suggestive trumping movement: for
the reified book and the sign, we get the obliterating pentecostal
harmony that makes all books redundant. No wonder the dreamer
tells us that 'A wish was now engendered in my fear | To cleave
unto this man' (*Prel.* v. 115–16); the poet would be out of business
in such an eternity. No wonder, too, that the blast is siren music, a
joyous, even seductive note woven in with its destructiveness; it
might engender a quite opposite wish. This is reassuring: it bears
out the nostalgia I suggested earlier, as I hoped it might. But
Wordsworth's equivocation is worth staying with a little longer.
The pied piper narrative as such need not detain us, for its hectic
rhythms lead inexorably to the moment of awakening. What
Wordsworth himself lingers on in the midst of his hurry is the
production of meaning within the dream. As with the Arab
Quixote,

> the very knight
> Whose tale Cervantes tells, yet not the knight,
> But was an arab of the desert too,
> Of these was neither, and was both at once.

> (*Prel.* v. 123–6)

a parade of pedantic exactitude creates uncertainty: 'neither, and
. . . both at once'. Is this truth or fiction, dream or charade? Or is it
the transaction between them that Wordsworth is enacting here?
The two books are firmly labelled ('one that held acquaintance with
the stars . . . Th' other that was a god, yea many gods . . .', v. 104,
107), yet, in testifying to his faith, Wordsworth undercuts the
symbolizing process itself:

> Strange as it may seem
> I wondered not, although I plainly saw
> The one to be a stone, th' other a shell,
> Nor doubted once but that they both were books,
> Having a perfect faith in all that passed.

> (*Prel.* v. 110–14)

Of course, such double perception is a common experience in
dreaming, but 'although I plainly saw . . . Nor doubted once' has
the faintly comical ring of nonsense verse such as that of Lewis

Carroll, where absurd substitutions at once unsettle proprieties of naming and refer to the craziness of things ('He thought he saw ——; He looked again, and found it was ——'); properly speaking, book seems quite as inconsequential as stone or shell. What we are left with is the arbitrariness endemic in language, and the faith that is necessary if we are to engage in any act of representation or reading; so that the movement is from *stone* to *shell* to *books*, and thence to (what is really a personification, but has instead the intensifying adjectival 'perfect') *faith*. As Wordsworth writes in a theatrical context, 'Delusion bold (and faith must needs be coy)' (*Prel.* vii. 308). Why coy? Presumably because it is in bad company. Showmanship and illusion, more restrained here than in the mountebank world of London, bring a more respectable belief. The passage from literal to metaphoric, from thing to word, becomes the chaste woman as opposed to the bold hussy— operating within the symbolic laws of language rather than on the streets of outrageous representation (compare Pope's noisy operatic Harlot in *The Dunciad*: 'O Cara! Cara!', iv. 45 ff.).[4] Or so Wordsworth would have us believe, for the purification of language from all taint of unchastity—from representationalism itself—is the necessary fiction of *The Prelude* in general and the dream of the Arab Quixote in particular.

Meanwhile, what about that word 'anxiety'? One woman purified in the interest of Wordsworthian quietness is Mary of Buttermere—rescued from her fallen state in the popular theatre of Book VII where she figures as a seduced, abandoned, bigamously unmarried mother, and restored to innocence on her native ground: 'Without contamination does she live | In quietness, *without anxiety*' (vii. 353–4; my italics).[5] Here 'anxiety' seems almost synonymous with consciousness, perhaps even with desire, though

---

[4] Cf. also Pope's mischievously parodic purification in *The Dunciad*, the hack poet's burning of his own works: 'Go, purify'd by flames ascend the sky, | My better and more Christian progeny! | Unstain'd, untouch'd, and yet in maiden sheets; | While all your smutty sisters walk the streets' (*The Dunciad*, i. 227–30).

[5] Wordsworth might well have wished to lay Mary of Buttermere to rest: her marriage to the bigamist and imposter, Hatfield, took place 2 days before his own marriage to another Mary on 4 Oct. 1802. The story broke during Oct. and Coleridge, who presumably knew about Annette Vallon and her child, made sure it received coverage in the London papers by supplying a succession of articles to the *Morning Post* during the next 3 months; see *The Collected Works of Samuel Taylor Coleridge: Essays on His Times*, ed. D. V. Erdman (3 vols.; Princeton and London, 1978), i. 357–416.

obviously carrying overtones of disquiet—'disquietude', as Wordsworth's friend calls it. How, if at all, does it relate to the Arab
Quixote's 'maniac anxiousness'? Under 'anxiousness', the *OED*
cites (in 1658) 'An anxiousness about their everlasting state'. In
1798, it is Southey on a father's anxiousness. This combination of
anxiety about the future (shall I be saved?) and solicitude about
one's offspring (are my children/books safe?) seems especially
relevant to Wordsworthian usage. It is not a question of *Angst*,
whether Freudian neurotic dread or Heideggerian metaphysical
insecurity; rather the movement here comprises both salvation and
salvage, desire and recuperation. For a poet, particularly, the
question becomes: will I be saved if I write? Will my writings
survive? In a more general sense, all writing expresses a demand
that can never be satisfied. Language inscribes both loss and desire;
desire perpetuates itself in the symbolic articulations and metonymic
movement of language. Desire, like the maniac's anxiousness, sets
something in motion. Wordsworthian usage elsewhere gives us the
child of the spots of time, 'Scudding away from snare to snare . . .
hurrying on, | Still hurrying, hurrying onward' (*Prel.* i. 319–21),
troubling the calm of nature with his 'anxious visitation'; or seeing
in the death of his father a correction of his earlier 'desires' on 'That
day . . . when from the crag | [He] looked in such anxiety of hope'
(*Prel.* xi. 370–1). Wishing to snare woodcock or go home for the
Christmas holidays are innocent enough desires in themselves, even
if they prove to be misplaced. What matters to Wordsworth is not
their object; it is the power of the child's anxiety to set his
imagination to work, creating spectral beings out of mountain
winds ('Low breathings coming after me') or 'indisputable shapes'
out of the mist to haunt him retrospectively like the ghost of
Hamlet's father.[6] In this, the spots of time prefigure the movement
of baffled desire in the crossing of the Alps—the movement which is
for Wordsworth that of the imagination itself: 'Effort, and
expectation, and desire, | And something evermore about to be . . .'
(vi. 541–2). The loud prophetic blast of harmony, then, stirs its
hearer because it announces an apocalyptic end which is not an
end, but a going beyond.

Vital or life-giving anxiousness in Wordsworth's poetry charac-

---

[6] De Selincourt and Darbishire suggest Hamlet's 'questionable shape' as the
source of Wordsworth's phrase: see *The Prelude*, ed. de Selincourt, rev. Darbishire,
p. 615.

teristically gives rise to both motion and spectrality: to intimations
of a ghostly life beyond the image which at once blocks it out and
conjures it into being (a process described by Coleridge as 'the
substitution of a sublime feeling of the unimaginable for a mere
image').[7] This is tricky terrain, and exorcisms may be necessary. So
it proves in Book VIII of *The Prelude*, where Wordsworth pays
tribute to the visionary Lake District shepherds of his childhood.
'Call ye these appearances', he writes,

> A shadow, a delusion?—ye who are fed
> By the dead letter, not the spirit of things,
> Whose truth is not a *motion* or a shape
> Instinct with vital functions, but a block
> Or waxen image which yourselves have made,
> And ye adore.
>
> (*Prel.* viii. 428–36; my italics)

The familiar opposition between 'the dead letter' and 'the spirit of
things' makes this an exemplary passage for both Wordsworth and
his readers; paganizing the image as the worship of golden calves, it
Christianizes the symbol—as well it might. For what we glimpse is
a different kind of apparition. The fractional pause at the end of the
line—'Whose truth is not a motion or a shape'—picks up the
spectrality of the 'indisputable shapes' of mist recalled by the
troubled boy. The 'shape | Instinct with vital functions' comes as an
afterthought, but here too there are spectral reminiscences; the
'grim shape' of the cliff in the boat-stealing episode, 'As if with
voluntary power instinct', pursues the child, 'With measured
motion, like a living thing' (i. 407, 411). One begins to see what
Wordsworth is up against when one looks back at the visionary
shepherd himself, a few lines before. Comically befogged—'In size a
giant, stalking through the fog, | His sheep like Greenland bears'
(viii. 401–2)—he is offered to us as a type of the Christian sublime:

> His form hath flashed upon me glorified
> By the deep radiance of the setting sun;
> Or him have I descried in distant sky,
> A solitary object and sublime,

---

[7] See S. T. Coleridge, *Seven Lectures on Shakespeare and Milton*, ed. J. Payne
Collier (London, 1856), 65; repr. in J. A. Wittreich, Jr. (ed.), *The Romantics on
Milton* (Cleveland, Ohio, 1970), 201.

> Above all height, like an aerial cross,
> As it is stationed on some spiry rock
> Of the Chartreuse, for worship.
>
> (*Prel.* viii. 404–10)

'Call ye these appearances ... A shadow, a delusion': no—call them rather the transcendental signifier, the word made flesh and redeemed for eternity. But once again, there is a disconcerting reminiscence. Though Wordsworth has invoked the authority of sacred texts, and added a cosy touch with his recollection of Thomson's *Seasons* (the shepherd of 'Autumn' who 'stalks gigantic' through 'the general fog'),[8] it is his own account of the rout of religion from the Grande Chartreuse, in *Descriptive Sketches*, that troubles the textual surface here: 'A viewless flight of laughing Demons mock | The Cross, by angels planted on the aerial rock.'[9] Presumably this strange, hybrid reanimation of precursor texts is what prompts Wordsworth's unguarded description of the shepherd as a 'creature—spiritual almost | *As those of books*' (viii. 417–18; my italics)—an admission hastily retracted with 'but more exalted far, | Far more of an imaginative form' and followed by the strategic banishing of literary pastoral ('not a Corin of the groves ... But ... a man | With the most common', viii. 420–4).

Behind every aerial cross is a flight of demons; behind every text is a prior text. So much is clear. What is odd about the shepherd is that Wordsworth relies on a submerged Romantic topos (if it can be dignified by that term) which already brings disquiet with it: that of the Brocken-Spectre. Coleridge, who had climbed the Brocken on the Whit Sunday of 1799 in search of the phenomenon/phantom, makes use of it as an image of that ideal self which art (specifically, Shakespeare's art) throws back at us.[10] But Coleridge's idealized 'being of gigantic proportions, and of such elevated dignity that you only know it to be yourself by similarity of action' takes an altogether stranger form in De Quincey's 'Apparition of the Brocken'. Identified with the 'Dark Interpreter' of *Suspiria de Profundis*, the Brocken-Spectre becomes an estranged portion of

---

[8] See 'Autumn', ll. 727–9.

[9] *Descriptive Sketches*, ed. E. Birdsall, 1836: ll. 69–70. This section of *Descriptive Sketches* did not find its way into Book VI of *The Prelude* until 1816/19 (see 1850: vi. 414–88 and *The Prelude*, ed. de Selincourt, rev. Darbishire, pp. 198, 200 app. crit.).

[10] *Seven Lectures on Shakespeare and Milton*, p. 101. Cf. also Coleridge's poem, 'Constancy to an Ideal Object'.

self, like Shelley's Jupiter or a Blakian Emanation. Though De Quincey uses mirror language, the image is reflected back at him through a glass darkly:

the apparition is but a reflex of yourself; and, in uttering your secret feelings to *him*, you make this phantom the dark symbolic mirror for reflecting to the daylight what else must be hidden for ever.

Such a relation does the Dark Interpreter, whom immediately the reader will learn to know as an intruder into my dreams, bear to my own mind. He is originally a mere reflex of my inner nature.[11]

Before arriving at this discovery, De Quincey forces his spectral *doppelgänger* to undergo a series of exorcizing rituals—making the sign of the cross, reconsecrating an anenome ('the sorcerer's flower') and a pagan stone ('the sorcerer's altar') to the service of the pentecostal Christianity celebrated at Whitsun. By putting the Dark Interpreter through his motions, De Quincey tries the faith and tests the obedience of the Brocken-Spectre, baptizing superstition for religion. But (like the unconscious), the Dark Interpreter has his own ways of evading the censor:

as the apparition of the Brocken sometimes is disturbed by storms or by driving showers, so as to dissemble his real origin, in like manner the Interpreter sometimes swerves out of my orbit, and mixes a little with alien natures. I do not always know him in these cases as my own parhelion. What he says, generally is but that which I have said in daylight, and in meditation deep enough to sculpture itself on my heart. But sometimes, as his face alters, his words alter; and they do not always seem such as I have used, or *could* use. No man can account for all things that occur in dreams. Generally I believe this—that he is faithful representative of myself, but he also is at times subject to the action of the god *Phantasmus*, who rules in dreams.[12]

The god *Phantasmus* typically makes his presence felt in meteorological disturbance ('disturbed by storms or by driving showers'). Dreams become treacherous deeps, unknown seas worked to turmoil by hurricanes. The weather of *The Prelude* is rarely so tempestuous, but 'the characters | Of danger or desire' can make the earth 'Work like a sea' (i. 497–501). It is this sea change that transforms the sublimely Christianized shepherd from the reflex of Wordsworth's ideal into its antithesis—the ghastly Discharged

[11] *Confessions of an English Opium-Eater and Other Writings*, ed. G. Lindop (Oxford and New York, 1985), 156. [12] Ibid. 156.

Soldier, for instance, or the reified Blind London Beggar, or the Arab Quixote; those Dark Interpreters who serve as a 'symbolic mirror for reflecting to the daylight what else must be hidden for ever'. In other words, the language of the dream.

'In dreams always there is a power not contented with reproduction, but which absolutely creates or transforms.' Not Freud, but De Quincey again.[13] Language, too, absolutely creates or transforms ('as his face alters, his words alter'). Subjected to the god *Phantasmus*, the characters sculptured on the heart lose their fixity and disclose 'the mysterious handwritings of grief or joy which have inscribed themselves successively upon the palimpsest of your brain'.[14] It is an aspect of the Wordsworthian supernatural that the semantic rules of the Uncanny (*heimlich* becomes *unheim-lich*, estranging the familiar) hold good, or bad, for a word like 'motion'. Chambers's mid-eighteenth-century *Cyclopaedia* offers an appropriately dynamic definition drawn from ancient philosophy: 'The ancient philosophers considered *motion* in a more general and extensive manner. *They defined it, a passage out of one state into another*: and thus made six kinds of motion, viz. Creation, generation, corruption, augmentation, diminution, and lation, or local motion' (*OED*; my italics). There is something of the same spectrum of meaning in Wordsworthian usage ('Creation' at one extreme, the glad animal movements of 'Tintern Abbey' at the other); but its oscillations on a different axis, between quiet and disquiet, give it a special role in relation to the unsanctified movements of the imagination. Primitive animism attends upon the motions of the winds, as well as visionary power; is perhaps necessary to them, as a religion of fear may provide the altar-stone for pentecostal Christianity. The other voice of the loud prophetic blast of harmony is death, the unassimilably alien aspect of spiritual life. So, 'Those hallowed and pure motions of the sense' (i. 578) which link life and joy are set against 'sounds | Of undistinguishable motion, steps | Almost as silent as the turf they trod' (i. 330–2) which link life and death. There is the common suggestion of winds in both motions ('even in that tempestuous time', 'Low breathings coming after me'), but it is the uncanny animation which makes one an intimation of the ghostly, the other, an intimation of immortality. Again, it is the spectral striding in the boat-stealing episode ('the huge cliff . . . With measured motion, like a living thing | Strode

[13] *Confessions of an English Opium-Eater . . .*, 157.   [14] Ibid. 149.

after me', i. 409–12) which makes it a haunting; whereas in the invocation to 'Thou soul . . . That giv'st to forms and images a breath | And everlasting motion' (i. 429–31), breath is part of the incommunicable inspiration of the Holy Ghost. The 'motions that are sent he knows not whence' to the man 'Incumbent o'er the surface of past time' (iv. 260, 263) scarcely ruffle its surface, but to the child plundering the raven's nest,

> With what strange utterance did the loud dry wind
> Blow through my ears; the sky seemed not a sky
> Of earth, and with what motion moved the clouds!
>
> (*Prel.* i. 348–50)[15]

My point is not that the Wordsworthian supernatural needs guilt to make it ghostly (Wordsworth himself tells us as much), but that motion becomes uncanny when it is unsettled from Latinate abstraction into an indeterminate physicality—as Freud puts it, betraying us to the superstitiousness we think we have overcome.[16] To put it another way, if all language is dead metaphor, then a movement towards the literal ('a passage out of one state into another') may, in reminding us of that originating death, summon ghostly presences.

Spectrality and the Intertext

In Book V of *The Prelude*, Wordsworth praises 'dreamers' (i.e. authors of romances) as 'Forgers of lawless tales . . . Who make our wish our power, our thought a deed, | An empire, a possession' (v. 547–8, 552–3). Making thought a deed is one function of the Dark Interpreter, language. Its movements may be profoundly disquieting, since it puts us in possession of our thoughts. But it is a disquiet central to the alliance of language and imagination; without such dream-work, what should the lawless forger be up to except lying? The lies of blocks or waxen images, as opposed to truth in motion—the Wordsworthian spectacular of static mirror representation ('those mimic sights that ape | The absolute presence

---

[15] One might add the effect—chiasmus with a difference—of bringing the semantic poles into close juxtaposition in the skating episode, with 'The rapid line of motion' spinning one way, earth rolling 'With visible motion her diurnal round' another (*Prel.* i. 482, 486); here glad animal movements are brought into the same orbit as the motions of the spheres.

[16] See 'The "Uncanny" ' (1919), *The Complete Psychological Works of Sigmund Freud*, trans. and ed. Strachey, xvii. 250.

of reality . . . as in mirror', *Prel.* vii. 248–50)—constitute a crucial antithesis to the Wordsworthian supernatural. Spectacle, the tyranny of the eye ('a transport of the outward sense, | Not of the mind', *Prel.* xi. 187–8), furnishes the theatrical underworld of *The Prelude*, that mingled threat to and seduction of the imagination called London. It might as well have been called Vanity Fair; framed by Wordsworth's puritan ethic, it offers the this worldly profits of the eye in place of the other worldly spiritual gains of the mind. 'Great God!' writes Wordsworth, 'that aught *external* to the living mind | Should have such mighty sway' (*Prel.* viii. 700–2; his italics). When he wants to admit its legitimate pleasures, he has to subsume spectacle into spectrality, animating the show in the visionary cinema of the imagination. The Cave of Yordas, in Book VIII of *The Prelude*, provides him with the chance for a retrospective trumping of London by a replay in the mind's eye; darkness becomes the screen on which to project a world of internalized images, subverting instead of aping 'The absolute presence of reality' with their shadowy motion:

> Substance and shadow, light and darkness, all
> Commingled, making up a canopy
> Of shapes, and forms, and tendencies to shape,
> That shift and vanish, change and interchange
> Like *spectres*—ferment quiet and sublime,
> Which, after a short space, works less and less
> Till, every effort, every *motion* gone,
> The scene before him lies in perfect view
> Exposed, and lifeless *as a written book*.
>
> (*Prel.* viii. 719–27; my italics)

Wordsworth's simile arrests the familiar liveliness of shapes and spectral motion in an alien stillness. The lifelessness of the printed page 'lies in perfect view' as an unintelligible blank. (There is a quietly submerged play of another kind going on here: compare Pope's 'Did the dead Letter unsuccessful prove? | The brisk Example never fail'd to move', *The Dunciad*, i. 193–4.) Such seeing is dead—unless it opens on to the endless vista of romance: 'Ships, rivers, towers, the warrior clad in mail, | The prancing steed, the pilgrim with his staff . . . A spectacle to which there is no end' (*Prel.* viii. 738–41). Spectrality saves spectacle for the imagination, as the shadow redeems the substance; romance, in turn, legitimizes the spectral. The experience evoked in these lines is, of course, reading itself. Is this the 'texture midway betwixt life and books' with which we began? Neither of the mind nor visible, but wrought by the mind's eye on the page, it animates the dead letter until (in Wordsworth's magical phrase) it is 'streaming, | Like a magician's airy pageant' (*Prel.* viii. 733–4). Reading the writing rather than seeing it, we have enchantment, illusionism, 'ferment quiet and sublime'—a sublimity which results from making the visible a little hard to see on the printed page.[17]

The Cave of Yordas saves the city from satire and gives it back to romance. Book VII of *The Prelude* is demonic not only in its imagery ('What a hell | For eyes and ears, what anarchy and din | Barbarian and infernal', vii. 659–61) but in its exuberant parody of Pandemonium, itself already parodic of Creation:

> A Universe of death, which God by curse
> Created evil, for evil only good.
> Where all life dies, death lives, and Nature breeds,
> Perverse, all monstrous, all prodigious things,
> Abominable, inutterable, and worse
> Than Fables yet have feign'd, or fear conceiv'd,
> *Gorgons* and *Hydras*, and *Chimeras* dire.
> (*Paradise Lost*, ii. 622–8)

In the same way, Wordsworth parodies the sanctified apocalypse of the Vale of Gondo ('Characters of the great apocalypse, | The types and symbols of eternity', *Prel.* vi. 570–1) with the rhetorical nadir of Book VII: 'O, blank confusion, and a type not false | Of what the mighty city is itself . . .' (vii. 696–7). The self-transcending natural legibility of the Alps is usurped by urban illegibility, a system of signs where 'differences . . . have no law, no meaning, and no end' (vii. 704–5). But why the difficulty in reading London? Is the text meaningless simply because Wordsworth's puritan ethic will have it so, because Vanity Fair, though it may tempt the Pilgrim with his staff, must leave him finally unmoved? Or is it rather the mistrust of the do-it-yourself enthusiast for the ready-made, akin to the progressive parent's worry that Action Man will oust creative play?

> A work that's finished to our hands, that lays,
> If any *spectacle* on earth can do,
> The whole creative powers of man asleep.
> (*Prel.* vii. 653–5; my italics)

[17] See H. Bloom, 'Visionary Cinema in Romantic Poetry', *The Ringers in the Tower* (Chicago, 1971), 37–52.

One could furnish a doctrinal justification for Wordsworth's underworld easily enough. But an aesthetic and, above all, a literary reading gives access to the textual rather than moral structuring of Book VII, and in addition reveals what is at stake for *The Prelude* as a whole.

In London, Wordsworth, the imaginative showman, confronts us with the misbegotten forms of a materialized imagination in order to dissociate his own creative vision from its fallen counterpart—rather as Blake depicts the malformed monsters of Urizenic creation, weighted and hunched with resentful and anguished physicality, by way of contrast to the freedom of an unfettered imagination. Bartholomew Fair is an infernal jumble of 'out-o'-th'-way, far-fetched, perverted things'; a 'parliament of monsters' like Milton's, 'Where all life dies, death lives, and Nature breeds, | Perverse':

> albinos, painted Indians, dwarfs,
> The horse of knowledge, and the learned pig,
> The stone-eater, the man that swallows fire,
> Giants, ventriloquists, the invisible girl,
> The bust that speaks and moves its goggling eyes,
> The waxwork, clockwork, all the marvellous craft
> Of modern Merlins, wild beasts, puppet-shows,
> All out-o'-th'-way, far-fetched, perverted things,
> All freaks of Nature, all Promethean thoughts
> Of man—his *dulness*, madness, and their feats,
> All jumbled up together to make up
> This parliament of monsters.

(*Prel.* vii. 681–92; my italics)

Perverted Nature has undergone literary mediation at the hands of Dulness; the prototypes for these parodic activities are the scatalogical games of *The Dunciad*, themselves grubbily parodic of the Devil's party. Behind 'The bust that speaks and moves its goggling eyes' is Pope's stuffed effigy of the poet, 'senseless, lifeless! idol void and vain! . . . a copy of a wit' (*The Dunciad*, ii. 46–8), the man of straw by means of which Pope dissociates his own activities in *The Dunciad* from those of the Grub Street hack he satirizes. So what Wordsworth is doing in these freak shows is saving himself for an art that is both natural and sublime—an art that can create, not a ventriloquist's dummy, but the visionary shepherd of Book VIII.

But there is more to it. Wordsworth's disapproving verdict, 'trivial objects, melted and reduced | To one identity' (*Prel.* vii. 703–4), applies to a satiric mode as well as to a scene. Ostensibly, he is banishing from *The Prelude* the techniques of the eighteenth-century city poetry which it has in fact appropriated. Book VII borrows its energy from the wit that blurs significant differences in the insurrectionary turmoil and apocalyptic unsoundness of Johnson's *London*—'and now a Rabble Rages, now a Fire', 'falling Houses thunder on your Head' (ll. 14, 17)—or, at the end of 'A Description of a City Shower', tumbles 'Dung, Guts, and Blood, | Drown'd Puppies, stinking Sprats, ... Dead Cats, and Turnip-Tops' (ll. 61–3) in an indiscriminate flood down the conduit of Swift's disgust. Though Wordsworth makes satire stand in for a mode of imagination, and uses parodic poetry to represent ventriloquistic creation, his own creativity is itself Promethean; Promethean, that is, not only in its creation of misshapen clay mannikins ('all the marvellous craft | Of modern Merlins'), but in its stealing of Promethean fire. He is deeply implicated in a theft that is also a gift, at once hubristic and humanistic. Parody not only steals energy from a prior text but, by a double movement, simultaneously distorts it and appropriates its power. On one level Wordsworth assimilates into *The Prelude* the Juvenalian disreputability and indignation which his chosen mode would seem to exclude; on another, he cancels and purifies Juvenalian satire by reverting to the demonic Sublime. But, in order to do so, he has to erase the ghost of an indecorous text: a ghost that is writing itself, surfacing—like the uncanny—where it should remain hidden. The Blind London Beggar is at once the spectre of spectacle (the two words have the same root meaning: *specere*, to look or see, and *spectāre*, to look) and the means of its exorcism. Like the 'blank confusion' of Bartholomew Fair, the beggar offers a version of what one might call the negative Sublime, the mind overborne by an unintelligible illegibility.[18] An embodiment of absence, the blind, propped beggar is the most threatening of all Wordsworth's Dark Interpreters; he 'smites' the sight like an assault on vision itself. 'Once', writes Wordsworth,

[18] Cf. the subtle and complex reading of this episode and its role in Book VII offered by Hertz, *The End of the Line*, pp. 40–60; and see also Weiskel, *The Romantic Sublime*, pp. 136–43, 167–204.

> 'twas my chance
> Abruptly to be smitten with the view
> Of a blind beggar, who, with upright face,
> Stood propped against a wall, upon his chest
> Wearing a written paper, to explain
> The story of the man, and who he was.

> (*Prel.* vii. 610–15)

Why is this view such a blow to the mind ('My mind did at this spectacle turn round | As with the might of waters', vii. 616–17)? Is it because the label at once parodies, diminishes, and controverts all attempts at self-representation, and with it Wordsworth's entire project in *The Prelude*? No characters, no written paper, can inscribe being; and so the beggar is doomed to non-being, to Death, in fact—his sublime archetype in Book II of *Paradise Lost*.

The 'execrable shape' of Death with his 'horrid strides' is the darkest and most shadowy—the most shapeless and unshapely—of all shapes haunting *The Prelude*:

> The other shape,
> If shape it might be call'd that shape had none
> Distinguishable in member, joint, or limb,
> Or substance might be call'd that shadow seem'd,
> For each seem'd either; black it stood as Night,
> Fierce as ten Furies, terrible as Hell . . .

> (*Paradise Lost*, ii. 666–71)

Here, if ever there was one, is an example of 'the conferring, the abstracting, and the modifying powers of the Imagination' which Wordsworth had illustrated with the 'intermediate image' of his own Leech Gatherer.[19] But once again, Milton's presence in Book VII has been overlayed by Pope's, the demonic or negative Sublime dulled into word-bound pedantry. The 'Spectre' who rises up with cane and birch among the crowd in Book IV of *The Dunciad* is that of the Grammar School tyrant himself (Dr Busby):

> Since Man from beast by Words is known,
> Words are Man's province, Words we teach alone.

---

[19] Coleridge uses this passage to illustrate the mind's power 'to reconcile opposites and qualify contradictions, leaving a middle state of mind more strictly appropriate to the imagination than any other, when it is, as it were, hovering between images'; see *Seven Lectures on Shakespeare and Milton*, ed. Collier, pp. 64–5.

When Reason doubtful, like the Samian letter,
Points him two ways, the narrower is the better,

(*Dunciad*, iv. 149–52)

As Pope's note informs us, 'The matter under debate is how to confine men to Words for life' (iv. 175 n.). Wordsworth embarks on the work of liberation through the Letter itself. The Arch-Grammarian may ponder the Digamma ('tow'ring o'er your Alphabet, like Saul, | Stands our Digamma, and o'er-tops them all', iv. 217–18), but he cannot take both forks of the Samian letter ('The letter Y, used by Pythagoras as an emblem of the different roads of Virtue and Vice', iv. 151 n.). Not so Wordsworth. By a sleight of hand, the Blind London Beggar becomes a symbol of spiritual life in death,

on the shape of this unmoving man,
His fixèd face and sightless eyes, I looked,
As if admonished from another world.

(*Prel.* vii. 621–3)

His label, similarly, becomes 'a type | Or emblem of the utmost that we know'. Know of what? 'Both of ourselves and of the universe' (vii. 618–20)—knowledge both of self and of other, the knowledge that language puts us in possession of. Wordsworth originally wrote: 'The whole of what is written to our view, | Is but a label on a blind man's chest' (MS X; see *Prel.* vii. 617–20 n.). The change from aphorism to recognition vivifies the dead letter ('Did the dead Letter unsuccessful prove?' etc.), but what really brings both it and the beggar alive, infuses them with the spirit of things, is not a brisk example but a single word—'*utmost*'. Earlier Wordsworth has mused on the 'mystery' of the faces that pass him by: now he confronts the mystery of meaninglessness and converts it into a species of revelation; he reads it. By its nature, language does not force us to choose all or nothing, one or the other. The label can be at once nothing and all, neither and both at once, like the Arab Quixote or Milton's Death ('each seem'd either'). As Wordsworth noted apropos of 'The Immortality Ode', 'Archimedes said that he could move the world if he had a point whereon to rest his machine. Who has not felt the same aspirations as regards the world of his own mind?' Wordsworth's lever for turning the mind round 'As with the might of waters' is the sign itself; at once fixed and mysterious, like London's face, it allows a vital traffic between the visible and the invisible world.

   Is this why Wordsworth produces with such pleasure the figure of the Sadler's Wells actor, 'The champion, Jack the Giant-killer'?

> lo,
>
> He dons his coat of darkness, on the stage
> Walks, and atchieves his wonders, from the eye
> Of living mortal safe as is the moon
> 'Hid in her vacant interlunar cave'.
> Delusion bold (and faith must needs be coy)
> How is it wrought?—his garb is black, the word
> INVISIBLE flames forth upon his chest.
>
> (*Prel.* vii. 303–10)

An engaging piece of mock heroic? Yes, but something more. Though Wordsworth himself is coy, his ravishment spills over in the boldness of the delusion. One might suspect him of having been seduced, like Mary of Buttermere (though the forms of theatrical entertainment in his case, like those of marriage in hers, could be said to have licensed spectacle—whose proper place, after all, is on the stage).[20] But Wordsworth himself speaks of reading as going to the theatre: rereading pages which once entranced him, he finds them now 'Dead in my eyes as is a theatre | Fresh emptied of spectators' (*Prel.* v. 574–5). His early literary tastes, like enjoying Sadler's Wells, may have been replaced by more grown-up entertainment; but the showman's trick remains his own: 'all the host | Of shadowy things do work their changes there' (v. 622–3). Only the flaming word labels the coat as invisible—making it, in Milton's unimaginable phrase (the phrase to which Pope gave new currency at the opening of the fourth book of *The Dunciad* with his last ditch plea for Enlightenment), 'darkness visible'. It is not surprising to stumble on a visual pun in the context of burlesque. What is disconcerting is the glimpse of a different Miltonic text behind the Coat of Darkness (a gaping garment, or *trompe-l'œil* obfuscation?): *Samson Agonistes*. On the face of it, the allusion— 'Hid in her vacant interlunar cave'—is so incongruous that we are reminded once more of *The Dunciad*; the court of Dulness is a literary solecism in its own right, and her reign is inaugurated by farce:

[20] See *OED* for the theatricality of 'spectacle' and its restricted technical sense, 'a piece of stage-display or pageantry as contrasted with real drama'.

> There motley Images her fancy strike,
> Figures ill pair'd, and Similies unlike.
> She sees a Mob of Metaphors advance,
> Pleas'd with the madness of the mazy dance:
> How Tragedy and Comedy embrace . . .
>
> (*Dunciad*, i. 65–9)

And of course Wordsworth *is* being sportive, offering us a motley imagery of his own. But still, the breach of decorum remains an unsettling performance: to make tragedy and comedy embrace, to draw the curtailment of Samson's (and Milton's) powers into the orbit of a shape-changer—this is real boldness, prostitution even.

The oscillation between tragicomic possibilities in this moment of mock heroic brings to light a hidden structure of thought—an obfuscated text—which proves to be the link between Sadler's Wells and the dream of the Arab Quixote, between London and Books. A brisk move at this point might be to tie the interlunar cave in with the texture midway betwixt life and books; it offers yet another intermediate image lodged in the interstices of poetic language, another instance of darkness visible. One could also ponder the metaphysics of presence and absence ('under-presence', as Wordsworth cunningly redefines it in Book XIII), or invoke the movement of visionary insight which celebrates Wordsworth's oblivious crossing of the Alps, when the light of sense goes out in flashes and reveals the invisible world. Or one could recapitulate on the problems of self-representation, of 'character'; Mrs Ramsay, in *To the Lighthouse*, experiences her inner self as 'a wedge of darkness' lodged in the intervals between the strokes of the lighthouse beam (later she is a triangular shadow in Lily Briscoe's picture, thrown by an invisible person—the shadow of presence, death, bringing her back to life in art). All this, and more, would bear on *The Prelude*. But it is Milton's text that yields most, with its memorable elegy for the poet's lost sight:

> The Sun to me is dark
> And silent as the Moon,
> When she deserts the night,
> Hid in her vacant interlunar cave . . .
>
> (*Samson Agonistes*, ll. 86–9)

Its tragic play on darkness, desertion, and silence, its moon that 'speaks' when visible, makes of Samson's own utterance an echoing silence: 'Myself my Sepulcher', as the moon is buried in its interlunar cave. A symbol of death in life, Samson becomes a speaking absence, an embodiment of lack as well as sightlessness. Earlier Milton has identified light and Logos and made Samson mourn his exclusion from both as a bereavement which amounts to death by word ('decree'):

> O first created Beam, and thou great Word,
> 'Let there be light, and light was over all';
> Why am I thus bereav'd thy prime decree?
>
> (*Samson Agonistes*, ll. 83–5)

What follows, a lament for the siting of seeing in the eye, takes us directly to Wordsworth's lament for the frailty of books as the shrine of imagination ('Why, gifted with such powers to send abroad | Her spirit, must it lodge in shrines so frail?', *Prel.* v. 47–8):

> Since light so necessary is to life,
> And almost life itself, if it be true
> That light is in the Soul,
> She all in every part; why was the sight
> To such a tender ball as th' eye confined?
>
> (*Samson Agonistes*, ll. 90–4)

But (and this is not in any way to enter into argument with Samson) without sight there could not even be the particular word-blindness induced by the Blind London Beggar's label; without the tyranny of the eye there could not be the contrary motion of the Wordsworthian supernatural; without a text, one's own or that of a precursor, there would be no signs for the imagination to work with, no dead letter to become characters of danger or desire, and no books to obliterate or save.

The Dream of Language

And now, back to the dream of the Arab Quixote. Freud would presumably classify it as an instance of *Traume von oben*,

That is to say . . . formulations of ideas which could have been created just as well in a waking state as during the state of sleep, and which have derived their content only in certain parts from mental states at a comparatively deep level. That is why these dreams offer for the most part a content which has an abstract, poetic, or symbolic form.[21]

---

[21] *The Complete Psychological Works of Sigmund Freud*, trans. and ed. Strachey, xxi. 203.

His comment relates, in fact, to the famous source of Wordsworth's 'dream', an actual dream of 10 November 1619 recounted in Baillet's *Vie de Descartes* (1691)—the third of three, and the least frightening (the others include apocalyptic whirlwinds and claps of thunder).[22] Like Wordsworth's, the dream concerns two books: a *Dictionary* which Descartes interprets while still asleep as standing 'merely for the sciences gathered together', and 'a collection of poems entitled *Corpus Poetarum*' which 'marked more particularly and expressly the union of philosophy with wisdom'—a superior mode of knowledge ascribed to 'la divinité de l'enthousiasme, et . . . la force de l'imagination'. The dream is well known, and the topos a traditional one (the Book of Nature and the Book of Revealed Scripture). But—like that of Wordsworth—the text is usually read in terms of its own rereading, the interpretation supplied by Descartes himself.[23] Predictably enough, he made sense of it in the light of his intense anxiety about the proper course of study to pursue, his ambition to create a unified system of knowledge, and his hopes for divine inspiration in the task. No less than Wordsworth's Arab Quixote, he was a visionary pitting himself against overwhelming odds. What Descartes himself (and his later readers) omit from the text is its nonsense—its inconsequential dream-play with vanishing books and lost texts. It might in fact be called the dream of the vanishing texts; texts highly relevant, as it happens, to Wordsworth's 'dream'. The form of the dream is this: Descartes finds a book on his table, the dictionary, without knowing how it had come there, and then happens on a second with no less surprise. Opening it, he chances on the line '*Quod vitae sectabor iter*' ('What path in life shall I pursue?') and simultaneously a stranger presents him with some verses beginning '*Est et non*'. Descartes recognizes the author as Ausonius (a fourth-century Christian poet) and begins to search for the poem in his *Corpus Poetarum*, but cannot find it; meanwhile the stranger questions him about the provenance of the book, the dictionary disappears and returns in a different form, and Descartes—still unable to find '*Est et non*'—offers to turn up '*Quod vitae sectabor iter*' instead, until

---

[22] See N. K. Smith, *New Studies in the Philosophy of Descartes* (London, 1952), 33–9, for the trans. of Baillet's account (*Vie de Descartes*, book II, ch. 1, pp. 81–6) from which quotations below are also taken. The two Ausonius texts are from book VII, *Eclogues* ii and iv, respectively.

[23] See e.g. G. Poulet, 'The Dream of Descartes', *Studies in Human Time*, trans. E. Coleman (Baltimore, 1956), 50–73.

he is deflected by some engravings in what proves to be an unfamiliar edition. Finally both man and books vanish.

What stands out in all this is the capricious behaviour of the books themselves. Baillet is inclined to put Descartes's dreams down to late night drinking, but it sounds more like late night reading. Whatever the cause, though, a later reader could not fail to be struck by the irritating mixture of corporeality and elusiveness in both books and texts. The book as object could hardly be more prominent. (A related fantasy inspires Pope's mischievous picture of the hack poet at work in *The Dunciad*, surrounded in his poetic frenzy by unfinished writings and pillaged books, and driven finally to build a sacrificial pyre to Dulness out of 'twelve volumes, twelve of amplest size'; book-burning always being a dangerously attractive fantasy to bibliophiles, especially when it is the Moderns who go up in smoke.) There is no evidence that Wordsworth himself had first-hand knowledge of Baillet's *Vie de Descartes*, and it has been suggested that Beaupuy narrated the dream to him under the trees of Blois in 1792. But this seems a long gestation period (the dream of the Arab Quixote was composed in February/March 1804), and at the time concerned Wordsworth was evidently more preoccupied with day-dreams inspired by Ariosto, Tasso, and Spenser than with philosophic dreams. Coleridge, however, was reading Descartes throughout the years 1797 to 1803 (especially during 1801), and, as usual, projecting a book on him.[24] It would be pleasing to think that Wordsworth not only discussed the dream with Coleridge, but read it himself—he was, after all, a bookish man as well as (by his own account) a bookish child. Moreover, had he done so, he would have been singularly, or rather, doubly receptive to Descartes's vanishing texts. His own poetic mission was similarly a source of anxiousness, while the first of Ausonius' lines ('*Quod vitae . . .*') meshes nicely with the neo-Miltonic quest announced in the 'glad preamble' ('The earth is all before me . . . I cannot miss my way', *Prel.* i. 15, 19). As for '*Est et non*' (the Pythagoraean 'Yea' and 'Nay', or truth and falsity in human knowledge), Ausonius' verses mischievously provide a textbook example of the 'neither, and both at once'

[24] For the suggestion that Beaupuy provided Wordsworth with his source, see Smyser, 'Wordsworth's Dream of Poetry and Science', pp. 272–3; Wordsworth's preoccupations at this period are recorded in *Prel.* ix. 450–64. For Coleridge's interest in Descartes see J. Lindsay, 'Coleridge's Marginalia in a Volume of Descartes', *PMLA* 49 (1934), 184–95, and *Collected Letters of Samuel Taylor Coleridge*, ed. Griggs, ii. 677–703.

principle at work in the dream of the Arab Quixote: light may be synonymous with day, but the fact of light does not prevent it being night after all; on this yes-and-no, writes Ausonius, 'the whole throng of rhetoricians depends in its wordy contests'.[25] Think of the Coat of Darkness and its inscription, 'INVISIBLE'; think also of Aristotle's deconstruction of the form of words that defines the sun as 'the brightest star that moves above the earth' (what becomes of the definition when the sun is hidden in its intersolar cave?).

In a different context, J. Hillis Miller has used this Aristotelian example to expose what he calls 'a blind spot'—the rhetorical catachresis or misnaming which attends all referentiality in language.[26] The dream of the Arab Quixote similarly uncovers the fiction on which both Wordsworth's poetry and the black-coated actor depend. Appropriately enough, *The Prelude* loses the philosopher and comes up with the romancer; instead of Descartes, for whom madness and rational discourse were incompatible, we find Cervantes and his fiction-ridden hero—the catachrazy hero, one might call him, in his mistaking of windmills for giants and his habitual misreading of the text of reality as that of romance. We are back in the hinterland between 'life' and 'books'. In a sense, the relation between the authors of Wordsworth's two literary sources is the relation also between stone and shell; one symbolizing abstract, deductive reasoning, the other, the ungrounded truth of the imagination (and maybe the two are not so distinct as Descartes would have us believe). For a philosopher attempting the impossible, Wordsworth substitutes the Romantic idealist—'not a man out of his senses', in Coleridge's phrase, but a man so possessed by imagination 'as to make him disregard the evidence of sense'.[27] He tilts with metaphors, and, though Sancho Panza may stand for the reality principle, he can never be the real hero. Wordsworth's own fall guy is the 'dwarf man' of Book V (' 'tis a child, no child, | But a dwarf man', v. 294–5)—a moral paragon and miniature pedant, his path 'chok'd with grammars' like the victims of Pope's spectral pedagogue. He too is a bookish child ('in learning and in books | He is a prodigy'), and a good reader and

[25] See *Ausonius*, trans. H. G. E. White (London and Cambridge, Mass., 1919), i. 173.

[26] See J. H. Miller, 'Stevens' Rock and Criticism as Cure', *Georgia Review*, 30 (1976), 29–30.

[27] See *Specimens of the Table Talk of the Late Samuel Taylor Coleridge*, ed. H. N. Coleridge (London, 1835), ii. 87.

speller: 'he can read | The inside of the earth, and spell the stars' (v.
319–20, 332–3). But, unlike the young Wordsworth, he knows no
fear, 'Unless it leap upon him in a dream'.

At this point in Book V, Wordsworth's rather ponderous satire
on infant self-possession gives way abruptly to the real theme of
'Books', romance. In a rush of generous impatience, Wordsworth
wishes on him and all children the heroes of popular romance who
figure on the London stage in Book VII and reappear in the
visionary after-images of the Cave of Yordas:

> Oh, give us once again the wishing-cap
> Of Fortunatus, and the invisible coat
> Of Jack the Giant-killer, Robin Hood,
> And Sabra in the Forest with St. George!
> The child whose love is here, at least doth reap
> One precious gain—that he forgets himself.
>
> (*Prel.* v. 364–9)

Or rather, Wordsworth wishes on him 'faith', the simple belief of
the Sadler's Wells audience. The first book as object that he
represents himself as having coveted is 'A little yellow canvass-
covered book, | A slender abstract of the *Arabian Tales*' (v. 483–4).
The Arabian Nights, by a happy Romantic pun, gives him the
composite hero of the dream: an Arabian Knight (remember the
sublime pun thrown up by the deep and gloomy breathing place of
the Snowdon vision: 'The soul, the imagination of the whole', xiii.
65). Such accidents of dream-language are among the 'precious
gains' of self-forgetfulness. By contrast, Wordsworth was fully
conscious of the continuity between the child's imagination and his
adult self. What is *Don Quixote*, after all, but a grown-up's version
of Jack the Giant-killer, a text recovered from his earliest schoolboy
reading and given a new layer of meaning?[28] Books become spots
of time, recuperating memory into consciousness, creating an
intertext or interspace between past and present which bridges the
gulf between the divided consciousness of the adult ('I seem | Two
consciousnesses—conscious of myself, | And of some other being',
Prel. ii. 31–3), while at the same time reminding us that our only

---

[28] For Wordsworth's early reading, see *Prelude*, ed. de Selincourt, rev. Darbishire, p. 540. As Geoffrey Hartman puts it, 'the spirit of poetry [is born] from the
grave clothes of Romance': see 'False Themes and Gentle Minds', *Beyond
Formalism* (New Haven and London, 1970), 289.

access to consciousness itself is by way of textuality, whether the text is that of memory or (and it amounts to the same thing) that of *The Prelude*.

De Quincey, who elsewhere writes perceptively about the dream of the Arab Quixote, has this to say about books in contrasting 'The Literature of Knowledge and the Literature of Power':

of this let everyone be assured—that he owes to the impassioned books which he has read, many a thousand more of emotions than he can consciously trace back to them. Dim by their origination, these emotions yet arise in him, and mould him through life like forgotten incidents of his childhood.[29]

Like forgotten incidents, forgotten books mould the language of the dream; even if their custodian is dispatched into an infinitely receding distance on his burial mission, they have a habit of coming to the surface. At this point it seems worth risking a connection between romance and dream. Romance, one might say, makes superstition manageable by turning it into 'faith'. Equally, it stands for the autonomy of the imagination, bringing self-forgetfulness. Dreams, too, though they may induce a frightening solipsism or abyss of idealism, enclose the dreamer in his own mind: 'I was the dreamer, they the dream,' Wordsworth writes of Cambridge (*Prel.* iii. 28); the London crowd becomes 'A second-sight procession, such as glides | Over still mountains, or appears in dreams' (vii. 602–3); the calm of nature makes the child forget that he has bodily eyes:

> what I saw
> Appeared like something in myself, a dream,
> A prospect in my mind.
>
> (*Prel.* ii. 369–71)

This is a different self-possession from that of the infant prodigy, and because one would expect such imaginative possession to be an intensely pleasurable experience in both reading and writing ('Visionary Power | Attends upon the motions of the winds . . .'), it is worth looking sharply at the well-known passage where Wordsworth develops the opposite view. In the third 'Essay upon Epitaphs' (1810), he writes of words as 'too awful an instrument

---

[29] 'The Poetry of Pope', *De Quincey as Critic*, ed. Jordan, p. 273. For De Quincey's discussion of the dream of the Arab Quixote, see *Recollections of the Lakes and the Lake Poets*, ed. D. Wright (Harmondsworth, 1970), 161–71.

for good and evil to be trifled with', and goes on to elaborate his
rather morbidly self-flaying fantasy about being taken over and
deranged by them:

If words be not . . . an incarnation of the thought but only a clothing for it,
then surely will they prove an ill gift; such a one as those poisoned
vestments, read of in the stories of superstitious times, which had power to
consume and to alienate from his right mind the victim who put them on.[30]

(The reference is to Hercules, driven mad with pain by the garments
which his wife had smeared with poison, thinking it a love-potion;
when he tore off his clothes, his skin came too.) It is important to
note that what Wordsworth is really talking about here are other
people's words—the second-hand, 'tainted' language of the previous
century. We are witnesses to a casting-out, as with Pope's
caricature of the hack poet Bayes, resting on his borrowed laurels:
'Next, o'er his Books his eyes began to roll, | In pleasing memory of
all he stole . . .' (*The Dunciad*, i. 127–8). But the anxiety of
influence—surfacing almost too predictably—only makes manageable a larger and more inescapable anxiety: that our texts have
always been written before, that the loud prophetic blast of
harmony is pentecostal and speaks with many voices—'Had voices
more than all the winds' (*Prel.* v. 108)—and that in submitting to
textuality, we put on inherited garments. The dream of the Arab
Quixote is an attempt to launder them while still remaining
enfolded in the texture of language.

　　Wordsworth's dream of language in *The Prelude* might be said
to make a virtue of unreadability; harnessing the defamiliarizing
movement of language itself, he opens a space for what can only
ever be written in the condensations and displacements of the
dream-text. Perhaps De Quincey, who thought that encyclopaedias
in general, and Newton's *Principia* in particular, 'transmigrated
into other forms', put it best (anxiety of influence and all) when he
wrote that the Literature of Power, unlike the Literature of
Knowledge, remains 'triumphant forever as long as the languages
exist in which they speak or can be taught to speak':

Human works of immortal beauty and works of nature in one respect
stand on the same footing; they never absolutely repeat each other; never
approach so near as not to differ; and they differ not as better and worse,
or simply by more and less: they differ by undecipherable and incommunic-

[30] *Prose Works*, ii. 84–5.

able differences, that cannot be caught by mimicries, that cannot be reflected in the mirror of copies, that cannot become ponderable in the scales of vulgar comparison.[31]

'The literature of power', he concludes, 'builds nests in aerial altitudes of temples sacred from violation'—in the mind, that intertextual edifice which *The Prelude* tries endlessly to defend against the violations, seductions, and transformations enacted by the dream-work, or the language of the dream.

[31] *De Quincey as Critic*, ed. Jordon, pp. 271–2.

CHAPTER 5

THE ART OF MANAGING BOOKS
Romantic Prose and the Writing of the Past*

THE butt of Wordsworth's satire in Book V of *The Prelude*, his book on books, is an infant prodigy—'a child, no child, | But a dwarf man' (v. 294–5). This stunted and pre-programmed mini-adult is the product of educational management by 'mighty workmen of our late age':

> they who have the art
> To manage books, and things, and make them work
> Gently on infant minds as does the sun
> Upon a flower—the tutors of our youth . . .
> Sages, who in their prescience would controul
> All accidents, and to the very road
> Which they have fashioned would confine us down
> Like engines . . .
>
> (*Prel.* v. 373–83)

Nature's education acts otherwise on the Boy of Winander, allowing the unforeseen to enter 'unawares' into his mind through the accident of self-forgetfulness. The Wordsworthian curriculum includes truancy, 'act[s] of stealth | And troubled pleasure' (i. 388–9), tutelary spirits of beauty and fear (especially fear), and even, in the case of Lucy and the Winander Boy, premature death. Though Wordsworth's own education at Hawkshead Grammar School was traditionally bookish,[1] his out-of-school activities were those he chiefly chose to recall, and when *The Prelude* does mention childhood reading it is to claim that the sight of a drowned man, 'a spectre shape— | Of terror even' (v. 472–3), could be

---

* Reprinted from Mary Jacobus, 'The Art of Managing Books: Romantic Prose and the Writing of the Past,' in *Romanticism and Language*, edited by Arden Reed. Copyright © 1984 by Cornell University Press. Used by permission of the publisher.

[1] Wordsworth claimed that 'no man in England had been more regularly educated': see *Prelude*, ed. de Selincourt, rev. Darbishire, p. 543. For his 'nine years from nine to nineteen . . . at Hawkshead, then a celebrated school', see T. W. Thompson, *Wordsworth's Hawkshead*, ed. R. Woof (London, 1970).

assimilated without trauma by a boy used to fairy tales and romances. Book learning, then, gets short shrift from an educational point of view, and the whole drift of Book V is towards subsuming literature under the heading of nature—towards naturalizing it as 'only less | For what we may become . . . Than Nature's self' (v. 220–2).

Wordsworth's satire in 'Books' is predictably anti-utilitarian, aimed as it is at the educational forerunners of the Gradgrind system in *Hard Times*.[2] But his attack on regimentation and conditioning—rote learning designed to turn children into 'engines'—discloses the unease that underlies much Romantic writing about literacy. Though Wordsworth sets out to commemorate 'all books which lay | Their sure foundations in the heart of man' (v. 199–200), he is anxious lest they cut the ground from under nature as she works through 'external accidents' (in his own words about the Winander Boy) 'to plant, for immortality, images of sound and sight, in the celestial soil of the Imagination'.[3] The fear covertly expressed in Book V is that it is not we that write, but writing that writes us; that the writing of the past, rather than 'the spirit of the past' (xi. 341), determines 'what we may become'; and that the language of books is 'unremittingly and noiselessly at work' (in Wordsworth's memorably obsessed phrases) to derange and to subvert the language of incarnated thought on which Romantic theorists pin their hope of linguistic salvation.[4] The temporal threat contained in the passage from Book V, the control of books over infant minds, is amplified in the 1850 version of *The Prelude*, where 'tutors of our youth' become 'keepers of our time'— picking up the Satanic suggestions in Wordsworth's glossing of the 'mighty workmen of our later age' as those 'Who with a broad highway have overbridged | The froward chaos of futurity' (v. 371–2), bringing death into God's timeless world. Management of books, or rather by books, means management of time too; these

---

[2] See D. V. Erdman, 'Coleridge, Wordsworth, and the Wedgwood Fund', *BNYPL* 60 (1956), 425–43, 487–507, esp. pp. 493–5, for an account of the educational schemes of the 1790s and their impact on Wordsworth in Book V of *The Prelude*. For the earlier and fuller version of *The Prelude* lines in MS 18A, see *PW* v. 345–6.

[3] 1815 'Preface'; *Prose Works*, iii. 35 app. crit.

[4] 'Language, if it do not uphold, and feed, and leave in quiet, like the power of gravitation or the air we breathe, is a counter-spirit, unremittingly and noiselessly at work to derange, to subvert, to lay waste, to vitiate, and to dissolve', *Essays upon Epitaphs*, III: *Prose Works*, ii. 85.

'sages' seek to control the future as well as the untoward. Perhaps this is why Wordsworth goes on almost at once in Book V to introduce the Winander Boy, whose attempts to manage owls with his mimic hootings are baffled by nature's 'external accidents' and whose formal education is cut short by the unforeseeable accident of death. 'Slumbering' (Wordsworth's euphemism for 'dead'), he is released both from writing out a hundred lines and, like Wordsworth himself, from being written out by tens of hundreds of them—laid asleep in nature so that the wordy, university-educated poet can attain to the art of book management. Preserving and laying to rest in one move the fantasy of a self that can neither write nor be written, the dead child is father to the *Prelude*'s man.

The episode of the Winander Boy, then, bears obliquely on the orality of Romantic theories about language—the pervasive notion that 'the voice | Of mountain torrents' (v. 408–9) speaks a language more profound than that of books and is carried farther into the heart. Wordsworth's naturalization of 'voice' here serves to avert the threat of anarchy that voices bring with them. The Winander Boy, blowing 'mimic hootings to the silent owls', has reverted to an innocently pre-linguistic phase of repeated sounds (difference without meaning, or babble); but his 'feverish and restless anxiety' also initiates a riotous Babel that is 'mocked' in turn by nature's silence ('pauses of deep silence mocked his skill', v. 405):

> And they would shout
> Across the wat'ry vale, and shout again,
> Responsive to his call, with quivering peals
> And long halloos, and screams, and echoes loud,
> Redoubled and redoubled—concourse wild
> Of mirth and jocund din.
>
> (*Prel.* v. 399–404)[5]

The distinction between parroting and echoing (who is mimicking whom—the owls the boy or the boy the owls?) is lost in the doubling and redoubling of 'concourse wild'. 'Din', though jocund here, brings to mind the confusion of another concourse altogether,

[5] 'The Boy . . . is listening, with something of a feverish and restless anxiety, for the recurrence of the riotous sounds which he had previously excited', ibid. iii. 35 app. crit. For a de Manian reading of this episode, see C. Chase, *Decomposing Figures: Rhetorical Readings in the Romantic Tradition* (Baltimore, 1986), 13–31. See also J. Hollander, *The Figure of Echo: A Mode of Allusion in Milton and After* (Berkeley and London, 1981), 18–20, for Wordsworth's relation to echo as a figure of representation.

Wordsworth's uproarious London in Book VII of *The Prelude*. *Paradise Lost*, too, provides not only a series of usages connected wth martial strife, but an archetypal usage that must surely have been in Wordsworth's mind, however subliminally—the most confused din of all, the building of the tower of Babel:

> each to other calls
> Not understood, till hoarse, and all in rage,
> As mocked they storm; great laughter was in heaven
> And looking down, to see the hubbub strange
> And hear the din; thus was the building left
> Ridiculous, and the work Confusion named.
>
> (*Paradise Lost*, xii. 57–62)

'Oh, blank *confusion*, and a type not false | Of what the mighty city is itself' (vii. 696–7; my italics):[6] Wordsworth's verdict on Bartholomew Fair, the epitome of London's 'Babel din', links urban anarchy and uproar with Nimrod's vainglorious architecture. Glimpsed behind the Winander Boy's jubilant dialogue with the owls is a wishful revision—a re-enactment that is also a restoration—of Milton's elegiac motif in Book XII of *Paradise Lost*, where the loss of a unified originary language is brought about by Nimrod's attempt to rival heaven's towers with his own.

In *The Prelude*, the boy's skill is mocked not by laughter but by silence—saving him, despite himself, from the fall he has initiated. But for the poet there can be no salvation *avant la lettre*. George Eliot, imagining the roar of unlimited sensibility that lies on the other side of silence, wads it thankfully with stupidity.[7] Wordsworth, imagining silence on the other side of uproar, uses his own writing to still the din that threatens when 'voice' becomes plural (voices) and to confine proliferation when singleness splits into uncontrolled redoubling. In this sense writing, though subordinated by Romantic theory to 'the voice of the living Speaker',[8]

---

[6] 'Babel' is marginally glossed as 'Confusion' by the Authorized Version of the Bible; Wordsworth presumably knew this popular etymology.

[7] 'If we had a keen vision and feeling of all ordinary human life . . . we should die of that roar which lies on the other side of silence. As it is, the quickest of us walk about well wadded with stupidity', *Middlemarch*, ch. 20.

[8] 'Spoken Language has a great superiority over written Language in point of energy or force. The voice of the living Speaker, makes an impression on the mind, much stronger than can be made by the perusal of any Writing', H. Blair, *Lectures on Rhetoric and Belles Lettres* (1783), ed. H. F. Harding (2 vols.; Carbondale, 1965), i. 136.

limits as well as inscribes an original fall, like Los attempting to bind Urizen's fallen universe lest it get yet further out of hand. Ordering the chaotic multiplicity of the self, writing not only defends against incoherence, but, because it is always of and from the past, defends against presence—and against the future too; only a hair's breadth separates the characteristic Romantic attempt to 'enshrine the spirit of the past | For future restoration' (xi. 341–2) from that overbridging of 'The froward chaos of futurity' denounced in Book V of *The Prelude*. What De Quincey calls 'the language of books' troubles Romantic writers in much the same way that writing troubles them—because it uncovers aspects of their practice which their theories attempt (even exist) to repress.

I want to explore these hidden contradictions by looking closely at what three major prose writers of the Romantic period have to say about language. Thomas De Quincey's essays on style and rhetoric, William Hazlitt's 'On Familiar Style', and Charles Lamb's 'Genteel Style in Writing' develop some of the questions that I have tried to introduce by way of *The Prelude*. These questions are ultimately bound up with the writing of Romantic autobiography. That what emerges looks at first sight disconcertingly like a poetics of quotation rather than of prose uncovers my central concerns— not with prose style as such, but with the part played by previous writing in constituting it; not with literary influence in any simple sense, but with the relation between the language of books and the inscribing of temporality.[9] In other words, I argue that the language of books *is* the writing of the past, and the writing of the past is the language of books.

The Language of Books

Writing in the 1840s, De Quincey identified as a prevalent cultural malaise the 'contagion of bookishness' that had infected the urban populace through the rise of journalism. A diverting anecdote in his essay on style brings the book-learned author (De Quincey prided

---

[9] Two essays that have played a part in shaping these concerns are J. Ehrmann, 'The Death of Literature', *NLH* 3 (1971), 31–47, and P. de Man, 'The Rhetoric of Temporality', *Blindness and Insight: Essays in the Rhetoric of Contemporary Criticism* (2nd edn., Minneapolis, 1983), 187–228. For a relevant structural analysis of quotation in the European novel, see H. Meyer, *The Poetics of Quotation* (Princeton, 1968).

himself on his own classical erudition)[10] face to face with
an egregious example of lodging-house literacy—a landlady 'in
regular training, it appeared, as a student of newspapers'. These
are the words that 'she—this semi-barbarian—poured from her
cornucopia':

First, 'category'; secondly, 'predicament' (where, by the way, from the
twofold iteration of the idea—Greek and Roman—it appears that the old
lady was 'twice armed'); thirdly, 'individuality'; fourthly, 'procrastination';
fifthly, 'speaking diplomatically, would not wish to *commit* herself,' who
knew but that 'inadvertently she might even *compromise* both herself and
her husband'? Sixthly, 'would spontaneously adapt the several modes of
domestication to the reciprocal interests,' &c.; and finally—(which word it
was that settled us: we heard it as we reached the topmost stair on the
second floor; and, without further struggle against our instincts, round we
wheeled, rushed down forty-five stairs, and exploded from the house with
a fury causing us to impinge against an obese or protuberant gentleman,
and calling for mutual explanations; a result which nothing *could* account
for, but a steel bow, or mustachios on the lip of an elderly woman;
meantime the fatal word was), seventhly, 'anteriorly'. Concerning which
word we solemnly depose and make affidavit that neither from man,
woman, nor book, had we ever heard it before this unique rencontre with
this abominable woman on the staircase.[11]

Belonging as she does to a long line of comic pedants stretching
back to Dogberry and beyond, De Quincey's landlady talks quite as
much like a court of law as a book—the difference being (in De
Quincey's words) 'the total absence of all *malaprop* picturesque-
ness'. One could read the encounter as a piece of covert grumbling
about the loss of a rich source of linguistic comedy, the pleasure of
the educated in the misappropriation of language by their social
inferiors, or as a stroke of Juvenalian satire against the talking
woman to whom grammarians yield and rhetoricians succumb.[12]
In any case, one does not have to be a particularly shrewd reader to
notice that De Quincey's facetiousness ('impinge against an obese
or protuberant gentleman, and calling for mutual explanations')

[10] Ironically, De Quincey attributes his fluency in ancient Greek 'to the practice
of daily reading off the newspapers into the best Greek I could furnish *extempore*'
(*Confessions of an English Opium-Eater*, ed. Lindop, p. 6).

[11] *De Quincey as Critic*, ed. Jordan, pp. 71–2. De Quincey's essays on style and
rhetoric were originally published in *Blackwood's Edinburgh Magazine* between
July 1840 and Feb. 1841 and in Dec. 1828, respectively.

[12] See G. Steiner, *After Babel* (London, 1975), 41, and Juvenal's 6th satire.

depends, like his rhetorical *suspensio*, on the lodging-house
mistress's logorrhoea—just as the would-be lodger ends by mimicking her courtroom mumbo-jumbo with his 'solemnly depose and
make affidavit'. But there is more going on here than the theft of
comic thunder. Outrage focuses on a single word, and one that
(deferred by a ballooning parenthesis) could scarcely be more
explosive for De Quincey himself: 'anteriorly'. He is literally put to
flight by the past, colliding with the quotidian in the form of
obesity. The language of books at once resurrects the past and
murders it; as Latin is a defunct language, so 'the fatal word',
'anteriorly', speaks the language of death intoned by the funereal
leitmotifs of De Quincey's writing: '*all is lost*'; 'everlasting
farewells! And again, and yet again reverberated—everlasting
farewells!'[13]

The cryptic narrative contained in the landlady's 'anteriorly'
('formerly') returns us to that false point of origin, at once ultimate and penultimate, the long ago death of De Quincey's sister,
on which both his infant sufferings and his writings are posited.[14]
But the accident on the topmost stair is doubly fatal in that
it not only rifles the tomb of the past but defeminizes language; the
landlady becomes a mustachioed Amazon ('twice armed')—a bad
mother, pouring words instead of plenty from her maternal
cornucopia. Shortly before relating his anecdote, De Quincey had
identified the 'mother tongue' or 'old mother idiom' as surviving
particularly among women—'not, Heaven knows, amongst our
women who write books ... but amongst well-educated women
not professionally given to literature'; 'The pure racy idiom of
colloquial or household English', he insists, 'must be looked for in
the circles of well-educated women not too closely connected with
books.'[15] (Dorothy Wordsworth, in De Quincey's *Recollections of
the Lake Poets*, is just such a woman—the Boy of Winander, as it
were, to the prodigiously learned landlady.)[16] Instead of looking to
Wordsworth's low and rustic life for the language of passion, De
Quincey looks to the sister and to the home. Like his anti-blue-
stocking prejudice, De Quincey's representation of women as the
site of nature, feeling, and purity is a common Romantic

[13] *Confessions of an English Opium-Eater*, ed. Lindop, pp. 77, 91.
[14] For defunct language, anasemia, and 'the exquisite corpse', see J. Derrida,
'Fors', *Georgia Review*, 31 (1977), 64–116.
[15] *De Quincey as Critic*, ed. Jordan, pp. 64, 67, 69.
[16] See *Recollections of the Lakes and the Lake Poets*, ed. Wright, pp. 199–204.

construction. But women in his writing are especially accident prone; if not dead (like his sister), nearly drowned (like his mother), or lost (like the prostitute Ann), they risk being run over by an English mail-coach. The young woman threatened with the accident of sudden death is a favourite and vivid fantasy of De Quincey's, and the language of headlong disaster is apt to spill over from *The English Mail-Coach* into what he has to say about style. Of contemporary writing, he complains: 'Whatever words *tumble out* under the blindest *accidents* of the moment, those are the words retained; whatever *sweep* is impressed by chance upon the *motion* of a period, that is the arrangement ratified'; elsewhere he speaks of modern speed-reading as 'this Parthian habit of aiming at full gallop', while his own subjection to 'the mighty Juggernaut of social life'—forcing his brain to 'work like a steam-engine' to meet the demands of periodical publication—implicates him in the 'hurry and inevitable precipitancy' threatening the young lady of *The English Mail-Coach*.[17]

De Quincey's references to a 'monster model of sentence' and 'dire monotony of bookish idiom . . . like some scaly leprosy or elephantiasis' infect the monstrous runaway machine and crocodilian driver of *The English Mail-Coach* with the disease of book language. The famous distinction between an '*organology*' and a '*mechanology*' of style is an attempt to free writing—his writing— from the death-dealing machine and to sublimate it in funereal organ music, as the dying children of his childhood visions are borne up to God or the woman of *The English Mail-Coach* is snatched to heaven in his dreams. 'Style', he insists,

may be viewed as an *organic* thing and as a *mechanic* thing . . . Now, the use of words is an organic thing, in so far as language is connected with thoughts, and modified by thoughts. It is a mechanic thing, in so far as words in combination determine or modify each other. The science of style as an organ of thought, of style in relation to the ideas and feelings, might be called the *organology* of style. The science of style, considered as a machine, in which words act upon words, and through a particular grammar, might be called the *mechanology* of style . . . it is of great importance not to confound the functions; that function by which style

---

[17] *De Quincey as Critic*, ed. Jordan, pp. 64–82 (my italics); Masson, xii. 159; v. 304, 307. For the relation between opium and eloquence in De Quincey's writing, see M. G. Cooke, 'De Quincey, Coleridge, and the Formal Uses of Intoxication', *YFS* 50 (1974), 26–40.

maintains a commerce with thought, and that by which it chiefly communicates with grammar and with words.[18]

What De Quincey is worried about is that the two functions might indeed be confounded—that the mechanology of style, gaining momentum of its own, might overrun thought and cause a fatal accident in which the feminine (the language of feeling) is the casualty. The fiction that language can retain a saving commerce with thought, independent of linguistic and grammatical machinery, is not, of course, confined to De Quincey; but the anxiety which Wordsworth figures as fear of fatal poisoning by borrowed robes (the second-hand language of the previous century)[19] takes a distinctively catastrophic form in his writing. De Quincey—willy-nilly—is a helpless passenger on an out-of-control vehicle that threatens death to what he holds dear. Drugged and powerless, barely able to shout his warning, he is at once the agent of disaster, its herald, and its witness. What is figured in *The English Mail-Coach*, in other words, is the untenability of De Quincey's attempt to distinguish between an organology and a mechanology of style. As his facetiousness about lodging-house literacy disguises an inevitable stake in literacy itself, so the melodramatic scenario of *The English Mail-Coach* is generated partly by guilt. Not only does he share the landlady's 'contagion of bookishness', but, like the sleeping coachman, he risks committing (wo)manslaughter if he is to write at all.

Hence De Quincey's persistence in attempting to sublimate prose to the condition of funereal music. The Sublime means Milton ('In Milton only, first and last, is the power of the sublime revealed'),[20] and so when De Quincey turns to the prose of an admired and influential predecessor in his essay on rhetoric, music and Milton set the tone: 'Where, but in Sir T[homas] B[rowne], shall one hope to find music so Miltonic, an intonation of such solemn chords as are struck in the following opening bar of a passage in the *Urne-Buriall*—"Now, since these bones have rested quietly in the grave under the drums and tramplings of three conquests," &c.'[21] In De Quincey's writing, too, death sounds solemn chords (the 'hollow, solemn, Memnonian, but saintly swell' breathed in the bedchamber of his sister's corpse, and 'the blare of the tumultuous organ' that

[18] *De Quincey as Critic*, ed. Jordan, pp. 70, 82–3.
[19] See *Essays upon Epitaphs*, III; *Prose Works*, ii. 84–5.
[20] *De Quincey as Critic*, ed. Jordan, p. 255.   [21] Ibid. 114.

sublimates the deaths of infants in *Suspiria de Profundis*).[22] *Urne-Buriall*'s breathings from the depths prefigure the most profound motifs of De Quincey's writing (death, time, the past—an 'eternity not coming, but past and irrevocable').[23] But they also produce echoes of a different kind—the doubling and redoubling of the Winander Boy's mimic hootings. When De Quincey embarks on his own redoubling of *Urne-Buriall* (itself already an echo chamber for Sir Thomas Browne's meditations on mortality), is he echoing or merely parroting, revising or merely belated?

What a melodious ascent of a prelude to some impassioned requiem breathing from the pomps of earth, and from the sanctities of the grave! What a *fluctus decumanus* of rhetoric! Time expounded, not by generations or centuries, but by the vast periods of conquests and dynasties; by cycles of Pharoahs and Ptolemies, Antiochi and Arsacides! And these vast successions of time distinguished and figured by the uproars which revolve at their inaugurations; by the drums and tramplings rolling overhead upon the chambers of forgotten dead—the trepidations of time and mortality vexing, at secular intervals, the everlasting sabbaths of the grave! [24]

'Language', it has been said, 'always comes to us from elsewhere (whence its character of echo, of quotation . . .).'[25] De Quincey vexes the sabbaths of the grave with trepidations that are both echoes and quotations; with language that comes from elsewhere—from the past. But (one might claim) his variation on the famous 'organ peal' of *Urne-Buriall*'s final and most sonorous chapter displaces, as echo does, the rhetoric of Browne's seventeenth-century original:

Now since these dead bodies have already outlasted the living ones of *Methuselah*, and in a yard under ground, and thin walls of clay, outworn all the strong and specious buildings above it; and quietly rested under the drums and trampling of three conquests; What Prince can promise such diuturnity unto his Reliques, or might not gladly say,

Sic ego componi versus in ossa velim.

[22] *Confessions of an English Opium-Eater*, ed. Lindop, pp. 105, 112.

[23] See H. A. Page [A. H. Japp], *Thomas De Quincey: His Life and Writings* (2 vols.; London, 1877), i. 340.

[24] *De Quincey as Critic*, ed. Jordan, p. 114.

[25] Ehrmann, 'The Death of Literature', p. 39. For a different approach to De Quincey and literary influence, see A. Reed, 'Abysmal Influence: Baudelaire, Coleridge, De Quincey, Piranesi, Wordsworth', *Glyph*, 4 (1978), 189–206.

Time which antiquates Antiquities, and hath an art to make dust of all things, hath yet spared these *minor* Monuments.[26]

Browne's urns are both tombs and wombs, 'making our last bed like our first';[27] their buried story is an originating death. Exhuming Browne's language, De Quincey sets going a perpetual-motion machine—recycling words whose meaning, like that of 'anteriorly', is always former, always buried, and always a repetition of the past, while achieving a paradoxical priority: his is the melodious prelude.

In 1821, the Tory *Quarterly Review* accused Hazlitt of being a 'SLANG-WHANGER'—that is, 'One who makes use of political or other gabble, vulgarly called slang, that serves to amuse the rabble'.[28] In the politics of style, 'gabble' invokes the presumptuous anarchy of Babel while 'slang' denounces radicalism as rabble-rousing. As Hazlitt wrote scathingly in *A Letter to William Gifford Esq.* (1819), the most furious outburst in his sustained political war with the Tory reviewers, 'When you say that an author cannot write common sense or English, you mean that he does not believe in the doctrine of divine right.'[29] His 1821 essay 'On Familiar Style' is thus both a rearguard action against the *Quarterly*—'I have been (I know) loudly accused of revelling in vulgarisms and broken English'—and an attempt to redefine style in terms of the Bourgeois Revolution. What starts as self-defence turns into an economics of language. Familiar style is not vulgarity, but common use; devaluing pedantry at one extreme and slang at the other, the essay sets out to legitimize a different currency, that of the market-place. Hazlitt as honest broker uses only legal tender, coin made current by 'the stamp of custom'. His distinction between slang and common usage turns on an example both incisive (as he wished his

---

[26] Sir Thomas Browne, *Religio Medici and Other Works*, ed. L. C. Martin (Oxford, 1964), 118.

[27] Ibid. 102.

[28] *Quarterly Review*, 26 (Oct. 1821), 108; the reviewer was John Matthews. For Hazlitt's dealings with the *Quarterly* and the *Quarterly's* dealings with Hazlitt, see R. B. Clark, *William Gifford: Tory Satirist and Editor* (New York, 1930), 213–20, and R. M. Wardle, *Hazlitt* (Lincoln, Nebr. 1971), 242–7, 286–7. See D. Bromwich, *Hazlitt: The Mind of a Critic* (New York and Oxford, 1983), 275–313, for a discussion of the politics of allusion in Hazlitt, and esp. for Hazlitt's relationship to Burke; and see also O. Smith, *The Politics of Language, 1791–1819* (Oxford, 1984), 147–52.   [29] Howe, ix. 14.

prose to be) and socially paranoid (as he was himself), salted with a grain of popular learning (*cum grano salis*):

> I should say that the phrase *To cut with a knife*, or *To cut a piece of wood*, is perfectly free from vulgarity, because it is perfectly common: but to *cut an acquaintance* is not quite unexceptionable, because it is not perfectly common or intelligible, and has hardly yet escaped out of the limits of slang phraseology. I should hardly therefore use the word in this sense without putting it in italics as a licence of expression, to be received *cum grano salis*. . . . I conceive that words are like money, not the worse for being common, but that it is the stamp of custom alone that gives them respect, and would almost as soon coin the currency of the realm as counterfeit the king's English. . . . As an author, I endeavour to employ plain words and popular modes of construction, as, were I a chapman and dealer, I should common weights and measures.[30]

The spectacle of Hazlitt the republican invoking the King's English might at first sight seem an odd one; but for him the bloodless revolution of 1688 had meant the introduction of a Bill of Rights by which the King derived his authority not from God but from the people—from the Lords and Commons, the guarantors of constitutional rights. Hazlitt, in fact, answers the *Quarterly Review* by putting himself firmly on the side of New Whig commerce ('common weights and measures') rather than Tory 'Legitimacy', which he elsewhere calls 'this foul Blatant Beast . . . breathing flame and blood'—a monstrous Error, regurgitating such books as Burke's *Reflections on the Revolution in France*.[31]

For Hazlitt, 'the want of ideas' means inflation. Plagiarizing Hamlet's irritable 'words, words, words', he attacks the 'florid style' that is the reverse of the familiar: ' "What do you read?"— "Words, words, words."—"What is the matter?"—"Nothing," it might be answered.' Polonius as windbag provokes a Hamlet-like railing against the flowers of rhetoric—'When there is nothing to be set down but words, it costs little to have them fine. Look through

---

[30] Ibid. viii. 243–4. See also J. Derrida, 'White Mythology', *NLH* 6 (1974), 5–74, esp. 6–17, for coins and metaphors; and M. Shell, *The Economy of Literature* (Baltimore, 1978), for the relation between literary exchanges and exchanges that constitute the political economy.

[31] Howe, vii. 10. Spenser's Blatant Beast, interestingly, is full of tongues that 'Ne Kesars spared . . . nor Kings' (*The Faerie Queene*, VI. xii. 28). For Hazlitt's changing political stance and his alignment with the Hanoverian loyalties and constitutional Whiggism of the dissenting tradition, see J. Kinnaird, *William Hazlitt: Critic of Power* (New York, 1978), 101–28.

the dictionary, and cull out a *florilegium*, rival the *tulippomania*. *Rouge* high enough, and never mind the natural complexion.' Painted ladies and rouged tulips figure the strumpetry of language that Hazlitt, like Marvell's Puritan mower against gardens, denounces less because art has meddled with nature than because nature has learned to counterfeit rather than cultivate plainness ('The Tulip, white, did for complexion seek; | And learn'd to interline its cheek', 'The Mower against Gardens', ll. 13–14). Or—to exchange one metaphor for another—the 'merely verbal imagination' becomes a social dragonfly, spawning in Hazlitt's own prose a further proliferation of empty, iridescent, deflationary images:

Such writers have merely *verbal* imaginations, that retain nothing but words. Or their puny thoughts have dragon-wings, all green and gold. They soar far above the vulgar failings of the *Sermo humi obrepens*—their most ordinary speech is never short of an hyperbole, splendid, imposing, vague, incomprehensible, magniloquent, a cento of sounding commonplaces.[32]

Horace's 'words creeping along the ground' (his modestly termed satiric 'conversations') are momentarily overreached by glittering hyperboles before they thud to earth as 'sounding common-places'. This is Hazlitt's equivalent to De Quincey's distinction between 'mechanology' and 'organology'; but, in Hazlitt's case, the 'merely verbal imagination' is floated by the fiction of reference—of a saving commerce, less with thought than with things. 'Imaginations, that retain nothing but words' have lost their purchase on reality. For Hazlitt this unreality is akin to possession, or madness: 'Such persons are in fact besotted with words, and their brains are turned with the glittering, but empty and sterile phantoms of things.' They are 'the poorest of all plagiarists, the plagiarists of words', inhabiting the world of writing instead of things—'Personifications, capital letters, seas of sunbeams, visions of glory, shining inscriptions, the figures of a transparency, Britannia with her shield, or Hope leaning on an anchor, make up their stock of trade.'[33] This is the same text of signs, inscriptions, and allegoric shapes that makes up Wordsworth's London, where the city as book is given over entirely to advertising:

---

[32] Howe, viii. 244, 246.   [33] Ibid. 246–7.

> Shop after shop, with symbols, blazoned names,
> And all the tradesman's honours overhead:
> Here, fronts of houses, like a title-page
> With letters huge inscribed from top to toe;
> Stationed above the door, like guardian saints,
> There, allegoric shapes, female or male . . .
>
> *(Prel.* vii. 174–9)

Rejecting 'personifications of abstract ideas' in the 1800 Preface to *Lyrical Ballads*, Wordsworth writes: 'I wish to keep the Reader in the company of flesh and blood.'[34] Ghostliness enters where representation becomes merely apparent, exposing appearances as apparitions, not flesh and blood. When 'objects are not linked to feelings, words to things, but . . . words represent themselves', the spectral text of language undoes what Hazlitt calls 'the web and texture of the universe'—revealing language as a weapon that cannot 'cut with a knife', but can only make feints and passes. The literal becomes a phantasm haunting the dematerialized text, as metaphor alternately effaces itself and returns to the surface.

'His words are the most like things' was how Hazlitt chose to praise Burke.[35] Fittingly, what he calls 'the true worth and hidden structure both of words and things' are underwritten by the most conservative as well as the most eloquent defender of the status quo. That Hazlitt's political obverse should be the prose writer he admired above all others epitomizes the ambidextrousness not only of literary inheritance but of language itself. Ironically, it was Burke's most self-interested (and ironic) defence of hereditary privilege that had made Hazlitt his ephebe in the 1790s: 'We first met with some extracts from Mr. Burke's *Letter to a Noble Lord* in the year 1796, and on the instant became converts to his familiar, inimitable, powerful prose-style.'[36] Burke at the top of his form, warding off the Duke of Bedford's attack on his pension with the weapons he had earlier used to defend the hereditary rights of kings, becomes the hero of Hazlitt's levelling essay 'On the Prose Style of Poets' (1822). The centrepiece of both essays is Burke's most authoritative celebration of the constitution, of privilege, and of legitimacy. This, for Hazlitt, is prose with its feet on the ground— useful, energetic, and pedestrian (as the prose style of poets is not);

---

[34] *Prose Works*, i. 130.   [35] Howe, vii. 309.
[36] Ibid. xvi. 222. The irony was not lost on Hazlitt: see ibid. vii. 186.

above all, prose in which a 'vague and complicated idea' is grounded on the bedrock of things:

As long as the well-compacted structure of our church and state, the sanctuary, the holy of holies of that ancient law, defended by reverence, defended by power—a fortress at once and a temple—shall stand inviolate on the brow of the British Sion; as long as the British Monarchy—not more limited than fenced by the orders of the State shall, like the proud Keep of Windsor, rising in the majesty of proportion, and girt with the double belt of his kindred and coeval towers; as long as this awful structure shall oversee and guard the subjected land, so long the mounds and dykes of the low, fat, Bedford level will have nothing to fear from all the pickaxes of all the levellers of France. As long as our Sovereign Lord the King, and his faithful subjects, the Lords and Commons of this realm—the triple cord which no man can break; the solemn, sworn, constitutional-frank pledge of this nation; the firm guarantees of each other's being, and each other's rights; the joint and several securities, each in its place and order, for every kind, and every quality of property and of dignity—As long as these endure we are all safe together—the high from the blights of envy and the spoliations of rapacity; the low from the iron hand of oppression and the insolent spurn of contempt. Amen! and so be it: and so it will be,

> *Dum domus Æneae Capitoli immobile saxum*
> *Accolet; imperiumque pater Romanus.*[37]

Burke is invoking the authority of the *Aeneid* and Anchises' prophecy from Book IX ('so long as the house of Aeneas shall dwell on the capitol's unshaken rock, and the Father of Rome hold sovereign sway') in order to base his defence of property rights on the foundations of Rome. Burke cites Virgil: Hazlitt quotes Burke. The appropriation of authority (in Burke's case to support his view of the Constitution, in Hazlitt's to support his view of prose style) involves a form of quotation that not only displaces meaning but reinvests it—since for Hazlitt the emphasis is not simply on defending the rights of men against the divine right of kings, but the right of prose writers to vie with poets, and ultimately his own right to vie with Burke.

For Burke, who (in the words of the 1850 *Prelude*) 'the majesty proclaims | Of Institutes and Laws, hallowed by time' (vii. 525–6), the language of books—here, of the *Aeneid*—is the language of legitimacy; 'Legitimacy, the very tomb of freedom', Hazlitt called

---

[37] Ibid. xii. 11–12; cf. *The Works of Edmund Burke* (5 vols.; London, 1855–64), v. 137–8.

it.[38] Legitimacy must be deposed if liberty is to flourish. Hazlitt's writing about Burke is doubly subversive, first displacing 'the vague and complicated idea' of the English Constitution with the figure of Burke himself, then appropriating his powers. The proud Keep of Windsor is only a pawn in the battle of words; Burke (according to Hazlitt) 'seized on some stronghold in the argument, and held it fast with a convulsive grasp . . . He entered the lists like a gladiator.' Burke as gladiator becomes Hazlitt the prose pugilist—'Every word should be a blow: every thought should instantly grapple with its fellow.'[39] Hazlitt's temperamental pugnacity makes his the pugilistic style as well as the familiar style (it is no accident that his favourite among Lamb's essays was the miniature mock epic, 'Mrs. Battle's Opinions on Whist'). The fight is ostensibly political—against what Hazlitt on a different occasion called 'the "old proud keep" of intolerance and privilege, fenced by "its double belt of kindred", ignorance and pride,' subverting the conservative imagery of Burke's *Letter to a Noble Lord* to make a radical point;[40] but it is also 'familiar' in another sense, that is, familial. Burke had defended hereditary privilege in order to parry attacks on the pension he had earned: Hazlitt's misreading of Burke contends with an admired predecessor and political adversary in order to wrest from him not his pension but his 'power'—a key term, of course, in the aesthetics of both. Burke (in Wordsworth's *Prelude* lines) 'Exploding upstart Theory, insists | Upon the allegiance to which men are born' (1850: vii. 529–30): Hazlitt embarks on an Oedipal struggle. For Wordsworth too, the elder Burke was a patriarchal figure:

> I see him,—old, but vigorous in age,—
> Stand like an oak whose stag-horn branches start
> Out of its leafy brow, the more to awe
> The younger brethren of the grove.

> (*Prel.* 1850: vii. 519–22)

It is thus all the more surprising that Hazlitt's essay should cast him as the rebel of the prose sublime: 'Burke's style is airy, flighty, adventurous. . . . It may be said to pass yawning gulfs "on the unsteadfast footing of a spear".'[41] The allusion here is (bizarrely) to Hotspur's incitement to rebellion by Worcester in *1 Henry IV*:

---

[38] Howe, vii. 10.   [39] Ibid. xii. 269, 11.   [40] Ibid. xvii. 324.
[41] Ibid. xii. 10.

I'll read you matter deep and dangerous,
As full of peril and adventurous spirit
As to o'er walk a current roaring loud
On the unsteadfast footing of a spear

(*1 Henry IV*, I. iii. 188–91)

Why did Hazlitt apply to Burke, of all people, the language of insurrection when it was not Burke but himself that was in revolt against *pater Romanus*? Is it because the son, in attempting to appropriate the authority of the father, must identify him as the same, while usurping him as other (conservative, repressive, and authoritarian)? Or, to put it another way, is Hazlitt himself both the good and the bad son, both Hal and Hotspur, desiring at once to inherit and to contest Burke's proprietary rights over language (while presumably recognizing him to be as much a self-made man as Bolingbroke)? But the ambivalence is not simply that of influence; it is also that of a writer who sees his inheritance guaranteed by the very legitimacy he challenges. The writing of Hazlitt the radical is constituted, so to speak, by Burke's conservative style. 'Always a usurper, meaning is never legitimate', writes Jacques Ehrmann; 'meaning', he goes on, '*commands* subversion (as one says of a geographical point that it commands a strategic place; that it both forbids and gives access at the same time.'[42] The proud old Keep of Windsor—at once the constitution and its chief defender—forbids and gives access in the same way. Hazlitt needs legitimacy in order to free liberty from her tomb.

'On Familiar Style' exempts Lamb from Hazlitt's general dislike of antiquarianism, recognizing him to be 'so thoroughly imbued with the spirit of his authors, that the idea of imitation is almost done away. . . . The matter is completely his own, though the manner is assumed.' Lamb's antiquarianism is a mask—like the fictional Elia, a means not simply of disguising eccentricity, but of shielding his identity; as Hazlitt puts it, 'The old English authors . . . are a kind of mediator between us and the more eccentric and whimsical modern, reconciling us to his peculiarities.'[43] The assumed manner mediates as much between past and present as between Elia and his readers; 'the film of the past hovers forever before him' to create a temporal interspace where what 'touches [Elia] most nearly . . . is

---

[42] Ehrmann, 'The Death of Literature', p. 44.   [43] Howe, viii. 245.

withdrawn to a certain distance, which verges on the border of oblivion'. Lamb, in fact, is a marginal writer only in the sense that he is a liminal one who imaginatively haunts the borders of life and death, ideas and reality:

Death has in this sense the spirit of life in it; and the shadowy has to our author something substantial in it. Ideas savour most of reality in his mind; or rather his imagination loiters on the edge of each, and a page of his writing recalls to our fancy the *stranger* on the grate, fluttering in its dusky tenuity, with its idle superstition and hospitable welcome.[44]

Lamb's written page is the '*stranger* on the grate' that in Cowper's *Task* (as in Coleridge's 'Frost at Midnight') 'play[s] upon the bars',

> in the view
> Of superstition, prophecying still,
> Though still deceiv'd, some stranger's near approach.
>
> *(The Task*, iv. 292–5)

The stranger hospitably summoned to inhabit it is Elia, that estranged and ghostly version of self brought to life in the hinterland of writing. This margin is a play space. The 'stranger', or the self doubled and fictionalized, is freed from the trials of empirical existence and in turn frees strangeness—eccentricity and whimsicality—for the uses of the imagination. The hovering spectre here is that of duplicity, paradoxically animated by writing that De Quincey contrasted with his own 'Rhythmus, or pomp of cadence' as 'the natural, the simple, the genuine'.[45] Lamb uses a different term in his essay 'The Genteel Style in Writing' (1826), which needs Shaftesbury's definition from the previous century to bring to light its veiled subject, the disguise of artifice as nature: 'The natural and simple manner which conceals and covers Art, is the most truly artful, and of the genteelest, truest, and best study'd Taste' (*OED*). Naturalness conceals art, taste is studied. Dissembling and study— the art of counterfeiting and of managing books—underwrite the 'truth' of the genteel style, which is really that of fiction.

Lamb is of all writers the most self-confessedly bookish ('Books think for me', he confides in his essay 'On Books and Reading') and the most at home in that retreat of the antiquarian imagination, a library. In 'Oxford in the Vacation', the Bodleian combines 'the mystery of retroversion' ('the past is everything, being nothing'),

---

[44] Ibid. xi. 178–80.   [45] *De Quincey as Critic*, ed. Jordan, pp. 448–9.

books, and—gardens. Why should ghostliness and books, antiquity and libraries, tend to evoke gardens in Lamb's writing? Is it so that knowledge can regain its innocence and the language of books lose its duplicity in the unfallen world of Eden? The library of 'Oxford in the Vacation' is a 'dormitory' for dead writers, a 'middle state' where they are not dead but sleeping, waiting to be restored to that 'happy orchard' into which death has not yet entered:

What a place to be in is an old library! It seems as though all the souls of all the writers, that have bequeathed their labours to these Bodleians, were reposing here, as in some dormitory, or middle state. I do not want to handle, to profane the leaves, their winding-sheets. I could as soon dislodge a shade. I seem to inhale learning, walking amid their foliage; and the odour of their old moth-scented coverings is fragrant as the first bloom of those sciential apples which grew amid the happy orchard.[46]

This kind of reading is called browsing (the apples of knowledge not picked, but enjoyed on the bough; learning inhaled, not as dust, but as paradisal fragrance). Dead knowledge is kept fresh by being embalmed in books as the Boy of Winander is embalmed in nature, a silent surrogate for the unnatural poet. Lamb's surrogate or *alter ego* in 'The Genteel Style in Writing' is Sir William Temple, a retired statesman whose 'plain natural chit-chat' and garden retreat give writing its gentility, naturalize the language of books, and restore Elian duplicity to original innocence. Though the manner is assumed, Lamb makes another's matter his own by an innocent form of plagiarism—quotation—which allows him to appropriate Temple's 'sweet garden essay' (*Upon the Gardens of Epicurus; or, Of Gardening, in the Year 1685*), turning rank to simplicity and learning to what he calls 'garden pedantry'. 'The rank of the writer is never more innocently disclosed, than where he takes for granted the compliments paid by foreigners to his fruit-trees', reports Elia, drifting into indirect chit-chat:

For the taste and perfection of what we esteem the best, he can truly say, that the French, who have eaten his peaches and grapes at Shene in no very ill year, have generally concluded that the last are as good as any they have eaten in France on this side of Fontainbleau; and the first as good as they have eaten in Gascony. Italians have agreed his white figs to be as good as any of that sort in Italy, which is the earlier kind of white fig there . . . His orange-trees, too, are as large as any he saw when he was young in France

46 Lucas, ii. 172, 9. 10.

... Of grapes he had the honour of bringing over four sorts into England, which he enumerates ...

And so on and so on, with the gentle tedium by which the genteel style makes pride harmless and purifies international politics as gardening. Temple's, in short, is a Horatian garden ('May I have books enough; and one year's store ...') designed as much to pastoralize learning as to make horticulture erudite.

Invoking Temple's role in the Battle of the Books ('the controversy about the ancient and the modern learning'), Lamb looks back to this lost classical tradition; 'Certain it is', he quotes Temple as saying, 'that ... the great heights and excellency both of poetry and music fell with the Roman learning and empire.'[47] For Temple (fancifully or not), such learning can be found in courts and cottages; but, for Lamb, it has taken refuge in libraries. A tradition that Temple could still pretend was alive in the latter part of the seventeenth century inscribes for Lamb the site of a *hortus conclusus* where, in Temple's phrase, the mind can be protected from 'the violent passions and perturbations' of the world. Learning for Lamb, in other words, has passed from being ancient to being antique, becoming an aspect of Temple's antiquarian appeal. The language of books, in refusing modernity, not only mediates between past and present, but guarantees the radical alterity or strangeness of the self that generates the fiction of Elia. Lamb's version of Romantic irony is bound up with his antiquarianism. The language of (old) books makes the self both safe and other, at once protecting and estranging it; if threatened, he can 'retire, impenetrable to ridicule, under the phantom cloud of Elia'.[48] Calling Temple's style a 'humour of plainness', he uses the same word in the context of the fictional alias who bears the letter of his name (L-ia) when he signs off in the Preface to *Last Essays* (1833): 'The *humour* of the thing ... was pretty well exhausted; and a two years' and a half existence has been a tolerable duration for a phantom' (my italics). It is this 'half existence' that Lamb goes on to define as natural. Describing the writings of his 'friend' (his 'familiar', one might call Elia) as 'unlicked, incondite things— villainously pranked in an affected array of antique modes and phrases', he asserts that 'they had not been *his*, if they had been other than such; and better it is, that a writer should be natural in a

[47] Ibid. 200–2. See *Five Miscellaneous Essays by Sir William Temple*, ed. S. H. Monk (Ann Arbor, 1963), 20–1, 25.   [48] Lucas, ii. 29.

self-pleasing quaintness, than to affect a naturalness (so called) that should be strange to him'. Quaintness is the natural mode of a strange identity. The duplicitous doubling of Lamb and Elia—the splitting of self into two (or more)—takes this alienation effect a stage further; as Lamb writes, defending Elia against the charge of egotism, 'What he tells us, as of himself, was often true only (historically) of another':

If it be egotism to imply and twine with his own identity the griefs and affections of another—making himself many, or reducing many unto himself—then is the skillful novelist, who all along brings in his hero, or heroine, speaking of themselves, the greatest egotist of all . . . And how shall the intenser dramatist escape being faulty, who doubtless, under cover of passion uttered by another, oftentimes gives blameless vent to his most inward feelings, and expresses his own story modestly?[49]

The modesty of fiction is the mask of egotism. Dispersing his identity among many or 'reducing many unto himself', Elia becomes the chameleon poet—'the least of an egotist', in Hazlitt's phrase.[50] The dead humorists of the South-Sea House, like Wordsworth's 'Old humourists . . . Of texture midway betwixt life and books' (*Prel.* iii. 610–13) are 'persons of a curious and speculative turn of mind. Old fashioned . . . Humourists . . . Odd fishes' who form a gallery of eccentric phantoms conjured out of the past as surrogates for Elia himself; so many Uncle Tobies 'summon[ed] from the dusty dead'.[51]

Temple, then, is an idealized version of Elia, and the language of books (his books) doubles for the language of the self. Writing, we know, is already a kind of quotation, and 'The Genteel Style in Writing' uses quotation to create a fictional space where the self can be made and unmade. For Schlegel, Romantic irony is an ever-present authorial intrusion or self-conscious narrative that draws attention to its own fictionality, as Lamb's writing does by its play of endlessly dividing selves and its motley (Elia's *toga virilus*, which sits uneasily on him, making him a humorist in his own right; a Yorick, or even a Hamlet). The irony that Schlegel calls 'this amazement of the thinking spirit at itself, which so often dissolves in a light, gentle laugh', is also 'the only entirely involuntary and nevertheless completely conscious dissimulation', making everything

---

[49] Lucas, ii. 151. The preface was originally published in 1823.
[50] Howe, v. 47.   [51] Lucas, ii. 3, 6.

'at once jest and yet seriousness, artless openness, and yet deep dissimulation . . . It contains and incites a feeling of the insoluble conflict of the absolute and the relative, of the impossibility and necessity of total communication. *It is the freest of all liberties*'.[52] Quotation as Lamb practises it here is just such a freedom, an ironic disguise that liberates and authorizes self-representation through the dissimulation of writing. More than half the essay is given over to quoting Temple, whose garden pedantry becomes an embowering refuge for Elia and whose final words in his own essay *Of Poetry* form the conclusion of Lamb's. Temple's defence of poetry and music against those who despise them 'as toys and trifles too light for the use or entertainment of serious men'—as play—culminates in a momentary closure of the teasing gap between mask and actor, Temple and Elia: 'When all is done', he concludes, 'human life is at the greatest and the best but like a froward child, that must be played with, and humoured a little, to keep it quiet, till it falls asleep, and then the care is over.'[53] Here ventriloquism speaks with the voice of the ventriloquist. The genteel style puts Elia himself among the skilful beggars whose impositions he defends in his 'Complaint of the Decay of Beggars in the Metropolis': 'When they come with their counterfeit looks, and mumping tones, think them players. You pay your money to see a comedian feign these things, which, concerning these poor people, thou canst not certainly tell whether they are feigned or not.'[54] Lamb's counterfeiting is the same; at once the freest of all liberties and the only entirely involuntary form of disguise, it makes the language of books a necessary fiction for 'these things, which . . . thou canst not certainly tell whether they are feigned or not'.

The Language of Temporality

For Wordsworth in Book IV of *The Prelude*, 'Incumbent o'er the surface of past time', the inability to disentangle past from present or depth from surface reflections brings a special kind of perplexity:

> As one who hangs down-bending from the side
> Of a slow-moving boat upon the breast

---

[52] F. Schlegel, *Dialogue on Poetry and Literary Aphorisms*, trans. E. Behler and R. Struc (Philadelphia, 1968), 131 (my italics).

[53] Lucas, ii. 202; see *Five Miscellaneous Essays by Sir William Temple*, ed. Monk, p. 203.   [54] Lucas, ii. 120.

Of a still water, solacing himself
With such discoveries as his eye can make
Beneath him in the bottom of the deeps,
Sees many beauteous sights—weeds, fishes, flowers,
Grots, pebbles, roots of trees—and fancies more,
Yet often is perplexed, and cannot part
The shadow from the substance . . .

(*Prel.* iv. 247–55)

Though the discoveries are 'solacing', the office 'pleasant', there is
also the danger of tumbling in and drowning 'in the bottom of the
deeps', as Lycidas visits 'the bottom of the monstrous world'
(*Lycidas*, l. 158). The submerged image of watery dissolution makes
this idly self-reflexive activity more edgy than it looks. The pleasant
interfusion of past and present is naturalized by Wordsworth's
simile, with its written-in parting of shadow from substance; and if
the poet seems to risk total immersion it is because his imagery has
itself been too successful in blurring boundaries ('cannot part | The
shadow from the substance' after all). Put another way, although
Romantic autobiographers characteristically desire to reintegrate
past and present selves—or, like Wordsworth, to replace self-
mirroring with a naturalized fusion of image and reflection—the
closing of the gap would obliterate autobiography altogether.
Attempting to overbridge, not 'The froward chaos of futurity' (*Prel.*
v. 372), but the 'Two consciousnesses' of past and present
('conscious of myself, | And of some other being', ii. 32–3), writing
simultaneously brings that 'other being' into alien half-existence
and makes the split manageable. Parting the shadow from the
substance, writing thus becomes the language of temporality, a
means of structuring the self in time. Inscribing both temporal
alterity and an origin that is always lost, it is at once a form of
archaeology and a means of ordering the past. What is salvaged is
also 'managed' so that the burden of the past can neither swamp the
present nor be swamped by it.

De Quincey's famous image of a palimpsest in *Suspiria de
Profundis*—the 'membrane or roll cleaned of its manuscript by
reiterated successions'—purports to be a multilayer inscription in
which the successive writings of the past are simultaneously present
and eternally retrievable. But the palimpsest is also an image of
management, controlling the unruly discontinuities of past experiences as it creates them, and (in theory at least) preventing a

perplexed interweaving of texts, since only one can be read at a time. Though De Quincey becomes facetiously digressive about the possibilities of the multilayer book (making sense for one age, nonsense for the next, reread by the one after), he is really preoccupied by the mythic unattainability of origins: 'We have backed upon each phoenix in the long *regressus* and forced him to expose his ancestral phoenix, sleeping in the ashes below his own ashes.' The infinite regression forces archaeology beyond history into myth and opens up an apocalyptic retrospect. A work not so much of exorcism as of conjuration, it unleashes the demonic hubbub of incoherence and Bacchic laughter stored in the human brain:

The image, the memorial, the record which for me is derived from a palimpsest . . . is but too repellent of laughter; or, even if laughter *had* been possible, it would have been such laughter as oftentimes is thrown off from the fields of ocean, laughter that hides, or that seems to evade mustering tumult; foam bells that weave garlands of phospheric radiance for one moment round the eddies of gleaming abysses; mimicries of earth-born flowers that for the eye raise phantoms of gaiety, as oftentimes for the ear they raise the echoes of fugitive laughter, mixing with the ravings and choir voices of an angry sea.[55]

The image is only sublimely laughable, and the laughter that of the mathematical sublime invoked by De Quincey's footnote to 'the fields of ocean'—the overwhelming plurality of Aeschylus' 'multitudinous laughter of the ocean billows'. The mockery of Pandemonium installs destructiveness in the depths of the imagination, like the tumult of 'Kubla Khan', with its ancestral voices prophesying war. For Freud, the instinctual source is 'a chaos, a cauldron, full of seething excitations'.[56] If id were to swamp ego, if writings were to be overwhelmed by sound waves—the '*fluctus decumanus* of rhetoric'—the tumultuous flood would have the apocalyptic force of the ocean in Wordsworth's dream of the Arab Quixote. This is surely the subliminal link between the image of the palimpsest and the episode of the drowning woman (resurrected from *Confessions of an English Opium-Eater*) which De Quincey goes on to introduce—another version of simultaneity, in which the past events of the drowning woman's life are flashed before her eyes

[55] *Confessions of an English Opium-Eater*, ed. Lindop, pp. 143–4.
[56] *The Complete Psychological Works of Sigmund Freud*, trans. and ed. Strachey, xxii. 73.

'as in a mirror', 'arraying themselves not as a succession, but as parts of a coexistence'. The woman of *Suspiria de Profundis* drowns, in effect, in her own depths. For the mind of each individual, De Quincey reminds us (like Freud with his image of the magic writing-pad) 'there is no such thing as *forgetting*'.[57] Like consciousness, the written page (the film of the past?) interposes its surface as a barrier between the present and total recall. The palimpsest, then, 'contains' the past in a double sense.

Writing contains; deciphering recovers. The two-way traffic is De Quincey's version of the man hanging over the side of his boat, another attempt at unperplexing the relation between experience and reflection. The act of deciphering establishes the gap between consciousness and being ('some other being') across which meaning is generated. This temporal time-lag is the subject of one of De Quincey's most crucial footnotes, inserted in his text after the words 'I felt' in an attempt to check an otherwise engulfing visionary experience—his childhood vision of dying infants borne up to heaven amid the blaze of stained-glass windows and the blare of organs. The fantasy of overcoming death's 'dreadful chasm of separation' brings with it a moment when De Quincey becomes at once apocalyptic victim and apocalyptic agent, and when his triumph over separation threatens to turn the dreamer into the dream itself, the visionary into his vision, as feeling annihilates the self: 'sometimes under the transfigurations of music I felt of grief itself as a fiery chariot for mounting victoriously above the causes of grief.' This vertiginous merging is steadied by De Quincey's elaborate secondary revision or rereading of his dream text:

'*I felt*'. The reader must not forget, in reading this and other passages, that though a child's feelings are spoken of, it is not the child who speaks. *I* decipher what the child only felt in cipher . . . I . . . did not, as a child, *consciously* read in my own deep feelings these ideas. No, not at all; nor was it possible for a child to do so. I the child had the feelings; I the man decipher them. In the child lay the handwriting mysterious to *him*; in me the interpretation and the comment.[58]

---

[57] *Confessions of an English Opium-Eater*, ed. Lindop, pp. 69, 145; cf. *The Complete Psychological Works of Sigmund Freud*, trans. and ed. Stachey, v. 621: 'In the unconscious nothing can be brought to an end, nothing is past or forgotten.'

[58] *Confessions of an English Opium-Eater*, ed. Lindop, pp. 112–13. For another account of De Quincey as autobiographer, see S. J. Spector, 'Thomas De Quincey: Self-effacing Autobiographer', *SiR* 18 (1979), 501–20.

It is as if Wordsworth had broken off from a spot of time to footnote the existence of two consciousnesses. 'Forgetting' ('The reader must not forget'), or self-loss, is of course just what De Quincey's dream visions aim to induce, as the spots of time aim to obliterate the gulf between the two consciousnesses; yet remembering must be invoked to ward off possession by the otherness of dream and by the past itself. Though De Quincey deeply desires to cross the 'chasm of separation', to do so would be to enter the boundless eternity inhabited by the dead infants of his vision. The child is written; the adult deciphers. The 'other being' is the text: 'I' supply the interpretation and the comment (but am already written). Meaning resides 'anteriorly', one might say with De Quincey's landlady, in the regressive movement of dreams and the unconscious. If Freudianism involves an archaeology of the unconscious, an uncovering of mythic regressions and a deciphering of the ever prior,[59] so too does writing itself—a system in which previous layers of text shape the present with their buried structures, as the landlady's 'anteriorly' conceals De Quincey's past within it like a time bomb.

For Hazlitt, the attempt to derive the meaning of the present from past inscription spells legitimacy. Burke had founded immemorial constitutional rights on wills that transmit inheritance from one generation to the next: 'From Magna Charta to the Declaration of Right, it has been the uniform policy of our constitution to claim and assert our liberties, as an *entailed inheritance* derived to us from our forefathers, and to be transmitted to our posterity.'[60] Tom Paine contends the opposite in *The Rights to Man* (1791): 'I am contending for the rights of the *living*, and against their being willed away, and controlled and contracted for, by the manuscript-assumed authority of the dead; and Mr. Burke is contending for the authority of the dead over the rights and freedom of the living.'[61] What Burke calls 'monumental inscriptions'—'records, evidences, and titles'—guarantee legality on the authority of the past.[62] But, for Paine, this is the dead hand

[59] See P. Ricoeur, *Freud and Philosophy*, trans. D. Savage (New Haven, 1970), 439–40. See also J.-M. Rey, 'Freud's Writing on Writing', *YFS* 50 (1974), 301–28.

[60] *The Works of Edmund Burke*, ii. 306; the emphasis is Burke's. For Burke's use of the family as a central symbol, see J. T. Boulton, *The Language of Politics in the Age of Wilkes and Burke* (London, 1963), 112–14.

[61] *The Rights of Man*, ed. Collins, p. 64.

[62] *The Works of Edmund Burke*, ii. 308.

ruling over the living; more Casaubon's will than a Bill of Rights. While Burke's 'manuscript-assumed authority of the dead' meant the perpetuation of the status quo, books and writing might mean for Hazlitt—as Paine's *Rights of Man* had demonstrated—a new form of popular power; a force for liberty rather than legitimacy. In 'The Influence of Books on the Progress of Manners' (1828), Hazlitt defines 'public opinion' as 'the atmosphere of liberal sentiment and equitable conclusions' brought about by books. 'The reading public', in his view, is 'a very rational animal, compared with a feudal lord and his hoard of vassals'. Perhaps because the essay was unsigned, Hazlitt opens the offensive with more than usual belligerence: 'Books govern the world better than kings or priests. There have always been plenty of the latter with full and undisputed powers, of which they have made as bad a use as possible. It is only of late that books and public opinion have borne much sway.' Books are the supreme example of a democratically constituted government, one that modern times alone have made possible; to them are ascribed the curbing of arbitrary power and the transmuting of might to right, with Hazlitt citing as evidence 'the way in which books have already battered down so many strongholds of prejudice and power'.[63] Neither anarchy nor tyranny, he claims, can exist after the invention of printing—indeed, the French Revolution itself, he argues elsewhere, 'might be described as a remote but inevitable result of the invention of the art of printing'.[64] This Utopian fantasy is inspired not simply by the wish to make the language of books the enemy of legitimacy, instead of the means of inscribing ancient authority; nor by the early nineteenth-century increase in literacy which made it genuinely possible to see books as at once the agents of democratic revolution and the *vox populi*. What lies behind Hazlitt's optimism may be a dream of revolutionizing the status of the political writer himself—of turning his writing into direct action.

'On the Prose Style of Poets', though ostensibly a levelling attempt to reconstitute the republic of letters on the basis of prose, had given pride of place to the poet of prose writers ('Burke's eloquence was that of the poet ... The power which governed

---

[63] Howe, xvii. 326, 321, 325.

[64] *The Life of Napoleon* (1828); Howe, xiii. 38. See also the discussion of Hazlitt's politics of literacy by Chandler, *Wordsworth's Second Nature*, pp. 144–7 and n. 19.

Burke's mind was his Imagination')[65]—a personification of the anti-levelling principle that Hazlitt's essay on *Coriolanus* identifies as that of poetry itself: 'The language of poetry naturally falls in with the language of power ... The principle of poetry is a very anti-levelling principle.'[66] Hazlitt's popularist *jeu d'esprit*, 'The Fight' (1822), celebrates a different kind of power in a pugilistic slanging match designed to democratize prose by aligning it punningly with 'the FANCY' rather than the imagination ('Truly, the FANCY are not men of imagination').[67] Hazlitt declares himself as a ringside supporter and 'lover of the FANCY', that is, prizefighting— the republican symbol in a sporting sketch whose racy colloquialism turns boxing into heroic knockabout, while identifying Hazlitt himself as a lover not just of the FANCY but of fancy's language, slang. Virginia Woolf writes of Hazlitt: 'There is always something divided and discordant even in his finest essays, as if two minds were at work who never succeed save for a few moments in making a match of it.'[68] 'Making a match of it' is just what Hazlitt's popular heroes manage to do—externalizing conflict and containing it within the ring or the fives court (as Lamb confines violence to the card table in 'Mrs. Battle's Opinions on Whist'). Hence his envy of the apparently effortless skill of the Indian jugglers and the athleticism of the ace fives player, Cavanagh, whose sporting obituary concludes the essay. 'The Indian Jugglers' (1821) is a dazzling *tour de force* that sets out to beat the jugglers at their own trade, and whose sustained rhetorical metaphor makes writing its displaced subject. Lamenting his own botched efforts, Hazlitt contrasts the effect of seeing the jugglers with 'hearing a speech in Parliament, drawled or stammered out by the Honourable Member or the Noble Lord', while turning Cavanagh himself into the opposition writer of the sporting world: 'Cobbett and Junius together would have made a Cavanagh.' A man of the present as well as the people ('the noisy shout of the ring happily stood him in stead of the unheard voice of posterity'), Cavanagh is said to do more good and make less noise than those who make speeches and answer them. He is the Burke of players, stripped of conservatism and revised as a popular orator whose blows are no longer

---

[65] Howe, vii. 302–3 (but cf. vii. 312–13, for Hazlitt's qualification).
[66] Ibid. iv. 214.   [67] Ibid. xvii. 80.
[68] *Collected Essays of Virginia Woolf*, ed. L. Woolf (4 vols.; London, 1966–7), i. 158–9.

metaphorical: 'As it was said of a great orator that he never was at a loss for a word, and for the properest word, so Cavanagh always could tell the degree of force necessary to be given to a ball, and the precise direction in which it should be sent.'[69] Hazlitt has made him the popular winner in the match 'People *vs.* Parliament', shifting the arena of power to the fives court and ruling legitimacy unsporting. But perhaps there is more yet. In laying Cavanagh to rest, Hazlitt kills off the man of action (as Wordsworth embalms the Winander Boy) so that the writer can take his place. If—as Auden has it—poetry makes nothing happen, every political writer's most cherished dream is still that he may by his writing take the law into his own hands.

Hazlitt attempts to bring writing into the present: Lamb defends against the present by consigning writing to the past. The Elian version of Romantic irony involves not simply disguise, but a splitting of self that simultaneously opens a gap between past and present. In this double time scheme, one dimension is paradoxically lacking. Writing for Lamb is only half Janus-faced ('what half Januses are we, that cannot look forward with the same idolatry with which we for ever revert!'), and the Elian 'mental twist' of retrospection prevents the future from having any reality: 'The mighty future is as nothing, being every thing! the past is every thing, being nothing!'[70] In 'New Year's Eve', Lamb demands rhetorically whether all good things, even '*irony itself*', go out with life ('Can a ghost laugh, or shake his gaunt sides, when you are pleasant with him?'). Not so; for it is death that brings irony into being, as a doubled, affectionate relation to oneself: 'Skipping over the intervention of forty years, a man may have leave to love himself', he asserts, writing off his present identity as 'this stupid changeling of five-and-forty' in order to make room for 'the child Elia—that "other me", there, in the back-ground'.[71] This is the form of irony that Carlyle calls 'the playful teasing fondness of a mother to her child',[72] the love of the creator for his creation—playful, protective, and characterized by permanent regret, for the defence of irony can be maintained only at the price of life, making

[69] Howe, viii. 78, 87, 89.   [70] Lucas, ii. 9.
[71] Ibid. ii. 28–30. See de Man, *Blindness and Insight*, pp. 211–14 for Baudelaire's version of this 'dedoublement' or 'ironic, two-fold self' brought into being only at the expense of an empirical self.
[72] T. Carlyle, *Critical and Miscellaneous Essays* (5 vols.; London 1905), i. 16.

the living self either an ageing changeling or a gaunt-sided ghost. Lamb concludes the Preface to *Last Essays*, his official epitaph on Elia, by claiming that 'the key' to his writing lies in 'the impressions of infancy'. A key to unlock it, or a thread by which it, and Elia too, can be unravelled as a fiction? The same Preface mentions 'that dangerous figure—irony'. For de Man, irony is a dangerous figure because it ushers in what Baudelaire calls 'vertige de l'hyperbole'; as he puts it, 'The moment the innocence or authenticity of our sense of being in the world is put into question, a far from harmless process gets under way. It may start as a casual bit of play with a stray loose end of the fabric, but before long the entire texture of the self is unravelled and comes apart'[73]—comes apart as writing. This vertiginous unravelling of the text is the far from harmless process that Schlegel initiates in his essay 'On Incomprehensibility', in which he envisages becoming entangled in uncontrollably proliferating ironies, his only escape 'an irony that might be able to swallow up all these big and little ironies and leave no trace of them at all'.[74]

Lamb's most poignant essay of lost childhood, 'Dream-Children; A Reverie' (1822), involves just such an entanglement and just such an undoing—a 'reverie' into which the writer himself vanishes, and in which what is mourned is as much the fragility of fiction as the evanescence of childhood. If loss gives 'Dream-Children' its pathos, it is the ephemerality of representation that makes it ghostly— makes it, in fact, central to Lamb's marginal dream-play of spectral selves. Objecting to the 1800 subtitle of Coleridge's 'Ancient Mariners' ('A Poet's Reverie'), Lamb told Wordsworth: 'it is as bad as Bottom the Weaver's declaration that he is not a Lion but only the scenical representation of a Lion. What new idea is gained by this Title, but one subversive of all credit . . . of its truth?'[75] His own subtitle subverts truth to fiction from the outset. 'Narrative teases me', Elia elsewhere confesses, and 'Dream-Children' narrates a double story ('Children love to listen to stories about their elders

[73] *Blindness and Insight*, p. 215.

[74] *Friedrich Schlegel's 'Lucinde' and the Fragments*, trans. P. Firchow (Minneapolis, 1971), 267; see *Blindness and Insight*, pp. 221–2, and cf. Ehrmann, 'The Death of Literature', p. 46: 'We make and unmake ourselves at one and the same time . . . what is "made" at one end is unmade at the other—just like a loop of film.'

[75] *The Letters of Charles and Mary Anne Lamb*, ed. E. W. Marrs, Jr. (3 vols.; Ithaca, NY, 1975–8), i. 266.

when *they* were children'). It begins by invoking a prior tale of
pathos, the ballad of the Children in the Wood which Wordsworth's
1800 Preface to *Lyrical Ballads* (in the best tradition of eighteenth-
century ballad criticism) had singled out for its enduring simplicity.
In Lamb's teasing tale—already at several removes from its naïve
original—the pathetic ballad is reinscribed in the 'long *regressus*'
(De Quincey's phrase) or fictional perspective of narrative itself.
Elia's imaginary listeners are represented as gathered round him to
hear about their great-grandmother, who had lived in the great
house 'which had been the scene . . . of the tragic incidents which
they had lately become familiar with from the ballad of the
Children in the Wood'. Lamb hints delicately at their great-
grandmother's housekeeper status by writing that she had lived
there '*in a manner as if* it had been her own' (my italics). Everything
in 'Dream-Children' is 'in a manner as if'; even the story of the
Children in the Wood is carved on the old wooden chimney-piece,
until the carving is replaced by unstoried marble.

   Like the motif of fictional obliteration, this double inscription
(the Children in the Wood: children in wood) is repeated
throughout the telling of Lamb's story, placing it in a realm
between the real and the imagined; the 'apparition of two infants'
haunting the old house, for instance, doubles with Elia's listeners,
who in turn put back a bunch of grapes uneaten when they hear of
his childhood restraint in the old garden ('the nectarines and
peaches hung upon the walls, without my ever offering to pluck
them, because they were forbidden fruit, unless now and then')—
'willing' (we are told) 'to relinquish them for the present as
irrelevant'. The 'irrelevance' of the present ushers in the motif of
lack in the figure of John L., who is kind to the lame-footed Elia
and later becomes lame himself. This crippled *alter ego*, haunting
Elia as the two dead children haunt the fictional house, initiates the
unravelling process that finally undoes the entire dream-text:
'when he died, though he had not been dead an hour, it seemed as
if he had died a great while ago, such a distance there is betwixt life
and death.' The final movement of 'Dream-Children' calls up the
children's 'pretty dead mother' only to collapse reverie into
'nothing; less than nothing, and dreams':

suddenly, turning to Alice, the soul of the first Alice looked out at her eyes
with such a reality of re-presentment, that I became in doubt which of them

stood there before me, or whose that bright hair was; and while I stood gazing, both the children gradually grew fainter to my view, receding, and still receding till nothing at last but two mournful features were seen in the uttermost distance, which, without speech, strangely impressed upon me the effects of speech; 'We are not of Alice, nor of thee, nor are we children at all. . . . We are nothing; less than nothing, and dreams.'[76]

This is surely the most uncanny moment in all Lamb's writing, as well as the most poignant—the moment when Elia's imaginary world, 'receding, and still receding' like a Cheshire cat into the realm of the phantasmal, is swallowed up by his own irony; when the 'reality of re-presentment' turns out to be that of a dream.

'Dream-Children' tells us, if we did not know already, that writing is 'nothing; less than nothing, and dreams'—a marginal or liminal phenomenon that has no existence beyond the printed page, but one that 'without speech, strangely impresse[s] . . . the effects of speech'. The spectral effect lies in the very 'reality of re-presentment', as the ghostliness of printing ('strangely impressed') lies in the effect of speech—what Wordsworth, in *The Prelude*, calls 'the mind's | Internal echo of the imperfect sound' (i. 64–5). Here, even the writing self is remorselessly discomposed by the spectrality of signs: 'immediately awakening, I found myself quietly seated in my bachelor arm-chair, where I had fallen asleep . . . but John L. (or James Elia) was gone for ever.' Lamb's ironic self-dissolution prevents 'Dream-Children' from toppling into simple pathos, while opening up dizzying vistas of non-being. His vertiginous inversion of creation is the nightmare side of reverie; only writing as precariously loitering on the edge of ideas and reality as Lamb's could admit both to the same page. Though few Romantic writers go so near the edge as Lamb, his brinkmanship offers a paradigmatic view of what it is that nature, or music, or direct action, attempts to cover over when Romantic prose—Wordsworth's, De Quincey's, or Hazlitt's—confronts the language of books. And like Wordsworth's attempt to part the shadow from the substance, De Quincey's deciphering of the palimpsest, or Hazlitt's attempt to hone language to a cutting edge on the substance of things, Lamb's ironic knitting and unknitting of the texture of being reminds us that in each case the 'other being' ('I, the child', the writer as pugilist, or 'that "other me" ') is an alienation effect brought into half-existence by the language of books; immune to the present or

[76] Lucas, ii. 75, 226, 100–3.

impotent to alter it, such book language is itself half Janus-faced, or less than nothing. Casting about for an epic subject at the start of *The Prelude*, Wordsworth recoils disheartened from the histories of Britain, myth, liberty, heroism, or the everyday left unsung by previous epic poets—recoils, in effect, from the history of past writing and from the writing of the past:

> the whole beauteous fabric seems to lack
> Foundation, and withal appears throughout
> Shadowy and unsubstantial.
>
> (*Prel.* i. 226–8)

It is not so much the burden of the past that inhibits him as this glimpse of the insubstantiality inherent in all writing—in auto-biography as well as epic. The remaining thirteen books of *The Prelude* attempt to clothe transparency and provide foundations for a fabric that cannot be gainsaid, the history of Wordsworth's own mind. Romantic prose writers like De Quincey, Hazlitt, and Lamb remind us what 'The Growth of a Poet's Mind' owes to the art of managing books. They also tell the one story Wordsworth could not afford to tell at any price—that the language of books can only ever be the history of itself.

CHAPTER 6

'DITHYRAMBIC FERVOUR'
The Lyric Voice of *The Prelude**

LOOKING back to the excitement with which *The Prelude* had
begun—a mood later described as one of 'distraction and intense
desire' (xiii. 374)—Book VII starts by recalling the 'dithyrambic
fervour' of the opening book. Named here as the 'glad preamble',
these introductory lines are recollected in terms both of the natural
Sublime and of the Sublime of poetry itself:

> Five years are vanished since I first poured out,
> Saluted by that animating breeze
> Which met me issuing from the city's walls,
> A glad preamble to this verse. I sang
> Aloud in dithyrambic fervour, deep
> But short-lived uproar, like a torrent sent
> Out of the bowels of a bursting cloud
> Down Scawfell or Blencathara's rugged sides,
> A waterspout from heaven.   (*Prel.* vii. 1–9)[1]

Wordsworth's 'torrent sent | Out of the bowels of a bursting cloud'
is more than just a means of naturalizing the landscape of poetic
inspiration—though it is that too; as in the waters of the Wye,
'rolling from their mountain-springs | With a soft inland murmur'
('Tintern Abbey', ll. 3–4), we recognize the source of a poetic
Helicon. But as Geoffrey Hartman puts it, Wordsworth's 'narrative
can almost be said to begin with "an Ode, in passion utter'd" '
(*Prel.* v. 97).[2] Although he does not enlarge on this connection
between the 'glad preamble' and the apocalyptic blast heard in the
shell of Book V, his allusion to the ode—both form and 'passion'—

* Reprinted from Mary Jacobus, 'Apostrophe and Lyric Voice in *The Prelude*,' in
Lyric Poetry: Beyond New Criticism, edited by Chaviva Hosek and Patricia Parker.
Copyright © 1985 by Cornell University Press. Used by permission of the publisher.

[1] These lines maintain the fiction that *Prel.* i. 1–54, the 'glad preamble', were the
first lines to be written.
[2] 'Words, Wish, Worth: Wordsworth', in H. Bloom (ed.), *Deconstruction and
Criticism* (London, 1979), 190.

is worth pursuing. The torrent of eloquence poured out here has quite specific associations with the sublime and (by popular misconception) 'irregular' ode, certainly the highest form of lyric poetry for the eighteenth century, and the one in which the poet was also thought to speak most directly in his own voice.[3] Translating Horace's praise of Pindar in one of his own *Pindarique Odes*, Cowley had written:

> *Pindars unnavigable Song*
> Like a swoln *Flood* from some steep *Mountain* pours along
>   The *Ocean* meets with such a *Voice*
> From his enlarged *Mouth*, as drowns the *Oceans* noise.
> So *Pindar* does new *Words* and *Figures* roul
> Down his impetuous *Dithyrambic Tide* . . .[4]

As Cowley notes, the '*Dithyrambic Tide*' of Pindaric eloquence is a risky one to navigate: 'For which reason, I term his Song *Unnavigable*; for it is able to drown any *Head* that is not strong built and well *ballasted*.'[5] Voice not only drowns the ocean's noise, but threatens to drown the reader too, and perhaps even the writer himself. Keeping one's head above water may even mean shutting one's ears. The traditional metaphor of a river for poetic eloquence—here, a torrent of words—might make one want to look again at Wordsworth's contrasting invocation to the River Derwent in Book I of *The Prelude*. The stream that 'loved | To blend his murmurs with my nurse's song' (i. 272–3) makes 'ceaseless music'; but unlike the torrential waterspout of the 'glad preamble'—a rush of intense but short-lived inspiration—its 'steady cadence' both 'composes' the infant's thoughts and, in another sense, the entire poem. Did Wordsworth, perhaps, find his own dithyrambic tide unnavigable, preferring to emphasize not the voice of the Sublime but the voice of nature?

---

[3] See N. Maclean, 'From Action to Image: Theories of the Lyric in the Eighteenth Century', *Critics and Criticism Ancient and Modern*, ed. R. S. Crane (Chicago, 1952), 409. See also, for a sustained discussion of the ode, P. H. Fry, *The Poet's Calling in the English Ode* (New Haven and London, 1980).

[4] *The English Writings of Abraham Cowley*, ed. A. R. Waller (2 vols.; Cambridge, 1905), i. 178. Cf. also Gray's 'Progress of Poesy: A Pindaric Ode', where 'the rich stream of music winds along' from Helicon to precipice: 'Now rolling down the steep amain, | Headlong, impetuous, see it pour' (ll. 7, 10–11).

[5] *The English Writings of Abraham Cowley*, ed. Waller, i. 180.

There are good reasons for his retreat from the Sublime. Cowley goes on to observe of Pindar's Dithyrambics that they were '*Hymns* made in honour of *Bacchus* . . . a bold, free, enthusiastical kind of Poetry, as of men inspired by *Bacchus*, that is *Half-Drunk*'; hence the two Greek proverbs he cites, 'You are mad as a *Dithyrambique Poet*' and 'There are no *Dithyrambiques* made by drinking water' (an Attic version, presumably, of 'You can't make an omelette without breaking eggs').[6] Remembering himself as a young poet in the throes of composition, Wordsworth speaks of hushing his voice and 'composing' his gait so that passers-by would not suppose him mad ('crazed in brain', *Prel.* iv. 116–20); 'kindled with the stir, | The fermentation and the vernal heat | Of poesy' (iv. 93–5), he too is like one half-drunk—just as chanting his favourite poets, when a boy, had brought fancies 'More bright than madness or the dreams of wine' (v. 592). At Cambridge, youthful intoxication took the form of getting drunk in Milton's rooms. Apostrophe and libation blend in a heady brew: 'O temperate bard!',

> I to thee
> Poured out libations, to thy memory drank
> Within my private thoughts, till my brain reeled,
> Never so clouded by the fumes of wine
> Before that hour, or since.
>
> (*Prel.* iii. 303–7)

Drinking to Milton's memory takes on an aspect at once sublime and Bacchic—inebriated with his poetry while disrespectful of Milton's own temperance. Milton himself comes to mind in this context not only as the bard of temperance but as the poet most obsessed with the terror of Bacchic orgies. His own apostrophe to Urania at the start of Book VII of *Paradise Lost*—clearly in Wordsworth's mind as he wrote his opening to Book VII of *The Prelude*—invokes protection against just such a Comus-like crew of drunken revellers:

> But drive far off the barbarous dissonance
> Of Bacchus and his revellers, the race
> Of that wild rout that tore the Thracian bard
> In Rhodope, where woods and rocks had ears
> To rapture, till the savage clamour drowned
> Both harp and voice . . .
>
> (*Paradise Lost*, vii. 32–7)

[6] Ibid. 180.

Wordsworth could praise Milton for 'a voice whose sound was like
the sea' ('Milton', l. 1)—a voice, presumably, in which all others
would be lost; but Milton's own anxiety was that his voice would
be drowned by savage clamour and the poet dismembered,
Orpheus-like, by hordes of Thracian women under the influence of
their Bacchic cult. Wordsworth himself had translated this part of
the Orpheus and Eurydice story from Virgil's *Georgic IV* in 1788,
and it is hard to imagine that the legend can have been absent from
his mind either at the time of the original literary orgy in Milton's
rooms, or later, when recollected in *The Prelude*:

> Him, mourning still, the savage maenads found
> And strew'd his mangled limbs the plain around;
> His head was from its neck of marble torn
> And down the Oeagrian Hebrus slowly born.[7]

The figure used by Cowley of the Pindaric Sublime ('it is able to
drown any *Head* that is not strong built and well *ballasted*')
coincides with the traditional figure of the poet's voice being
drowned by barbarous dissonance, and his severed head borne
down the flood. Both appear to be articulations of the dread that
poetic individuality might be lost—whether by being subsumed into
the Sublime or by being dispersed into the meaningless multiplicity
of 'clamour'. The Orphic fantasy might be said to involve for
Wordsworth, as for Milton, the threat that discomposing Bacchic
dithyrambs, or possession by the voices of others, would lead to the
individual poet's dismemberment.

   One safeguard against such imaginary dismemberment is provided
by the compensating fantasy of fully naturalized Orphic song. As
Frances Ferguson aptly writes, the dying head gives nature a
speaking voice ('Ah! poor Eurydice, it feebly cried, | Eurydice, the
moaning banks replied').[8] For her, the echoic structure is that of
epitaph itself; but one might also see in it the Wordsworthian desire
to appropriate the speaking voice of nature in an attempt to render
his own imperishable. Drowned neither by the voice of the
Sublime—Milton's voice—nor by the clamour of all the other
voices by which the poet risks being possessed, the voice of nature

---

[7] *PW* i. 285, ll. 71–4. For the date, see Reed, *Wordsworth: The Chronology of the Early Years, 1770–1799*, p. 21.

[8] *PW* i. 285, ll. 77–8. See F. Ferguson, *Wordsworth: Language as Counter-Spirit* (New Haven and London, 1977), 163–5.

permits a loss of individuality which is at once safe and unifying. In nature, the poet can take refuge against dismemberment. Hailing *The Prelude* in 'To William Wordsworth', Coleridge calls it 'An Orphic song', 'A song divine of high and passionate thoughts | To their own music chaunted' (ll. 45–7. He clearly has in mind the ethical severity and high seriousness of the Orphic tradition (a 'Theme hard as high! . . . Of Duty, chosen Laws controlling choice', ll. 11, 44), to which Wordsworth himself alludes when outlining his poetic aspirations early in Book I:

> I yearn towards some philosophic song
> Of truth that cherishes our daily life,
> With meditations passionate from deep
> Recesses in man's heart, immortal verse
> Thoughtfully fitted to the Orphean lyre.
> But from this awful burthen I full soon
> Take refuge . . .

> (*Prel.* i. 230–6)

Orphism too has its problems. As Wordsworth well knew, the phrase 'Orphean lyre' occurs at the start of *Paradise Lost*, Book III, just before Milton undertakes to sing of Heaven and immediately after his perilous but successful descent into Hell ('With other notes than to the Orphean lyre | I sung of Chaos . . .', *Paradise Lost*, iii. 17–18). Milton may simply be making a doctrinaire point (his notes are other than Orphean because Christian, not pagan),[9] but there is also the possibility that his notes are not Orphic because he—unlike Orpheus—has successfully completed his mission. The 'awful burthen' would have been for Wordsworth not just that of living up to Milton's Christianized 'song', but that of assuming his strength; this is the same 'load of Immortality' which Keats too found burdensome when taking up his own poetic mission.[10]

A fragment written in the copy of *Paradise Lost* which belonged to Wordsworth at Cambridge refers to the Miltonic altar kindled on Religion's holy hill as having the power to elicit, not only 'Airs of high melody from solemn harp | And voice of Angel in accordance sweet', but also the voice of the Sublime:

[9] Compare Elegy VI, where Diodati's poetry is associated with Bacchus and Milton's own with the *Nativity Ode*, or Christianizing of pagan myth.

[10] *The Letters of John Keats*, ed. H. E. Rollins (2 vols.; Cambridge, Mass., 1958), i. 370.

Anon the trump of God, with dreadful blast
Rock'd all the mountain; on their flashing clouds
The silent cherubs trembled . . .[11]

'Undismayed | Stood the blind prophet.' But could Wordsworth
stand likewise undismayed before this dreadful blast? If we seem to
be in the familiar terrain of the belated poet's anxiety about his
apparently indestructible precursor, this is no more than saying that
Wordsworth, while appearing to differ (and to defer), can only
repeat. Milton's own invocation to Urania at the start of Book VII,
after all, had voiced the embattled and solitary poet's fears about
his survival, and, in particular, fears about the adequacy of his
poetic performance. Wordsworth, too, at the start of his Book
VII—about to re-enter the city and encounter its discomposing
influences—invokes his personal sources of protection, a choir of
redbreasts and, in place of Urania's heavenly light, a humble glow-
worm. These earth-born voices and sources of illumination surely
have the special function of disarming the threat of the Sublime
which Milton's invocation had brought uncomfortably close.
Although, looking back from the end of *The Prelude*, Wordsworth
can see himself as having been spurred on by the reproaches of
Book I to take flight on his own account ('Anon I rose | As if on
wings . . .', xiii. 377–8), in his case it is a flight 'Attempered to the
sorrows of the earth' (xiii. 383). In the anxious confrontation with
Milton, Wordsworth evades the dangers of the Sublime by making
earth, rather than Heaven or Chaos, his chosen sphere. Humanizing
his epic—giving it a less elevated lyric voice—simultaneously
protects the poet from Milton and from apocalypse, proving to be
his most secure guarantee of survival.

If the poet's urgent need to constitute himself as a poet leads him
to the dithyrambic fervour of the 'glad preamble', self-preservation
throws him back on naturalized Orphic song. On one hand the
dismembering voices of the past, or Bacchic possession; on the
other, the re-membering continuities of the Derwent, murmurings
which assimilate the poet's voice to nature and so preserve it. The
ode-like, inspirational passion of the 'glad preamble' ultimately
'vex[es] its own creation' (*Prel*. i. 47), its redundant energy
disrupting the flow of river and memory. By contrast, the fiction of
a poetry that originates in nature, like the voice of the Derwent,

[11] *PW* v. 362, ll. 6–10. For the date, see Reed, *Wordsworth: The Chronology of
the Early Years, 1770–1799*, p. 21.

ensures continuity while providing a safely trans-subjective voice
into which the poet's own can be merged. Wordsworth's claim is
not simply that nature speaks through him, but that he speaks with
nature's voice. The characteristic alternations in *The Prelude*—
between the uproarious waterspout and the murmuring stream,
inspiration and reflection, invocation and narrative—become a sign
of this tension between poetic self-assertion and self-immersion.
Wordsworth's final sleight of hand may well be that of divesting
himself of the Sublime while investing his poetic voice in nature.
The Romantic counterpart to Milton's successful flight from Chaos
to Heaven is the self-immersing Bard of Gray's 'Pindaric Ode' who
'spoke, and headlong from the mountain's height | Deep in the
roaring tide . . . plunged to endless night' ('The Bard', ll. 143–4)—
an ostensibly suicidal loss of individual identity which at once
destroys the poet's voice and vests nature with those qualities which
have proved dangerous to it. As we see in Book XIII, this leaves the
poet free to take refuge in pastoral, the address of one poet-
shepherd to another. If the ode is the Sublime (and therefore
dangerous) form of the lyric, then apostrophe could be said to be
the figure which most completely characterizes the sublimity of the
ode. *The Prelude* begins apostrophically but ends by addressing the
living—Dorothy and Coleridge—in a way designed to assimilate
the poet to a safer pastoral community. It is this formal progression
that most clearly marks the concession made by a poet whose lyric
voice survives finally at the price of seeming to renounce the
Sublime altogether. Paradoxically, only by making the torrential
and uproarious voice of inspiration that of nature itself can
Wordsworth sustain a voice of his own.

Invoking Apostrophe

> *Apostrophe*! we thus address
> More things than I should care to guess.
> Apostrophe! I did invoke
> Your figure even as I spoke.[12]

Apostrophe, as Jonathan Culler has observed, is an embarrassment.
Regularly ignored by writers on the ode, it might be seen 'as the
figure of all that is most radical, embarrassing, pretentious, and

[12] J. Hollander, *Rhyme's Reason: A Guide to English Verse* (New Haven and
London, 1981), 48.

mystificatory in the lyric'.[13] Critics turn away from it as it turns away from the discourse in which it is embedded; *apo-strophe*—literally, a turning away, the abrupt transition which, as Cowley puts it in his 1656 Preface, takes the Pindaric ode out of 'the common Roads, and ordinary Tracks of *Poesie* . . . The digressions are many, and sudden, and sometimes long, according to the fashion of all *Lyriques*, and of *Pindar* above all men living.'[14] Regarded as a digressive form, a sort of interruption, excess, or redundance, apostrophe in *The Prelude* becomes the signal instance of the rupture of the temporal scheme of memory by the time of writing. Wordsworth's 'two consciousnesses' (*Prel.* ii. 32) can then be seen as a division, not simply between me-now and me-then, but between discursive time and narrative time—a radical discontinuity which ruptures the illusion of sequentiality and insists, embarrassingly, on self-presence and voice; insists too that invocation itself may be more important than what is invoked. 'Apostrophe! I did invoke | Your figure even as I spoke' is a poet's joke that accurately mimes the bringing into being of the poet's voice by way of what it addresses. If apostrophe's characteristic function is to invoke the Muse, it is also, ultimately, a form of self-constituting self-address that says: 'to my soul I say "I recognise thy glory" ' (vi. 531–2). The question of the poet's vocation, translated into invocation, becomes the question of poetic voice. Like imagination in Book VI, voice halts the poet in his tracks, privileging self-address over narrating the past. The opening apostrophe of the 'glad preamble' may constitute Wordsworth as a poet but, in doing so, it loses hold of his subject; there is always this incompatibility between the lyric voice of *The Prelude* and its much-desired, 'distracting' epic progress—an incompatibility which typically presents itself as a problem of redundancy. Voice usurps on the ceaselessly murmuring Derwent, making the poet himself the interrupter of his poem.

The 'glad preamble' initiates not only *The Prelude*, but the problem of its composition. The erratic progress to which the opening lines of Book VII allude (' 'twas not long | Ere the interrupted strain broke forth once more . . . then stopped for years', vii. 9–11) may be nothing other than the symptom of Wordsworth's anxiety about writing a long poem. A 'distraction' (in another sense) from *The Recluse*, *The Prelude* could easily seem

---

[13] 'Apostrophe', *Diacritics*, 7 (Winter 1977), 60.
[14] *The English Writings of Abraham Cowley*, ed, Waller, i. 11.

a series of fragments, parts instead of a whole. Only in Book XIII, looking back from a completed poem, can Wordsworth retrospectively see the image of a longed-for completeness in the stream that has been traced from darkness (xiii. 172–84). Meanwhile, the distinct phases of the poem's composition evoked by the opening lines of Book VII present themselves, disturbingly, as fragmentation rather than composition. One recalls the 'fragment' inscribed in Wordsworth's undergraduate copy of *Paradise Lost*—itself a formal tribute to the hopelessness engendered in a beginning poet by the shadow of an epic precursor. Perhaps the 'glad preamble' should in the last resort be read, not simply as a dramatization of Wordsworth's anxiety about his poetic undertaking or as a record of the fluctuations of inspiration, but rather as a propitiatory gesture that frees the poet from the 'burden of [his] own unnatural self' and, in doing so, from the burdensome past of poetry. *The Prelude*'s opening apostrophe to the breeze would then become an image of liberation which, though predicated on the novelty of self-presence to one 'not used to make | A present joy the matter of [his] song' (i. 55–6), is directed ultimately at sloughing off his poetic precursors or consciousness of the past:

> O welcome messenger! O welcome friend!
> A captive greets thee, coming from a house
> Of bondage, from yon city's walls set free,
> A prison where he hath been long immured.
> Now I am free, enfranchised and at large,
> May fix my habitation where I will.
>
> . . . .
>
> . . . I breathe again—
> Trances of thought and mountings of the mind
> Come fast upon me. It is shaken off,
> As by a miraculous gift 'tis shaken off,
> That burden of my own unnatural self . . .
>
> (*Prel.* i. 5–10, 19–23)[15]

The poet's breathing and the breeze are at once the breath of pure, unconstructed sound ('O' or voice) and a prison break, an escape

[15] The omitted passage contains Wordsworth's famous allusion to the concluding lines of *Paradise Lost* ('The world was all before them, where to choose | Their place of rest, and Providence their guide', xii. 643–7). See Chandler, *Wordsworth's Second Nature*, pp. 188–99, for a discussion of the opening of *The Prelude*, Book I, in relation to Wordsworth's attempt to free himself from the culturally determined choices (and voices) of the past.

from the confines of memory and self-consciousness. In the same way, apostrophe itself breaks off from the demands of narrative as a moment of lyric redundancy or inspired escape. The 'vital breeze' becomes 'A tempest, a redundant energy, | Vexing its own creation' (i. 46–7), just as in the opening lines of Book VII the grove 'tossing its dark boughs in sun and wind— | Spreads through me a commotion like its own' (vii. 51–2). This tempest or commotion is not exactly a 'corresponding mild creative breeze' (i. 43), more a vexation or a kind of uneasiness.[16] The effect is that of voice itself, perceived as an interruption of the past from the present.

Wordsworth comments of the 'glad preamble', 'My own voice cheared me, and, far more, the mind's | Internal echo of the imperfect sound' (i. 64–5). The appeal to voice might usually be thought of as having the function of making the self whole. Whereas writing disperses, voice unifies, providing the illusion of single origin and temporal unity (no 'two consciousnesses' here). Yet, in this instance, Wordsworth writes of a doubling effect whereby the sound of his own voice has an internal echo, and one which, unlike echo as usually figured, perfects rather than incompletely repeating 'the imperfect sound'; it is voice here that functions like echo, since speech is imagined as secondary in its attempt to represent the silence of self-present meaning in consciousness. At this point it seems worth digressing to consider some of the more problematic aspects of the Romantic conception of voice. A small book by Francis Berry, *Poetry and the Physical Voice* (1962), brings to light the hidden implications of Wordsworth's position. Like Wordsworth, Berry appears to insist on the primacy of voice over writing (seeing the letter as a mere representation of sound), and his book laments the debasing of language as a mere means of communication, or 'instrument'. Yet this distinction between language as instrument and the poetic use of language as 'agent' proves oddly difficult to sustain. As Wordsworth had been, Berry too is anxious to restore to poetic voice the musicality which he believes once to have been synonymous with poetry itself. Yet even Wordsworth no longer insists on 'feigning that [his] works were composed to the music of the harp or lyre', happily substituting 'nothing more than an animated or impassioned

---

[16] Cf. Wordsworth's apostrophic reaction to the news of Robespierre's death ('Come now, ye golden times . . .') where the traveller is 'interrupted by uneasy bursts | Of exultation' (*Prel.* x. 541, 557–8).

recitation'.[17] Berry's terms—pitch, duration, volume, timbre, and so on—thus emphasize the sound of vocal 'music' to a degree never risked by Wordsworth himself. But, in doing so, they uncover the underlying myth of the voice of which Wordsworth's is a less extreme version; that is, the myth of the 'inner ear' (not a kind of memory but a kind of hearing) which leads us to suppose, according to Berry, that though 'modern poets compose silently . . . in composing they record what they are inwardly experiencing as vocal sound, usually their own voices however idealized . . . we could say they record the double experiences of hearing *and* saying';[18] this is what Wordsworth had called 'the mind's internal echo of the imperfect sound', likewise surrendering to an auditory myth of self-presence. But there follows for Berry an altogether less composing notion, that of the poet as 'a person obsessed, scored and spoored by vocal linguistic sound—'or, put another way, he is *possessed* by vocal sound as a man was said to be possessed by devils'.[19] What it amounts to is that voice, instead of bringing reassurance by guaranteeing the existence of a unified consciousness ('my own voice cheared me'), can equally take on the demonic aspect of possession. Whose are the voices the poet hears? Not necessarily his own, after all.

In the light of such demonic vocalism, Berry's notion of an individuated voice breaks down. His insistence that the attentive or 'listening' reader can recover or reconstruct the unique and authentic voices of, say, Tennyson, Milton, or—presumably—Wordsworth on the evidence of 'the printed signs on the page', is revealed as a fiction. Calling the self into being through apostrophe becomes rather a matter of calling another into being; perhaps an 'authorial' voice, but, equally, the variety of haunting, threatening, nightmarish, or apocalyptic voices heard throughout *The Prelude* in 'the voice | Of mountain-echoes' (i. 389–90), or in 'Black drizzling crags that spake . . . As if a voice were in them'

---

[17] 1815 'Preface', *Prose Works*, iii. 29.

[18] F. Berry, *Poetry and the Physical Voice* (London, 1962), 34. Cf. Derrida's paraphrase of this myth of the voice in 'The Voice that Keeps Silence', *Speech and Phenomena*, trans. D. B. Allison (Evanston, 1973), 77: 'When I speak, it belongs to the phenomenological essence of the operation that *I hear myself . . . . at the same time* that I speak. The signifier . . . is in absolute proximity to me. The living act . . . which animates the body of the signifier . . . seems not to separate itself from itself, from its own self-presence.'

[19] Berry, *Poetry and the Physical Voice*, pp. 36, 7.

(vi. 563–4), or the 'voice that cried | To the whole city, "Sleep no more!" ' (x. 76–7), or in a shell that broadcasts 'voices more than all the winds'—the voice of 'a god, yea many gods' (v. 107–8). The voice is always a doubling of self, and more often a multiplication or alienation. Berry's view of poetic language as agent, then, turns out to be characterized not by the individuality of the writer but by something closer to the supernatural—the gift of tongues or hearing voices ('he is *possessed* by vocal sound'). Conceived as a man more vocal than other men, the poet becomes an echo-chamber for all those voices heard while boat-stealing, descending the Vale of Gondo, unable to sleep in Paris after the September Massacres, or in the Arab dream. They speak through him, so that far from attesting to unity of origin or a stable identity, voice comes to imply all the destabilizing multiplicity of plural (or ancestral) voices— much as the composing 'voice' of the Derwent can become the discomposing voice of inspired poetry, 'the voice | Which roars along the bed of Jewish song', or the Miltonic 'trumpet-tones of harmony that shake | Our shores in England' (v. 203–4, 206–7). Given these transformations, Wordsworth's quest turns out not to be for an individual voice so much as for one that is transcendentally unified.

The apostrophic moments in Book I of *The Prelude* are, typically, callings into being of supernatural powers:

> Wisdom and spirit of the universe,
> Thou soul that art the eternity of thought,
> That giv'st to forms and images a breath
> And everlasting motion . . .
>
> (*Prel.* i. 427–31)

> Ye presences of Nature, in the sky
> Or on the earth, ye visions of the hills
> And souls of lonely places . . .
>
> (*Prel.* i. 490–2)

Wordsworth's invocations to the Muse summon up spirits, presences, souls—the supernatural machinery of an unexorcized nature, arising in the same breath as winds, hills, solitude. If Shelley demands of the wind, 'Be thou me, impetuous one!', Wordsworth could be said to ask of nature to give his voice whatever haunts and denatures landscape; whatever puts the individual origin of voice most in question. The Aeolian fantasy so beloved of Romantic poets, after all, is nothing more or less than the wish for the trans-subjective instrumentality which Berry would repress if he could, but fails ultimately to exorcize. Wordsworth's apostrophes to breezes, brooks, and groves, in which he wishes for himself 'a music and a voice | Harmonious as your own' (xi. 20–1), are the equivalent of asking to be played on too. The distinction which Wordsworth himself would have endorsed, between language as instrument (or, as he calls it himself, 'counter-spirit')[20] and language as agent, falls away to leave only breezes or breathings through the poet, 'obedient as a lute | That waits upon the touches of the wind' (iii. 137–8). Subsumed into transcendental nature, the poet's voice becomes orphic rather than bacchic, banishing rough music with the myth of natural harmony. Nature steps in to de-demonize voice, turning possession into Aeolianism and sanctifying vocalism as 'Eolian visitations' (i. 104). Instead of the voice of the poet, we have the voice of poetry—that is, nature. In order to achieve this status for his poetry, Wordsworth has to eschew the very fiction of individual voice · which is central to Romantic conceptions of the poet. The transcendental defends against possession, but it also takes away the poet's most distinctive and sought-after personal property, the voice that differentiates him from his predecessors, and from Milton in particular. That, perhaps, may be the trade-off—since not to be either Milton or unlike Milton has the effect of losing the Miltonic voice as well as one's own in the impersonally oceanic voice of nature, thereby drowning the ventriloquizing voices of the past in 'A waterspout from heaven' (vii. 9).

The Sound of Nature

What is involved for Wordsworth in sound itself? And what is the relation of voice to writing? The aftermath of the 'glad preamble' turns out to be largely one of discouragement: 'the harp | Was soon defrauded' (i. 104–5) and the hope of fixing 'in a visible home . . . those phantoms of conceit, | That had been floating loose about so long' (i. 129–31) was not to be fulfilled. The disembodied 'phantoms of conceit' remain unrepresented, perhaps unrepresent-able. A fragment from the *Peter Bell* MS, possibly an early attempt

[20] 'Essays upon Epitaphs', III; *Prose Works*, ii. 85.

at an introduction to the two-part *Prelude*, had explored. the problem of representation in terms directly relevant to the random vocalizings of the 'glad preamble':

> nor had my voice
> Been silent—oftentimes had I burst forth
> In verse which with a strong and random light
> Touching an object in its prominent parts
> Created a memorial which to me
> Was all sufficient, and, to my own mind
> Recalling the whole picture, seemed to speak
> An universal language. Scattering thus
> In passion many a desultory sound,
> I deemed that I had adequately cloathed
> Meanings at which I hardly hinted, thoughts
> And forms of which I scarcely had produced
> A monument and arbitrary sign.[21]

Bursting forth in verse becomes the equivalent of a private mnemonic; 'to my *own* mind | Recalling the whole picture', the voice only '*seemed* to speak | An universal language'. Writing to Godwin in 1800, Coleridge had asked, 'Is *thinking* impossible without arbitrary signs? &—how far is the word "arbitrary" a misnomer?' If Coleridge seems to want to destroy 'the old antithesis of *Words* & *Things*, elevating ... words into Things, & living Things too',[22] Wordsworth seems to be suggesting that at best— 'scarcely', or 'scarcely even'—poetry can produce 'A monument and arbitrary sign' for thought; and, at worst, make only desultory sounds. This is the Aeolian fantasy demystified, and along with it there collapses the entire Romantic fallacy of spontaneous lyric utterance, whether heard or overhead. In another fragment, Wordsworth alludes to 'slow creation' imparting 'to speach | Outline and substance'.[23] This sounds like fixing phantoms of conceit in a visible home, or writing poetry. It is as if representation only begins at the point where Aeolianism—the fiction of un- mediated expression—is eschewed; or perhaps, Wordsworth seems to imply, thinking can begin only where the monuments and

[21] *Prel.*, p. 495, fragment (*a*), ll. 1–13. The passage is also discussed by J. Wordsworth, 'As With the Silence of the Thought', in L. Lipking (ed.), *High Romantic Argument: Essays for M. H. Abrams* (Ithaca, NY, and London, 1981), 58–64.

[22] *Collected Letters of Samuel Taylor Coleridge*, ed. Griggs, i. 625–6.

[23] *Prel.*, p. 495, fragment (*b*), ll. 3–4.

arbitrary signs of language take over from sound (pure voice or breath) and speech (pure presence). In any event, it is clear that writing, the permanent record of thought, involves both the muting of voice—a kind of deafness—and the death of presence.

No wonder Aeolianism pervades *The Prelude*; it is Wordsworth's defence against that inability to hear oneself think (or speak) involved in writing itself. Going back to the opening of Book VII, we find Wordsworth experiencing 'Something that fits me for the poet's task' in the infectious 'commotion' of his favourite grove, 'Now tossing its dark boughs in sun and wind' (vii. 50–3). Presumably both grove and poet make a composing noise much like the one that is wasted on the deaf Dalesman, though not on his peaceful grave, memorialized in Wordsworth's final 'Essay upon Epitaphs':

> And yon tall Pine-tree, whose composing sound
> Was wasted on the good Man's living ear,
> Hath now its own peculiar sanctity;
> And at the touch of every wandering breeze
> Murmurs not idly o'er his peaceful grave.[24]

The Dalesman's epitaph is 'A monument and arbitrary sign' masquerading as the sound of murmuring trees, alias the composing sound of the poet's own voice (Wordsworth loved to compose aloud in a grove of trees, and may well have done so, murmurously, in the grove near Dove Cottage whose commotion he records at the start of Book VII). Why does the pine tree murmur 'not idly'? Is it because the entire epitaph, though ostensibly commemorating a man for whom the mountain vale was soundless and the storm-tossed landscape 'silent as a picture'—for whom all voices save those of books were unheard—actually celebrates the poet's own aural imagination as a means of denying the soundlessness of writing? The poet himself, Wordsworth implies, is not only murmurous but has inward ears that can hear; this is what makes him a poet. Imagined sound becomes a way to repress or deny writing and undo the privation of deafness or death. If a monument marks the site of a grave, voice—'Breathings for incommunicable powers' (iii. 188)—gives evidence of the poet's enduring life. For the poet, Wordsworth argues covertly, there can be no such thing as

---

[24] 'Essays upon Epitaphs', III; *Prose Works*, ii, 96 (*Excursion*, vii. 477–81). Cf. P. de Man on the Deaf Dalesman's epitaph, 'Autobiography as De-Facement', *The Rhetoric of Romanticism*, pp. 72–4.

silence, but only, as in the Dalesman's epitaph, 'audible seclusions'. The soundless world of the Dalesman's solitude and death is one that speaks to him. So much so that in *The Prelude* a moment of visionary seeing is as likely as not to be one of hearing, an attempt to communicate 'what e'er there is of power in sound | To breathe an elevated mood':

> I would stand
> Beneath some rock, listening to sounds that are
> The ghostly language of the ancient earth,
> Or make their dim abode in distant winds.
> Thence did I drink the visionary power.
>
> (*Prel.* ii. 324–30)

Visionary power—'by form | or image unprofaned'—is blindness, not insight; the heightened sense of hearing makes language into something ghostly, non-referential, ancient, and without origin, like the homeless voice of waters in the Snowdon episode.[25] Along with Francis Berry, Wordsworth wants to believe that the poet hears voices as well as speaking with tongues; but what he most desires to hear are the unheard sighings or breathings that writing ('arbitrary signs') must repress. This is the other side of babble, or Babel, the non-linguistic murmur of a composing voice that may be the poet's as he saunters 'like a river murmuring' (*Prel.* iv. 110) or, equally, invoked as that of the Derwent ('O Derwent, murmuring stream,' v. 509), but is above all that of a unified poetic presence that has no need of discourse.

Wordsworth's definitive statement of the ear's power occurs in his 'musical' ode, 'On the Power of Sound' (1828). As the preposterous 'argument' puts it, 'The Ear addressed, as occupied by a spiritual functionary, in communion with sounds, individual, or combined in studied harmony'.[26] The ode is all apostrophe, all voice, all ear:

> a Spirit aerial
> Informs the cell of Hearing, dark and blind;
> Intricate labyrinth, more dread for thought
> To enter than oracular cave . . .
>
> (ll. 3–6)

---

[25] Cf. also the 'breath-like sound, | A respiration short and quick' (*Prel.* iv. 175–6) which Wordsworth in his solitary musings often mistook for the panting of his dog.   [26] *PW* ii. 323.

The ear becomes the prime organ of vision, making audible 'Ye Voices, and ye Shadows | And Images of voice' (ll. 33–4). The poem's function is both to invoke Spirit (ear) and Muse (voice); or 'the mind's | Internal echo of the imperfect sound'. As John Hollander's account of the poem has shown, the ear is a place of echo and reverberation, sounding and resounding, a cave, a 'strict passage', a maze, a temple, a vault, a hollow place where music is made as well as heard.[27] Like the shell, whether a poeticism for the lute or the Romanticized sea shell, it is both sounded on and sounds, combining the Orphean properties of a stringed instrument and the Dionysian properties of a wind instrument.[28] In effect, it is nothing less than the ear of God. Wordsworth's originary myth of the voice ('A Voice to Light gave Being', l. 209) is also apocalyptic: 'A Voice shall . . . sweep away life's visionary stir' (ll. 211–12). Compare the dual functions of music and harmony in *The Prelude*, one to build up, the other to destroy; though 'The mind of man is framed even like the breath | And harmony of music' (*Prel.* i. 351–2), the shell's 'loud prophetic blast of harmony' (v. 96) in the Arab dream announces the end of the world, and the Sublime of revolutionary terror is accompanied by 'Wild blasts of music' (x. 419). Music can both frame and unframe, compose and shake, like the voice of Milton ('Those trumpet-tones of harmony that shake | Our shores', v. 206–7). Wordsworth's unstated argument in 'On the Power of Sound' reconciles this dual aspect of harmony, claiming that even after earth is dust and the heavens dissolved, 'her stay | Is in the WORD, that shall not pass away' (ll. 223–4). His ode is the optimistic, orthodox Christian sequel to the Arab dream, revised not to foretell 'Destruction to the children of the earth' (*Prel.* v. 98) but rather to prophesy salvation of and through the Word. As the type of the divine fiat, poetry itself is guaranteed survival— the consolatory message unavailable to the Arab or the dreamer in Book V of *The Prelude*—by means of its transformation into the transcendental, imperishable 'WORD'. Poetic utterance now promises 'to finish doubt and dim foreseeing' ('On the Power of Sound', ll. 211), dependent no longer on 'books' (the materiality of stone or shell), but on the special harmony of Christian assurance or faith in

[27] See the extended discussion in Hollander's 'Wordsworth and the Music of Sound', in G. Hartman (ed.), *New Perspectives on Coleridge and Wordsworth* (New York and London, 1972), 67–79.

[28] See J. Hollander, 'Images of Voice: Music and Sound in Romantic Poetry', Churchill College Overseas Fellowship Lecture, V (Cambridge, 1970), 12.

life—and therefore faith in hearing—beyond death. This is a word that can continue to hear itself and be heard, even after the apocalypse.

The guaranteeing of poetry as 'WORD' (voice transcendentalized as the Logos) in 'On the Power of Sound' reveals one function of sound, and particularly of voice, in *The Prelude*. What the deaf Dalesman can 'hear' are the immortal voices of the poets, secured against 'imperfection and decay':

> Song of the muses, sage historic tale
> Science severe, or word of holy writ
> Announcing immortality and joy
> To the assembled spirits of the just,
> From imperfection and decay secure.[29]

After the death of the poet, there still remains immortal verse. In lines like these, Wordsworth uses silent reading to free poetry from the monumentality and arbitrary signs of death. Disembodied sound—'The ghostly language of the ancient earth'—comes to be the archetype of poetry. In this light, the 'glad preamble' might be seen not only as a means of calling both poet and voice into being, but also as a way to fantasize their transcendence of material representation. In MS *A* of 'On the Power of Sound', Wordsworth had wondered what skill 'Shall bind these wanderers thro' loose air | In the precious chains of sight . . .' (ll. 169–74 app. crit.), much as in *The Prelude* he had hoped vainly 'that with a frame of outward life' he might 'fix in a visible home . . . those phantoms of conceit, | That had been floating loose about so long' (i. 128–31). How are we to read Wordsworth's self-proclaimed failure to fix or bind the insubstantial (and hence imperishable) 'phantoms of conceit'? The longing 'To brace myself to some determined aim' (i. 124) is synonymous in *The Prelude* with the epic enterprise itself, yet the poem finally evades even this enterprise by substituting the 'WORD'—lasting, but inaudible except to the mind—for an epic theme. It is left celebrating the spirit or 'voice' of poetry instead of the form. Like the cuckoo, 'No bird, but an invisible thing, | A voice, a mystery' ('To the Cuckoo', ll. 15–16), poet as well as poem becomes unavailable, 'disposse[d] . . . almost of a corporeal existence'.[30] An extended personal lyric, *The Prelude* is redeemed

---

[29] *Prose Works*, ii. 95 (*Excursion*, vii. 450–4).
[30] 1815 'Preface', *Prose Works*, iii. 32.

from time and death by the unheard voice of the poet, or, as Wordsworth calls it, 'Imagination', its declared subject. The entire poem becomes an apostrophe or 'prelude' designed to constitute the poet and to permit Wordsworth himself to join the ranks of Homer, the great thunderer, of the Bible, Milton, and even the ballad, as Voice rather than voice, Poetry rather than individual poet: that is, the Voice of Poetry which resounds not only in the ears of the living but in the ears of the deaf.

'Hear I not a Voice from Thee . . . ?'

Gray's 'Bard' sacrifices the individual poet so that his poetry may survive to prophesy the extinction of his oppressors. 'The torrent's awful voice' (l. 24) in which the individual is immersed becomes another name for the chorus of slaughtered poets who foretell the downfall of Edward and the rise of the Tudors. The association of Gray's Pindaric ode with Snowdon gives a specifically poetic dimension to 'the homeless voice of waters' which Wordsworth hears from the top of Mount Snowdon in the final book of *The Prelude*:

> from the shore
> At distance not the third part of a mile
> Was a blue chasm, a fracture in the vapour,
> A deep and gloomy breathing-place, through which
> Mounted the roar of waters, torrents, streams
> Innumerable, roaring with one voice.
> The universal spectacle throughout
> Was shaped for admiration and delight,
> Grand in itself alone, but in that breach
> Through which the homeless voice of waters rose,
> That dark deep thoroughfare, had Nature lodged
> The soul, the imagination of the whole.
>
> (*Prel.* xiii. 54–65)

Here again, sight is less profound than sound, as though visionary depths could only be plumbed by the ear; even in the *Descriptive Sketches* prototype for the passage, Wordsworth had rhymed 'sound' and 'profound'.[31] Significantly, too, Wordsworth's source for the original *Descriptive Sketches* passage, a stanza from

---

[31] 'Loud thro' that midway gulf ascending, sound | Unnumber'd streams with hollow roar profound', *Descriptive Sketches*, ed. Birdsall, 1793: ll. 504–5.

Beattie's *Minstrel* (1771), had merely contained 'the voice of mirth'; torrential and perhaps ancestral voices are Wordsworth's addition.[32] One might see Wordsworth himself as having lodged in this 'deep dark thoroughfare' not only the soul of nature, 'the imagination of the whole', but the soul of the Sublime—the voices of past poets, and also the dithyrambic fervour of the 'glad preamble', transferred here to nature as a means of protecting him from its self-destructive potential. Once the Sublime becomes the voice of nature, not his own, the poet can withdraw to a place of greater safety, no longer exposed to the dreadful blast of apocalyptic revelation liable to strike Milton's altar in its high place. This place of safety is the sheltered valley of pastoral, Theocritan pastoral in particular, where the poet competes not with the dead but, more in the spirit of shepherdly friendship, with the living. If Wordsworth effects the preservation of poetry by handing the Sublime over to nature in the Snowdon passage, he effects the preservation of the poet by transforming his voice into that of Coleridge's shepherd friend—local, personal, and particular.

The function of *The Prelude*'s apostrophes is to constitute the voice of the poet: the function of its addresses to Coleridge (and to some extent, Dorothy) is to save it by domesticating it. The punctuating addresses to Coleridge ('O friend') throughout *The Prelude* have served to comment on the poem's progress, or to signal pauses and regressions; but, towards the end of the poem, they take on much greater importance, occurring with special concentration and effect at the end of Book X and in the second half of Book XIII. In Book X, they become almost a kind of self-locution, a guarantee of the ability to address oneself—to self commune or 'regulate' oneself; Dorothy, we are told, 'Maintained for me a saving intercourse | With my true self' and 'preserved me still | A poet' (x. 914–15, 918–19) while Coleridge (inaccurately, since the period of his influence was yet to come) is retrospectively credited with having lent 'a living help | To *regulate* my soul' (x. 906–7; my italics) at the time of Wordsworth's supposed post-Revolutionary crisis. By the end of Book X, Wordsworth can represent the entire *Prelude* as having been written, not out of self-reproach, still less out of epic ambition, but for Coleridge's sympathetic ear ('A story destined for thy ear', x. 946), addressed to him in his restorative Sicilian exile:

[32] See J. Beattie, *The Minstrel* (London, 1771), part I, st. xxiii.

> Oh, wrap him in your shades, ye giant woods,
> On Etna's side, and thou, O flowery vale
> Of Enna, is there not some nook of thine
> From the first playtime of the infant earth
> Kept sacred to restorative delight?
>
> (*Prel.* x. 1001–5)

Sicily may be a lamentable example of the decay of an ancient classical civilization, but, as the *locus amoenus* of pastoral poetry, it is also—imaginatively at least—an idyllic refuge from the dark post-revolutionary times which Wordsworth has been recalling, and from the state of Europe in the time-present of the poem's writing (1804), with England now the only stronghold of resistance against Napoleon. Most of all, it is the island of the Theocritan idyll, of shepherds devoted to the Muse and engaged in companionable rivalry with one another. This is the context in which Coleridge becomes most clearly a talisman for poetic preservation, whether his own or Wordsworth's. The idyll to which Wordsworth specifically alludes in Book X, the seventh, belongs, appropriately enough, to the genre of the *propemptikon* (prayer for safe voyage), and contains as one of its two chief shepherd singers the goatherd Lycidas. Though Coleridge was literally *en voyage* at this moment in the poem's composition, the allusion to Idyll VII suggests that Wordsworth, at least by association, would have had in mind the tragic fate of Milton's Lycidas and that of the Orphic poet generally.[33]

In Theocritus' poem, Lycidas sings of the special preservation of Comates, a goatherd who was shut up in a chest by his master for over-zealously sacrificing his flock to the Muse. This is the story which Wordsworth retells in Book X: 'And, O Theocritus',

> not unmoved,
> When thinking on my own beloved friend,
> I hear thee tell how bees with honey fed
> Divine Comates, by his tyrant lord
> Within a chest imprisoned impiously—
> How with their honey from the fields they came
> And fed him there, alive, from month to month,
> Because the goatherd, blessed man, had lips
> Wet with the Muse's nectar.
>
> (*Prel.* x. 1019–26)[34]

---

[33] Theocritus' idyll is, of course, one of a number of possible sources for Milton's choice of name for Edward King.   [34] Cf. Theocritus, Idyll VII. 78–83.

Ostensibly an image of Coleridge's restoration to health by Sicily's
most famous product, Mount Hybla honey, the story of Comates
narrates the poet's salvation by natural powers in reward for his
dedication to poetry. It also provides a pastoralized version of
Milton's succouring by Urania at the start of *Paradise Lost*, Book
VII, in the time of his blindness and personal danger ('On evil days
though fallen, and evil tongues; | In darkness; and with dangers
compassed round', vii. 26–7). So traditional was this the idyll of
friendship—Lycidas implores fair weather for the sea-crossing
undertaken by his beloved friend, Ageanax—that Tennyson, in one
of the earliest composed lyrics of *In Memoriam*, can echo it with his
wish for a calm passage for Hallam's remains ('Fair ship, that from
the Italian shore | Sailest the placid ocean-plains . . .', st. ix). For
Wordsworth, as for Tennyson, it would obviously have recalled
Neptune's plea in 'Lycidas' that the winds were calm and the
Nereids at play at the time of the shipwreck, drawing into *The
Prelude*'s own field of allusion the fear that the poet's life and work
would be cut short by the Orphean fate that consists of the triumph
of barbarism over human wisdom and art. This is the fate with
which the post-revolutionary crisis had seemed to threaten Wordsworth himself, and, later, Europe in its entirety, as well as the
personal anxiety attending Coleridge's Sicilian sojourn.

Wordsworth reverts to the theme of poetic friendship and rivalry
celebrated by Theocritus' seventh idyll in his closing book. Here the
idyllic scene recalled is that of the Quantocks, the two shepherds
are Wordsworth and Coleridge, and the date is 1798, 'That
summer when on Quantock's grassy hills | Far ranging' (xiii.
393–4) they composed 'The Idiot Boy' and 'The Ancient Mariner'.
Remembering 'times . . . wherein we first | Together wandered in
wild poesy', Wordsworth writes of the intervening years as 'Times
of much sorrow, of a private grief | Keen and enduring' (xiii.
413–17). The note of elegy is sounded clearly for both himself and
Coleridge. But the comparatively anonymous public lyricism of the
Theocritan pastoral inhibits direct expression of private grief; the
address 'To William Wordsworth', not the Ode 'Dejection', is the
poem with which Coleridge fittingly responds to hearing *The
Prelude* read aloud.[35] At this stage in *The Prelude*, Dorothy and
Coleridge are invoked as calming agencies on the passionately

---

[35] See T. G. Rosenmeyer, *The Green Cabinet: Theocritus and the European
Pastoral Lyric* (Berkeley, 1969), 62–4.

dithyrambic poet of the earlier books—she as the 'Child of my parents, sister of my soul' who has tempered the Sublime ('which as Milton sings | Hath terror in it') by decking with flowers 'A rock with torrents roaring' and breathing the pastoral influence of a 'gentler spring' (xiii. 211–46); Coleridge as the 'most loving soul' who has provided 'mild | Interposition, closelier gathering thoughts | Of man and his concerns', thereby chastening, stemming, and balancing (Wordsworth's terms) 'the deep enthusiastic joy, | The rapture of the hallelujah' (xiii. 246–68). Marking as they do the transition in Book XIII from the celebration of the Sublime of nature and imagination in the Snowdon episode to the human supports of sister and fellow poet, the two long addresses to Dorothy and to Coleridge also place firmly in the past the dithyrambic fervour of the 'glad preamble' ('The deep enthusiastic joy, | The rapture . . .'). Redundant energy has been channelled into making the poet whole; each of these supporting figures mirror an aspect of Wordsworth's salvaged poetic identity, serving to reflect back on him the chastened, stemmed, and balanced qualities necessary if he is to confront, not the Sublime, but mortality: 'Oh, yet a few short years of useful life, | And all will be complete—thy race be run . . .' (xiii. 428–9). By providing a remembering image of his own subjectivity, the addresses to Dorothy and especially to Coleridge allow Wordsworth finally to claim the stable basis on which to prophesy:

> my powers so far confirmed, and such
> My knowledge, as to make me capable
> Of building up a work that should endure.
>
> (*Prel.* xiii. 277–9)

Ostensibly, Coleridge's greatly increased role at the end of *The Prelude* is important both to redefine the entire poem as 'this gift | Which I for thee design' (xiii. 411–12), and as the justification for its writing; by him at least it will be felt 'that the history of a poet's mind | Is labour not unworthy of regard' (xiii. 408–9). But the underlying importance of Wordsworth's imaginary colloquy with Coleridge lies in the function of the address itself. In speaking to another, the poet hears himself speak with a unity of sound and voice that comes to stand for consciousness itself. Or, to put it another way, to have an imaginary auditor is to fantasize the reproduction of one's speech in another without external mediation or deferral, and so to create the illusion of mastery over the process of signification.[36] Hence the new-found prophetic confidence at the close of Book XIII: 'United helpers forward of a day | Of firmer trust, joint labourers in the work . . . *we to them will speak* | A lasting inspiration' (xiii. 438–9, 442–3; my italics). As 'Prophets of Nature', Wordsworth and Coleridge are self-duplicating; poetic comradeship comes to stand for the simultaneity of speaking and being heard, prophecy and efficacy. Hence, too, the fantasy which Wordsworth now sees as having animated the entire poem, that of an instantly elevating dialogue with himself, the inner colloquy through which he at once knows and makes himself a poet:

> Call back to mind
> The mood in which this poem was begun,
> O friend—the termination of my course
> Is nearer now, much nearer, yet even then
> In that distraction and intense desire
> I said unto the life which I had lived,
> 'Where art thou? Hear I not a voice from thee
> Which 'tis reproach to hear?' Anon I rose
> As if on wings, and saw beneath me stretched
> Vast prospect of the world which I had been,
> And was; and hence this song, which like a lark
> I have protracted . . .
>
> (*Prel.* xiii. 370–81)

Hearing his own voice makes the poet airborne, calling into play images of soaring height, epic prospect, and unlimited power. This is self-possession, the sublime self-mastery which makes prophecy possible. The exchange between the voice of the life and the voice of the poet who has lived it—between 'the world which I had been | And was' and the language of his desire—brings *The Prelude* into being as a lyrical dialogue between past and present, between the discourse of memory and the discourse of poetic aspiration. If the lyric voice, as some would have it, is not so much heard as overheard, overhearing creates the doubling through which self-recognition or self-audition can occur. The lyric voice of *The*

[36] As Jacques Derrida puts it: 'To speak to someone is doubtless to hear oneself speak, to be heard by oneself; but, at the same time, if one is heard by another, to speak is to make him *repeat immediately* in himself the hearing-oneself-speak in the very form in which I effectuated it . . . The possibility of reproduction . . . *gives itself out* as the phenomenon of a mastery or limitless power over the signifier . . .' (*Speech and Phenomena*, trans. Allison, p. 80).

Prelude is the fiction of the poet talking to himself; the entire poem becomes a self-constituting apostrophe, a 'glad preamble' or necessary interruption to its own beginning which only comes to an end when the poet assumes his prophetic mission, and only becomes prophetic when it finally succeeds in obliterating the unheard or deafening 'voice' of writing with the transcendent, disembodied song of a bird: 'No bird, but an invisible thing, | A voice, a mystery' ('To the Cuckoo', ll. 15-16).

III
SEXUAL DIFFERENCE

CHAPTER 7

GENRE, GENDER, AND AUTOBIOGRAPHY
Vaudracour and Julia

The question of the literary genre is not a formal one: it covers
the motif of the law in general, of generation in the natural and
symbolic senses, of birth in the natural and symbolic senses, of
the generation of difference, sexual difference between the
feminine and masculine genre/gender ... of an identity and
difference between the feminine and masculine.

(Jacques Derrida, 'The Law of Genre')[1]

WHAT has sexual difference to do with *The Prelude*? In particular,
what can be said about the relation between the genre of
Wordsworth's autobiographical poem and questions having to do
with gender? My epigraph provides one approach to these
questions. It comes from an essay whose already involuted
paradoxes of classification and taxonomy need no further elaboration here (although I will be returning to Derrida in due course).
Rather, Derrida's summary announces in brief the argument which
I want to make apropos of *The Prelude* in particular, but also
apropos of genre theory in general. Questions of genre involve both
law and generation, or beginnings; both gender and sexual identity,
or difference. My point of departure (and in a sense, my pretext) is
provided by the Vaudracour and Julia episode—an episode whose
plot is for my purposes conveniently summarized by Derrida's
summary; but I hope also to suggest ways in which that episode
might serve as a rereading of current genre theory, especially in the
light of Derrida's critical reflections on the (il)legitimizing effects of
'the law of genre'. In other words, instead of reading the episode in
the light of theories of genre, I want to read theories of genre in the
light of an episode that involves questions of generation, law, and
sexual difference as a central aspect of its narrative.

In doing so, I have in mind especially attempts such as Alistair

---

[1] 'The Law of Genre', *Glyph*, 7 (1980), 221.

Fowler's to bring notions of generic transformation to bear on literary history in *Kinds of Literature* (1982). Rather misleadingly subtitled *An Introduction to the Theory of Genres and Modes*, Fowler's book might well be seen as an instance of the refusal of theory, in the interests of conserving an ultimately dynastic view of literary history. Genre, in effect, does away with the need for theory since it organizes literature in the forms in which we already know it; recognizability and an unbroken line of descent are the final criteria, and literary hierarchies remain fundamentally unchanged. The Vaudracour and Julia episode tells a story about illegitimacy, but, interestingly, the fate of the episode itself tells a story about literary hierarchy. I want to argue that the disreputable episode lost its place in Wordsworth's autobiography because it threatened to undo the legitimizing efforts that went into the authorized version of *The Prelude*. One way to explore the (non-)relation between views of genre as different as those of Derrida and Fowler is to tell the story of the Vaudracour and Julia episode as it is told not only by Wordsworth himself, but by the textual history of *The Prelude*, and then as it in turn retells the story of the law of genre—a story which also necessarily engages questions of gender along with questions of theory.

'With That Prelude Did Begin | The Record'

To begin at the end: the naming of Wordsworth's untitled posthumous poem by his widow can be seen as at once a legitimation, an act of propriety, and an appropriation. Here is his nephew Christopher's account of the naming of the 'anonymous' poem that became *The Prelude*, in the *Memoirs of William Wordsworth* (1851):

Its title, 'The Prelude', had not been fixed on by the author himself: the Poem remained anonymous till his death. The present title has been prefixed to it at the suggestion of the beloved partner of his life, and the best interpreter of his thoughts, from considerations of its tentative and preliminary character. Obviously it would have been desirable to mark its relation to 'The Recluse' by some analogous appellation; but this could not easily be done, at the same time that its other essential characteristics were indicated. Besides, the appearance of this poem, *after* the author's death, might tend to lead some readers into an opinion that it was his *final* production, instead of being, as it really is, one of his *earlier* works. They were to be guarded against this supposition. Hence a name has been adopted, which may serve to keep the true nature and position of the poem constantly before the eye of the reader; and 'THE PRELUDE' will now be perused and estimated with the feelings properly due to its preparatory character, and to the period at which it was composed.[2]

Guarded against the supposition that it is a later work ('his *final* production'), the reader knows where the poem belongs ('one of his *earlier* works'), and to whom—the poet's family; more particularly, his widow ('the best interpreter of his thoughts'). The title, then, not so much prefixes *The Prelude* as serves to fix it, or 'to keep the true nature and position of the poem constantly before the eye of the reader'. The widow's afterthought prepares us to be prepared. But for what? How can we know 'the feelings properly due to its preparatory character' without knowing what comes afterwards? And what if its 'true nature' were to have been an end, and not a beginning—the 'tail-piece' to the unwritten *Recluse* which Coleridge had first envisaged? Or supposing the famous antechapel turned out to be an annex instead—'the biographical, or philosophico-biographical Poem to be prefixed or annexed to the Recluse' (Coleridge again)?[3] At once an endless beginning and always an afterword to the life it narrates, Wordsworth's autobiography seems not to have a proper place after all. It belongs nowhere and has no fixed character, redundant to the non-existent text which its title is supposed to 'prelude'. In short, it is an impropriety, and one properly suppressed during the poet's lifetime.

It would be difficult to cut *The Prelude* from the record of Wordsworth's writings. But he did his best to excise another impropriety, also successfully suppressed during his lifetime. I mean, of course, his off-the-record love affair with Annette Vallon and the birth of their daughter Caroline:

> Oh, happy time of youthful lovers, (thus
> My story may begin) O balmy time,
> In which a love-knot, on a lady's brow,
> Is fairer than the fairest star in Heaven!
> So might—and with that prelude *did* begin
> The record; and, in faithful verse, was given
> The doleful sequel.

(1850: *Prel.* ix. 553–9)

---

[2] Wordsworth, *Memoirs of William Wordsworth*, i. 313.
[3] *Collected Letters of Samuel Taylor Coleridge*, ed. Griggs, i. 538; ii. 1104.

The record thus begun and aborted was the story of Vaudracour and Julia, published separately in 1820 and omitted altogether from the 1850 version of *The Prelude* in which these prelusive lines occur ('and with that prelude *did* begin | The record'). Removed from its originally autobiographical context, 'The doleful sequel' became yet another of Wordsworth's pathetic tales, a 'Poem Founded on the Affections'. The note added in 1820 indicates that the story was 'written as an Episode, in a work [i.e. *The Prelude*] from which its length may perhaps exclude it'.[4] But in a letter of 1805 to Sir George Beaumont, Wordsworth makes it hard for himself to exclude anything from his ever-expanding autobiography. Offering, in his own phrase, to 'lop off' any 'redundancies' that may later become apparent in the completed poem, he withdraws the offer in the same breath: 'this defect [i.e. redundancy], whenever I have suspected it or found it to exist in any writings of mine, I have always found incurable. The fault lies too deep, and is in the first conception.'[5] Contradictorily, Wordsworth seems to say that lopping off an incurable defect risks damaging an integrity which already includes redundancies. The cut would at once strike a blow to the integrity of the work, and yet admits that it lacks integrity to start with, since the 'fault' or 'defect' lies in its first conception. A story of impropriety, disowning, and cutting off as the result of a faulty conception, the Vaudracour and Julia episode suffers the same fate as its hero—surely the most lopped-off romantic lover since Abelard.

There is nothing in the 1850 version of *The Prelude* to tell us that Vaudracour and Julia are both victims of an *ancien régime* whose social and sexual codes of honour are founded on both the Name and the Law of the Father—on paternity, property, and propriety. Wordsworth contents himself with directing his imaginary reader elsewhere for 'The doleful sequel' to the story, and at this point in the 1850 text substitutes a clumsy twenty-line paraphrase which is striking for its omissions: 'Thou, also, there mayst read', he tells Coleridge (who may be presumed to have known the whole story anyway),

> how the enamoured youth [i.e. Vaudracour] was driven,
> By public power abused, to fatal crime,
> Nature's rebellion against monstrous law;

---

[4] *PW* ii. 59.   [5] *EY* 587.

How, between heart and heart, oppression thrust
Her mandates, severing whom true love had joined,
Harassing both; until he sank and pressed
The couch his fate had made for him; supine,
Save when the stings of viperous remorse,
Trying their strength, enforced him to start up,
Aghast and prayerless. Into a deep wood
He fled, to shun the haunts of human kind;
There dwelt, weakened in spirit more and more;
Nor could the voice of Freedom, which through France
Full speedily resounded, public hope,
Or personal memory of his own worst wrongs,
Rouse him; but, hidden in those gloomy shades,
His days he wasted,—an imbecile mind.

(1850: Prel. ix. 568–85)

To set the record straight: Vaudracour loses his liberty, his manhood, and his marbles because his noble father objects to a middle-class marriage (plebeian, as it becomes in 1820) with his childhood playmate; these are not star-crossed lovers, but class-crossed, and the paternal prohibition which mobilizes the law against Vaudracour means that the child he engenders outside marriage can never be legitimate—can never inherit the Name of the Father. The censored text of 1850 may tell us no more than the fact that by this time Wordsworth himself had become a Victorian father, a reading borne out by the 1820 denial of his earlier, more permissive speculation that the lovers had been carried away 'through effect | Of some delirious hour' (ix. 596–7; 'ah, speak it, think it, not!' is Wordsworth's expostulatory 1820 revision). But where beginning fictions are concerned, omissions like this tell tales. Modern readers of *The Prelude* know—too knowingly, perhaps—that the episode is a pretext; for Vaudracour read 'Heartsworth', or Wordsworth as lover; for Julia, read Annette.[6] But the biographical reading is a short cut. What should interest us is not so much the begetting of Caroline as the beginnings of *The Prelude*; not so much the (giving) life as the work.

In 1805, Wordsworth had introduced the episode as a digression from his main purpose in the Revolutionary books: 'I shall not, as my purpose was, take note | Of other matters . . . —public acts, |

---

[6] See Erdman, 'Wordsworth as Heartsworth; or, Was Regicide the Prophetic Ground of those "Moral Questions"?', *The Evidence of the Imagination*, p. 15.

And public persons ... —but I will here instead | Draw from
obscurity a tragic tale' (ix. 544–51). This turning away from
history, or domestication of epic, is prefigured at the start of *The
Prelude* when Wordsworth's survey of mythic and historical themes
for his projected poem comes home to 'Some tale from my own
heart, more near akin | To my own passions and habitual thoughts'
(i. 221–2). Although it too proved a false start, the untold 'tale
from [his] own heart' is resumed in Book IX. The Vaudracour and
Julia episode can be seen—not, I think, entirely fancifully—as the
point from which *The Prelude* departs as well as a redundancy; as
an opening as well as a cut. A history of error and transgression, the
episode is also symptomatic of the errancy of Wordsworth's
abandonment of historical and philosophical epic for that mixed
and transgressive genre, autobiography. Here a pause for classification seems in order. Wordsworth's 1815 'Preface' includes under
the heading of narrative the following taxonomy of genres or kinds:
'the Epopoeia, the Historic Poem, the Tale, the Romance, the
Mock-heroic, and ... that dear production of our days,
the metrical Novel'. The distinguishing mark of this class,
Wordsworth goes on, 'is, that the Narrator ... is himself the source
from which everything primarily flows'.[7] Where does this leave his
autobiography, which Wordsworth, we know, regarded as
'unprecedented' in literary history ('a thing unprecedented in
Literary history that a man should talk so much about himself', as
he wrote to Beaumont)?[8] Presumably, it leaves autobiography with
tales and romances. In other words, Wordsworth's lapse into 'that
dear production of our days, the metrical Novel' can scarcely be
dissociated from his larger lapse in talking so much about himself.
Cutting the Vaudracour and Julia episode makes amends for an
error that cannot be cut, the altogether redundant, too talkative
Prelude. Romance—which is well known to be in love with error—
is censored in the form of the Vaudracour and Julia episode, so that
autobiography can speak out at unprecedented length.

Revolution, Romance, and Sexual Difference

What kind of poem is *The Prelude*? We could settle for Coleridge's
'philosophico-biographical' and leave it at that as far as generic
legitimacy goes. But I would like to press the question a little

---

[7] *Prose Works*, iii. 27.   [8] *EY* 586.

further. Genre might be called the Frenchification of gender, and it was in France that (having left his French letters at home, as they say in England) Wordsworth discovered the literal implications of engendering. We know that France appeared to him under the sign of romance as well as revolution; 'Bliss was it in that dawn to be alive' (x. 692), but also: 'O balmy time, | In which a love-knot, on a lady's brow, | Is fairer than the fairest star in Heaven!' (1850: ix. 554–6). In a strikingly proleptic passage, Wordsworth describes how on his first arrival in Paris in 1791 he gathered up a stone from the ruins of the Bastille 'And pocketed the relick in the guise | Of an enthusiast' (ix. 66–7). Yet, 'Affecting more emotion than [he] felt', he is less moved by this symbol of the Revolution than by a picture then on show in Paris as a tourist attraction, 'the Magdalene of le Brun' (ix. 71–80). Le Brun, associated with Versailles and Richelieu, and a rapturously penitent Magdalene popularly (but incorrectly) thought to portray Louise de la Vallière, the mistress of Louis XIV, seem on the face of it to represent aesthetic lapses on the part of an aspiring Republican. But the incident foretells the Vaudracour and Julia episode, later in the same book, in a number of significant ways. The painting's erotic religiosity would have provided an imaginary visual parallel for the tale of hapless lovers forced—like Louise de la Vallière, who retired to a Carmelite convent—to sublimate their passion in religious houses (Julia is consigned to a convent by her mother while, according to the Fenwick note, the final refuge of the real-life Vaudracour was the convent of La Trappe).[9] Politically speaking, Wordsworth himself had fallen in love with a woman of royalist sympathies in a Loire landscape bearing the traces of royal erotic history ('that rural castle, name now slipped | From my remembrance, where a lady lodged | By the first Francis wooed', ix. 485–7). Finally, the Vaudracour and Julia episode redeems sexual love as romance (this is no casual affair, after all) and rededicates it to revolution.

Two critics have recently and persuasively argued for the centrality of the erotic motif in Book IX, offering their own readings of both le Brun's penitent Magdalene and the Vaudracour and Julia episode. For Alan Liu, elaborating what he calls 'the Genre of Revolution' in Books IX and X of *The Prelude*, the Magdalene is the female 'genius' of the revolutionary landscape; Wordsworth, writes Liu persuasively apropos of le Brun's painting,

[9] *PW* ii. 478.

wants to see a revolutionary country in which liberation arrives, not with the pike-thrusts of violence, but with the soft, fluid undulations of a necklace spilling from a box, of clouds rolling through a window, or of the clothes, hair, tears, and body, of a woman flowing out of old constraints.

He points out that Wordsworth misread both the penitent Magdalene and revolutionary France.[10] For Ronald Paulson, drawing on Liu's argument that Wordsworth is trying to fit the French Revolution into an aesthetic category or literary genre in order to make it manageable, 'love itself is the symbol of revolution' and 'The act of love . . . an act of rebellion, or at least a scandalous act, in the context of a society of arranged marriages, closed families, and decorous art and literature'. The story thus becomes for Paulson 'the hidden centre' or 'displaced paradigm' of Wordsworth's revolutionary experience which he reads as follows:

he falls in love with an alien woman (alien by class and nationality), challenges his father, runs away with her, but eventually succumbs to the external, paternal pressures. The act of loving with this slightly alien woman *is* the act of revolution.[11]

Thematically speaking, the Vaudracour and Julia episode clearly represents just such 'an act of rebellion, or at least a scandalous act' and it is no surprise that the later Wordsworth should have chosen to hush it up on political as well as personal grounds. But persuasive as these readings are, I want to risk an alternative reading, one which bears not only on the genre of *The Prelude* but on the gender of the poet (not to mention that 'slightly alien woman'). This is my justification for retelling the story which Liu and Paulson in their different ways have already told in the context of their common concern with genre and revolution in Books IX and X of *The Prelude*.

In brief, I want to suggest that the metonymic swerve of passion from fallen Bastille to fallen woman, from history to romance, puts a woman's face on the Revolution and, in doing so, makes a man of Wordsworth. Without 'a regular chronicle' of recent events, Wordsworth (he tells us) is unable to give them 'A form and body' (ix. 101–6); 'all things', he complains, 'were to me | Loose and

---

[10] ' "Shapeless Eagerness". The Genre of Revolution in Books 9–10 of *The Prelude*', *MLQ* 43 (1982), 10, repr. in *Wordsworth: The Sense of History*, pp. 362–87; Liu offers a particularly suggestive analysis of the le Brun 'Magdalene'.

[11] Paulson, *Representations of Revolution 1789–1820*, pp. 265, 268–9.

disjointed' (ix. 106–7). Lacking a body ('the affections left |
Without a vital interest', ix. 107–8), how can revolution engender
desire? Chaotic, formless, and multitudinous, revolutionary
uproar—the 'hubbub wild' of Milton's Pandemonium which strikes
Wordsworth on his arrival (ix. 56)—mocks all attempts to
textualize it for posterity: 'Oh, laughter for the page that would
reflect | To future times the face of what now is!' (ix. 176–7), writes
Wordsworth, dropping into the present tense. Superimposed on the
faceless face 'of what now is' we find that of le Brun's stylized
Magdalene, 'A beauty exquisitely wrought—fair face | And rueful,
with its ever-flowing tears' (ix. 79–80). Le Brun's expressive theory
of the passions was famous for transforming the face itself into an
intelligible or speaking text. Embodied as a beautiful woman
(whose expression, Liu points out, is closest to that of 'Ravishment'
or 'Rapture' in le Brun's scheme), revolution becomes readable.
Elsewhere, Wordsworth himself admits to having prized 'the
historian's tale' only as 'Tales of the poets'; only as romance—'as it
made my heart | Beat high and filled my fancy with fair forms' (ix.
207–10). Once more seduced by fair forms as he encounters the
reality of revolutionary France, Wordsworth substitutes the
Vaudracour and Julia episode for the historian's tale. But, like the
penitent Magdalene with her fair face, the episode gives form to
more than the unreadable, risible text of history. The story of
Vaudracour and Julia is also a means of constituting Wordsworth
himself as an autobiographical subject, and, specifically, as a
masculine one.

Paul de Man has written of the resistance of autobiography to
attempts to make it look less disreputable by elevating it into a
genre or mode and installing it 'among the canonical hierarchies
of the major literary genres'; rather, autobiographical discourse
becomes for him 'a figure of reading or of understanding that
occurs, to some degree, in all texts'. He goes on: 'The autobiographical moment happens as an alignment between the two
subjects involved in the process of reading in which they determine
each other by mutual reflexive substitution'; as a figure of face
(posited by language) and simultaneous defacement (since language
for de Man is privative).[12] Because the woman's face images his
own, reflecting the onlooker's desire much as the supposed

---

[12] See 'Autobiography as De-Facement', *The Rhetoric of Romanticism*, pp. 67–8,
70.

Magdalene (Louise de la Vallière) might be thought to reflect that of Louis XIV, the autobiographer can come into existence as a specular image of the reader. When the page has a face, it can speak to the future; or at any rate to Coleridge—another of the autobiographer's self-constituting mirror images or faces in *The Prelude*.

Hence gender (sexual difference) establishes identity by means of a difference that is finally excised. What we end up with is not difference (that 'slightly alien woman') but the same: man, or man–to–man. Like the Vaudracour and Julia episode, and like the feminized genre of romance, woman becomes redundant. Her role is to mediate between men, as the role of romance is to mediate between history and the historian's tale or page. The real hero of this tale is in fact Beaupuy, Wordsworth's surrogate narrator for the Vaudracour and Julia episode, as well as his mentor and idealized revolutionary self (his name, tellingly, combines beauty and power—a masculine or beau ideal). Their 'earnest dialogues' beneath the trees of the Loire valley are compared to those between Dion and Plato (ix. 446, 415–16), or between student and teacher. But Wordsworth's thoughts soon wander from philosophic debate about freedom (Dion liberated Sicily from tyrannical rule) to tales of damsels more or less in distress—fantasies drawn from Ariosto, Tasso, and Spenser: 'Angelica thundering through the woods', 'Erminia, fugitive as fair as she', satyrs mobbing 'a female in the midst, | A mortal beauty, their unhappy thrall' (ix. 454–64). Beaupuy himself is an errant knight who wanders 'As through a book, an old romance, or tale | Of Fairy' (ix. 307–8), and chivalry turns out to be the motivating force for his political idealism even when he points to a present-day reality, the hunger-bitten girl feeding her heifer by the wayside (' 'Tis against that | Which we are fighting', ix. 519–20). Beaupuy's political programme, in fact, is none other than to transfer to the people 'A passion and a gallantry . . . Which he, a soldier, in his idler day | Had payed to woman' (ix. 318–20). As Gayatri Spivak has noted in her provocative analysis of 'Sex and History in *The Prelude*', the transfer constitutes 'an unwitting display of class and sex prejudice'.[13] This embodiment of the people as an unhappy female

[13] 'Sex and History in *The Prelude* (1805): Books Nine to Thirteen', *Texas Studies in Literature and Language*, 23 (1981), 341. It seems worth noting in the context of the Vaudracour and Julia episode that Freud, in 'A Special Type of Choice

thrall in need of rescue suggests that their role (like that of the beauty surrounded by satyrs) is to mediate relations between men. Both politics (the people) and romance (woman) go under, leaving the philosophic dialogue addressed by one man to another; this dialogue Dorothy Wordsworth called 'the Poem addressed to Coleridge'[14]—a poem 'fair-copied' by the women of the Wordsworth–Coleridge circle, but not, or only rarely, addressed to them.

In the economics of chivalry, it is the woman who pays. Wordsworth, who in 1793 had called Burke's *Reflections on the Revolution in France* 'a philosophic lamentation over the extinction of Chivalry', knew the price. The Vaudracour and Julia episode reads like a critique of Burke's famous lament (inspired by the fate of Marie Antoinette) for the age of chivalry: 'It is gone, that sensibility of principle, that chastity of honour, which felt a stain like a wound, which inspired courage whilst it mitigated ferocity, which ennobled whatever it touched, and under which vice itself lost half its evil, by losing all its grossness . . .'[15] The Vaudracour and Julia episode translates 'that chastity of honour' as ruthless persecution of the lovers, even to the point where the father imprisons his son rather than recognize marriage to a commoner; even to the point of disregarding primogeniture rather than recognize an illegitimate child. Yet Wordsworth's own unmasking of the ideology which sustains the fictions of 'chivalry'—an ideology based on class and sexual inequality, and maintained by laws designed to perpetuate the interests of the upper classes— might be accused of participating in the values of an outmoded genre. If only by its contiguity with chivalric romance, the 'Tale' or 'metrical Novel' is anachronistic, identified with the values of the ruling class even when it tells of simple people, and complicit in the retreat from the specificity of history whereby romance conceals the social basis of the ruling class—its exploitation or oppression of the ruled.[16] Though Wordsworth claims for Beaupuy's narrative of Vaudracour and Julia 'The humbler province of plain history' (ix.

of Object made by Men' (1910), identifies the masculine fantasy of idealizing, debasing, and rescuing the beloved as a version of the wish to make her a (his) mother: see *The Complete Psychological Works of Sigmund Freud*, trans. and ed. Strachey, xi. 71–4.

[14] *EY* 664.   [15] See *Prose Works*, i. 35, 56 n.

[16] See Patricia Parker's argument in *Inescapable Romance: Studies in the Poetics of a Mode* (Princeton, 1979), 9.

643), the story—based in part on Helen Maria Williams's *Letters Written in France in the Summer of 1790* (1790)—preserves all the self-consciously literary qualities of sensibility and pathos common in late eighteenth-century fiction and metrical tales.[17] Vaudracour himself is a man of feeling whose single act of violence (the murder of one of the men sent by his father to arrest him) accentuates his passivity and feminization in the face of paternal authority. His final impotence, roused neither by 'the voice of Freedom, . . . public hope, | Or personal memory of his own worst wrongs' (1850: ix. 581–3) is the impotence of the pathetic tale itself to confront history, let alone revolution. Set in a pre-revolutionary era, it is a relic, literally a pre-text—its lovers for ever belated, as if caught in a time-warp from which *The Prelude* itself is able to escape by virtue of its impropriety or illegitimacy, that of a distinctively revolutionary non-genre, autobiography. Unlike Wordsworth (or for that matter the voluble Annette) who lived to tell his own tale, Vaudracour is silenced: 'From that time forth he never uttered word | To any living' (ix. 912–13). His imbecility is the autobiographer's unacted part. Though he had found it hard to get started on his epic, Wordsworth had not 'wasted' his days; his release from the past came not just through timely utterance but through an excess of talkativeness: 'a thing unprecedented in Literary history that a man should talk so much about himself'.

A Family Romance: Or, the Politics of Genre

Oedipal interpretations of the Vaudracour and Julia episode are fuelled by Wordsworth himself when he writes of 'A conflict of sensations without name' which he experienced after his return from revolutionary France on finding himself unowned and silent in the midst of a congregation praying 'To their great Father' for victory against the French (x. 265–73). Oedipal conflict becomes synonymous with the French Revolution—'in the minds of all ingenuous youth, | Change and subversion from this hour . . . that might be named | A revolution,' writes Wordsworth (x. 232–7). Paulson's Bloomian version of the Oedipal plot has Wordsworth

---

[17] See F. M. Todd, *Politics and the Poet* (London, 1957), 219–25. K. R. Johnston, *Wordsworth and the Recluse* (New Haven and London, 1984), 178–80, argues that—like Helen Maria Williams's tale—Wordsworth's too may in its own way have been intended as a tract for the times, less sentimental than cautionary.

staging a successful poetic rebellion against the literary father, Milton; 'the struggle with (as Bloom would put it) his poetic father reflecting in microcosm the oedipal conflict of the Revolution itself . . . the rebellion against Milton [is] a successful version of the Vaudracour–Julia story in which the father *is* defied.'[18] For Spivak, in the most ambitious attempt so far to read the Vaudracour and Julia episode in the combined light of gender, politics, and psychoanalysis, Wordsworth's disavowal of paternity (his fathering of Caroline) is crucial to the plot of both *The Prelude* and the Great Tradition which has it that 'the Child is father of the Man', i.e. 'man as son'. Paulson's Wordsworth reverses the fate of Vaudracour, who remains by contrast for ever son not father—his marriage forbidden, his freedom curtailed, and his child illegitimate. Spivak's reading is less indulgent of the Oedipal plot, seeing it as a ruse that allows Wordsworth to play at mothers and fathers, thereby acceding to an androgyny which finally excludes women in the interests of a restored imagination. 'Suppression of Julia, unemphatic retention of Vaudracour as sustained and negative condition of possibility of disavowal, his sublation into Coleridge . . . Imagination as the androgyny of Nature and Man— woman shut out. I cannot but see in it the sexual–political program of the Great Tradition.'[19] The plot, in short, is a (Great) Masterplot.

But what about the baby, to whom Vaudracour becomes so devoted after Julia's incarceration in a convent, and whom he curiously resembles in his own helplessness and dependence on Julia? When we recall the baby's omission from the 1850 text of *The Prelude*, we might pause to ask whether, in suppressing it, Wordsworth may not be providing us with another twist to the Oedipal narrative: that of the so-called 'family romance'. In his edition of *The Prelude*, Ernest de Selincourt takes time out to grumble about the Vaudracour and Julia episode in a footnote as 'among the weakest of [Wordsworth's] attempts in narrative verse'. 'Its most radical fault', he goes on,

lies in that part which was probably true to fact, but farthest removed from his own experience, i.e. the character of the hero, with whose meek resignation it is as impossible to sympathize as with the patience of a

---

[18] Paulson, *Representations of Revolution 1789–1820*, pp. 273–5.

[19] See Spivak, 'Sex and History in *The Prelude* (1805)', pp. 331, 336, and 326–36 *passim*.

Griselda. ... Wordsworth completely fails in presenting a character so unlike his own; and the matter-of-fact detail which he supplies, often so effective and moving in his narratives, only makes *Vaudracour and Julia* more ludicrous, till in [the lines narrating the death of the baby] it reaches a climax of absurdity difficult to parallel in our literature.[20]

'A hero', writes Freud in *Moses and Monotheism* (1939), 'is someone who has had the courage to rebel against his father and has in the end victoriously overcome him.'[21] The antithesis of such a hero and therefore (for de Selincourt) unlike Wordsworth himself, Vaudracour can only be a woman, or a patient Griselda. For woman, read 'neurotic', since according to Freud in 'Family Romances' (1908) the failure to liberate oneself from the authority of one's parents determines one class of neurotic. Freud's essay goes on to identify a characteristic form of fantasy in children and in the erotic and ambitious fantasies of adolescents—one never yielded up by such neurotic individuals; namely, the fantasy of being a stepchild or an adopted child. In the Moses story, it is the aristocratic father who disowns his child or condemns him to death (a role taken by Vaudracour's implacable father in the *Prelude* episode). Vaudracour, then, assumes the role of nurse to himself as abandoned infant when disowned by the father. This may shed light on the unparalleled 'climax of absurdity' denounced by de Selincourt, lines describing Vaudracour performing 'The office of a nurse to his young child, | Which ... by some mistake | Or indiscretion of the father, died' (ix. 906–8). Negligent nursing and negligent narrative coincide. Wordsworth's offhand aporia (is this a displaced suicide, a mercy killing, or an infanticide?) raises a bizarre line of questioning. Freud remarks on an interesting variant of the family romance in which a younger child robs those born before him of their prerogatives by imagining them illegitimate, so that 'the hero and author returns to legitimacy himself while his brothers and sisters are eliminated by being bastardized'.[22] When one recalls the lines which depict Vaudracour 'Propping a pale and melancholy face' (ix. 812) on one of Julia's breasts while the baby drinks from the other, this is a less far-fetched interpretation than might at first appear. Killing off the illegitimate child leaves Vaudracour (Wordsworth as Heartsworth) without a rival in his

[20] *The Prelude*, ed. de Selincourt, rev. Darbishire, pp. 592–3.
[21] *The Complete Psychological Works of Sigmund Freud*, trans. and ed. Strachey, xxiii. 12.
[22] Ibid. ix. 240.

mother's affections, while simultaneously relegitimizing him as his father's only son and heir.

A second aporia immediately follows the lines relating the death of the baby: 'The tale I follow to its last recess | Of suffering or of peace, I know not which—' (ix. 909–10). The last recess is presumably the grave—a 'sepulchral recess', like one of those included in the gothic edifice of which *The Prelude* is the antechapel. Literally, it is the end of the line; Vaudracour, the eldest son, dies without issue. The prominence of genealogy in the Vaudracour and Julia episode provides scope for the theoretical reversal I promised at the start. What light does the episode throw on genre theory, in particular, on the analogy given fresh currency by Alistair Fowler's *Kinds of Literature*, that of family resemblance? Preferring to see genres as characters or types rather than classes, Fowler invokes Wittgenstein's famous analogy between word-games and games in general: 'We see a complicated network of similarities overlapping and criss-crossing . . . I can think of no better expression to characterize these similarities than "family resemblances"; for the various resemblances between members of a family: build, features, colour of eyes, gait, temperament, etc., etc., overlap and criss-cross in the same way.' Fowler glosses this as follows: 'Representatives of a genre may then be regarded as making up a family whose septs and individual members are related in various ways, without necessarily having any single feature shared in common by all.'[23] (One recalls Wordsworth's grouping of different kinds of narrative according to a common line of descent: 'the Narrator . . . is himself the source from which everything primarily flows.') A 'sept', appropriately, is a clan or tribe claiming descent from a common ancestor. Though Fowler himself had earlier dismissed the view that genres form distinct classes (preferring to see genre in interpretative rather than taxonomic terms), the family analogy allows him to reintroduce qualities of distinctiveness, individuality, and integrity commonly associated with the concept of 'character'—a concept which buttresses our sense of the separateness of subjects against the dangers of (inter-)mixing. By means of the 'mutual reflexive substitution' or 'alignment between the two subjects involved in the process of reading' which de Man identifies as constitutive of autobiography,

[23] A. Fowler, *Kinds of Literature: An Introduction to the Theory of Genres and Modes* (Cambridge, Mass., 1982), 41.

genre puts a face on theory. Is genre theory, then, no more than 'a figure of reading or of understanding', a means of stabilizing the errant text by putting a face on it, and so reading into it a recognizable, specular image of our own acts of understanding? In this light, theories of genre become inseparable from theories of the subject, and hence inseparable from theories of writing. However mixed the genre or mixed-up the 'self', the source of writing ('the source from which everything primarily flows', in Wordsworth's phrase) is held finally to be a more or less integrated and coherent author, the individual named 'Wordsworth' who guarantees the stability and, finally, the legitimacy of the text by means of what Fowler elsewhere calls 'legitimate authorial privilege'.

The family analogy also throws light on what might be termed the politics of genre—a politics implicitly conservative. As Fowler himself goes on to point out, the basis of such family resemblances ('build, features, colour of eyes, gait, temperament, etc., etc.') is literary tradition; specifically, features such as influence, imitation, and inherited codes: 'Poems', writes Fowler, 'are made in part from earlier poems: each is the child . . . of an earlier representative of the genre and may yet be the mother of a subsequent representative.' The implications of this genealogical view of genre are clearly stated in Fowler's book: 'in the realm of genre, revolution or complete discontinuity is impossible.'[24] To break with literary tradition would be to break with the possibility of perceived resemblance. The result would be an unrecognizable text or a faceless page, like the one with which the French Revolution presented Wordsworth ('Oh, laughter for the page that would reflect | To future times the face of what now is!', *Prel.* ix. 176–7). To get over the difficulty inherent in his privileging of continuity (how then does literary change occur?) Fowler elaborates the family analogy in the direction of genetic mutation: 'Naturally', he goes on, 'the genetic make-up alters with slow time.'[25] *Naturally?* By consecrating genre as part of the order of nature, while simultaneously emphasizing the gradual evolution of genre in response to historical change, Fowler reveals himself to be a moderate (if not a conservative) rather than revolutionary, not only in the realm of genre theory, but in the realm of theory itself, where 'farouche structuralists' are said to be at work with 'mere bad effects of Yale

[24] Fowler, *Kinds of Literature: An Introduction* . . ., 42, 32.   [25] Ibid. 42.

formalism' and 'deconstruction is no more than a regrettable but unavoidable necessity' like 'political iconoclasm . . . inappropriately directed against legitimate authorial privilege'. Here Fowler sounds remarkably like Burke in *Prelude*, Book VII ('Exploding upstart Theory', 1850: vii. 529).[26]

The same could be said of Wordsworth, a Girondist Republican turned Tory, when it comes to literary tradition (and finally to politics too). We are back with Derrida's essay on 'The Law of Genre'—a law which Derrida ventriloquizes as follows: 'genres should not intermix. And if it should happen that they do intermix, by accident or through transgression, by mistake or through a lapse, then this should confirm, since after all, we are speaking of "mixing", the essential purity of their identity.'[27] The Vaudracour and Julia episode, in which intermixing occurs 'by accident or through transgression, by mistake or through a lapse', says in effect: let genres (classes) mix; there is no such thing as illegitimacy (the unrecognized baby), since the only law Wordsworth will recognize is the law of nature (the gradual transformation of class systems by social or literary intermixing). The baby becomes 'Nature's rebellion against monstrous law' (1850: ix. 571). But so long as the notions of authorship and identity remain intact, the law itself remains unchallenged, albeit in a naturalized form; entrusting oneself 'To Nature for a happy end of all' (ix. 604) turns out to be a futile recourse for Vaudracour and Julia. Their child can have no name, no future. '*Pater semper incertus est, sed mater certissima*' ('paternity is always uncertain, maternity is most certain', the old legal tag invoked by Freud in 'Family Romances') means that legitimacy must still be bestowed by legal process; by the father, and not the mother.[28] As necessity is the mother of invention, 'Nature' may similarly become the mother of *The Prelude*—nature, in all its 'essential' impurity. But it is only when *The Prelude* has been named by the poet's family that it becomes legitimate, a recognized and recognizable literary text. In the last resort, nature proves to be merely the common-law wife of a Wordsworth who subsequently married within the family (thereby,

[26] Ibid. 264–6.
[27] Derrida, 'The Law of Genre', p. 204.
[28] *The Complete Psychological Works of Sigmund Freud*, trans. and ed. Strachey, ix. 239 and n. For a brief political consideration of the role played by 'Nature' in the Vaudracour and Julia episode, see Chandler, *Wordsworth's Second Nature*, p. 79.

incidentally, refusing the principle of exogamy which is also the principle of intermixture). If *The Prelude* as autobiography is Romanticism's rebellion against the law of genre, it is a rebellion which ultimately turns back to the order of the past in the interests of a readable text. Engendered by the illicit mixing of aristocratic and middle-class genres—'the Epopoeia, the Historic Poem, the Tale, the Romance, the Mock-heroic, and ... the metrical Novel'[29]—*The Prelude* simultaneously defies the Law of the Father and preserves it.

But the Vaudracour and Julia episode reminds us that there is no history without error; that genre is always impure, always 'mothered' as well as fathered, and that 'lodged within the heart of the law itself, [is] a law of impurity or a principle of contamination'. Although the episode may serve to question the authority of epic as history, it stops short of questioning the law; specifically the law of its own lopping-off from *The Prelude*. The Vaudracour and Julia episode ultimately remained (in Christopher Wordsworth's sense of the term) 'anonymous', nameless like Vaudracour's child and disowned like Vaudracour himself; hence, at once unauthored and unauthorized—a mere prelude to *The Prelude* proper. But just as we can see in *The Prelude* itself the playing out of possibilities that are occluded by the silencing of Vaudracour and the death of the baby in its 'pre-text', so we can see in Derrida's elaboration of 'the law of genre' the playing out of possibilities which Wordsworth himself must occlude in the interests of installing his poem (however unprecedented) in what he calls 'Literary history': 'The genre has always in all genres been able to play the role of order's principle: resemblance, analogy, identity and difference, taxonomic classification, organization and genealogical tree, order of reason, order of reasons, sense of sense, truth of truth, natural light and sense of history'.[30] It might be argued that to appropriate *The Prelude*—a poem presumably innocent of post-structuralist literary politics—for Derridean literary theory merely repeats the proprietary gesture of Wordsworth's widow (' "THE PRELUDE" will now be perused and estimated with the feelings properly due to its preparatory character, and to the period at which it was composed').[31] Rather than simply refixing the face of genre with the face of Derrida, I would argue instead that the Vaudracour

[29] *Prose Works*, iii. 27.   [30] Derrida, 'The Law of Genre', p. 228.
[31] Wordsworth, *Memoirs of William Wordsworth*, i. 313.

and Julia episode reveals what is at stake in all such acts of appropriation, naming, or legitimation: not the genre (or even the character) of literature, but the literariness of genre, or the character of the poet. As the 'fair form' that puts a recognizable face on the page of literary history and thereby makes it readable, genre allows us to find our own faces in the text rather than experiencing that anxious dissolution of identity which is akin to not knowing our kind; or should one say, gender? In the context of *The Prelude*, this would amount to finding the author lacking either in issue or in the distinctive masculinity which aligns his poem with epic struggle rather than with the pathos of the feminized metrical tale; which is to say, it would amount to finding *The Prelude* unreadable.

CHAPTER 8

'SPLITTING THE RACE OF MAN IN TWAIN'

Prostitution, Personification, and *The Prelude*

'EVERY Jack will have his Jill.'[1] With what he calls 'This utopian and "romantic" proverb', Geoffrey Hartman begins a gnomic essay 'On the Theory of Romanticism'. An authorized gloss might run: 'Every intellectual desire will finally find its scholastic fulfilment.'[2] The role of woman (Jill) is to put man (Jack) in possession of his desire. High Romantic critical quests might be said to have been waylaid by this enchanting and discriminatory plot (also known as 'Natural Supernaturalism'); the metaphoric consummation or spousal union of masculine mind and feminine nature haunts A. O. Lovejoy's Romantic heirs, giving M. H. Abrams's shaping narrative its underlying form (that of the History of Ideas) and lingering on in Hartman's 'romantic' proverb.[3] As Gayatri Spivak has pointed out, the elision of sexual difference, or occlusion of woman, is a by-product of the Romantic master-plot.[4] Domesticated by her role in the Great (male) Tradition, Jill settles down with Jack in Dove Cottage to raise their brood of Romantic daughters; in the Romantic family, the only good daughter is a dutiful one (Dora), or a dead one (Kate—'Surprised by joy . . .').

I want to try to sketch a different Romantic plot, as well as an alternative profession for the Romantic daughter. What if the mind addressed its courtship, not to nature, but to the city (in Wordsworth's poetry, a city of dreadful art)? And what if the Romantic quester is accosted by a voice that speaks shamelessly, not from the world of the dead (*Siste viator*) but from the *demi-monde*? What if the long journey home were that of a prodigal

---

[1] G. Hartman, *The Fate of Reading and Other Essays* (Chicago and London, 1975), 277. [2] Personal communication.
[3] See M. H. Abrams, *Natural Supernaturalism* (New York, 1971).
[4] G. Spivak, 'Sex and History in *The Prelude* (1805): Books Nine to Thirteen', *Texas Studies in Literature and Language*, 23 (1981), 336.

daughter instead of the Romantic son and heir in Abrams's story? I have in mind the possibility of a prostituted and indiscriminate Romanticism, perhaps infected by the French disease. Hartman's essay asks us to make allowance 'for the seductive presence of romance motifs' in Romantic poetry, akin to the use of the *persona* in neo-classical and modern poetry.[5] My concern in this chapter is with the seductive presence of persons, or rather personifications, in Wordsworth's poetry, and with the turn towards Romance, or Spenserian allegory, which signals that seduction.[6] My argument will be not only that high Romanticism depends on the casting out of what defines its height—figurative language, and especially personification—but that the characteristic form of this figure is a Romantic woman. The fate of personification (the outcast of Romantic figuration) and of prostitution (the outcast of spousal verse) tells us how these rhetorical and figurative schemes are constituted and at what price. My example will be Mary of Buttermere in Book VII of *The Prelude*, and the girl prostitute, Ann of Oxford Street, from De Quincey's *Confessions of an English Opium-Eater*; my route will be digressive, accosted by the wandering forms of Romantic error (figured here as Milton's Spenserian allegory of Sin and Death), and I will conclude with a brief encounter with the economics of autobiography.

The Maid of Buttermere

On the face of it, sexual difference seems the most completely repressed aspect of *The Prelude*. Except for the Vaudracour and Julia episode, later excised, the theme of sexual desire is either banished to the realm of the pastoral or else thoroughly domesticated. Mary of Buttermere, to whose seduction Wordsworth alludes in Book VII, prompts the improbable pre-seduction fantasy that 'we were nursed . . . On the same mountains' (vii. 342–3)—risking Johnson's testy objection to Milton's similarly pastoral fiction in *Lycidas* ('For we were nursed upon the self-same hill', l. 23): we *know* they never drove afield together. In Book XI the same pre-Freudian view of the nursery crops up in connection with the virginal Mary Hutchinson, here named as 'Nature's inmate';

---

[5] Hartman, *The Fate of Reading*, pp. 277–8.

[6] I am indebted to Steven Knapp, *Personification and the Sublime: Milton to Coleridge* (Cambridge, Mass., and London, 1985), for suggesting the relation between allegorical romance and Romantic attitudes to personification.

'Even like this maid', Wordsworth insists, he loved nature ('nor lightly loved, | But fervently') without being enthralled by the later tyranny of the eye which he terms a 'degradation' (xi. 213, 223–6).[7] And, in Book XIII, Dorothy Wordsworth is invoked as 'Child of my parents, sister of my soul' (xiii. 211); here, as always in Romantic poetry, the motif of brother–sister love (whether overtly incestuous or not) swiftly assimilates sexual difference to narcissistic identity. No less than the maid and the wife, the sister simultaneously figures the repression of sexuality and the refusal of sexual difference. Women are all the same (as the young Wordsworth).

Romantic women routinely appear in *The Prelude* at moments when Wordsworth wants to emphasize the continuity of his mature poetic identity with an imaginary latency period, or undifferentiated sexuality, belonging to his Lake District boyhood. Far from being emblems of sexual difference, they function precisely as defences against it. Just as nature, at the opening of Book XI, interposes itself 'betwixt the heart of man | And the uneasy world—'twixt man himself . . . and his own unquiet heart' (xi. 17–19),[8] so the purified and purifying figure of woman interposes itself healingly between man and his own unquiet, pre-existing, inner division. But there is one important exception. In Book VII of *The Prelude*, what I will call the Maid of Buttermere sequence—beginning with an account of the Sadler's Wells melodrama, 'The Beauty of Buttermere', and ending approximately a hundred lines later with the words 'I quit this painful theme'—introduces a figure whose traumatic effect is to split 'the race of man | In twain' (vii. 426–7).[9] Like the beggars of London, the figure of the prostitute is almost synonymous with late eighteenth-century representations of the city. But Wordsworth's circuitous approach to the overwhelming visibility of prostitution at this period (in 1803, estimates put the number of London

[7] These lines belonged originally to drafts connected with 'Nutting', where 'Nature's inmate' presumably referred to Dorothy. See *The Prelude*, ed. de Selincourt, rev. Darbishire, p. 612.

[8] *Prel.* xi. 17–19 also belonged originally to drafts connected with 'Nutting'; see ibid. 610.

[9] See also L. Kramer, 'Gender and Sexuality in *The Prelude*: The Question of Book Seven', *ELH* 54 (1987), 619–37, for a detailed psychoanalytic reading of the Maid of Buttermere episode in relation to Wordsworth's larger repression of the theme of sexuality, and to related issues of representation figured in Book VII by the city; I am grateful to Professor Kramer for the opportunity to read his essay while working on my own.

prostitutes between 50,000 and 70,000) suggests an internal
obstacle to broaching 'this painful theme'.[10] His compulsively
digressive returns to the same point of fixation—rather as Freud, in
his essay on 'The Uncanny', relates his own involuntary return to
the red light district of an unknown city—signal one effect of that
traumatic 'splitting'; namely, repression. Or, as Blake puts it at just
about the time of Wordsworth's first encounter with London, the
Romantic family is blighted by the harlot's curse.

The most common literary form taken by the uncanny is
doubling. Mary of Buttermere raises the spectre of a theatrical
other, or dark interpretess, whose urban fall shadows her Lake
District purity. Wordsworth's brief account of 'The Maid of
Buttermere' as presented on the London stage in 1803,

> how the spoiler came, 'a bold bad man'
> To God unfaithful, children, wife, and home,
> And wooed the artless daughter of the hills,
> And wedded her, in cruel mockery
> Of love and marriage bonds.
>
> (*Prel.* vii. 323–7)[11]

introduces his 'memorial verse' on the bigamously unmarried
mother, a personal recollection of the real Mary Robinson as he
and Coleridge had met her during their walking tour of 1799 ('in
her cottage-inn | Were welcomed, and attended on by her', vii.
327–46). This tribute, he writes, 'Comes from the poet's heart, and
is her due'; it makes amends for her immodest stage career. But her
image cannot be laid so easily, rising up in the poet's path like an
unexorcized ghost when he attempts to resume his interrupted
account of the London theatre:

[10] See A. Parreaux, *Daily Life in England in the Reign of George III* (London,
1966), 122–8, 134–40. For a fuller account of prostitution in 18th-cent. London, see
F. Henriques, *Prostitution and Society* (3 vols.; London, 1963), ii. 143–91. During
the 18th cent., London was said to have twice as many prostitutes as Paris; in 1789,
the West End alone contained an estimated 30,000 prostitutes (see ibid. 144). For
literary representations of the prostitute, see also J. B. Radner, 'The Youthful
Harlot's Curse: The Prostitute as Symbol of the City in 18th-Century English
Literature', *Eighteenth Century Life*, 2 (1976), 59–63.

[11] As Kenneth R. Johnston writes, pointing out the anachronism whereby
Wordsworth introduces a play which he not only did not see in the 1790s but may
not in fact have seen later, 'Wordsworth's oddly self-implicating account of *The
Beauty of Buttermere*' seems to block his narrative and thematic progress as well: see
Wordsworth and The Recluse, pp. 160–3. For Mary Robinson, see also D. H.
Reiman, 'The Beauty of Buttermere as Fact and Romantic Symbol', *Criticism*, 26
(1984), 139–70.

> These last words uttered, to my argument
> I was returning, when—with sundry forms
> Mingled, that in the way which I must tread
> Before me stand—*thy image rose again*,
> Mary of Buttermere!

(*Prel.* vii. 347–51; my italics)

The unmarried mother comes athwart the poet like the 'unfathered vapour' of imagination in Book VI, halting him in the time of writing with the crisis of interpretative confusion which has been identified by Weiskel and others with the Romantic Sublime.[12] Here, however, an encounter with the 'unfathered' or unfathering Oedipal Sublime is replaced by an unlaid female apparition who blocks further poetic progress. The unsuccessful exorcism has to be repeated a second time in the succeeding lines ('She lives in peace ... Without contamination does she live | In quietness ... Happy are they both, | Mother and child!', vii. 351–4, 359–60)—but this time with an added sacrifice. Her new-born and unfathered child sleeps in earth ('Fearless as a lamb') in order that Mary may live on 'without contamination' as the Mary Magdalene of *The Prelude*. The infant's burial tranquillizes her unquiet life, allowing her to stand in for the purified, pre-sexual, Lake District poet (himself, one might note, the parent of an 'unfathered' child). This hushing up of the sexual drama is effected by making Mary no longer—or again not yet—a mother, still emphatically the *Maid* of Buttermere.

But the matter of sexuality cannot be laid to rest quite so easily as the babe. Or, someone, somewhere, is always getting laid. As if *The Prelude* were a Spenserian narrative in which the moment of interpretive difficulty produces an insistent doubling of allegorical persons, Duessa splits off from Una. In this theatrical city, how are we to recognize the difference between the Maid of Buttermere and a Sadler's Wells prostitute, between a Romantic woman and a painted theatrical whore?

>   foremost I am crossed
> Here by remembrance of two figures: one
> A rosy babe, who for a twelvemonth's space
> Perhaps had been of age to deal about
> Articulate prattle, child as beautiful

---

[12] See e.g. Weiskel, *The Romantic Sublime*, pp. 173–5, 200–4.

As ever sate upon a mother's knee;
The other was the parent of that babe—
But on the mother's cheek the tints were false,
A painted bloom.

(*Prel.* vii. 366–74)

In the semiotics of sexuality, 'painted bloom' is the sign of solicitation, and solicitation the sign of shamelessness; Sadler's Wells (like Drury Lane and Covent Garden, notoriously the haunt of prostitutes at the end of the eighteenth century) brings together anti-theatrical and sexual prejudices in one scene. But what about the rosy babe, who, we might note, differs in three important respects from Mary of Buttermere's dead, ungendered, new-born infant? He is alive, he is specified as male ('The lovely boy', vii. 396), and he is no longer 'infans' (i.e. he has been prattling for about a year). Not the mother ('scarcely at this time | Do I remember her', vii. 394–5) but this beautiful boy becomes the focus of Wordsworth's 'remembrance'. I want to emphasize the displacement from mother to child, since it will help to refine one common reading of the episode: namely, that it allows Wordsworth to depict himself as ultimately uncontaminated by the fall into writing or representation which London symbolizes in Book VII of *The Prelude*. And, once more, we should notice the disappearance of the mother during the decontamination process.

This mother-and-child pair, obviously parodic of the duo in the 'Blessed the infant babe' passage, implies a theory of pre-Oedipal relations previously unglimpsed in *The Prelude*—that of gathering dangerous passions from one's mother's eye; a theory, in fact, of maternal seduction. If the mother seduces, the child must be 'stopped' ('through some special privilege | *Stopped* at the growth he had', vii. 401–2; my italics), presumably lest he grow up gay as the result of a too-loving mother, like Freud's type of the homosexual artist, Leonardo da Vinci. Wordsworth fondly imagines the boy spared this fate, 'as if embalmed | By Nature',

destined to live,
To be, to have been, come, and go, a child
And nothing more, no partner in the years
That bear us forward to distress and guilt,
Pain and abasement . . .

(*Prel.* vii. 400–6)

We can glimpse here the shadow cast by an earlier family romance or incestuous primal scene. If the mother is Sin, accosting Wordsworth on his journey as she accosts Milton's Satan *en route* for chaos, then the final tendency of 'the years | That bear us forward' is not so much homosexuality as Death, Milton's name for Sin's incestuously conceived and incestuous son. Arrested development becomes the only alternative. This arrest or stoppage, it hardly needs pointing out, not only precludes growing up as distressed and guilty as the rest of us; it precludes the growth of a poet.

Like the Winander Boy in Book V, the embalmed child is arrested in a moment of indeterminacy, a pause that suspends him between mimic hootings or 'articulate prattle' on the one hand, and on the other the silent writing or reading of his own epitaph which Wordsworth characteristically undertakes at such self-reflexive moments.[13] Here a structure of address sketches the temporal relations between the two pairs (Mary of Buttermere with her nameless infant, and the painted woman with her rosy boy), installing Wordsworth himself in loving commiseration with his own future:

> he perhaps,
> *Mary*, may now have lived till he could look
> With envy on *thy* nameless babe that sleeps
> Beside the mountain chapel undisturbed.
>
> (*Prel.* vii. 409–12; my italics)

In these lines the poet in the time of writing addresses a purified Mary (the Mary of his Lake District past), just as the unembalmed, unstopped city boy might look with envy (*invidia*) on her nameless babe—a babe imagined as not only immune to time (euphemistically asleep), but immune to the division which besets all subjects, especially what has come to be known as the subject in language; hence, a babe immune to sexual division.[14] The unstopped boy occupies the same position as the guilty, autobiographically split Wordsworth who is also subject to growth; but his fall has been

[13] See Hertz, *The End of the Line*, pp. 218–19, for what he calls 'structures of minimal difference' in relation to the Winander Boy episode.

[14] The term *invidia* is Lacan's, as elaborated by R. Young, 'The Eye and Progress of his Song: A Lacanian Reading of *The Prelude*', *Oxford Literary Review*, 3 (1979), 78–98; for the connection between this passage and the 'Blessed the Infant Babe' passage in Book II, see esp. pp. 89–90.

displaced on to the forgotten mother. The reason why the mother is scarcely remembered 'at this time' is that she has been cast out—in the Kristevan terms which I will elaborate later, 'abjected'—so that Wordsworth can throw in his lot with the 'embalmed' and separate self figured by the beautiful boy. In order to save the boy, Wordsworth has to get rid of the mother.

It is not surprising, then, that the residual form taken by the mother is that of the prostitute. Cast out, she becomes (by a neat symbolic reversal) an outcast. As if possessed by its own internal momentum, the sequence digresses yet again from its theatrical context, this time to invoke the earlier journey when Wordsworth, *en route* from the Lake District to Cambridge in 1787, first heard and saw a cursing prostitute,

> for the first time in my life did hear
> The voice of woman utter blasphemy—
> Saw woman as she is to open shame
> Abandoned, and the pride of public vice.
>
> (*Prel.* vii. 417–20)

The Prelude represents the effect—or affect—as 'immense', a permanent and founding split in the autobiographical subject that is simultaneously trauma and repression:

> Full surely from the bottom of my heart
> I shuddered; but the pain was almost lost,
> Absorbed and buried in the immensity ·
> Of the effect: a barrier seemed at once
> Thrown in, that from humanity divorced
> The human form, splitting the race of man
> In twain, yet leaving the same outward shape.
>
> (*Prel.* vii. 421–7)

A pain 'absorbed . . . in the immensity | Of the effect' sounds remarkably like the pain of castration anxiety before naked female sexuality as Freud describes it—in his account, a pain buried by the immense effects of fetishism. Even as sexual difference is recognized, it is denied or disavowed by means of a defensive 'splitting' (what might be termed the both/and defence).[15] The barrier permits a

---

[15] See S. Freud, 'Fetishism' (1927): 'what happened [in the case of the fetishist] . . . was that the boy refused to take cognizance of the fact of his having perceived that a woman does not possess a penis . . . It is not true that, after the child has made

'divorce' which paradoxically allows the subject not to confront difference structured as division or as equally unacceptable alternatives (the either/or trauma). Characteristically, the fetishist clings to a representation associated with the last moment before his sight of the apparently castrated mother. Here that representation is 'the human form', or rather, 'man'—the ostensibly undifferentiated (male) body which serves as the measure of Romantic humanism while serving also to deny sexual difference.

Splitting becomes the means to defend an imaginary bodily integrity, warding off castration anxiety by means of the fantasy of organic wholeness with which Romantic humanism is invested, whether its subject is man or simply his imagination. In the context of Book VII of *The Prelude*, the book of representations, the painted or fallen woman becomes an emblem of representation itself, allowing Wordsworth to cling to the (here perilously sustained) fiction of a self that is not the subject of, or in, representation (and hence inevitably split). 'The overthrow | Of her soul's beauty' (vii. 432–3)—we might note that Wordsworth's soul is regularly feminized in *The Prelude*—is the ostensible trade-off for Wordsworth's immunity to division; but the female body is the actual price paid, since the overthrow of the prostitute's soul means the throwing over of her body. In other words, the passage allows us to see how the fetishistic compromise works for men (splitting keeps them whole), but only, and contradictorily, at the expense of women (splitting creates the division fallen/unfallen, and thus institutes a denigrated class). Once this compromise between incompatible ideas has been effected, Wordsworth can move on from the 'Distress of mind [that] ensued upon this sight' (vii. 428) to a more manageable 'milder sadness'. 'In truth', he writes, 'The sorrow of the passion *stopped* me here' (vii. 434–5; my italics). This stoppage is so effective that Wordsworth can finally 'quit this painful theme' (vii. 436)—shut his eyes to division—and return to his account of the London stage. 'Stopped' is the same word used of the beautiful boy's arrest ('through some special privilege | Stopped at the growth he had', vii. 401–2). It halts Wordsworth by returning him in fantasy to the moment before the distressing and

his observation of the woman, he has preserved unaltered his belief that women have a phallus. He has retained that belief, but he has also given it up. In the conflict between the weight of the unwelcome perception and the force of his counter-wish, a compromise has been reached . . .', *The Complete Psychological Works of Sigmund Freud*, trans. and ed. J. Strachey, xxi. 153–4.

anxiety-inducing sight of sexual difference. We should also notice that Wordsworth's insistance on the child being father to the man (the *post hoc ergo propter hoc* recipe for embalming infants) allows him to adopt the myth of nature as Romantic Mother without ever confronting maternal desire, whether the mother's for and in him, or his own for the mother. To call sexual difference the most completely repressed aspect of *The Prelude* amounts to saying that it is put a stop to, whether by the fiction of Natural Supernaturalism, or by systematic domestication, or, as here in Book VII, by being cast out in the figure of the prostitute.

Sexual Difference and 'My Single Self'

At this point, a digression by way of Wordsworth's Cambridge education permits an alternative approach to the question of sexual difference. I want to propose Milton as the obvious candidate for homo-erotic influence on, or in, *The Prelude*. Wordsworth represents Cambridge as an extension of his imaginary Lake District latency period ('Hushed meanwhile | Was the under-soul, locked up in such a calm . . .', iii. 539–40). Full term becomes a 'deep vacation', or period of prolonged unisex play with former alumni who were later destined for literature ('The nurslings of the Muses', iii. 473); Wordsworth calls sweet Spenser (the Muses' erstwhile 'Page of State', iii. 280) his brother, and in imagination bounds along in the footsteps of a stripling Milton—'A boy, no better, with his rosy cheeks | Angelical' (iii. 291–2). Successfully embalmed, the rosy babe of Book VII might have turned into this rosy-cheeked cherub, with his 'conscious step of purity and pride' (iii. 293). There were, of course, possibilities for what *The Prelude* calls 'dissolute pleasure' (iii. 535) in late eighteenth-century Cambridge as well as in London—possibilities only glimpsed in Christopher Wordsworth's *Social Life at the English Universities in the Eighteenth Century* (1874),[16] but surfacing in Coleridge's confused

[16] See e.g. Christopher Wordsworth on university 'Toasts' at Cambridge and Oxford, in *Social Life at the English Universities in the Eighteenth Century* (Cambridge, 1874), 363, 367–73, 397. 'Toasts' (like 'Beauties') were often the daughters of university tradesmen rather than open prostitutes; while Christopher Wordsworth documents the drinking habits of 18th-cent. undergraduates, he represses the question of sexuality outside imprudently contracted marriages. For prostitution at Oxford—a well-established problem for the university authorities in the mid-19th cent.—see A. J. Engel, ' "Immoral Intentions": The University of Oxford and the Problem of Prostitution, 1827–1914', *Victorian Studies*, 3 (1979), 79–107.

nightmare of 'a university Harlot' ('out rushes a university Harlot, who insists on my going with her . . . The Harlot in white with her open Bosom certainly was the Cambridge Girl [Sal Hall]').[17] Wordsworth's desires, however, seem to have been as sublimated as those of 'the Lady of Christ's', or, rather, they seem to have taken the form of that Miltonic strength-in-singleness embodied by the 'blind poet, who, in his later day | Stood almost single, uttering odious truth' (iii. 284–5). (One such odious truth, we might recall, was Milton's advocacy of divorce when spousal union failed or when, as in *Paradise Lost*, woman fell.)

Wordsworthian desire for singleness is figured in his Book III account of Cambridge by the wish to be a uniquely favoured or 'chosen' son: 'my single self', Wordsworth recalls, was 'bred up in Nature's lap, was even | As a spoiled child' (iii. 356–9). Associated at the outset with the autobiographical theme of *The Prelude* ('A theme | Single and of determined bounds', i. 668–9), the term 'single' becomes synonymous with inner life or 'what passed within me', and with the interiority privileged by spiritual autobiography ('Not of outward things . . . —words, signs, | Symbols or actions— but of my own heart | Have I been speaking', iii. 174–7). This secret, silent breathing-place of 'incommunicable powers' ('far hidden from the reach of words', iii. 185) abuts on the point of embattled solitude where the blind Milton 'Stood almost single, uttering odious truth' (iii. 285). The assertion that 'Points have we all of us within our souls | Where all stand single' (iii. 186–7) is an affirmation of the Miltonic strength which lies both in silence and in unpopular utterance, or utterance that falls on deaf ears. (The fallen woman, by contrast, announces herself all too loudly by 'utter[ing] blasphemy', as if all female public utterance was an obscenity and should be hushed up.) The *locus classicus* for the depiction of a fall from and recovery of this singling, God-given, and above all masculine strength-in-silence is *Samson Agonistes*, which Romantic poets, including Wordsworth, tended to read as Milton's spiritual autobiography. Wordsworth's allusions to *Samson Agonistes* in Book VII have been exhaustively and fruitfully studied in *Prelude* criticism.[18] But with the assistance of a recent essay by

[17] *The Notebooks of Samuel Taylor Coleridge*, ed. K. Coburn (3 vols.; London, 1957–73), i. 1726.
[18] See e.g. Chase, 'The Ring of Gyges and the Coat of Darkness: Reading Rousseau with Wordsworth', *Decomposing Figures: Rhetorical Readings in the Romantic Tradition*, pp. 32–64.

Jim Swan, 'Difference and Silence: John Milton and the Question of Gender', I want to sketch an alternative reading of the relations between the two, one potentially able to illuminate the relation between masculine creativity, silence, and sexual difference. Since, as Swan emphasizes, Milton is above all the poet who 'bestowed on us a vision of solitary male creativity that dominated English literary culture for centuries',[19] Samson's 'case' as chosen son may be especially instructive for the case of Wordsworth, the spoiled brat of *The Prelude*.

Close readers of Book VII will recall that Wordsworth quotes *Samson Agonistes* four lines before the start of the Maid of Buttermere sequence, in the motley company of Jack the Giant-killer, whose coat of darkness hides him 'safe as is the moon | "Hid in her vacant interlunar cave" ' (vii. 306–7). Although the quotation is facetious, it is far from innocent. The thematic link between the London stage and the Maid of Buttermere lies, presumably, in the implicit contrast between the shameless immodesty of the theatre and the modest trust of the maid.[20] In a 'Delusion bold' like that of John Hatfield's audacious seduction of Mary, the actor wears the word 'INVISIBLE' on his chest. Read for its rhetorical rather than thematic bearing on *The Prelude*, *Samson Agonistes* might be thought of as confronting Wordsworth (like the Blind London Beggar's label elsewhere in Book VII) with 'the utmost that we know'—with the limits of poetic possibility or the (im)possibility of meaning; that is, with a de Manian view of poetry's privative muting of language or voice (a privation figured as blindness in Milton's poem).[21] Equally, *Samson Agonistes* might be read as figuring the sublimity of Miltonic blindness; here the issue is not so much privation as legibility. Wordsworth's eyes are 'smitten with the view' of the blind beggar, echoing Samson's boast that his blind strength 'with amaze shall strike all who behold' (*Samson Agonistes*, l. 1645), as if obliterating the spectacle of urban chaos. When Samson assaults the pillars 'As with the force of winds and waters pent' (l. 1647), the sublime convulsion washes into *The Prelude*, making Wordsworth's mind 'turn round | As with the might of waters' (vii. 616–17). Just as Samson's terminal

---

[19] J. Swan, 'Difference and Silence: John Milton and the Question of Gender', in S. N. Garner, C. Kahane, and M. Sprengnether (eds.), *The (M)other Tongue: Essays in Feminist Psychoanalytic Interpretation* (Ithaca, NY, and London, 1985), 144.

[20] 'Faith must needs be coy', *Prel.* vii. 308.

[21] See Cynthia Chase's reading in *Decomposing Figures*, pp. 58–62.

violence could be read as a consoling fiction of performative language (like his glorious deeds, which 'though mute, spoke loud the doer') in the face of Milton's actual powerlessness to gain a hearing, so the Beggar (in this reading) serves the defensive function of substituting reading for unreadability. The (bare) legibility of 'The story of the man, and who he was' takes the place of 'an unmanageable sight' (vii. 615, 709), much as Wordsworth substitutes the autobiography of a discrete, single self for 'differences | That have no law, no meaning, and no end' (vii. 704–5).[22] Read not as Milton's autobiography but as a reading of autobiography itself, *Samson Agonistes* is an indispensable subtext for reading Book VII of *The Prelude*.

But what of sexual difference? Swan is alone in pointing out that Samson's blindness results specifically from his seduction—from succumbing to a femininity that is figured as speech. It is this emphasis which I want to pursue in relation to Book VII of *The Prelude*: Samson's self-betrayal, writes Swan, is of 'a silence which is also a secret—or rather, *the* secret of the self'; his fall 'implies that the encounter with sexual difference is somehow connected with the transformation of silence into speech'.[23] Swan's reading of *Samson Agonistes* goes something like this: the repeated references to Samson's secret are a displacement of Milton's own anxiety about prying into, and blasphemously publishing, sacred truths (Marvell's ironic encomium on *Paradise Lost*, Swan notes, specifically compares Milton to Samson, ruining the temple 'to revenge his sight'). Samson's crime is also publication: 'I God's counsel have not kept, his holy secret | Presumptuously have published' (ll. 497–8). Once Samson betrays the secret of his strength (which is silence), he suffers a fall into language, becoming effeminate, like Dalila, who overwhelms him with words—the talking woman, as usual, serving as a misogynist trope. By his own account, Samson 'for a word, a tear . . . divulged the secret gift of God | To a deceitful woman' and 'vanquished with a peal of words (O weakness!) | Gave up my fort of silence to a woman' (ll. 200–2,

---

[22] Cf. Neil Hertz's reading for the discrimination between seeing and reading: 'The encounter with the Beggar triangulates the poet's self in relation to his double, who is represented . . . as an emblem of minimal difference fixed in relation to itself. The power of the emblem is that it reestablishes boundaries between representor and represented and . . . keeps the poet-impresario from tumbling into his text', *The End of the Line*, p. 60.

[23] Garner, Kahane, and Sprengnether (eds.), *The (M)other Tongue*, p. 144.

235–6). But even before his enslavement by the Philistines, he declares, 'foul effeminacy held [him] yoked | Her bond-slave' (ll. 410–11). When Dalila tells Samson during their ritual exchange of ex-marital accusations and counter-accusations, 'To what I did thou show'dst me first the way', Samson concedes her point: 'I led the way; bitter reproach, but true' (ll. 781, 823). It is not just that *Samson Agonistes* equates orality and sexual intercourse as sources of infection by treacherous femininity; rather, Samson is seen by himself as already self-betrayed, feminized by an internal weakness. As he puts it, 'I to myself was false ere thou to me' (l. 824).

Swan's essay casts the problem of masculine psychosexual identity in Chodorowian terms. In this scheme, the child's first identification is with the mother. Whereas, 'in maturity, women look back to an origin of identity with one who is the same . . . men look back to an identity with one who is different'. In order to distinguish themselves from the mother, men, 'more than women, will feel compelled to assert an identity separate and distinct from others'—compelled, that is, by their original self-division to make a stronger, more insistent assertion of distinct and separate identity. There is thus a fundamental asymmetry in the way men and women experience their assumption of (gender) identity.[24] In *Samson Agonistes*, Swan argues, Milton represents individuality both as nostalgia for primal unity with the mother prior to being singled out (as neither/nor), and as the agonistic separation or division (either/or) that comes later. The boy-child's sense of not being fully separate from the mother, yet not at one with her either, structures Samson's struggle 'to reassert his identity as the one man singled out by God for heroic action'.[25] Sexual difference becomes a figure for, or displacement of, issues involving 'strong' or 'single' masculine poetic identity because the terms 'masculine' and 'feminine'—even though an arbitrary set of markers—allow for the assertion of a fixed difference (either/or). By contrast, the temporally prior neither/nor structure of undifferentiated wholeness can only be represented as the muteness and absence of the maternal moon,

---

[24] Ibid. 160. Cf. also ibid. 160 n. for Chodorow's formulation of the problem of gender identity: 'Underlying, or built into, core male gender identity is an early, nonverbal, unconscious, almost somatic sense of femaleness that continually . . . challenges and undermines the sense of maleness', N. Chodorow, 'Feminism and Difference: Gender, Relation, and Difference in Psychoanalytic Perspective', *Socialist Review*, 46 (1979), 63.

[25] Garner, Kahane, and Sprengnether (eds.), *The (M)other Tongue*, p. 158.

hid in her vacant interlunar cave, or, alternatively, as Samson's lost secret of silence—the secret that is his divinely appointed rather than self-published strength.[26]

Thus, Swan argues, the arrival of a woman on the scene demands that Milton/Samson assume a single, distinct identity figured conveniently in terms of gender identity, or strong manhood. For Swan, one might add, Renaissance representations of woman have less to do with the relation between unity and division (Una and Duessa) than with the problem of representing 'the double and divided *subject*, who suffers a fall into language'.[27] I want, however, to suggest a slightly different way of formulating questions relating to the subject and to language. Following Chodorow, Swan apparently assumes both that boys somehow always will be boys, and that the constitution of identity differs for boys and girls (girls 'naturally' identify with their mothers, while boys undergo an identity crisis). The question of identification is naturalized and elided with the process by which the constitution of gender identity takes place; the radical separation involved in the constitution of gender identity for *all* subjects is therefore played down. Kristeva's theory of the emergence of the pre-Oedipal subject has the advantage (in this instance at any rate) of avoiding the assumptions implicit in the Chodorowian paradigm. That is, Kristeva neither begs the psychoanalytic question of the constitution of the (for Chodorow, already) gendered subject, nor does she distinguish between the process which constitutes masculine and feminine subjects in terms of an inevitable same-sex identification (feminine) vs. different sex origin (masculine). One reason for this difference in emphasis lies in the fact that while Kristeva may seem to favour the pre-Oedipal, it is a pre-Oedipal structured from the outset by a third term, the father. A Kristevan account of the pre-Oedipal also reveals, as Swan's does not, why the process demands not only differentiation, but a maternal scapegoat.

Kristeva posits the earliest emergence of the pre-Oedipal subject

---

[26] Swan at this point is brought to question Chodorow's object-relations-derived account by way of Juliet Mitchell's more Lacanian position. His own footnoted formulation runs as follows: 'At the primitive, originative core of identity is not femaleness or maleness but an undifferentiated wholeness that is neither. Most discussions of this issue that are based entirely on object relations theory tend to view the beginning of gender as both/and, both masculine *and* feminine. But that comes later as a reading of difference back upon a moment that is *neither/nor*', ibid. 162 n.   [27] Ibid. 168.

in terms of an archaic, always present split, the minute gap existing between the mother (not yet a subject in the full sense) on which depends the process she calls 'abjection'. This split Kristeva sees as demarcating an archaic paternal space, or imaginary father. Collusively, the child comes to identify, not with the mother, but with this gap or *vide*—even if it is only the mother's imaginary desire for something other than her child (Lacan would call it the phallus). The emergent, not-yet-subject is constituted by the primal narcissism of identification with the mother's images, with the Imaginary, or the Other (the place of the imaginary father); by means of this narcissistic crisis, it becomes a subject of and in signification—in Lacanian terms, the subject is enabled finally to take up a position, via the Imaginary, in the Symbolic realm. A necessary by-product of the process of abjection is the 'abjecting' of the mother, or of what symbolically blurs the boundaries of the emergent, still archaic self, threatening to collapse it back into an indifferentiated maternal origin.[28] How would this scheme work in Milton's *Samson Agonistes* and Wordsworth's *Prelude*? If language in *Samson Agonistes* is what assaults the boundaries of single self ('my fort of silence'), then words themselves—which, as we have seen, are associated with weakness and with the talking woman— must be cast out; we might note in passing that by the end of the poem non-verbal noise has been appropriated for the strong man. Samson's final identification, then, is not with the pre-Oedipal silence and absence of the moon (with what can be imagined as a pre-linguistic era preceding the Symbolic or paternal realm, the mother's cave-like *chora*); it is with the archaic space of the paternal Logos, or sun—with God the Father, whose originating divine act (his Word) provides the ground for Samson's and Milton's fantasy of speaking deeds or the language of presence ('deeds which spoke loud the doer'). The presence of God in Samson's act is what makes the actor able to declare himself without loss of strength.

It is in this sense only—a sense predicted on the myth of an originating but unuttered or unutterable paternal Word—that we

---

[28] For Julia Kristeva's theory of maternal 'abjection', see *Powers of Horror: An Essay on Abjection*, trans. L. S. Roudiez (New York, 1982), esp. pp. 1–18, 32–55 *passim*, and the further elaboration in 'Freud and Love: Treatment and its Discontents' (originally published as 'L'abjet d'amour'), *The Kristeva Reader*, ed. T. Moi (New York, 1986), 238–71. See also Neil Hertz's brief but helpful discussion in *The End of the Line*, pp. 231–3.

would be justified in alluding to a 'fall into language'. Positing such
a fall involves entering into Samson's and Milton's interpretive
collusion, their fantasy of language as feminine, enfeebled by its
divorce from the power and presence of God. *Samson Agonistes*
pits feminine chatter or weakness against language as performance,
which is either the secret of Samson's silence or the thunderous
utterance of his strength. If, in Book VII of *The Prelude*, London
means nothing less than the necessity of becoming a subject of, and
in, signification—a process which involves both producing and
being produced by the split between sign and thing, or the temporal
and significatory difference between words and what they name—
then the bandage for that wound of problematic identification-in-
and-as-division is Wordsworth's 'abjection' of the city itself.
Located as the source of the production and reproduction of signs,
the city is like a woman whose soul has been overthrown, or a man
who has been feminized by publishing his secret. By associating
London with the blasphemy (words out of place, just as dirt may be
called matter out of place), 'painted bloom', and 'open shame' of
the prostitute, Wordsworth taints the city with the ambiguity which
threatens the constitution of the (masculine) single self, while
purifying his own utterance. Besides throwing light on the question
of poetic identity, and on the constitution of the signifying subject
(the growth of the poet), Kristeva's theory of abjection thus helps to
explain the function of the prostitute in Book VII of *The Prelude*,
and in particular to clarify her relation to the city as simultaneously
a representation and a casting out of the fallenness of poetry or
language itself.

Later in Book VII, 'The feeble salutation from the voice | Of some
unhappy woman' (vii. 639–40) haunts an imaginary emptying out
and silencing of the London scene during a night-piece whose
effect, like that of Wordsworth's 'Sonnet Composed Upon West-
minster Bridge', is to assimilate the city to natural archetypes; or
rather, to impose on it the arrested sleep of death. In Milton's
allegory, Death is the child of Sin, born incestuously of a difference
that is insufficiently different, and giving birth to the error of
endlessly multiplying repetition which forever returns to its origin
in the womb of the mother. By making the solitary woman accost
him—by arresting her, so to speak, as solitary women on the streets
of eighteenth-century London were regularly arrested for loitering
with intent—Wordsworth casts out the dangerous possibility of

being himself mistaken for a nocturnal loiterer, or fallen woman. He too, after all, was the product of a late eighteenth-century sociological drift from country to city that turned him (like Poor Susan) into a Lake District outcast from his father's house. But Wordsworth also makes the prostitute prefigure all that is soul-destroying about the 'unmanageable sight' of the city, for which Bartholomew Fair is the culminating type, with its blank confusion and unnatural, man-made ('Promethean') freaks. Casting out woman as prostitute, the form that 'split[s] the human race | In twain' protects Wordsworth himself from division by projecting the split as sexually differentiated; two voices are there—the voice of the fallen (woman) and the voice of the chosen (son). The gap or 'barrier' created by Wordsworth's first sight of a prostitute effects a saving 'divorce' between his soul and the body of representation; between Wordsworthian poetic identity and the figures or signs that constitute him as a poet. Or, to put it another way, prostitution in *The Prelude* screens the process by which the Romantic poet separates himself from the natural unity he purports to espouse, in order to permit an illicit intercourse with the painted bloom of Sin and the self-spawning reproductive capacities of Death. In this version of the Miltonic allegory, for Sin read 'figurative language', and for Death read 'writing', or the unnatural multiplication of signs figured by and in the city.[29]

Autobiography and the Prodigal Daughter

De Quincey's *Confessions of an English Opium-Eater* opens with an apology to the reader 'for breaking through that delicate and honourable reserve, which, for the most part, restrains us from the public exposure of our own errors and infirmities'. English feelings, De Quincey continues, are revolted by the spectacle 'of a human being obtruding on our notice his moral ulcers or scars, and tearing away that "decent drapery" ' by which they should be concealed.[30] Consequently, most English confessions proceed from those whose

[29] As Catherine Gallagher has pointed out, prostitution is a common metaphor for 'one of the ancient models of linguistic production: the unnatural multiplication of interchangeable signs: see 'George Eliot and *Daniel Deronda*: The Prostitute and the Jewish Question', in R. B. Yeazell (ed.), *Sex, Politics, and Science in the Nineteenth-Century Novel. Selected Papers from the English Institute* (Baltimore and London, 1986), 41.

[30] De Quincey, *Confessions of an English Opium-Eater*, ed. Lindop, p. 1.

status is socially ambiguous or deviant—from 'demireps, adventurers, or swindlers'. This is not the case, he observes, in French literature, where decent and self-respecting citizens may perform 'acts of gratuitous self-humiliation' that are confined in England to the criminal classes. Autobiography is the French disease, the immodest exhibition of moral ulcers which taints literature with 'the spurious and defective sensibility of the French', i.e. the feminine and demi-reputable sensibility of a Jean-Jacques Rousseau. De Quincey identifies confession not only with the 'demirep' or prostitute, but with the effeminate foreignness that infects his own 'English' confessions from within, much as femininity (the weakness of self-betrayal or self-publication) infects Samson. Or, as de Man puts it apropos of Rousseau, excuses are catching; there can never be enough of them to keep up with the infection of rhetorical effects.[31] Autobiography, in a word, is sick, and of itself.

De Quincey's self-advertised 'guilt and misery' are terms commonly applied to the fallen woman ('Let other pens dwell on guilt and misery', Jane Austen begins the last chapter of *Mansfield Park*, alluding there to the fall of Maria Rushworth). In the *Confessions*, the sister-double with whom De Quincey can never be reunited except in opium visions or death is the fifteen-year-old prostitute, Ann of Oxford Street. Hers are the extenuating circumstances which Mary Wollstonecraft had pleaded in *A Vindication of The Rights of Woman* (1791): 'many innocent girls . . . are, as it may emphatically be termed, *ruined* before they know the difference between virtue and vice . . . prostitution becomes [their] only refuge.'[32] Ruined before she knows (the) difference, Ann stands in for the young De Quincey, who traces his route to opium addiction back to his own weeks as a starving and destitute adolescent streetwalker. 'Being myself at that time of necessity a peripatetic, or a walker of the streets', he recalls, 'I naturally fell in more frequently with those female peripatetics who are technically called Street walkers.' Ann's peripatetic wanderings—a harlot's progress or quest of error—images the deviance of De Quincey's later addiction But the metaphor of the prostitute's wandering toward dissolution and death ('the central darkness of a London brothel, or . . . the

[31] See P. de Man, 'Excuses (*Confessions*)', *Allegories of Reading: Figural Language in Rousseau, Nietzsche, Rilke, and Proust* (New Haven, 1979), 278–301.
[32] M. Wollstonecraft, *A Vindication of the Rights of Woman*, ed. M. Kramnick (Harmondsworth, 1975), 165.

darkness of the grave',[33] stands for more than opium addiction. Ann's wanderings on the London streets and De Quincey's never-ending quest for her become a metaphor for his own attempt to recover the past through memory. The retrospective and confessional movement of autobiography is De Quincey's primary addiction, which is also the compulsion of autobiography to repeat.

By some oversight, De Quincey has either never enquired or forgotten Ann's surname, and he calls his inability to trace her his 'heaviest affliction'. Like his opium habit, his quest for Ann in the labyrinthine streets of London can never attain its imaginary goal, reunion with a lost self; though 'perhaps even within a few feet of each other' they are divided by 'a barrier . . . amounting in the end to a separation for eternity!'[34] Eternal separation severs empirical being-in-the-world from purgatorial being-in-the-text. This is the writerly fate to which De Quincey is perpetually condemned. In his dealings with the money-lenders, for instance, he finds it difficult to establish his credit-worthiness—his credibility—until he produces letters addressed to him as proof of his identity: 'It was strange to me', writes De Quincey, 'to find my own self, *materialiter* considered . . . accused, or at least suspected, of counterfeiting my own self, *formaliter* considered.' Here De Quincey, alert to his own legal usage, is '(to use a forensic word) *soliciting*' (his italics).[35] He solicits money on the basis of his name and his patrimony; Ann solicits money on the basis of her body, but—a significant difference—at the price of losing her paternal name ('It is a general practice . . . with girls of humble rank in her unhappy condition . . . to style themselves . . . simply by their Christian names, *Mary, Jane, Frances*, &c.').[36] By commodifying her sexuality (entering the oldest profession), she also loses the means to purchase a new surname in exchange for an old one; the marriage market—the realm of 'social' (re)production—is barred to her as a fallen woman. Ann becomes the non-exchangeable outcast of patriarchal economics by selling herself; De Quincey commodifies his identity by pawning it to the brokers. Both enter the capitalist and mercantile system symbolized by the city at the price of alienation from their fantasized origins (the Romantic family) and loss of imaginary unity between 'material' self (body) and 'formal'

---

[33] *Confessions of an English Opium-Eater*, ed. Lindop, pp. 20, 22.
[34] Ibid. 34.   [35] Ibid. 25, 23.   [36] Ibid. 27.

self (name of the father); hence De Quincey's initial, self-confessed identification with 'demireps, adventurers, or swindlers'.

The crime to which the subject-in-writing must confess is the one that debars her or him from natural identity or guaranteed wholeness; what she or he has for sale is signs, or a signature. The loss of integrity between body and name, or this splitting of imaginary self-identity, might also be seen as a metaphor for authorship. As Catherine Gallagher has argued apropos of George Eliot, both prostitution and usury—another form of unnatural reproduction—come increasingly to be identified with authorship in the nineteenth century; during the Victorian period, she writes, 'The activities of authoring, of procuring illegitimate income, and of alienating one's self through prostitution seem particularly associated with one another.'[37] Late eighteenth- and early nineteenth-century changes in the legal and economic status of the author—the emergence of copyright law, the growth of a popular readership, increasing dependence on the market-place—brought the legally commodified text into being, along with the modern notion of authorship ('*formaliter* considered', in De Quincey's phrase). In a displaced fashion, De Quincey's financial dealings with the money-lender figure the self-sale by the commodifier of a 'confessional' autobiography whose very saleability requires the guarantee of authenticity, or legal identity. This may, indeed, be the reason why De Quincey prefers to think of Ann 'as one long since laid in the grave . . . of a Magdalen; taken away, before injuries and cruelty had blotted out and transfigured her ingenuous nature.'[38] Like the beautiful boy embalmed in *The Prelude*, she is laid in her grave in order to save the author from a fate worse than death, that of the fallen writer—self-sold, self-divided, and self-seduced into the error of confessional, demi-reputable autobiography.

De Quincey's *Confessions* end with a vision of his reunion with Ann in the tranquillity of a Judaean Easter Sunday. The religious landscape of this culminating vision merges the garden of resurrection with the Lake District landscape that is now De Quincey's home. Wordsworth's Poor Susan looks longingly northward to 'a single small cottage, a nest like a dove's', to which she is urged 'Poor outcast! return' ('to receive thee once more | The house of thy

---

[37] Gallagher in *Sex, Politics, and Science in the Nineteenth-Century Novel*, p. 43.
[38] *Confessions of an English Opium-Eater*, ed. Lindop, p. 34.

Father will open its door', ll. 17–18).[39] In De Quincey's *Confessions*, Oxford Street—the scene of his wanderings with Ann—is both the scene of his first opium purchase and the road to the north which leads to the Lake District, to Dove Cottage, and to Wordsworth: 'oftentimes on moonlight nights . . . my consolation was . . . to gaze from Oxford-street up every avenue in succession . . . for *that*, said I, travelling with my eyes up the long vistas . . . "*that* is the road to the North," and therefore to [Grasmere], and if I had the wings of a dove, *that* way I would fly for comfort.'[40] Ann's place at his side is later taken by Peggy Simpson, the Lake District girl whom De Quincey seduced but married, and whom at the time of writing— significantly, he has had to return to the city in order to meet his obligations to the *London Magazine*—he imagines 'sitting alone in that same valley, and mistress of that very house [Dove Cottage] to which my heart turned in its blindness, nineteen years ago'. What he calls 'the impotent wishes of childhood' surface again in the refrain-like motif of his desire for an always distant, always lost maternal comfort: 'Oh, that I had the wings of a dove . . . and *that* way I would fly for comfort.'[41] In De Quincey's version of the long journey homeward, the present can only repeat the fixations of the past. His demonic parody of Wordsworthian domesticity turns Dove Cottage itself into the scene of the *Oresteia*, with Dorothy Wordsworth's part taken by Peggy-as-Electra, witness to the furious pains of opium which now possess him. The wages of sin are the deaths of infant children, orchestrated by sighs of farewell 'such as the caves of hell sighed when the incestuous mother uttered the abhorred name of death'.[42] In De Quincey's incestuous family romance, it goes without saying, these sibling deaths are desired (as perhaps even Kate Wordsworth's death was desired) so that the mother may be more certainly and uniquely possessed.

[39] As Lamb observed mischievously, 'The last verse of Susan . . . threw a kind of dubeity upon Susan's moral conduct. Susan is a maid servant. I see her trundling her mop and contemplating the whirling phenomenon thro' blurred optics; but to term her a poor outcast seems as much as to say that poor Susan was no better than she should be, which I trust was not what you meant to express', *The Letters of Charles and Mary Anne Lamb*, ed. Marrs, iii. 147. For an interesting argument relating to Poor Susan and her outcast status, see P. J. Manning, 'Placing Poor Susan: Wordsworth and the New Historicism', *SiR* 25 (1986), 351–69. See also D. Simpson, 'What Bothered Charles Lamb About Poor Susan?', *SEL* 26 (1986), 589–612.

[40] *Confessions of an English Opium-Eater*, ed. Lindop, p. 35.

[41] Ibid. 36–7.

[42] Ibid. 77.

Signs of absence or 'everlasting farewells!' signal the central darkness or lack at the core of being. Facelessness—the sign of lost identity—figures the dispersal of self as an undifferentiated London crowd. Like Wordsworth in Book VII of *The Prelude*, unable to read the faces of the city streets ('The face of every one | That passes by me is a mystery', vii. 597–8), or violently confronted by the minimal characters of a blind man's label, De Quincey experiences the autobiographical text itself as a lawless, meaningless multiplication of difference—as textuality without a face. Hence his attempt to anchor the wanderings of self-loss by fixing identity on the (ever-to-be) recovered face of Ann: 'I suppose that, in the literal and unrhetorical use of the word *myriad*, I may say that on my different visits to London, I have looked into many, many myriads of female faces, in the hope of meeting her.'[43] 'The tyranny of the human face'—a legacy of this obsessive self-reading—becomes one of the pains of opium as De Quincey's addiction enters its demonic phase. The infinitely agitated characters of the addictive sublime ('the sea appeared paved with innumerable faces, upturned to the heavens: faces, imploring, wrathful, despairing, surged upwards by thousands, by myriads, by generations, by centuries')[44] represent death by self-multiplication, or death by signs. Ann's face never surfaces from the apocalyptic flood to render De Quincey's identity 'literal and unrhetorical' (that is, non-figurative) with the illusion of a stabilizing, specular reflection.

This fixing of an illusory or 'literal' identity was to be Wordsworth's function, as De Quincey describes it in his *Recollections of the Lakes and the Lake Poets*. The long-delayed meeting with Wordsworth at Dove Cottage in 1807 brings De Quincey 'face to face' with 'that man whom, of all the men from the beginning of time, [he] most fervently desired to see', and their confrontation is the autobiographical climax of his essay on Wordsworth.[45] The meeting is momentous not only because it signifies the return of the prodigal to the house of his father, but because it permits a powerful, specular, assertion of identity. De Quincey believes that his resemblance to Wordsworth lies in the singular defect they share, 'namely . . . a peculiar embarrassment and penury of words'. This singular defect is swiftly redefined as a distinction, 'a most

[43] *Confession of an English Opium-Eater*, p. 34.
[44] Ibid. 72.
[45] *Recollections of the Lakes and the Lake Poets*, ed. Wright, p. 127.

distinguished talent "pour le silence" '.[46] Hard up for words, De
Quincey needs a literary identity card; he finds it not only in his
resemblance to Wordsworth, but in the filial relationship which
permits his return to the bosom of the Romantic family. The
question of resemblance turns out to be crucial to De Quincey in a
number of ways. His memoir is curiously, disproportionately
concerned not so much with their shared defect of silence, but with
Wordsworth's defective physique ('it impressed a spectator with a
sense of absolute meanness, more especially when viewed from
behind, and not counteracted by his countenance'). Not Wordsworth's physique but Wordsworth's face ('one which would have
made amends for greater defects of figure')[47] becomes the talisman
of his greatness and, by extension, the guarantee or reflection of De
Quincey's own identity—as if 'face' could be detached from 'figure'
to become an emblem of poetic greatness, or rather, a figure for it,
like the head of a poet fronting his Poetical Works.

Wordsworth's face, De Quincey asserts, is a national face, that of
an Englishman (long rather than round). No one could mistake him
for a round-faced Frenchman; the defect of *his* sensibility is
strength-in-silence, not Rousseau's confession of feminine weakness. Forehead, eyes, nose, mouth (especially mouth)—the catalogue
builds up an identikit portrait. But the portrait is not, as it turns
out, of Wordsworth. Milton's is the poetic face or front, De
Quincey insists, which resembles Wordsworth's even more closely
than the Carruthers portrait of 1817.[48] Richardson's laurel-
crowned engraving, the frontispiece to De Quincey's long-sought
edition of *Paradise Lost*, confronts him with a shock of recognition
which he ventriloquizes by a dramatic rehearsal of Richardson's
anecdote about Milton's last surviving daughter, who, when she
saw the Richardson portrait, 'burst out into a rapture of passionate
recognition; exclaiming—"This is my father! this is my dear
father!" '.[49] In Wordsworth's face, De Quincey finds himself as
prodigal daughter; it was, after all, the poet's infant daughter,
Kate, with whom De Quincey most deeply identified, and it was
Kate's premature death which unleashed his mourning for the
original self-loss prefigured in the childhood death of his sister

[46] Ibid. 124.   [47] Ibid. 136, 137.
[48] See F. Blanshard, *Portraits of Wordsworth* (Ithaca, NY, 1959), plate 5 and
pp. 53–9.
[49] *Recollections of the Lakes and the Lake Poets*, ed. Wright, p. 140.

Elizabeth, and repeated over and over in the face of the lost girl prostitute, Ann.

If De Quincey re-enters the literary fold (symbolized by the Romantic family at Dove Cottage) in the guise of Milton's daughter, what are the implications for his literary relations to Wordsworth? As a dutiful daughter rather than a dead one, De Quincey becomes the amanuensis who gives Wordsworth his eyes—or (since blindness is an image of privation) the voice, symbol of poetic presence, that issues from such a poet's face. Domesticating the great poet as 'a household image', like Shakespeare, De Quincey memorializes Wordsworth in the prime of his powers by restoring to the portrait (as close readers of Shakespeare's portraits have also attempted) the empirical existence of the man: 'Commensurate with the interest in the poetry will be a secondary interest in the poet—in his personal appearance, and his habits of life, *so far as they can be supposed at all dependent upon his intellectual characteristics.*'[50] When De Quincey asks, in Westmoreland fashion, ' "*what-like*" was Wordsworth?' his answer is, tautologic- ally: Wordsworth resembles his life as told in *The Prelude*; that is, it exhibits 'a most remarkable (almost a providential) arrangement of circumstances, all tending to one result'—namely, the writing of his poetry.[51] Everything in Wordsworth's life tends to make him 'Wordsworth', the poet of the autobiographical *Prelude*. The providential dispensation allows for the convergence of the life and the poetry, insisting on the identity of Wordsworth the man and his representative autobiographical text. Some of this naturalized poetic identity inevitably rubs off on De Quincey too, personifying the biographer (a chosen daughter) as *The Prelude* personifies the autobiographical poet ('I was a chosen son', iii. 82), and under- writing his own claims to literary distinction.

We might ask what further function this providential scheme serves and how it is connected with the person—the persona—of Wordsworth. Wordsworth's London in Book VII of *The Prelude* is a gigantic shopping centre. With its 'string of dazzling wares, | Shop after shop', its 'symbols, blazoned names, | And all the tradesman's honours overhead', and its 'fronts of houses, like a title-page | With letters huge inscribed from top to toe' (vii. 173–7), the city becomes

---

[50] *Recollections of the Lakes* . . . , pp. 144–5.   [51] Ibid. 134, 148.

FIG. 1. The Carruthers Portrait of Wordsworth (1817)

Nectens aut Paphia Myrti, aut Parnasside Lauri

FIG. 2. Frontispiece to the Richardson edition of *Explanatory Notes and Remarks on 'Paradise Lost'* (1734)

a symbol of the eighteenth-century consumer revolution. One visible aspect of this revolution was advertising, which often took the allegorical form of life-size statues, 'physiognomies', busts, or portraits—'allegoric shapes, female or male . . . physiognomies of real men . . . Boyle, Shakespear, Newton . . . the attractive head | Of some quack-doctor, famous in his day' (vii. 179–83). Elsewhere in *The Prelude*, Wordsworth uses the word 'front' to refer to his own poem ('On the front | Of this whole song is written . . .', vi. 669–70). In poetic or highly rhetorical usage, 'front' means forehead, and, by extension, the whole face as expressive of character. Elsewhere in Book VII, 'Advertisements of giant size . . . Press forward in all colours on the sight',

> These, bold in conscious merit—lower down,
> That, fronted with a most imposing word,
> Is peradventure one in masquerade.
>
> (*Prel.* vii. 210–14)

This most imposing word, according to MS X, was 'Inviting' (compare the masquerading word, 'INVISIBLE', on the actor's chest).[52] Counterfeiting identity ('masquerade') and soliciting money, perhaps under false pretences, advertising takes its place alongside the 'inviting' masquerades of the eighteenth-century leisure industry associated with Ranelagh and Vauxhall Gardens. Just as public places, and especially crowd-activities such as masquerades and theatres, were also the scene of prostitution, so advertising had notoriously become the language of euphemistic 'invitation' by the end of the eighteenth century (indeed, 'advertisements of an indelicate or immoral tendency' were the object of contemporary denunciation).[53] If a blind London beggar touting his own story is the other face of the adman or conman, the blind London poet (Milton) is the other face of the impecunious Grub Street hack whose financial solicitations placed him in the same

[52] 'That, peradventure, one in masquerade | Inviting is the leading word . . .' (MS X): *The Prelude*, ed. de Selincourt, rev. Darbishire, p. 232 app. crit.

[53] See e.g. N. McKendrick, 'George Packwood and the Commercialization of Shaving: The Art of Eighteenth-Century Advertising or "The Way to Get Money and be Happy" ', in N. McKendrick, J. Brewer and J. H. Plumb (eds.), *The Birth of a Consumer Society: The Commercialization of Eighteenth-Century England* (Bloomington, 1982), 146–94, esp. p. 151 n. For the association of public parks and gardens such as Ranelagh and Vauxhall with prostitution, see Henriques, *Prostitution and Society*, ii. 159.

relation to the commodification of texts as the prostitute stood in relation to the commercialization of leisure and the commodification of sex.

This textual commodification is the socio-economic reality of writing which the providential scheme in Wordsworth's poetry, and especially his legacy from Calvert, serves to screen. For De Quincey, whose own hand-to-mouth existence as a journalist made him the outcast or prostitute of contemporary letters, Wordsworth's pastoral seclusion would have had redemptive connotations; not for nothing does his saving vision of Ann take place at Easter. Yet not even Wordsworth is entirely immune to the fall figured by De Quincey's addictive autobiography. For all its refusal of the city and its strategic relocation of poetry in the north, *The Prelude* too is a piece of effrontery or self-advertisement—an invitation to enter into an illicit reading relationship with a man named Wordsworth. Rhetorically speaking, 'Wordsworth' is a personification, like the 'allegoric shapes, female or male, | Or physiognomies of real men' in the London streets. Personification is well known to be the most devalued figure in late eighteenth-century and Romantic critical discourses about poetic diction. 'I wish to keep my Reader in the company of flesh and blood', writes Wordsworth in the 1800 'Preface' to *Lyrical Ballads*, eschewing 'personification of abstract ideas'.[54] As Stephen Knapp has argued persuasively in *Personification and The Sublime*, critical ambivalence towards allegorical personification is symptomatic of a wider Romantic ambivalence about figurative language.[55] Significantly, in their notes to Wordsworth's remarks on personification in the 1800 'Preface', the editors of Wordsworth's *Prose Works* refer the reader to one of the 'interludes' in the third edition of Darwin's *The Loves of the Plants* (1791). 'The Muses are young ladies, and we wish to see them dressed', writes Darwin, introducing sexual difference into art as if by analogy with vegetable reproduction.[56] Not only must poetry be decently clothed, however, but personification itself is only allowed into poetry if properly 'dressed', that is, it must be veiled or invisible, rather than shamelessly painted or nakedly displayed. Darwin's preferred example of personification in action, therefore,

[54] *Prose Works*, i. 130.

[55] See *Personification and the Sublime*, pp. 1–7, and, for Wordsworth and personification, pp. 98–129 *passim*.

[56] See *Prose Works*, i. 172 n. and E. Darwin, *The Botanic Garden: Part II, The Loves of the Plants* (Lichfield, 1789), 43.

is the modestly silent 'person' (a woman, naturally) of Shakespeare's 'concealment' in *Twelfth Night*: 'She never told her love . . . concealment, like a worm i' th' bud . . .'[57] If to declare one's love is tantamount to a sexual invitation, or even a harlot's curse, then to fail to conceal the presence of personification is to cease to be a respectable poet.

In their notes to the 'Preface' of 1800, the editors of the *Prose Works* go on to footnote Hugh Blair's *Lectures on Rhetoric and Belles Lettres* (1783)—the source of many of Wordsworth's central poetic arguments in the 'Preface'—for his views on prosopopoeia. The rhetorical figure associated by de Man specifically with autobiography, prosopopoeia is for Blair the highest form of personification, 'when inanimate objects are introduced . . . as speaking to us, or hearing and listening when we address ourselves to them'.[58] Prosopopoeia gives voice to the face of Wordsworth, inviting us to identify the autobiographical front of *The Prelude*— its masquerade of identity—with the figure of the poet. Figuratively speaking, it masquerades as a self that is 'literal and unrhetorical', concealing the representational and economic structures which produce such a person. That these structures should involve reference to an allegorical fall which is itself a privileged example of the fall into allegory gives special resonance to the Maid of Buttermere sequence and the accompanying figure of the prostitute in Book VII of *The Prelude*. In the eighteenth-century debate over the propriety of figurative language, Milton's allegory of Sin and Death—as Knapp has argued—provided the test case.[59] Johnson's criticism of the introduction of figures into the literal narrative of Satan's journey ('Sin is indeed the mother of Death . . . but when they stop the journey of Satan, a journey described as real . . . the allegory is broken . . . to this there was no temptation, but the author's opinion of its beauty') makes the Puritan Milton the most notorious victim of seduction by Spenserian romance, or 'beauty'.[60]

[57] Ibid. 44: '. . . the person of Concealment is very indistinct, and therefore does not compel us to attend to its improbability, in the following beautiful lines of Shakespeare: "She never told her love; | But let Concealment, like a worm i' th' bud, | Feed on her damask cheek." '

[58] See *Prose Works*, i. 173 n., and cf. de Man, *The Rhetoric of Romanticism*, pp. 67–82.

[59] See *Personification and the Sublime*, pp. 51–65, for the 18th-cent. debate over Miltons's Sin and Death.

[60] S. Johnson, *Lives of the English Poets*, ed. G. Birkbeck Hill (3 vols.; Oxford, 1905), i. 185–6; see *Personification and the Sublime*, pp. 62–3.

When the painted woman and her beautiful boy rise up in Wordsworth's path, what they figure is the seduction of figuration itself, along with the error of romance (the romance of error). Like the beautiful boy, Romanticism is saved for the History of Ideas or the history of consciousness—for the high Romanticism of Lovejoy and Abrams, or for what Hartman calls a 'viable *poetic* form of enlightenment (or post-enlightenment) thought'[61]—only if it can be 'stopped' before the castrating encounter with Sin or sexual difference. The prostitute who 'split[s] the race of man | In twain' figures the concealed shame of Romantic personification, outcast in *The Prelude* as the seductively feminine face of the autobiographical persona in an age of textual and sexual commodification.

[61] Hartman, *The Fate of Reading*, p. 277.

CHAPTER 9

'BEHOLD THE PARENT HEN'
Romantic Pedagogy and Sexual Difference

Behold the parent hen amid her brood . . .

. . . Early died

My honoured mother . . .

(*Prel.* v. 246, 256–7)

WHAT does it mean when we meet the following sentence in the Acknowledgements of a major book on Wordsworth: 'On the front of this whole study is written my obligation to Harold Bloom and Geoffrey Hartman, who, early and late, teacher and mentor, have led me forward in my way by intellectual prowess and spiritual example'?[1] Readers of *The Prelude* will recognize the legacy of Wordsworthian pedagogy in the mildly archaic phrasing and rhythms of Kenneth Johnston's acknowledgement. Led forward in his way as Wordsworth is led by nature, Johnston's is only at one remove from a Wordsworthian education (*educare* = to rear or bring up; *educere* = to lead). This is what the great teachers offer, especially to students of high Romanticism—not critical practice, still less literary theory, but what one might call leadings from above ('intellectual prowess and spiritual example'). Like the Leech Gatherer, these critics are simply there ('not stood, not sat, but "*was*" ') in the sublime landscape of Wordsworth studies.[2]

---

[1] Johnston, *Wordsworth and the Recluse*, p. xxv. Johnston's own pages on Book V of *The Prelude* and its educational theme (*Wordsworth and the Recluse*, pp. 139–46) provide a shrewd and witty summary of that book's often perplexing movement.

[2] To Sarah Hutchinson, 14 June 1802, *EY* 366. See also M. B. Ross, 'Naturalizing Gender: Woman's Place in Wordsworth's Ideological Landscape', *ELH* 53 (1986), 392: 'Wordsworth's best readers . . . have accepted Wordsworth's terms . . . and have passed the inheritance on'; though this essay has a somewhat different pedagogical emphasis from Ross's, I have learned from his incisive account of 'Three Years she Grew' and 'Nutting'. Cf. also R. Young, ' "For Thou Wert There": History, Erasure, and Superscription in *The Prelude*', in *Demarcating the Disciplines* (Glyph Textual Studies, NS I), 103–28; commenting on the 1850

When Wordsworth writes in *The Prelude* that 'On the front | Of this whole song is written . . .' (vi. 669–70), he is referring to his own high Romantic argument about the mind's independence of external forms. But the front, both title page and face, is a visible advertisement for the poet's mind. At once guaranteeing and conferring a legible poetic identity, the writing on the front of the song is another name for autobiography.[3] When Johnston lets us know that his critical descent goes back to Wordsworth by way of Bloom and Hartman, his acknowledgement establishes a pedagogical genealogy, much as Wordsworth names his chief literary forebears (Spenser and Milton) at moments of epic indebtedness, emulation, and anxiety such as poets own to at the front of big poems (and critics at the front of big books). But it is not so much that Johnston's book looks like a book by Bloom, or Hartman, or for that matter Wordsworth; rather, what is important is that it, or he, can 'look' at all, in the sense of laying claim to a recognizable critical identity. By linking matters of pedagogy to matters of autobiography, Johnston repeats the most persistent of the autobiographical tropes sustaining *The Prelude*.

My aim in this preamble is not to embarrass Johnston for inhabiting a world where Romantic criticism can seem (at least to its practitioners) continuous with or contiguous to Romantic poetry. Scarcely anyone who has written seriously about Wordsworth during the last two decades could avoid making some such acknowledgement. But by situating himself in a recognizable tradition of Romantic pedagogy (one which has specialized in producing big books with imposing fronts), Johnston raises a question about gender specificity. I want to ask: to what extent does installing oneself in this tradition also mean constituting oneself as looking like Wordsworth, or Bloom, or Hartman— i.e. masculine? And why have the intellectual prowess and spiritual example of these and other teachers and mentors made it, until

reception of *The Prelude* as exposing the deadness of English university training, Young remarks: '*The Prelude*'s subsequent career in the institution testifies to its continuing ability to surprise those who had regarded it as wholly theirs: the "Limits of Pluralism" debate, for instance, was conducted around a critical work (M. H. Abrams's *Natural Supernaturalism*) that centers on *The Prelude*, espouses its values, and reduplicates its form' (p. 105).

[3] Cf. London 'fronts of houses, like a title-page | With letters huge inscribed from top to toe' (*Prel.* vii. 176–7) for the link between advertising and autobiography.

quite recently, hard to raise questions of sexual difference—especially feminist questions—in the context of high Romantic criticism? What does it mean to confront the model of pedagogical autobiography advanced by Wordsworth if one happens to be a woman student, or a feminist critic, or even an autobiographical woman poet? (One answer would be: it means becoming an amanuensis—a de Manuensis; or again, it might mean becoming 'Nature'.)[4]

I am not going to air the fate of women graduate students in the institution of Romantic scholarship, here. Instead, I want to explore the representation of pedagogy in *The Prelude* and the history of that pedagogy (its contested Rousseauism), along with its bearing on a specific resistance to reading, that is, to reading sexual difference as one constituent of high Romanticism. It was in the context of education, after all, that Rousseau generated the first really extended account of sexual difference, in Book V of *Émile, or On Education* (1762), as well as provoking the first extended feminist critique of that sexual ideology, Wollstonecraft's *A Vindication of The Rights of Woman*. Wordsworth's own criticism of contemporary educational theory in Book V of *The Prelude* is also widely held to be aimed at Rousseau and his followers.[5] What are the implications of Romantic pedagogy for women? If Hartman and Bloom have taught us how to read Wordsworth by their intellectual prowess and spiritual example, what form might the lesson take for feminist readers? And if *The Prelude* is the account of an education from which women happen to be excluded—an education which is also an autobiography—what can it teach women if not how to be men, or else 'early dead' like Wordsworth's mother? I will begin with *Émile* before coming back to the implications of Wordsworth's educational model in *The Prelude* and elsewhere.

But first, my title. In Book V of *The Prelude*, the injunction to 'Behold the parent hen amid her brood' immediately follows a passage in which Wordsworth broaches his educational theme with an attack on the 'pest' of contemporary educational theories

[4] For Wordsworth's instructive effect on one major 19th-cent. woman writer, George Eliot, see M. Homans, *Bearing the Word: Language and Female Experience in Nineteenth-Century Women's Writing* (Chicago and London, 1986), 120–52. Homans's essay begins with the scene of the sister's instruction in 'Tintern Abbey' and 'Nutting'.

[5] See esp. Chandler, *Wordsworth's Second Nature*, pp. 93–119.

unleashed by Rousseau. 'This verse', he writes, 'is dedicate to Nature's self | And things that teach as Nature teaches' (v. 230–1). Leading-strings ('Stringed like a poor man's heifer at its feed', v. 240) compare unfavourably with the model of free-range education offered by the parent hen. Despite 'the maternal bond', her brood is allowed to 'straggle from her presence'. But, 'Early died my honoured mother'. The maternal presence is an absence, the Wordsworthian family destitute. What remains is a memory of this primal teacher fantasmatically coloured by the word 'brood', in this instance a noun, but elsewhere among the most affectively charged of Wordsworthian verbs for the activity of the imagination that characterizes the sublime incubator, Milton's broody Holy Spirit. 'The metaphor *broods*' (as in 'Over his own sweet voice the Stock-dove *broods*'), according to Wordsworth in the 1815 'Preface', assists 'in marking the manner in which the bird reiterates and prolongs her soft note, as if herself delighting to listen to it, and participating of a still and quiet satisfaction, like that which may be supposed inseparable from the continuous process of incubation.'[6] Incubation and repetition hatch imagination and voice, in a process that seems less reproductive than self-engendering.

If we go back to the *Prelude* passage, the little Wordsworthian brood turns out to be self-hatched, and perhaps self-engendered too. The mother must be absent or dead in order for the child to be father to the man, and the note of the poet's voice satisfyingly reiterated and prolonged. Signification seems to depend on the mother's absence, as it does, for instance, in Kristeva's account of the Bellini madonnas, or her more developed theory of maternal abjection.[7] Another way of putting it would be to say that *The Prelude* is not, as it represents itself, an account of Wordsworth's education at the hands of nature. Rather, it is an educational treatise directed at the missing mother. While seeming to pay a filial tribute to barnyard education, Wordsworth actually administers the lesson to the parent hen who leaves him destitute. *The Prelude* repeats the self-constituting trope which makes *Émile* an account of how the child becomes father to the man without the help of his mother. Looked at this way, the lesson of Wordsworthian

---

[6] *Prose Works*, iii. 32.

[7] See J. Kristeva, 'Motherhood according to Giovanni Bellini', *Desire in Language: A Semiotic Approach to Literature and Art*, ed. L. S. Roudiez (New York, 1980), 237–70.

pedagogy is 'how to get hatched without a parent hen', and—to misquote another Wordsworthian poem—'Let Nature be your teacher' ('The Tables Turned', l. 16) really means 'Let *me* be Nature's teacher'. If maternal nature is the ground or background for Wordsworthian identity, *The Prelude* teaches her to know her place.

Reading, Writing, and Femininity

> I know a young person who learned to write before learning to read, and who began to write with the needle before writing with the quill. Of all the letters, she first wanted only to make O's. She incessantly made big and little O's, O's of all sizes, O's inside one another, and always drawn backward.
>
> (J.-J. Rousseau, *Émile*)[8]

In the introduction to his translation of Rousseau's *Émile*, Allan Bloom identifies it as both 'a *Phenomenology of the Mind* posing as Dr. Spock' and 'the first *Bildungsroman*' (pp. 3, 6), implicitly recognizing the conjunction of education and autobiography as a founding Romantic trope. Rousseau's Utopian scheme teaches the boy how to survive in a state of nature, then introduces him to society. His one-man civilization in the first three books is socialized under the aegis of sublimated sexuality in the last two. Rosseau's account of Émile's quest for and courtship of Sophie in Books IV and V constitutes the deferred romantic climax of his pedagogical narrative, and in Book V he turns explicitly to the question of sexual difference. But the issue has already been broached when Rousseau defines his reader, back at the start of Book I: 'It is to you that I address myself, tender and foresighted mother . . .' (p. 37). A footnote invokes breast-feeding: 'The first education is the most important, and this first education belongs incontestably to women; if the Author of nature had wanted it to belong to men, He would have given them milk with which to nurse the children. *Always speak, then, preferably to women in your treatises on education . . .*' (p. 37 n.; my italics). Speaking to women

---

[8] *Émile, or On Education*, trans. and ed. A. Bloom (New York, 1979), 369; subsequent references to *Emile* in the text are to this edition. For an important critique of Rousseau's theory of sexual difference, see Patricia Parker's extended discussion of the relation between Milton's *Paradise Lost*, *Émile*, and Freud in 'Coming Second: Woman's Place', *Literary Fat Ladies: Rhetoric, Gender, Property* (New York and London, 1987), 178–233; Parker traces the reversal whereby the *maître* or father displaces the (bad) mother (see pp. 210–11).

about education means speaking to mothers. But, a few pages later, we learn that 'Women have stopped being mothers; they will no longer be; they no longer want to be. If they should want to be, they hardly could be' (p. 46). Because women no longer want to be mothers, men cannot become either children or fathers (children who are fathers to men). Rousseau, therefore, addresses *Émile* to an absent mother-teacher. But fortunately the mother is not really needed after all: 'to make a man, one must be either a father or more than a man oneself' (pp. 49–50). The self-authoring pedagogue makes the mother redundant. Rousseau's boast in Book V as he sees his work almost complete—'I am Émile's true father; I made him a man' (p. 407)—is that of Victor Frankenstein, whose motherless child embodies all the Oedipal violence of high Romantic poetry.[9]

Wordsworth's mother really did die early. But Rousseau's *Émile* suggests that if she were not already dead, she would need to be killed off; that autobiography comes into being on the basis of a missing mother.[10] Mentor not mother plays the central role in *Émile*. Throughout his Telemachean romance, Rousseau projects himself as the *sujet*, not only *supposé savoir*, but one who knows better than nature herself. By a supplementary activity called pedagogy, he teaches nature what she does not know about being natural. Like Sophie in Book V, she has to be educated by skilful ruses, cunning deceptions, and elaborate educational artifices.[11] She has to be taught, in fact, how to seduce. Wollstonecraft—who covertly identified with Rousseau on the score of his allegedly feminine sensibility (while viewing feminine sensibility itself as a masculine plot of entrapment)—indignantly denounced his educational scheme for its libertinism ('voluptuous reveries', 'a system of cunning and lasciviousness').[12] *Émile* is a seducer's manual, a kind

---

[9] See M. Jacobus, 'Is there a Woman in this Text?', *Reading Woman: Essays in Feminist Criticism* (New York and London, 1986), 99–103.

[10] As Barbara Johnson argues in 'My Monster/Myself', *Diacritics*, 12 (Summer 1982), 2–10, apropos of women's autobiographies; repr. in *A World of Difference* (Baltimore and London, 1987), 144–54.

[11] Cf. J. de Jean, '*La Nouvelle Héloïse*, or the Case for Pedagogical Deviation', *YFS* 63 (1982), 115: 'the Rousseauian educator may proclaim himself the champion of nature, but with his teaching he is actually working against nature.' My thinking throughout this chapter is indebted to the special issue of *YFS* on 'The Pedagogical Imperative: Teaching as a Literary Genre', ed. B. Johnson.

[12] Wollstonecraft, *A Vindication of the Rights of Woman*, ed. Kramnick, pp. 167, 174.

of *Joy of Sex Education* in which spontaneity is learned and deferral practised to heighten pleasure. What Rousseau teaches is the management of desire via traditionally feminine arts of enticement, arousal, and delay. Every sexual surrender must wear the face of acquaintance-rape (as Sophie understands when she limits her availability to Émile even after marriage). At the same time, the system which prescribes modesty to women also assumes an aggressive feminine sexuality far in excess of need; unbridled feminine desire constantly threatens to overwhelm the passively desiring male. The frontispiece which dominates Book V of *Émile* pointedly depicts Circe submitting to Ulysses—the one man whom, in Rousseau's explanation, 'she was not able to transform'.[13]

To rescue Émile from this fate, Rousseau constructs his theory of women's education, along with the theory of sexual difference which underpins it.[14] The progress of Émile's courtship of Sophie makes the creation of civilized man dependent on successfully restraining feminine sexuality. As Allan Bloom observes in his introduction, 'No segment of *Émile* is more "relevant" than is this one nor is any likely to arouse more indignation, for Rousseau is a "sexist" ' (p. 23).[15] Rousseau assumes that women exist to please men and to make them feel strong by sexually submitting to them: equality stops with sexual difference, even though, apart from sexual difference, men and women are alike, i.e. male ('In everything not connected with sex, woman is man', p. 357). There is no difference, yet sex makes all the difference ('In everything connected with sex, woman and man are in every respect related and in every respect different', p. 357). But as always in such discussions, defining difference proves difficult:

[13] See Parker, *Literary Fat Ladies*, pp. 207–8, for a detailed discussion of the significance of this illustration of the Circe story to Book V of *Émile*.

[14] For a useful discussion of Rousseau's theory of female education, as well as its Greek precursors and subsequent feminist revisions such as Wollstonecraft's, see J. R. Martin, *Reclaiming a Conversation: The Ideal of the Educated Woman* (New Haven and London, 1985), esp. pp. 38–69.

[15] Bloom goes on: 'The particular force of Rousseau's argument for us comes from the fact that he begins from thoroughly modern premises—not deriving from Biblical or Greek thought—and arrives at conclusions diametrically opposed to those of feminism', *Émile*, pp. 23–4. As Patricia Parker shows, Rousseau's premises are in fact both biblical and Miltonic, if not Greek; see *Literary Fat Ladies*, esp. pp. 191–201. Cf. also J. Schwartz, *The Sexual Politics of Jean-Jacques Rousseau* (Chicago and London, 1984), esp. pp. 84–9, for an unconvincing attempt to vindicate Rousseau for feminism against Wollstonecraft's arguments.

The difficulty of comparing [woman and man] comes from the difficulty of determining what in their constitutions is due to sex and what is not. On the basis of comparative anatomy and even just by inspection, one finds general differences between them that do not appear connected with sex. They are, nevertheless, connected with sex, but by relations which we are not in a position to perceive . . . The only thing we know with certainty is that everything man and woman have in common belongs to the species, and that everything which distinguishes them belongs to the sex . . . it is perhaps one of the marvels of nature to have been able to construct two such similar beings who are constituted so differently.   (*Émile*, p. 358)

Rousseau's bafflement anticipates Freud's at the start of his lecture, 'On Femininity', where lack of self-evidence ('relations which we are not in a position to perceive') is also the problem; for Freud too, empirical inquiry cannot solve the riddle of sexual difference.

Freud's bafflement is a ruse for introducing psychoanalysis (gender is psychically constructed): Rousseau's 'difficulty' is a ruse for introducing education. Far from being innate, sexual difference is pedagogically constructed. The natural woman is 'formed', and formed to suit and perfect the natural man:

Once it is demonstrated that man and woman are not and ought not to be constituted in the same way in either character or temperament, it follows that they ought not to have the same education. . . . After having tried to form the natural man, *let us also see how the woman who suits this man ought to be formed so that our work will not be left imperfect.*

(*Émile*, p. 363; my italics)

Forming the natural woman assumes an original rapport with nature. Yet nature has got it wrong somehow. Although 'Everything that characterizes the fair sex ought to be respected as established by nature' (p. 363), it transpires that (Wollstonecraft again) 'Nature was supposed to have acted like a step-mother', i.e. unnaturally.[16] For Rousseau, the mother's task is to oversee the constitution of gender, and above all to prevent the confusion of masculine and feminine: 'judicious mother, do not make a decent man [*honnête homme*—a gentleman?] of your daughter, as though you would give nature the lie' (p. 364). This is the context for the remark about women's education relating to men which particularly infuriated Wollstonecraft: 'The good constitution of children initially depends on that of their mothers. The first education of

[16] *A Vindication of the Rights of Woman*, ed. Kramnick, p. 178.

men depends on the care of women. Men's morals, their passions,
their tastes, their pleasures, their very happiness also depend on
women. *Thus the whole education of women ought to relate to
men*' (p. 365; my italics). The education of women must relate to
men so that they can become masculine. But we already know that
mothers are no longer willing to be mothers. Because the very
constitution of sexual difference is jeopardized by the mother's
abdication, Rousseau as educator (pedagogy as supplement) must
step in to prevent the dangerous confusion of gender which Book V
of *Émile* everywhere represents as imminent.

'In the confounding of the sexes that reigns among us, someone is
almost a prodigy for belonging to his own sex' (p. 393). If sexual
difference is pedagogically constructed, the sexual prodigy is one
who has learned Rousseau's lesson well. Masculine identity (so his
theory of sexual pedagogy implies) depends on an image of
femininity designed to reflect the image of man. Hence the spectre
of gender confusion which generates Rousseau's recurrent references
to Ninon de L'Enclos, the *honnête homme* (so called for having
only one lover at a time) who gives nature the lie—an emancipated,
free-loving, proto-feminist and letter writer of the seventeenth
century who tried, in the words of Bloom's note, 'to liberate herself
from the constraints of her condition' (p. 493 n.); or, as Rousseau
tells it, 'she had made herself a man. Wonderful' (p. 386). Hence
also the policing of women. Rousseau's libertine system gives
licence only to men, since it rests on a code of constraint for
women, as Wollstonecraft angrily pointed out. 'Girls', writes
Rousseau, 'ought to be constrained very early. . . . All their lives
they will be enslaved to the most continual and most severe of
constraints—that of the proprieties . . . teach them above all to
conquer themselves . . . a decent woman's life is a perpetual combat
against herself. It is just that this sex share the pain of the evils it has
caused us' (p. 369). A decent woman's life is rendered a perpetual
conflict, not (as Wollstonecraft was to argue) because her education
has made her weak and wayward, but because Rousseau's system
makes women the scapegoat for desire. Hence the justice of their
sufferings. *Émile* is a treatise on the arousal, management, and
subjugation of a desire which is identified throughout with
disruptive femininity, and especially with feminine narcissism.

Femininity in *Émile* comes to be allied with what Rousseau refers
to as 'this fatal science', reading and writing. Like femininity,

literacy spells desire in excess of need ('There are very few girls who do not abuse this fatal science more than they have need of it', p. 368). Writing verses, pamphlets, and letters makes a woman either unmarriageable or a plague to her husband—'making her a man after the fashion of Mademoiselle de L'Enclos' (but in any case, her literary productions are always ventriloquistic: 'It is known who the discreet man of letters is who secretly dictates [her] oracles', p. 409). Yet reading and writing have their place in Rousseau's own educational scheme, since, like pedagogy, they provide a necessary supplement to nature. Through her reading of Fénelon's *Télémache* (and perhaps also of Fénelon's anti-feminist *De l'education des filles*?), Sophie learns to recognize Émile as her lover and to adopt her role as Eucharis. By means of Fénelon's book, Rousseau himself lets us know that he is 'Mentor'. We learn how to read *Émile* by our prior reading, just as Sophie learns how to love by hers. Though he bans all books but *Robinson Crusoe* (that bourgeois parable of masculine self-sufficiency) until Émile has almost reached maturity, Rousseau introduces them when the quest for Sophie begins in earnest. Hitherto allied with imagination, and therefore potentially seductive, reading becomes an instrument of deferral that sublimates desire in the interests of civilization. As Wollstonecraft points out, the last two books of *Émile* are a kind of sexual reverie ('when he describes the pretty foot and enticing airs of his little favourite!').[17] Rousseauian pedagogy is a discourse of desire; reading about sex defers doing it, as the authors of *The Joy of Sex* knew when they gave us *More*. Sexual pedagogy in *Émile* is a dangerous supplement disguised as virtuous sublimation.

Rousseau casts out the seductive pleasures of reading and writing by way of feminine narcissism. Femininity is not just maternity abdicating its job, or a too-desirous woman, but a vain little girl enamoured of her reflection. The risk that women might prefer themselves, leaving men without the mothers on whom their masculinity depends, is a threat that Rousseau manages by means of narcissism itself. Just as Freud pessimistically lets slip the inference that the basis of all love is narcissistic, so in Rousseau's scheme *amour propre* or vanity provides the motive for all self-improvement—but especially the improvement of women. Wollstonecraft took exception to what she called Rousseau's

<hr />

[17] *A Vindication* . . . , p. 107.

'ridiculous stories, which tended to prove that girls are *naturally* attentive to their persons', for instance this one, his story of O ('that a little miss should have such a correct taste as to neglect the pleasing amusement of making O's, merely because she perceived that it was an ungraceful attitude':[18]

I know a young person who learned to write before learning to read, and who began to write with the needle before writing with the quill. Of all the letters, she first wanted only to make O's. She incessantly made big and little O's, O's of all sizes, O's inside one another, and always drawn backward. Unfortunately, one day when she was busy with this useful exercise, she saw herself in a mirror; and finding that this constrained attitude was not graceful for her, like another Minerva she threw away the pen and no longer wanted to make O's.

(Émile, p. 369).

Feminine vanity—innate, mythic, and universal (Minerva threw away her flute when she saw that playing distorted her face)— enters the scene along with feminine writing. Already synonymous with constraint, the little girl's proliferating concentric and auto-erotic O's (call it doodling) also become the sign of an imaginary feminine completeness or *jouissance*; like Milton's Eve, this young person likes her own image better than Adam's—until taught that, in the hierarchy of Edenic signs, she must refer only to him. Rousseau's solution? Because she is vain, the little girl likes having her own underclothes; when other people refuse to mark them for her, she has to learn how to do it herself (hence, she begins to write with a needle before a quill). 'The rest of her progress can easily be conceived' (p. 369). She masters signs in the interests of her person, then signs master her person by assimilating her to a system of regulated desire which inscribes her femininity in relation to a masculine viewer. All her Os become clothes, the mark at once of feminine modesty and of feminine sexuality caught in the masculine gaze which (Rousseau tells us) delights in taking them off.

This exemplary instance of Rousseau's pedagogical ruse (feminine narcissism turned to the ends of needlework) raises a rather different aspect of his educational theory. Apropos of Wasserman's reading of *The Rape of the Lock*—a poem which can be read as similarly designed to put Belinda in her proper place (the Baron's bed)—Neil Hertz has commented on Wasserman's pedagogical

[18] Ibid. 129.

'uneasiness about *one* form of the relation of signs and reality, the beautiful woman's fascination with her reflected image'. He goes on: 'in this region where semiotic and sexual questions seem to be converging', we might expect 'some further fine-tuning of the notion of narcissism in the form of a denunciation of autoerotic behaviour'.[19] The story of O could be read in terms of Rousseau's authorial anxieties about the dangerous supplement (auto-eroticism/ writing). Nor is it only a question of the production of signs seeming narcissistically self-imbricating. For Rousseau, signs are themselves seductive. Elsewhere in *Émile*, he laments the obscenity of the French language: 'it seems to me that the chasteness of a language consists not in the careful avoidance of indecent meanings but in not having them . . . to avoid them, one must think of them, and there is no language in which it is more difficult to speak purely, in every sense, than in French' (p. 324). As Freud found in Dora's case, the possibility of *double entendre* lurks in every word, and especially in French; he does not need to teach his hysterical pupil sexual terms, since she is previously instructed, and by word of mouth.[20] For Rousseau too, a chaste reading of *Émile* is impossible, unless for Émile himself.

If signs are always by definition unchaste, it is likely that she whose 'fascination with her reflected image' (Hertz again) is a traditionally misogynist trope will bear the brunt of any attempt to purify reading and writing. Rousseau's model of pedagogy rests on a theory of signs in which words constantly threaten to usurp reality: 'What was said most vividly was expressed not by words but by signs. One did not say it, one showed it'; better still, 'never substitute the sign for the thing except when it is impossible for you to show the latter, for the sign absorbs the child's attention and makes him forget the thing represented' (pp. 322, 170). Betrayed by signs at the outset, Rousseau associates them with the feminine narcissism which he then converts to masculine ends. On Sophie's chastity rests his claim to be a chaste educator (just as, conversely, Freud's claim to professional propriety depends on Dora's prior seduction). Because Sophie has learned the value of appearances to the extent of making artifice appear natural, Rousseau's educational mode—seduction through signs—can seem to have closed the gap

[19] Hertz, 'Two Extravagant Teachings', *The End of the Line*, p. 157.
[20] For Dora, orality, and *double entendre*, see Jacobus, *Reading Woman*, pp. 185–92.

between saying and showing, signs and reality, or auto-eroticism
and sublimated marriage.

It is not surprising, therefore, to find in *Émile* a treatise on
rhetorical reading. Rousseau's deconstructive method begins early,
with what he calls 'the plague of childhood' (p. 116), or childhood
reading. The fables of La Fontaine seduce by veiling the truth and
telling lies. But, paradoxically, they are in any case impossible to
understand. Rousseau's reading of the fable of the Crow and the
Fox is an exemplary instance of the impossibility of reading
without error. Rousseau picks apart La Fontaine's fable line by
line: '*Master Crow, on a tree perched, Master*! What does this word
signify in itself? What does it signify in front of a proper name?
What meaning has it on this occasion? What is a crow? What is *a
tree perched*? One does not say: "on a tree perched"; one says:
"perched on a tree". Consequently one has to talk about poetic
inversions; one has to tell what prose and verse are' (p. 113). And
so on. Images not made according to nature, language current only
in verse, fictional narrative, verbal redundancy, figurative speech,
irony, and, above all, incomprehensible general maxims—net
result: children can only misread, or read 'in a way opposite to the
author's intention' (making fun of the vain crow, taking a fancy to
the fox). Here the impossibility of chaste reading becomes the
impossibility of reading at all. Like the fox's address to the crow, all
writing, all reading, becomes an invitation to flatter one's narcissism
by imagining that signs and reality correspond. Rousseau here plays
fox, the teacher-seducer who tricks Master Crow into losing his
hold on the mastery of meaning.

The story of Rousseau's *O* is the story of narcissism seduced and
managed by a pedagogical ruse. The story of Sophie is the story of
narcissism raised to a high art, that of nature (for nature, read
'culture'). The difference between 'the young person who learned to
write before learning to read' and Sophie herself is simply that
Sophie has learned her lesson better. Or, in more literary terms, the
moral of Sophie's education is that women must be the guarantors
and safe-keepers, not only of masculinity, but of language made
chaste, naturalized, and brought into imaginary correspondence
with reality. 'Sophie' is a sign which corresponds to the artful
or cultivated alliance of nature, art, and beauty. Little girls'
conversation, after all, is to be judged not by its utility ('What is it
good for?') but by its effect on the hearer ('What effect will it

have?', p. 376). Rousseau not only teaches Sophie perfect command of the rhetoric of appearances; he also makes her understand that when it comes to the art of signs there is in fact nothing but effects, or appearances. That understanding is what Rousseau as well as Sophie simultaneously displays and veils as the culmination of the education (or rather, the seduction) of Émile. Sophie-like, Rousseau writes of his creation of the imaginary woman, 'I shall, if you please, have told fictions, but I shall still have explicated my method, and I shall still be pursuing my ends' (p. 402). The ends of Rousseau, like the ends of Sophie, are seductive pedagogy. This makes Mentor's real other not Émile, but the woman formed to perfect him—the signifier at once of feminine desire and writing, whose instability as a sign of chastity anticipates her adulterous betrayal in Rousseau's projected sequel, *Émile et Sophie*.[21]

The Making of a Lady

> This Child I to myself will take;
> She shall be mine, and I will make
> A Lady of my own.
>
> ('Three Years She Grew', ll. 4–6)

I want to suggest now that—like Rousseau's account of the education of Émile—Wordsworth's account of the growth of a poet's mind also demands a complementary story of the growth of a natural woman. In 'Three Years she Grew', nature sets out to 'make | A Lady of [her] own' (ll. 5–6). As in *Émile*, where natural education assumes a prior split between child and nature, education is by definition unnatural; nature makes her own what should already be hers ('A lovelier flower | On earth was never sown', ll. 2–3). In Freud's familiar account, the making of a lady involves the tortuous process of acculturation which differentiates the little girl from the little boy whom she initially resembles, installing her in the hierarchical institution of gender with all its attendant woes (penis envy, female masochism, repression of clitoral sexuality,

---

[21] See *Émile et Sophie, ou les solitaires* in *Œuvres complètes de Jean-Jacques Rousseau*, ed. B. Gagnebin and M. Raymond (4 vols.; Paris, 1959–69), iv. For the plot, see ibid., iv, pp. clxi-clxvii, and Schwartz, *The Sexual Politics of Jean-Jacques Rousseau*, pp. 96–8, where the unfinished epistolary novel is assimilated to Schwartz's argument about the dependence of men on women in Rousseau's writing.

frigidity, neurosis, hysteria, and, of course, a weak super-ego). In Wordsworth's poetry, the making of nature's own lady involves a similarly life-denying process of differentiation to which Lucy herself is sacrificed ('she is in her Grave, and Oh! | The difference to me', ll. 11–12). One might gloss the poem, unkindly, by saying that the poet's consciousness of difference is constituted by making Lucy lose hers (just as, in Freud's account, masculinity might be said to be constituted at the price of a repressive model of femininity as defect). Assimilated into the educational scheme of her Mentor—or should one say tormentor, since nature's scheme involves a kind of teaching that twists Lucy into non-human shapes (rocks, stones, and trees)?—Lucy's end is to become 'mute' and 'insensate': 'Hers shall be the silence and the calm | Of mute insensate things' (ll. 17–18).[22]

Maternal nature plays a Rousseauian part in 'Three Years she Grew', laying down the law so as to regulate even spontaneity: 'Myself will to my darling be | Both law and impulse' (ll. 7–8). In the 1802 text, the same lines run: 'Her Teacher I myself will be, | She is my darling . . .', making explicit the equation of love and despotic natural pedagogy. But the real villain is not a too-loving Teacher; it is Wordsworth himself, who first loads Lucy with metaphor and then lays her in her grave. Nature only does what the poet says when she compares Lucy to a sportive fawn, or promises her 'beauty born of murmuring sound', or turns her into the landscape which is all that remains of her at the end of the poem ('This heath, this calm and quiet scene', l. 40). Lucy here is not just a memory; she becomes the ground or background for Wordsworthian figuration. He writes on her. However loving, all acts of naming or poetic making such as those lavished on Lucy might be said to involve the constitution of the speaking or writing subject at the expense of a silenced object. In this respect, poetic activity—the metaphoric transfer of meaning—has something in common with the transferential processes of pedagogy ('gynagogy', in its seductive heterosexual mode).[23] All teaching is counter-transferential to the extent that it attempts to reconstitute the

---

[22] See Ross, 'Naturalizing Gender', pp. 392–402, for an extended commentary on the denial of subjectivity involved in 'Three Years she Grew'; as Ross observes, 'Lucy's education by a tyrannical Nature accords surprisingly well with the education of young ladies in eighteenth- and nineteenth-century patriarchal society' (ibid. 400).

[23] See J. Derrida, 'All Ears: Nietzsche's Otobiography', *YFS* 63 (1982), 250.

student in the teacher's image. Both are forms of self-inscription. The Lucy poems are 'about' Wordsworth in the sense that their drama of virgin consummation thematizes this poetic drama of self-making. The true end of nature's 'Lady' is to provide Wordsworth with a blank page.[24]

As a commentary on the way masculine poetic genius inscribes itself on feminized virgin sensibility—that excess of organic sensibility which in 'Three Years she Grew' makes Lucy an instance of natural *in*sensibility—I want to turn to De Quincey's portrait of the Wordsworth family in *Recollections of the Lake Poets*. De Quincey is the first in a long line of biographical commentators who have written about Wordsworth by paraphrasing the as yet unpublished *Prelude* (though there is an edge in his recounting of the providential scheme—as De Quincey tells it, Providence is pecuniary; Wordsworth keeps getting rich because his benefactors keep dying off). But De Quincey also initiates the story known as 'William and Dorothy Wordsworth', offering what amounts to a double portrait: 'I have thought that it would be a proper *complement* of the whole record, to subjoin a very especial notice of his sister' (De Quincey's italics).[25] What is the function of Dorothy's 'complementarity' in this domestic portrait of the poet? And what is the function of the condition that De Quincey calls 'maidenly'? The connection between Dorothy's excessive organic sensibility and her lack of viability, whether as woman or as writer, could be read as an indirect comment on Wordsworth's own apparently asexual solitude and disregard of other writers, as well as his (providential) detachment from the commercial world of letters inhabited by the less fortunate De Quincey. But it is tempting to view the biographical fact of Wordsworth having a sister as being as much a necessary fiction for De Quincey as Rousseau's representation of Émile, or Wordsworth's representation of himself as an orphan. His 'notice' of Dorothy is especially revealing *vis-à-vis* her function in constituting the poet as masculine.

De Quincey's narrative of his long-deferred meeting with the Wordsworth family at Dove Cottage in 1807 makes the notoriously untalkative Mary Wordsworth a kind of stock-dove, brooding maternally in what De Quincey calls 'a quiescent, reposing,

---

[24] See S. Gubar, 'The Blank Page and the Issues of Female Creativity', in E. Abel (ed.), *Writing and Sexual Difference* (Chicago and London, 1982), 73–94.

[25] *Recollections of the Lakes and the Lake Poets*, ed. Wright, p. 206.

meditative way'.[26] But Dorothy (who, by contrast, suffers from a speech impediment) affects him differently. Her 'gypsy tan' and 'wild and starting' eyes identify her with the younger Wordsworthian self of 'Tintern Abbey'. She also recalls Rousseau's first, rejected sketch of Sophie ('by dint of elevating her soul I have disturbed her reason', *Émile*, p. 405). This Ur-Sophie (Eve before she accepts Adam) rejects all suitors because none resembles her ideal. In sketching his first impressions of Dorothy, De Quincey links her 'maidenly condition' and the 'excessive organic sensibility' which will prove fatal to her in the end:

some subtle fire of impassioned intellect apparently burned within her, which, being alternately pushed forward into a conspicuous expression by the irrepressible instincts of her temperament, and then immediately checked, in obedience to the decorum of her sex and age, and her maidenly condition, (for she had rejected all offers of marriage, out of pure sisterly regard to her brother and his children,) gave to her whole demeanour and to her conversation, an air of embarrassment and even of self-conflict, that was sometimes distressing to witness. Even her very utterance and enunciation often, or rather generally, suffered in point of clearness and steadiness, from the agitation of her excessive organic sensibility ... At times, the self-counteraction and self-baffling of her feelings, caused her even to stammer ...[27]

Where Mary is a matron of few words ('*God bless you!*'), Dorothy stammers with a self-bafflement which De Quincey diagnoses as the product of temperament struggling with 'the decorum of her sex'. 'Checked, in obedience to ... her maidenly condition', Dorothy is like Rousseau's decent woman locked in 'a perpetual combat against herself' (p. 369). Her instincts may be irrepressible, but her condition is maidenly ('checked'); there are some things she simply cannot say, some growth that must be denied her mind.

Why is Dorothy a virgin? This is an absurd question, of course. Ungraceful and even unsexual, De Quincey calls her, while echoing Wordsworth's touching fraternal fiction in *The Prelude*, where he attributes to her a feminizing influence that marries the Sublime to the Beautiful:

she it was ... that first *couched* his eye to the sense of beauty—humanized him by the gentler charities, and engrafted, with her delicate female touch, those graces upon the ruder growths of his nature, which have since

---

[26] Ibid. 129.   [27] Ibid. 131–2.

clothed the forest of his genius with a foliage corresponding in loveliness and beauty to the strength of its boughs and the massinesss of its trunks.[28]

(Notice that femininity here is a kind of parasite or secondary growth, grafted on to the primary stock of masculinity.) I want to linger on the word 'touch', as well as on De Quincey's own suggestive, oddly italicized '*couched*'. 'Nutting'—at once a poem of instruction and Wordsworth's most obviously sexual and sexualizing approach to the question of nature's gender—enjoins that delicate female touch on a 'dearest Maiden!' usually equated with Dorothy herself: 'with gentle hand | Touch,—for there is a Spirit in the woods' (ll. 54–5). (As Rousseau puts it, 'Woman's empire is an empire of gentleness', *Émile*, p. 408.) Calling the bower 'A virgin scene!' identifies the 'Spirit in the woods' with the 'dearest Maiden!' at the end. Incongruously (since it is not her hand but his that ravishes the 'virgin scene!') the soi-disant rapist makes a virgin the student of his quietist teaching about nature. In this doubling of bower and maiden, we see something of Rousseau's tack with Sophie; at once seductive and virginal, she remains chaste to the end (or does she?). Commentators tend to point to an element of fierce masculine self-differentiation in the boy's rapine.[29] But there is less agreement about what precisely is being differentiated, or why differentiation should take the form of a gendered drama in which bower and maiden yield up exactly what it takes to make the rough boy an *honnête homme* (a gentleman). I want to suggest that the casting of this drama in terms of sexual difference is a guise for a linguistic drama to which virginity is ambiguously central.

Hardy in *Tess of the D'Urbervilles* describes Tess's rape as a kind of masculine writing which marks not just her underclothes but her skin: 'Why was it that upon this beautiful feminine tissue, sensitive as gossamer, and practically blank as snow as yet, there should

---

[28] *Recollections of the Lakes* . . . , p. 132. Cf. *Prel.* xiii. 231–4: 'A rock with torrents roaring . . . thou didst plant its crevices with flowers, | Hang it with shrubs that twinkle in the breeze . . .'

[29] See e.g. Ross, 'Naturalizing Gender', pp. 393–5 and 408 n. 3. Cf. also Geoffrey Hartman's deployment of the mutilated bower of 'Nutting' as an emblem of the way in which the child's imagination 'is joined to rather than separated from nature' by means of 'a desecration clearly due to *stength* of spirit'—an act 'both interesting and reprehensible, heroic and against nature'; see *Wordsworth's Poetry, 1787–1814*, pp. 73–5. For an interesting reading of 'Nutting' that is especially alert to questions of sexual difference, as well as women's exclusion from literature, see also J. Arac, 'Wordsworth's "Nutting": Suspension and Decision', *Critical Genealogies: Historical Situations for Postmodern Literary Studies* (New York, 1987), 34–49.

have been traced such a coarse pattern as it was doomed to receive . . .?' ('The Maiden', ch. xi). Tess's maidenhood is the blank sheet on which Alec D'Urberville (and, arguably, Hardy too) inscribes his name. She bears his signature and becomes his property. In *Émile*, Sophie's conjugal modesty renders this feat of self-inscription endlessly repeatable on Émile's part (it follows that the 'dearest Maiden!' must never, never, touch herself). 'Nutting' represents nature much as Rousseau represents Sophie—inviting rape because seemingly chaste. The young Wordsworth becomes a kind of gentleman trickster, like Alec D'Urberville, 'a Figure quaint, | Trick'd out in proud disguise of Beggar's weeds' (ll. 7–8), associated both with theft and with sexual depredation ('Figure *quaint*'—the *double entendre* sexualizes the boy's disguise as that of an Autolycus). Virgin nature has her fruits stolen from her: Dorothy ('dearest Maiden!') has just enough gentleness taken from her to make her a plausible recipient of Wordsworth's lesson ('with gentle hand | Touch'). But what has Wordsworth really stolen from bower and maiden? Though the psychological aspect of his compunction (whether boy's or man's) is beautifully rendered, it conceals a traditional trope—that of woman sexually knowing before the event, never naturally either altogether 'virgin' or entirely 'gentle' (a similar uncertainty surrounds Tess's sexuality).[30] Wordsworthian figurativeness is 'quaint' (i.e. sexually suggestive) in the sense that it provides the poet with the opportunity for luxurious masculine self-inscription, while hinting that he is already forestalled.

In Rousseau's sense, Wordsworthian language is bound to be unchaste because impure thoughts and meanings can never be kept at bay. 'Fearless of a rival'? Surely not. The bower was 'deform'd and sullied' even before he came on the scene. Although we are told

---

[30] This reading is supported by draft material associated with 'Nutting', among them the version that opens with a wild maiden apparently bent on unmaidenly pleasures ('Ah! what a crash was that!'); the fate of this strange Lucy figure, with her 'keen look | Half cruel in its eagerness' and 'cheeks | Thus [   ] flushed with a tempestuous bloom', is to be suitably restrained by the poet: 'Come rest on this light bed of purple heath . . .' (in MS *JJ*, Q recto, her lap becomes a resting-place for his head); see *PW* ii. 504–5, and *The Prelude*, ed. de Selincourt, rev. Darbishire, pp. 610, 641. For the dates of these drafts, see also Reed, *Wordsworth: The Chronology of the Early Years 1770–1799*, pp. 331–2. Apart from their *frisson* of fraternal eroticism, the drafts suggest a pedagogical agenda not very different from that of the final version of 'Nutting'. I am grateful to David Erdman for reminding me of this nutty crux.

that the 'dear nook' bears no phallic scars—'not a broken bough |
Droop'd with its wither'd leaves' (ll. 16–19)—the Edenic language
marks a prior lapse. In Wordsworth's *Prelude* self-parody of his
earlier use of tired pathetic fallacy, not a foxglove can droop
without a 'drooping' woman being retrospectively imported for the
flower to sympathize with.[31] The only difference between this self-
parody and 'Nutting' is that literary self-consciousness has put on
its weekend clothes ('Beggar's weeds'). Like a courtier who has
wandered into the Forest of Arden, the poet is in that luxurious
mood of anticipatory pleasure when 'The heart . . . Wast[es] its
kindliness on stocks and stones'.[32] The pay-off for voluptuous
deferral is a compensatory moment of pleasurable violence: 'Then
up I rose, | And dragged to earth both branch and bough, with . . .
merciless ravage.' Figuratively, the violence of 'Nutting' could be
read as the story of a youthful attempt to repossess the waste of
nature—nature which (like the mother) is always prepossessed.
Ravaged by the 'Figure quaint', the landscape loses a virginity lost
before the poem began. For readers with a literary memory, this too
patient, too seductive bower was long ago the place of a blissful
fall. If raping virgins (or mothers) attempts to erase the tormenting
signature of a prior rival (arguably the father), then, by the same
token, inscribing oneself on nature—naturalized inscription—
attempts to erase a literary rival (arguably Spenser). But if 'Nutting'
makes Wordsworth a man, it is at the price of initiating him into
the secret of manhood: *Cosi fan tutte.* Inside every *honnête homme*
lurks a libertine philosopher.

The Wordsworthian strip-tease of sexualized nature provides an
imaginary glimpse of what nature was like before anyone else had
interfered with her. Like Rousseau when he makes Sophie put on
clothes, Wordsworth makes nature modest so that he can be the
one to reveal all. But what 'Nutting' ultimately exposes is surely the
myth of virginity; nature is always culture (in this case, *The Faerie
Queene*) and language always sullied by prior users. If to figure is
to rape, rape—the acting out of masculine fantasies of self-

[31] See *Prel.* viii. 551–4: 'If such a sight were seen, would fancy bring | Some
vagrant thither with her babes and seat her | Upon the turf beneath the stately
flower, | Drooping in sympathy . . .'

[32] Marlon B. Ross, noting in passing the auto-erotic implications of 'waste',
comments on the sexual as well as affective implications of 'touch' ('What is
"touching" to the male here would seem to be constricting to the female'); see
'Naturalizing Gender', pp. 395–6, 394.

inscription—might also be said to be generated by figuration. But there is nothing inherently masculine about self-inscription. Inscription only comes to seem masculine because women are consistently viewed as the ground of masculinity, or, like the bower, as endowed with feminine interiority, the 'quiet being' which it gives up to the rapacious poet. The scenario is familiar— nature silenced in order that the poet may speak, bower made virginal so that he can sully it, maiden told to be gentle so that he may be rough. But it is not just a matter of the same violent gender drama getting played out between the lines in the sexual ideology of 'Nutting'. Rather, a drama that is figurative gets turned into a sexual drama, so that being a poet (reaping treasure, 'rich beyond the wealth of kings') can seem a natural gentleman's activity, just as, on a narrative level, nutting can seem naturally boyish.

A poem of instruction, 'Nutting' could read as teaching a lesson about men's and women's respective positioning within culture. Marlon B. Ross, for instance, has persuasively argued that 'Wordsworth needs the hierarchy of gender (male over female, masculine locution determining feminine location); he needs a female listener . . .' By casting 'Nutting' as a drama of masculine self-determination, he goes on, 'Wordsworth effaces the issue of the growth of the female mind'.[33] With Rousseau's help, this ideological reading could become a teaching about reading itself. 'Nutting' not only makes virginal nature the poet's blank page; it also makes a gentle maiden the poet's pupil, then refuses to let her grow up to enjoy a spot of pleasurable roughness. De Quincey tells us that Dorothy had been 'in effect, trained and educated' by her brother and by 'his admirable comments on the daily reading which they pursued in common'.[34] Here too she resembles Émile's student, Sophie, who has only read enough to identify him with Telemachus; by analogy, Dorothy is maidenly precisely in her supposed ignorance of other, non-Wordsworthian readings. The proper object of women's study, writes Rousseau, is 'the mind of man—not an abstraction of the mind of man in general, but the minds of the men around her, the minds of the men to whom she is subjected'. But this course of study contains a paradox, since Rousseau's women turn out to be better readers than men—better readers, that is, of men's unconscious desire ('Men will philosophize about the human heart

[33] Ibid. 395.
[34] *Recollections of the Lakes and the Lake Poets*, ed. Wright, p. 200.

better than she does; but she will read in men's hearts better than they do'). To read her own heart—to become a desiring subject in her own right—is to misread: 'The world is the book of women. When they do a bad job of reading it, it is their fault, or else some passion blinds them.' Conscious of Émile's desire, yet blind to her own, Sophie's only route to fulfilment is double-speak; given her subordination, she must learn 'how to communicate . . . the sentiments that she wishes to communicate without appearing even to dream of it' (*Émile*, p. 387). Her lips must say 'no!' while her accent says 'yes!' (the bower must say 'hands off!' while inviting rape in every recess). Rousseau constructs the feminine reader so that men can represent themselves as correctly read whatever violence they commit. Either way, 'no' means 'yes', and women ask for it.

This femininized *suject supposé(e) savoir* allows us to take Rousseau's de Manian fable of the Crow and the Fox a step further, suggesting not only the universal errancy of reading, and the inevitable duplicity of all communications, but the gender-specific power structures within which acts of reading and communication take place. Rousseauian reading tells us why Dorothy is 'checked'. De Quincey's account of her literary career illustrates how the replication of these power structures within the Romantic family may constrain actual women readers and writers. De Quincey goes so far as to suggest that intensive tutelage by her brother was an indirect cause of Dorothy's later sufferings ('that nervous depression which, I grieve to hear, has clouded her latter days').[35] His diagnosis has a certain feminist appeal. For all her feminine sensibility ('the answering and echoing movements of her sympathizing attention'), he thought Dorothy should have read and written more. 'Her knowledge of literature', he tells us, 'was irregular, and not systematically built up':

In whatever she read, or neglected to read, she had obeyed the single impulses of her own heart; where that led her, *there* she followed: where that was mute or indifferent, not a thought had she to bestow upon a writer's high reputation. . . . And thus the strange anomaly arose, of a woman deeply

[35] *Recollection of the Lakes* . . . , p. 205. For an account of Dorothy's last years and for the diagnosis of her condition as a type of pre-senile dementia related to Alzheimer's disease, see R. Gittings and J. Manton, *Dorothy Wordsworth* (Oxford, 1985), 269–79, and appendix 2, pp. 282–3. For other instances of the ill-effects of female literary education, see B. Kowalski-Wallace, 'Milton's Daughters: The Education of Eighteenth-Century Women Writers', *Feminist Studies*, 12 (1986), 275–96.

acquainted with some great authors . . . and yet ignorant of great classical works in her own mother tongue, and careless of literary history, unless where it touched upon some topic of household interest.[36]

A Great Books course would have taught her more than any number of impulses from a vernal wood. With hindsight, De Quincey finds himself wishing that she had after all been more of a blue-stocking (a derogatory term in his vocabulary)—'it would have been far better had Miss Wordsworth condescended a little to the ordinary mode of pursuing literature'—and that, instead of writing journals which served only as a lens for her brother's poetic eye, she had been 'in good earnest, a writer for the press'.[37] Intimating that women are culturally constructed after all, he sees that the 'defect' in Dorothy's education is its parodic relation to Wordsworth's own 'extreme, intense, unparalleled *onesideness*' and his literary isolationism ('Very few books sufficed him . . . Thousands of books . . . for Wordsworth were absolutely a dead letter').[38] Not Wordsworth, with his university education, but his sister Dorothy falls victim to the free-range Wordsworthian education preached by Book V of *The Prelude*.

'*I Was a Chosen Son*'

> But wherefore be cast down,
> Why should I grieve?—I was a chosen son.
>
> (*Prel.* iii. 81–2)

Feminist readings of Dorothy Wordsworth as yet another victim of Wordsworthian education must, however, take into account an aspect of her later derangement which is literary in another sense. When De Quincey writes that Dorothy's latter days were clouded by nervous depression, the extinction of her consciousness is predetermined by the entire metaphoric structure of Romanticism. Up till now, I have been arguing that literary self-consciousness and poetic identity are predicated in Wordsworth's poetry on the site of what is not, or no longer, conscious—call it the natural background, call it maternal absence, or just Lucy—and that such absence of mind or loss of consciousness is typically femininized. To forestall the objection that some of Wordsworth's victims are in any case masculine, I want to take as my final example the *locus classicus* of

---

[36] *Recollections of the Lakes and the Lake Poets*, ed. Wright, pp. 133, 202.
[37] Ibid. 204–5.   [38] Ibid. 189–90.

Wordsworthian education, the Winander Boy (the occasion for an exemplary pedagogical reading by De Quincey to which I will return later). In Book V of *The Prelude*, the episode of the Winander Boy is prefaced by Wordsworth's satiric sketch of a boy prodigy which may or may not be a hit at Rousseauian theories of education. As James Chandler has argued, Wordsworth's denunciation of 'Vanity' echoes the terms of Burke's earlier attack on Rousseauian education, based as it is on the deployment of *amour propre*, the masculine equivalent of feminine narcissism.[39] Clearly designed to cast out all theories but Wordsworth's own, this 'noontide shadow of a man complete'—this midget man— allows Wordsworth to develop a radical educational system based on 'error' or the privileging of happenstance; the laid-back parent hen, it is worth recalling, is free 'From feverish dread of error and mishap' (*Prel.* v. 277), unlike the sages who 'in their prescience would controul | All accidents' (v. 380–1).[40] From an earlier version of these lines, we also learn that nature has to work long hours of overtime to educate the growing boy—'How manifold the expedients, how intense | The unwearied passion with which nature toils | To win us to herself . . .'[41] Even—or especially—an education in error requires discipline.

But natural education is a mixed blessing; the Winander Boy falls tragically silent, leaving the mute poet to read (and write) his epitaph. His is an error of dependency ('while he hung | Listening', v. 406–7) that results in a chance fall or accident (*accidere* = to fall), a mistake from which he learns—what? The Winander Boy could be read as another noisy drama of masculine self-assertion, its mimic hooter mocked by 'pauses of deep silence', much as, in 'Nutting', the rapacious nutter is reproached by the silent sky. Yet there is something at once liminal and regressive in the 'gentle shock of mild surprize' (v. 407) that seems to cast the boy back into an earlier developmental moment. It is tempting to install the passage in a Kristevan narrative of abjection, as an intimation of a time prior to signification proper, when scarcely the glimmerings of differentiation existed between nature and consciousness or infant and mother. In such a state of liminal dependency, the Kristevan

---

[39] See *Wordsworth's Second Nature*, pp. 109–16.
[40] In the version of these lines preserved in MS 18a, 'all error is block'd out | So jealously that wisdom thrives apace . . .'; see *The Prelude*, ed. de Selincourt, rev. Darbishire, pp. 545–6.   [41] See *PW* v. 346.

subject emerges through his identification, not with the mother, but with her images ('the visible scene | Would enter unawares into his mind')—casting in his lot with the 'solemn imagery' which at once screens and demarcates the vacancy between them.

But even without the help of Kristeva, one could say that a scene of vigorous self-articulation gives way, not so much to loss of self, as to receptivity to the images on which that self is posited. With its Monet-like indeterminacy, the passage verges towards that characteristic Wordsworthian mode which dissolves a visible scene in uncertainty in order to reconstitute it in the steady bosom of the poet. As echo effects give way to mirror effects (owls/boy; boy/nature; sky/lake; poet/grave), supposedly stable distinctions between signs and reality, subject and object, become blurred. The Winander Boy (ostensibly the subject of the passage) is displaced by nature, seemingly caught in a moment of abstraction, as if looking away, or just self-absorbed, for once the object of her own contemplation:

> With all its solemn imagery, its rocks,
> Its woods, and that uncertain heaven, received
> Into the bosom of the steady lake.
>
> (*Prel.* v. 411–13)

The flickering question in this moment of indeterminacy (which is sky, which watery reflection?) gets quickly overwritten by a different question, one of survival; the terminal accident of life is death. As nature is displaced in turn by the mute poet at the graveside, the sequel replies to an unuttered question (what would it feel like to be thus received?) with the answer: it would be like dying young. But the threat to subjectivity in that all-enfolding bosom is countered by strenuous exertions on the part of the poet, who leaves us with a reassuring narrative of the continuity of childhood ('a race of young ones like to those | With whom I herded')—a collective boyhood which permits the recovery of a noisy juvenile self and his 'gladsome sounds'. An education in error need not be fatal for the growing boy after all.

The residue of the Winander Boy's death is separated Wordsworthian subjectivity. Though the boy is muted (like the poet after his death, 'I have stood | Mute'), the seeing Wordsworthian eye or 'I' ('methinks I have before my sight . . .', v. 421–3) is left to fix the uncertain moment in which it glimpses itself going under. I want, however, to draw attention to the part played in this process by a surrogate educator, or Alma Mater. If we continue to read the Winander Boy passage to its end, we find a sublimated version of that earlier caretaker, the parent hen—higher in the pecking order, but still a little absurd:

> Even now methinks I have before my sight
> That self-same village church: I see her sit—
> The thronéd lady spoken of erewhile—
> On her green hill, forgetful of this boy
> Who slumbers at her feet . . .
>
> (*Prel.* v. 423–7)

Like the madonna in Bellini's paintings, 'the thronéd lady' is oblivious of her slumbering boy. Her mind is on something else (perhaps an archaic paternal space, her ministry, or her tithes—who knows). Neither lady nor simply a whitewashed building, the village church approximates nicely to Kristeva's category of not-yet objects, or 'abjects' (as does a parent hen). The seeing eye of *The Prelude* emerges ('I see her sit') by identifying with what she sees: Wordsworth has earlier described 'The thronéd lady spoken of erewhile' as 'sending out | A gracious look all over its domain' (iv. 14–15).[42]

And what does she see? Why, boys at play, of course—the 'race of real children' who attended Hawkshead Grammar School (single sex in the 1780s). It is business as usual on the hill. Those who have appropriated Kristeva's maternal theory, whether for signification or for feminism, may have failed to deal with its theological legacy—the fact that the madonna's baby is always a boy. What is left at the end of the process that installs the subject in signification is emphatically a 'chosen *son*' (iii. 82; my italics); in these comforting scenarios of mother and child, the generic babe is masculine ('no outcast *he*'). What is outcast is the mother. In her place stand signs—or rather, 'books and Nature' (v. 447), another problematic pair, like nature and its reflected imagery, or the beautiful woman and her image, but one in which the indeterminacy of signs and reality has been stabilized by way of the masculine eye they constitute. The way is now clear for the poet to offer his

---

[42] Cf. Neil Hertz's reading of the 'two consciousnesses' passage (*Prel.* ii. 27–33) in the light of Kristeva's theory of abjection, at the very end of *The End of the Line*, pp. 233–8. Hertz's reading is especially alert to the economy of sacrifice and restitution in what he calls 'these scenarios of end-of-the-line signification', or structures of minimal differentiation (ibid. 233).

erroneous teaching, impervious to all accidents. Whether as nurturer or as teacher, mother nature recedes into her proper place. Here it is tempting to invoke Derrida (that other Jacques) on the absence of women from an educational scene which is by definition masculine ('*nous tous*' not '*nous toutes*'): 'With the notable exception of the mother, of course. But this makes up part of the system, for the mother is the faceless, unfigurable figure of a *figurante*. She creates a place for all the figures by losing herself in the background, like an anonymous persona.' Derrida continues (and what can he be describing but Wordsworth's Alma Mater in *The Prelude*?) that although 'All returns to her' she only survives 'on the condition of remaining in the background'.[43] One could rephrase this as follows: the mother survives—but on the condition of remaining the background itself, that which makes figuration possible.

By way of self-commentary, I want to return in closing to the question of reading. In an essay I referred to earlier, Marlon Ross urges us 'to refuse to become a Wordsworthian reader', specifically, 'to refuse to become the aggressive male reader' inscribed in Wordsworth's canonical poetry.[44] I want to ask what it would mean to become a non-Wordsworthian reader—one, unlike Dorothy, resistant to Wordsworth's lesson. A feminist reading that merely ransacked *The Prelude* for its sexual ideology could be accused of the same transgression as Wordsworth's own nutter, or Rousseau's *honnête homme*, Ninon de L'Enclos ('She made herself a man. Wonderful'). The spectre of a woman reading Wordsworth as if she were a man is itself as misogynistic as Rousseau's reaction to this historical instance of female emancipation; yet it seems worth speculating about what might constitute an alternative mode. The ideological reading is necessarily destined to return to its own beginnings in a variety of contestatory political, social, or feminist beliefs. Yet the passions that blind the feminist reader to the text are one form of error that she might want to endorse. To paraphrase Rousseau on women readers, since 'The world is the book of women', the feminist reader would be one who 'will read in men's [texts] better than they do'—while deliberately misreading in the blinding light of her own desire. Of course, such a reading of *The Prelude* is itself didactic. Even error is deliberate, even

---

[43] Derrida, 'All Ears: Nietzsche's Otobiography', p. 250.
[44] Ross, 'Naturalizing Gender', p. 392.

blindness a form of knowledge; even resistance an aspect of recognition. Another direction to take, however, would be that of Wordsworth's own poetry, teasing out the errors and uncertainties that ruffle the all too steady outlines of his sexual ideology by way of an inquiry into the mishaps of literary language and the accidents of reading.

At this point, De Quincey's pedagogical rereading of the Winander Boy passage takes on new relevance. The episode comes to De Quincey as an example of the psychological effects of vigilance or concentration suddenly relaxed. Wordsworth and De Quincey have been waiting impatiently at night for the sound of the carrier bringing the newspaper, when, as he lifts his ear from the road, 'a bright star fell suddenly upon [Wordsworth's] eye, and penetrated [his] capacity of apprehension with a pathos and a sense of the infinite, that would not have arrested [him] under other circumstances'. Wordsworth goes on to cite the Winander Boy passage, which De Quincey can only represent by glossing and repetition—by recapitulating the effects of Wordsworth's poetry and evincing his own sense of the infinite:

in that instant, the scene actually before him, the visible scene, would enter unawares—

> 'With all its solemn imagery'

This complex scenery was—What?

> 'Was carried *far* into his heart,
> With all its pomp, and that uncertain heav'n received
> Into the bosom of the steady lake.'

This very expression, 'far', by which space and its infinities are attributed to the human heart, and to its capacities of re-echoing the sublimities of nature, has always struck me as with a flash of sublime revelation. On this, however, Wordsworth did not say anything in his commentary . . .[45]

Like the Winander Boy, De Quincey engages in a kind of mimic rivalry with Wordsworth as the owl: if he hallooes, will Wordsworth's poetry reply? The answer is 'no'. De Quincey discovers not only that mimicry is not Wordsworth's real subject, but also that it fails to account for the echo effects of his poetry—a poetry 'carried *far* into his heart', penetrating his capacity of readerly apprehension in a way that recalls Jane Gallop's definition

---

[45] *Recollections of the Lakes and the Lake Poets*, ed. Wright, pp. 160–1.

of pederasty as a paradigm for classic Western pedagogy ('A greater man penetrates a lesser man with his knowledge').[46]

The Winander Boy is for De Quincey himself the story of a lesser man penetrated by a greater—a sequence of derivative dependencies in which effects hang on prior effects ('Even the attention was an effect, a derivative state; but the second stage, upon which the poet fixes his object, is an effect of that effect . . .'), and explanations necessarily depend on what they purport to explain ('but for this conditional and derivative necessity, but for this dependency of the essential circumstances upon the boy's power of mimickry . . .'). If the point was not even the slackening of the boy's attention, still less his skill in mimicry, what then, he asks, '*was* the subject of the poet's reverie' by the grave? In his role of explainer, De Quincey is baffled. After all, 'A poem ought to explain itself'. He has stumbled on something finally unfathomable or irreducible—a point where pedagogical mimicry falls silent: 'It is a fact which cannot be controverted . . . that scarcely one in a thousand of impassioned cases, scarcely one effect in a thousand of all the memorable effects produced by poets, can, upon any theories yet received amongst us, be even imperfectly explained.'[47] If teaching here takes the form of repetition, pedagogy finds its limits in the incompleteness of explanation, which is also the limit of literary knowledge. The Winander Boy resists the rape of reading by intimating that the residue of Wordsworth's poetry is not so much an untouchable Spirit in the lines, as a linguistic component which explanations such as De Quincey's always attempt, and must always fail, to explain.[48] This is what De Quincey latches on to as a 'sublime revelation', a moment when the mind seems capable of re-echoing the poetry, yet falls silent—on the brink, as it were, of an uncertain reflection.

This moment of silence or uncertainty in De Quincey's rereading of the Winander Boy passage is interesting not simply for its

[46] J. Gallop, 'The Immoral Teachers', YFS 63 (1982), 118.

[47] *Recollections of the Lakes and the Lake Poets*, ed. Wright, pp. 162–3.

[48] See Barbara Johnson's preface to 'The Pedagogical Imperative', YFS 63 (1982), pp. iii–vii. Both pupils and critics of de Man (pupils and critics both) have observed that a Spirit lurking in the lines is sometimes revealed as the unreconstructed residue of idealism in de Man's theory of literature. For two readings of the pedagogical role of 'error' in de Man, see B. Johnson, 'Rigorous Unreliability', *The Lesson of Paul de Man*, YFS 69 (1985), 73–80, repr. in *A World of Difference*, pp. 17–24, and S. Corngold, 'Error in Paul de Man', in J. Arac, W. Godzich, and W. Martin (eds.), *The Yale Critics: Deconstruction in America* (Minneapolis, 1983), 90–108.

irreducibility and its oddly unstable, momentary effect of equilibrium (the poetry seemingly contemplating or commentating on itself), but because it coincides with an earlier moment we have noticed in Rousseau—the moment when sexual difference seems similarly irreducible, similarly resistant to explanation. We could rephrase this impasse as follows. If assertive masculinity is one mode of teaching reading (difference), and penetrative pederasty another, De Quincey's instructive failure allows us to glimpse a third alternative—the moment when language itself leaves the teacher sublimely unable to account for either literary effects or sexual difference. Wordsworthian pedagogy or the teaching of error endorses that check before the unknowable (its resistance to being known) as the accident on which both teaching and reading depend. To call it masculine or feminine, as one may at certain moments wish to do in the interests of the ideological reading, is only, but necessarily, to draw attention to the limits which the institution of sexual difference imposes on the errancy of language for teachers and readers alike. Let us not forget that while Wordsworth himself is allowed to wander freely in pursuit of signs, for Lucy Gray one slip means the end. To take a more flagrant and problematic instance of the relation between gender and pedagogy, De Quincey as mentee can re-echo the sublimities of his Mentor Wordsworth, turning the teacher's poetic effects to his own account, whereas Rousseau's woman of letters must always risk being seen as ventriloquistically dependent on her master's voice ('It is known who . . . secretly dictates [her] oracles', *Émile*, p. 409); or else, to revert to the scene of 'Nutting', the unchasteness of language is displaced on to a feminine mentee, deforming her text and sullying her virginity. Whether the talk is of pedagogy, of reading, or of sexual difference, irreducibility is not to be mistaken for equality. This is an error we might all want to learn from.

CHAPTER 10

AFTERWORD

Romantic Analogy; or, What the Moon Saw

AMONG the many natural chasms, fractures, or gulfs in the landscape of Wordsworth's poetry, the most visionary—the most charged with symbolic significance—is also the least substantial. I mean, of course, the one glimpsed from the top of Snowdon in Book XIII of *The Prelude*. The culminating episode in Wordsworth's autobiographical narrative, the climbing of Snowdon has a special status not only because it serves as the ground for Wordsworth's most sustained account of a theory of imagination which has only evolved during the course of his poem, but because it allows him to confront, self-consciously, an externalized or naturalized model for the mind, considered as an aesthetic object. For all its philosophical explicitness, however, it also seems to reach back into the shadowy regions associated with the early spots of time in *The Prelude*. It could, indeed, be read as an account of the origins of signification—of the coming into being of a signifying self only precariously distinguished from nature—even as it provides the peg on which Wordsworth hangs his elaborated theory of the imagination. In this sense, the Snowdon episode is exemplary. It provides a metaphorical representation of the entire narrative of *The Prelude*—a representation not so much of its plot or thesis (the instating of nature as a counterpart to the human imagination which none the less always transcends it), as of its precondition. That precondition is the possibility of metaphorization—a possibility which the Snowdon episode at once addresses and then denies by labelling its representation of natural appearances not as metaphor, but as analogy. Analogy is a term that elides or erases metaphoricity by attempting to claim an actual or essential reality for what is figurative, and so rendering the fictions of the creating mind as if they were independently existing entities. The question provoked by the Snowdon episode is why Wordsworth, in order to aggrandize the mind, should go so far towards claiming that what the mind sees in nature is really there—and then go beyond his own claim to say that the mind in any case always transcends what it sees. What is at stake in his troping of metaphor as analogy? And what can be learned from the long 'Analogy' passage originally intended to amplify the Snowdon episode with a series of similarly impressive natural appearances? Finally, why should the issue of analogy have surfaced at the moment when Wordsworth believed his autobiographical poem to be drawing to a close?[1]

What the Moon Saw

The climbing of Snowdon leads not to a sense of mountain conquest, nor even to the sense of 'dejection' that attends the crossing of the Alps, but rather to a dissolution of boundaries figured not only by mist (as in the crossing of the Alps) but by a fissure—a lack of substance in what is already insubstantial. When the sea of mist usurps the real sea, and the voice of an autobiographical 'I' gives way to the disembodied, impersonal voice of waters, naturalized narrative also falls away to leave a scene which Wordsworth, even without the explanatory passage that follows, clearly intends to be read as a self-conscious metaphor for the workings of the mind:

> from the shore
> At distance not the third part of a mile
> Was a blue chasm, a fracture in the vapour,
> A deep and gloomy breathing-place, through which
> Mounted the roar of waters, torrents, streams
> Innumerable, roaring with one voice.

> (*Prel.* xiii. 54–9)

Wordsworth calls this unified absence—somewhere between breath and voice, at once scarcely audible and deafening—'an under-presence'. If the ambiguously transformed cloudscape, neither land nor sea, forms 'The perfect image of a mighty mind', the voice within the chasm images with equal ambiguity 'whatso'er is dim | Or vast in its own being' (xiii. 69–73). This interior dimness and vastness is apprehended in the overcoming of landscape by

---

[1] The 'Analogy' passage—'Even yet thou wilt vouchsafe an ear'—appears in MS W of *The Prelude* and belongs to late Feb. or early Mar. 1804, when it was intended to follow on after the ascent of Snowdon as part of Book V of the briefly envisaged five-book *Prelude*. See *Prel.* 496–9, and *The Prelude*, ed. de Selincourt, rev. Darbishire, pp. 623–8 and app. crit.

mistscape, and of silence by disembodied sound. Emptiness becomes the most powerful presence in the Snowdon landscape—the presence that is typically manifested as voice or breath elsewhere in Wordsworth's poetry.

Other gaps in *The Prelude*, most notably the 'vacancy' between older and younger selves in Book II, produce similar transformations of absence into disturbing presence; the wider the vacancy between Wordsworth and his remembered past, 'Which yet [has] such self-presence in my mind', the more the autobiographical persona is fractured ('I seem | Two consciousnesses') and unsettled by the sense of an alien, interior presence—'conscious of myself, | And of some other being' (ii. 30–3). Here Wordsworth terms his past self 'self-presence' rather than under-presence, but the implication is of a similarly haunting, indwelling division, at once strange and integral to identity. This account of cleft consciousness in Book II of *The Prelude* is immediately followed by the image of a split rock, 'A grey stone | Of native rock' (ii. 33–4) now gone to build 'A smart assembly room'—an emblem not just of change at home, but of the division experienced by Wordsworth himself once higher education had effectively severed him from his native landscape. The fracture thus seems to mark the quarrying of socialized consciousness from the solitary, unified selfhood that *The Prelude* posits as always in the past, or the hewing of the bedrock of childhood memory in order to build a public identity in the time present of writing.[2] Either way, this sign of consciousness doubled and divided becomes a marker for the self-reflexive yet differential processes involved in the writing of an autobiographic poem. Splitting is the origin of remembering, of writing, of autobiography, and ultimately of subjectivity. Even recollection in tranquillity has its beginnings in the recognition that consciousness, in order to be consciousness at all (let alone recollection), begins in division.

Moments such as this in *The Prelude* bear the weight of self-conscious signification with emblematic explicitness. At other moments, symbolic landscapes may inscribe meanings that have no need of mediation, as in the Vale of Gondo in Book VI, or—alternatively—undergo the naturalized transcendental apotheosis of Snowdon in Book XIII. The function of these moments, however, is not just thematic or even philosophical. They bear on

---

[2] See Hertz, *The End of the Line*, pp. 233–9, for a reading of the 'two consciousnesses' passage in relation to the split stone.

the history of signification and of signifying possibility, a history on which *The Prelude* itself depends. As an autobiography, *The Prelude* necessarily has its origin in an always prior self-division. Its melding of landscape into a seemingly autonomous, self-sufficient language for both doubling and depicting the action of the writing, desiring, or imagining subject could be read as a defence against that precondition of internal division. Positing a mirroring or specular relation between nature and imagination externalizes (and hence manages) the split as an exterior, consolidating reflection rather than as internal division. 'Having tracked . . . Imagination— up her way sublime' (xiii. 289–90), the retrospectively imposed trajectory of *The Prelude*, Wordsworth also provides an account, along the way, of the metaphorical constitution of his poetic landscape. In this landscape, the Sublime of imagination and the Sublime of nature are treated not simply as analogous, but as mirror images for one another, and hence as mutually stabilizing. And yet, the ground always seems about to fall away beneath the onlooker's feet; poised as a spectator on the brink of the chasm, the poetic self that wants to see its reassuring double also sees the possibility of its fragmentation and extinction. It is this precarious-ness, and its relation to signification, that I want to explore in terms which attempt to relate a psychoanalytic reading to a reading that draws attention to the status of Romantic metaphoricity, both here and elsewhere in *The Prelude*.

In Book XIII, an analogue for the usurpation of absence by under-presence is provided by the installation in the natural scene of a supernature ('the homeless voice of waters') that goes by the name of both 'soul' and 'imagination'. The 'fracture in the vapour' that is its home from home contains the implication of menace as well as loss always attendant on the suggestion of cleft origins. The breathing-place is gloomy, the waters roar, and in the distance the ancestral voices of 'Kubla Khan' are to be heard, prophesying war. Despite aestheticizing the chasm with the language of spectatorship ('The universal spectacle throughout | Was shaped for admiration and delight', xiii. 60–1), Wordsworth does not succeed in holding at bay a sense of the imminent collapse of the spectator into this perilous breach. The wholeness of the self is fractured by its threatened immersion in the larger whole (or hole) that is simultaneously absence and a too present presence. What confronts the eager mountaineer and view seeker is in the last resort a nothingness from which issues a voice. Not his own voice, however, but nature's; and not nature's (self-identical) voice either, but that of nature's imagination, at once its own and differentiated from it: 'in that breach . . . had Nature lodged | The soul, the imagination of the whole' (xiii. 62–5). This dissociated voice—imagination rendered as both other and dangerously vocal, roaring from the abyss with cumulative, differential power—suggests that in the very moment of the self-possessed subject's disappearance, signification may arise in its most sublime (most subject-shattering) manifestation. It also suggests, by analogy as it were, that the gap or *vide* which divides or cleaves the subject (in Kristevan terms, the pre-Oedipal infant from the barely differentiated maternal) may be the *sine qua non* for signification itself.[3] The view from Mount Snowdon images the source of all signification, all images; Wordsworth terms it nature, but Kristeva would call it the pre-Oedipal, the soul that nature lodges in the abyss, corresponding to the earliest, most fragile sense of self. Once the split of primal repression has taken place, this first narcissistic crisis confronts the child with the place-holding, alien entity between itself and the mother which Kristeva identifies, not precisely with the father, but with an archaic paternal space. The space makes subjectivity possible, but only at the cost of self-differentiation.

We might recall that in Kristeva's account, images (or rather, identification with the mother's images—with her desire) at once cover over and protect the vacancy between mother and child. Like Wordsworth, Kristeva turns out to be writing in a tradition associated with the Sublime, where the imminent annihilation of the subject is the price paid for an apprehension of boundlessness, and only the installation of borders can fend off the threat of non-being. Her account uncannily recapitulates the vision from Mount Snowdon in its rendition of a 'zero degree' of imagination, or an imagination emptied of all but its own possibility:

Thus . . . the *emptiness* that is intrinsic to the beginnings of the symbolic function appears as the first separation between what is not yet an *Ego* and what is not yet an *object*. Might narcissism be a means for protecting that emptiness? But against what?—A protection of emptiness (of 'arbitrariness', of the 'gaping hole') through the display of a decidedly narcissistic

---

[3] See 'Freud and Love: Treatment and its Discontents', *The Kristeva Reader*, ed. Moi, pp. 238–71, pp. 240–3, 246–8, 256–60.

parry, so that emptiness can be maintained, lest chaos prevail and borders dissolve. Narcissism protects emptiness, causes it to exist, and thus, as lining of that emptiness, ensures an elementary separation. Without that solidarity between emptiness and narcissism, chaos would sweep away any possibility of distinction, trace and symbolization, which would in turn confuse the limits of the body, words, the real and the symbolic. The child . . . not only *needs* the real and the symbolic—it signifies itself as child, in other words as the subject that it is . . . precisely in that zone where *emptiness and narcissism*, the one upholding the other, constitute the zero degree of imagination.[4]

If language—identification with the words of the other—is the Oedipal domain, and therefore the domain of the Sublime, Kristeva's pre-Oedipal realm would be this 'zone where *emptiness and narcissism*' provide the necessary basis for the Oedipal Sublime. Kristeva's account of the coincidence of the gap or *vide* with the possibility of allying oneself with what fills it (what Wordsworth calls 'the soul, the imagination of the whole') provides a psychoanalytic account of the precarious moment of ontological safety on the edge of destruction which characterizes most versions of the mountain Sublime (apprehension of danger and desire linked with the fending off of any imminent extinction for the subject).[5] But it would also explain why an element of narcissism must enter in—why such moments in *The Prelude* characteristically involve mirroring effects, offering, for example (as here), the stabilizing sense that nature's role is to image the workings of imagination. In the last resort, scenes of specular mirroring stand in for—gesture towards—the saving metaphoricity which Kristeva defines as 'movement towards the discernible, a journey towards the visible'.[6] This is a reassuring movement. Only by holding on to the visible can the subject avoid fatal immersion in the maternal breach, thereby not only avoiding loss of self but clinging to the power to signify. Thus the focus for the transferential process in psycho-analytic treatment as Kristeva formulates it is 'not a narcissistic merger with the maternal container but the emergence of a *metaphorical object*'.[7] Kristeva calls this emergence of a meta-phorical object 'love', as opposed to metonymic desire; Words-worth, in his gloss on the Snowdon passage, similarly associates

---

[4] *The Kristeva Reader*, ed. Moi, p. 242.
[5] See e.g. Wordsworth's own account of the Sublime, *Prose Works*, ii. 353–4.
[6] *The Kristeva Reader*, ed. Moi, p. 247.   [7] Ibid. 248.

with the Sublime of nature a non-relational 'higher love . . . a love that comes into the heart | With awe', a love that 'proceeds | More from the brooding soul, and is divine' (xiii. 161–5).

Turning back to Wordsworth's account of the climbing of Snowdon, with Kristeva in mind, we might remark that his initial appearance as picturesque traveller and landscape spectator (as the wholly self-absorbed, seemingly unified, and unproblematic subject of his own narration) is fractured at the precise moment when he is startlingly arrested and dwarfed by the nakedness of the (surely feminine) moon: 'and lo, | The moon stood naked in the heavens at height | Immense above my head' (xiii. 40–2). What the moon saw is what Wordsworth sees. Spectator and moon between them divide the envisioner of the mistscape into an already split subjectivity (the panting, earthbound, prosaic self of a realistic narrative on the one hand, the immensely high sublime eye of symbolic narrative on the other): 'Meanwhile, the moon looked down upon this shew'. Although the moon looks down on the show 'in *single* glory' (my italics), it actually serves to double the seeing eye of the poet ('*we* stood'), presenting both with an image of their fracture. In Wordsworth's formulation, the mistscape too has its mirror, 'Nature'—the agent who (in turn) 'lodges' in it yet another faculty called imagination. In a gesture of infinite regress, nature installs in the abyss of its own subjectivity something (a soul) that ought not to be there, a supernumary presence or noise in excess of the visible. 'Imagination' stands for both man and moon, both mistscape and nature. The other of both, it is for ever displaced ('homeless'), constituted by its divided identification with the desire and images of another (the moon-mother). For Kristeva, it is this constitution in self-alienation, the earliest form of which is separation from the mother, that allows the most rudimentary form of signifying subject to come into being. Her account of the Oedipal as the overlay of an already triangulated pre-Oedipal elaborates a structure which might be called not simply the natural Sublime, but (doubly naturalized) the maternal Sublime.[8]

In his 'meditation' on the scene, Wordsworth, as usual, explicitly identifies nature as 'she':

[8] See Hertz, *The End of the Line*, pp. 230–1, 49–53, for the way in which Kristeva serves to modify or revise the version of the Oedipal Sublime provided by Thomas Weiskel in *The Romantic Sublime*, and for an earlier consideration of what Hertz calls 'the Oedipal moment' in Weiskel.

                                                above all,
        One function of such mind had Nature there
        Exhibited by putting forth, and that
        With circumstance most awful and sublime:
        That domination which she oftentimes
        Exerts upon the outward face of things,
        So moulds them, and endues, abstracts, combines,
        Or by abrupt and unhabitual influence
        Doth make one object so impress itself
        Upon all others, and pervades them so,
        That even the grossest minds must see and hear ...

                            (*Prel.* xiii. 73–83)

That nature plays the same role as the pre-Oedipal in Kristeva's scheme—installing boundaries and laying down the rudiments of a signifying system for the primitive, barely separate subject—hardly needs further underlining. Wordsworth's own interpretation of the Snowdon vision makes nature the mother of imagination; because it has a life of its own, it provides the ground for claiming that the imagination too is autonomous, even though they both obey the same laws. At this point I want to pursue the question of metaphoricity. We, and Wordsworth, and the moon (a figure for Wordsworthian sublimity, as well as for the seeing eye), are led to see the Snowdon landscape as a 'natural' metaphor for the imagination, for the mind, and for the activity of nature itself. Wordsworth represents this vision, however, not as metaphorical, but as a matter of 'resemblance', 'counterpart', or (in the term which is crucial to the episode's discursive aftermath), 'analogy':

                                    the express
        Resemblance—in the fullness of its strength
        Made visible—a genuine counterpart
        And brother of the glorious faculty
        Which higher minds bear with them as their own.

                            (*Prel.* xiii. 86–90)

Compare Wordsworth's later use of the term 'counterpart' in Book XIII, in conjunction with 'mirror'. Wordsworth is invoking 'Nature's secondary grace, | That outward illustration which is hers', when nature's works are viewed 'As they hold forth a genuine *counterpart* | And softening *mirror* of the moral world' (xiii.

282–3, 286–7; my italics).[9] The two passages relate to each other somewhat on the lines of the Coleridgeian primary and secondary imagination; in the first instance, nature has a mind of its own, in the second, it provides moral analogies. But both passages use the term 'counterpart' in place of metaphor, with a literalness that seems to deny the metaphoricity involved. Why should this be? And why should the natural and the human imagination be inscribed within a family hierarchy as siblings (brothers)—offspring of a single greater power (the divine imagination, presumably)—rather than in terms of the mediated and displaced relation associated with linguistic processes?

Clearly what is at stake is the wish for metaphor to have a literal referent or grounding. When Wordsworth writes of finding himself 'on the shore . . . of a huge sea of mist', opposing it to 'the real sea', he draws our attention to the metaphoricity of that misty sea. By a linguistic sleight of hand, the sea of mist becomes more actively oceanic than the ocean it obscures—'Far, far beyond, the vapours shot themselves | In headlands, tongues, and promontary shapes . . .' (xiii. 47–8). Wordsworth, however, goes on to claim that nature's ability to transform and usurp on itself is not a metaphor but an 'analogy' for the mind's usurpations on nature. Traditionally, eighteenth-century rhetoricians distinguished between the passionate fictions of metaphor—the shapings of human emotion and expressivity—and natural or divine correspondences actually existing between nature and God as a system of given relations. Analogy, or, as Wordsworth calls it here, 'counterpart', might seem on the face of it to be functioning as just another trope; specifically, a trope for metaphor, but one designed to reverse the process which (it has been argued) took place during the eighteenth century, whereby analogy was transferred gradually from the realm of objective reality (divine analogy) to that of subjectivity, or the creating and perceiving mind.[10] In order to explore the question of

---

[9] Cf. the 1850 version—'Apt illustrations of the moral world, | Caught at a glance, or traced with curious pains' (1850 *Prel.* xiv. 319–20). The drift of the argument of Book XIII at this point suggests that this secondary power is envisaged as a bridge between 'imagination' and the faculty next addressed, 'fancy'; see xiii. 289–94, and cf. the explicit association with Fancy in 1850 *Prel.* xiv. 318.

[10] See E. Wasserman, 'Nature Moralized: The Divine Analogy in the Eighteenth Century', *ELH* 20 (1953), 39–76. Wordsworth would certainly have known the most famous 18th-cent. articulation of the divine analogy, J. Butler's *The Analogy of Religion, Natural and Revealed, to the Constitution and Course of Nature* (London,

analogy more fully, and its seeming power to make substantial or present what metaphor renders insubstantial or absent (turning the sea of mist into a more real sea, or absence into under-presence), I want to look at the long, important, and, until recently, critically neglected passage from MS *W*, composed during 1804, which Wordsworth originally intended to follow on immediately after the Snowdon episode.[11] Here he not only uses the term 'analogy' to define certain natural phenomena, but provides a selection of other supposed analogies or 'living pictures' to embody his 'pleasing argument' that nature's workings are analogous to those of the imagination.

Providence, Signs, and the 'Analogy' Passage

The so-called 'Analogy' passage, written in the early spring of 1804 for the brief moment when *The Prelude* was envisioned as a five-book structure culminating in the climbing of Snowdon, represents in its own way a fracture in the text of Book XIII—as Wordsworth puts it parenthetically, '(Passage which will conduct in season due | Back to the tale which I have left behind)', (ll. 9–10). How does the 'Analogy' passage 'conduct' back to the tale which Wordsworth had left behind, given its apparently random collocation of associations and miniature narratives? Reading the passage in the light of Wordsworth's 'tale' at this point in *The Prelude* (his story of nature and imagination as each other's counterpart) may elucidate the Snowdon passage, indicating exactly how the usurping mistscape is supposed to offer an analogy to the mind. But one could also read it in the light of Wordsworth's need to deny the tropological status of metaphor. On the face of it, this series of tumultuous or disturbing scenes (a storm over Lake Coniston, a sleeping horse frozen into immobility, Columbus dipping towards the poles, Sir Humphrey Gilbert engulfed at sea before the eyes of his fellow voyagers, Mungo Park and Dampier anticipating their

---

1736), from his undergraduate years at Cambridge, where it was one of the set books. Bringing Newtonian science and Lockian philosophy to bear on religious problems, Butler's book looks to the constitution of nature—natural analogy—for evidence of a divine or 'intelligent' author of nature.

[11] See Appendix for the entire text. For two discussions of the 'Analogy' passage, see also R. Schell, 'Wordsworth's Revisions of the Ascent of Snowdon', *PQ* 54 (1975), 592–603, and J. F. Kishel, 'The "Analogy Passage" from Wordsworth's Five-Book *Prelude*', *SiR* 18 (1979), 271–85.

respective deaths in the desert heart of Africa and an open boat on the South Seas) appear to have little in common with the climbing of Snowdon. But read closely, they point to two underlying concerns crucial to Wordsworth's temporarily abandoned tale: not only the concern with Providence—with personal election and survival (clearly relevant to the poetic fears and aspirations associated with the composition of *The Prelude*)—but the reassurance offered by signs themselves. The 'sign' here is the Covenant, a contract or promise of redemption. Metaphoricity, figured as nature's power to transform or aestheticize itself before the spectator's gaze, becomes the guarantee provided by the Covenant. When Wordsworth alludes to the 'manner in which Nature works . . . upon the outward face of things' (ll. 10–11), we might expect in addition that the question of identity (a 'face' moulded and exalted, given distinct or separate character) will be connected with autobiography—that endowing nature with the power to 'speak' represents a symbolic displacement of the signifying power claimed by the autobiographical poet.

The element of danger common to these 'analogies' seems to point to that dangerous edge of things where either separation (signification) or loss of self (the extinction of signs) may befall the individual. The first 'living picture' which Wordsworth uses to embody his 'pleasing argument' is another landscape, this time marked by the turbulence of storm ('It was a day | Upon the edge of autumn, fierce with storm,' ll. 33–4). 'Wrought into commotion', this borderline landscape ('Upon the *edge* of autumn') is indeterminate too in another way, hovering between the visible and the finally unvisualizable Sublime of Milton's war in heaven, whose 'ten thousand thousand saints' (*Paradise Lost*, vi. 767) give Wordsworth his 'Ten thousand thousand waves' (l. 40).[12] But Wordsworth must have had another passage still more strongly in mind, Milton's account in *Paradise Lost*, Book XI, of Noah's Ark and the rainbow Covenant. When Wordsworth mentions not just a 'horse and rider stagger[ing] in the blast' but a boat that is not there ('he who looked upon the stormy lake | Had fear for boat or vessel *where none was*,' ll. 45–7; my italics), the absent boat is the Ark, and its principal passenger is Noah, 'The one just man alive' (*Paradise Lost*, xi. 818), whose survival is guaranteed by the rainbow which forms the reassuring climax of *Paradise Lost*,

---

[12] See ibid. 282–3 for the Miltonic allusion here.

Book XI. Milton's account of the great storm weathered by Noah, when the elements exceed their boundaries and oceanic inundation threatens the mount of Paradise itself, is in its own way a precursor of the moments of usurpation (a term presumably borrowed from Milton) which Wordsworth locates respectively in the Simplon Pass and the Snowdon landscape:

> all the cataracts
> Of heaven set open on the earth shall pour
> Rain day and night, all fountains of the deep
> Broke up, shall heave the ocean to *usurp*
> Beyond all bounds, till inundation rise
> Above the highest hills: then shall this mount
> Of Paradise by might of waves be moved
> Out of his place, pushed by the horned flood,
> With all his verdure spoiled, and trees adrift
> Down the great river to the opening gulf . . .
>
> (*Paradise Lost*, xi. 824–33; my italics)

If a link were needed to connect the vision from Mount Snowdon and the storm over Lake Coniston, this passage surely provides it. The inundating ocean, the usurpation of boundaries, and the suggestion that the Paradisal mount itself might be immersed in 'the opening gulf', all indicate that, as well as his own earlier description of sunrise in a misty Alpine landscape from *Descriptive Sketches*, Wordsworth had in mind this more threateningly apocalyptic scene.[13] He may rewrite Milton's flood as the misty apotheosis of the Snowdon landscape (a familiar feat of natural supernaturalism), but both oceans contain the same subtext. Immense natural threat is made tolerable by a sign from God.

The Covenant provides the clearest link between the storm over Coniston and the story of Noah. In Milton's rendition of Genesis, Noah

> over his head beholds
> A dewy cloud, and in the cloud a bow
> Conspicuous with three listed colours gay,
> Betokening peace from God, and Covenant new.
>
> (*Paradise Lost*, xi. 864–7)

---

[13] See *Descriptive Sketches*, ed. Birdsall, 1793, ll. 495–505.

In the 'Analogy' passage, Wordsworth sets against the confused tumult of the storm 'A large unmutilated rainbow . . . With stride colossal bridging the whole vale' (ll. 50–2). The rainbow is described in terms at once aesthetic and visionary, as if its wholeness ('unmutilated') were set in defiance of fragmentation; as if it were a sign, not a natural phenomenon—which is what God (in Milton's account) had in any case promised that rainbows would henceforward always be:

> The substance thin as dreams, lovelier than day,
> Amid the deafening uproar stood unmoved,
> Sustained itself through many minutes space,
> As if it were pinned down by adamant.

> (ll. 53–6)

When, at the end of *Paradise Lost*, Book XI, Adam asks for an explanation of 'those coloured streaks in heaven',

> serve they as a flowery verge to bind
> The fluid skirts of that same watery cloud,
> Lest it again dissolve and shower the earth?

> (*Paradise Lost*, xi. 879, 881–3)

the Archangel Michael tells him that the rainbow is God's 'Covenant never to destroy | The earth again by flood, nor let the sea | Surpass his bounds' (xi. 892–4), and that all future rainbows will be a reminder of his promise. With this passage in mind, Wordsworth hardly needed to invoke the Covenant explicitly to make his point—that the airy substance of the rainbow not only defends the Coniston landscape against dissolution into chaos, but that, as the Noah or chosen son of *The Prelude*, he himself is promised immunity from destruction. Moreover, the rainbow has another function. It ensures that Wordsworth's tropes will be read not as metaphors but as adamantine analogies ('As if it were pinned down by adamant'). The ultimate reassurance provided by the rainbow Covenant lies in betokening a natural, hence God-given, sign system—a divine language that guarantees the subject's relation to signification. Just as metaphor is adamantine sign, so the fixture of signs preserves their user from mutilation.

The sleeping horse in the passage that follows shares with the Snowdon landscape and the adamantine rainbow a seeming capacity for natural self-transmutation:

> With one leg from the ground the creature stood,
> Insensible and still; breath, motion gone,
> Hairs, colour, all but shape and substance gone,
> Mane, ears, and tail, as lifeless as the trunk
> That had no stir of breath. We paused awhile
> In pleasure of the sight, and left him there,
> With all his functions silently sealed up,
> Like an amphibious work of Nature's hand,
> A borderer dwelling betwixt life and death,
> A living statue or a statued life.

(ll. 64-73)

Once more, Wordsworth attributes to nature the ability to cross into the aesthetic realm. This is poetry in stillness not motion ('a living statue or a statued life') which asks implicitly, like Keats's urn, if the price of aesthetic or figurative arrest may be empirical death—not, perhaps, a problem for a horse, but (potentially at least) a problem for the autobiographical poet. The obvious link here would be with the power of the imagination to dissolve, diffuse, dissipate, in order to recreate ('to one life impart | The functions of another', ll. 24-5) which Wordsworth illustrates in the 'Preface' of 1815 with his lines about the Leech Gatherer.[14] But is there, perhaps, another route to go? Wordsworth's very aestheticizing of the horse suggests a concern with the figural in its own right. The sleeping horse is 'amphibious' because neither dead nor alive, literally a figure for figurality, 'all his functions silently sealed up'. Paul de Man, writing of the deaf dalesman in *The Excursion*, argues for the way in which figuration involves a similar sensory privation, or stilling of the audible and sensible world. In de Man's words, 'the story of a deaf man who compensates for his infirmity by substituting the reading of books for the sounds of nature' constitutes 'a discourse that is *sustained* beyond and in spite of *deprivation*'—an allegory (like other figures of deprivation in *The Prelude*) of Wordsworth's own figurative mutilation or deprivation and his attempt at self-restoration through the figure of reading called autobiography.[15] We might recall that Wordsworth in Book I of *The Prelude* writes of his want of poetic power—his timorous procrastination—as a similar functional privation or blankness ('a more subtle selfishness, that now | Doth lock my

[14] See e.g. J. Wordsworth, *William Wordsworth: The Borders of Vision* (Oxford, 1982), 2-3.

[15] See 'Autobiography as De-Facement', *The Rhetoric of Romanticism*, pp. 72-4.

functions up in blank reserve', i. 247–8). What does Wordsworth's inability to get launched on his autobiographical poem have in common with a sleeping horse? The answer may well be a suspension of lived, empirical existence ('Ah, better far than this to stray about | Voluptuously through fields and rural walks', i. 252–3)—paradoxically, the very suspension enjoined by figurality. Striving to make oneself a figure for oneself (a living figure or a figured life) both holds, and holds at bay, the threat embodied by the figural, that of becoming 'A borderer dwelling betwixt life and death', neither fully alive nor entirely divested of life, but consigned to the hinterland of figuration.

Wordsworth's chief defence against the figural privation which constitutes him as an autobiographical subject is his insistence that nature too is an artist, composing 'living pictures' (l. 32) of its own ('those I mean | Which Nature forces on the sight when she | Takes man into the bosom of her works', ll. 74–6). Just to muddy the waters, he adds: 'Books are full of them' (l. 79). If nature's living pictures are to be found especially in books, then who is to say where nature ends and figuration (reading and writing) begins? In the miniature narratives that follow, Wordsworth returns to the imminent (and immanent) danger of extinction which gives both the Snowdon episode and the Coniston storm their undertow of threat while also, by a compensatory movement, provoking their persistent appeal to Providence. Columbus, Gilbert, Park, and Dampier are figures of solitary voyagers confronting impossible odds in their quest for new worlds or, like Park, in his journey of exploration into the interior of Africa. Survival is the issue, although for the first of these travellers, Columbus and his crew, loss of bearings—the disorientation of no longer knowing where they are in relation to a hitherto fixed point—figures the momentousness of the voyage of discovery.

> When first, far travelled into unknown seas,
> They saw the needle faltering in its office,
> Turn from the Pole.   (ll. 82–4)

In a narrative suggestive of 'The Ancient Mariner', Columbus has recently endured extremes of heat and drought from which he is only delivered by seemingly miraculous rain and mist.[16] Despite his

---

[16] See F. Colombo, *The Life of the Admiral Christopher Columbus by his Son Ferdinand*, trans. B. Keen (New Brunswick, 1959), 179.

personal privations, he yet has time to observe a moment when nature's laws appear to be suspended, and the old world loses its direction in the new. The needle falters, the North Star seems to change its altitude as the ship shifts in relation to the Pole. That faltering, uncertain moment makes Columbus (and Wordsworth with him) an observer of nature's estranging effects—for Columbus at least, at considerable personal risk. It is as if Wordsworth wants to suggest the power of nature's waters to turn round, as well as orient, the minds of its inmates, gesturing here towards the defamiliarization which nature itself can effect. Just as the spectacle of the Blind London Beggar makes the 'mind . . . turn round | As with the might of waters' (*Prel.* vii. 616–17), so the thought of Columbus dipping down towards the Pole becomes an apprehension, at once privative and sublime, 'of the utmost that we know | Both of ourselves and of the universe' (vii. 619–20).

The motif of personal extinction, whether actual or threatened, links the remaining travel narratives. In the case of Sir Humphrey Gilbert, Wordsworth tells of an engulfment accompanied by personal confidence (or carelessness) about survival so immense as to seem to the awed onlookers like exemplary Christian faith. This is the spectacle presented to Gilbert's followers in a second ship,

> When they beheld him in the furious storm
> Upon the deck of his small pinnace sitting
> In calmness, with a book upon his knee—
> The ship and he a moment afterwards
> Engulphed and seen no more.   (ll. 90–4)[17]

In Wordsworth's startling *mise-en-abyme*, Gilbert goes down reading ('a book upon his knee') with all the obliviousness of a man drowning in his own text. By using a book-derived episode about a figure immersed in a book as an analogy for nature's 'living pictures', Wordsworth may in the end be saying not just that

[17] Wordsworth's source is Edward Haie's report of Sir Humphrey Gilbert's voyage from Hakluyt's *Principall Navigations*; see *The Principall Navigations, Voyages, Traffiques, and Discoveries of the English Nation* (8 vols.; New York and London, 1907), vi. 35–6:' . . . giving foorth signes of joy, the Generall sitting abaft with a booke in his hand, cried out unto us in the Hind (so oft as we did approch within hearing) We are as neere to heaven by sea as by land . . . The same Monday night . . . the Frigat being ahead of us in the Golden Hinde, suddenly her lights were out, whereof as it were in a moment, we lost the sight, and withall our watch cryed, the General was cast away, which was too true. For in that moment, the Frigat was devoured and swallowed up of the Sea.'

reading (like writing) risks putting an end to the empirical life of the reader-writer, but that nature too is a book in which we can drown, as in any other sea of signs. One spin-off would be to deconstruct the traditional distinction between nature as original and book as representation, offering instead the (equally traditional) analogy between the Book of Poetry, or Revelation, and the Book of Nature on which Wordsworth draws in Book V with the Arab Dream.[18] The function of this analogy is ultimately stabilizing. If both nature and books are texts, textuality can thereby be deprived of its dangers—specifically, of its risk to the empirical self confronting the perils of figuration. Nature becomes a benign instance of the figurality of all things. Looked at like this, Gilbert's engulfment might be read as Wordsworth's counter-argument to himself for safety in textuality, as a kind of lifeline; hence Gilbert's sublime indifference to his fate. With just such confidence Wordsworth presumably wished to confront his own engulfment at the end of *The Prelude*.[19]

The last two travel narratives involve an explicit imagining or anticipation of one's own death. They therefore enact the threat to consciousness represented by the drowning of Gilbert, while at the same time reassuring us of the explorer's ultimate survival. Wordsworth's perspective resembles that of the onlookers as Gilbert's ship goes down ('Like spectacle | That traveller yet living doth appear | To the mind's eye . . .', ll. 94–6); he himself remains only a witness, by definition spared the same fate. Yet it seems also that the convergence of his own and another's consciousness is the basis for his identification, with Mungo Park at least. Park, the 'traveller yet living', left a graphic account of what he took to be his last moments in the desert:

as I was now too faint to attempt walking, and my horse too much fatigued to carry me, I thought it but an act of humanity, and perhaps the last I

---

[18] See *Prel.* v. 99–109.

[19] Joseph F. Kishel notices the oddity of this passage—'We read Wordsworth, and he tells us that he has read the story of Gilbert's drowning. In the story, Gilbert himself sits calmly on the deck of his endangered pinnace, reading yet another book'—but suggests only that 'This Chinese puzzle of distanced observers leaves us with a strong sense that Wordsworth is grappling with but not solving questions of conscious artistic control'; see 'The "Analogy Passage" ', pp. 281–2. Kishel's argument (designed to counter Hartman's 'apocalyptic' reading of the Snowdon episode) focuses on the question of Wordsworth's conscious or unconscious struggle for artistic distance at a turbulent moment in his career.

should ever have it in my power to perform, to take off his bridle and let
him shift for himself; in doing which I was suddenly affected with sickness
and giddiness; and falling upon the sand, felt as if the hour of death was
fast approaching. 'Here then, thought I, after a short but ineffectual
struggle, terminate all my hopes of being useful in my day and generation:
here must the short span of my life come to an end.'—I cast (as I believed) a
last look on the surrounding scene, and whilst I reflected on the awful
change that was about to take place, this world with its enjoyments seemed
to vanish from my recollection. Nature, however, at length resumed its
functions; and on recovering my senses, I found my self stretched upon the
sand, with the bridle still in my hand, and the sun just sinking behind the
trees.[20]

Wordsworth omits all but the briefest summary of Mungo Park's
thoughts on his impending death ('overcome with weariness and
pain . . . Sunk to the earth', ll. 98–100), focusing instead on his
awakening to find his horse by his side and his arm still within the
bridle, 'the sun | Setting upon the desert', 102–3). But Park's hopes
of being useful in [his] day and generation' must have resonated
with Wordsworth's own literary ambitions, if nothing else, while
Park's graphic account of the extinction and revival of consciousness takes him from self-loss to a sense of providential self-
recovery—from engulfment and back again, as if he had stepped
over the brink of Snowdon's 'deep and gloomy breathing place' and
returned to solid land; or as if Gilbert had only momentarily
appeared to go under.

In telling Dampier's story, Wordsworth remains similarly on the
brink, casting himself as reader: 'Kindred power | Was present for
the suffering and distress | *In those who read the story*' (ll. 103–5;
my italics). Wordsworth seems to be offering something like a
theory of the Sublime of reading, in which the power of 'suffering
and distress' to produce pleasure depends on the readers's own
immunity from the threat of bodily destruction. With Dampier's
story of imminent death by water we come full circle to the missing
Ark on Lake Coniston. As Dampier writes,

The sea was already roaring in white Foam about us; a dark Night coming
on, and no Land in sight to shelter us, *and our little Ark in danger to be
swallowed by every Wave*; and what was worst of all, none of us thought
ourselves prepared for another World. The reader may better guess, than I

[20] M. Park, *Travels in the Interior Districts of Africa . . . in the Years 1795, 1796
and 1797* (2nd edn., London, 1799), 177.

can express, the confusion that we were all in. I had been in many Imminent Dangers before now . . . but the worst of them all was but a play-game, in comparison with this.[21]

Dampier is by no means the one just man assured of personal salvation; on the contrary, his 'lingering view of approaching Death'—danger that comes on 'with such a leisurely and dreadful Solemnity'—provides ample time for reflection (as Wordsworth puts it, 'Bitter repentance for his roving life', l. 115), and also for interpreting the signs (Wordsworth's apocalyptic 'portents of the broken wheel | Girding the sun', ll. 108–9). In his deliberate appeal to the reader ('The reader may better guess, than I can express, the confusion that we were in'), Dampier draws attention to the drama of providential survival. Even in the midst of the storm, he has time to 'call to mind the many miraculous Acts of God's Providence towards [him]', and to negotiate the threat of death (in Words-worth's phrase) 'by prayer and trust in God' (l. 117). The reader who identifies with Dampier's peril without actually undergoing it becomes the guarantee of his survival; as in the case of Mungo Park, we know that if Dampier had perished, there would have been no travel narrative.[22]

Is this, perhaps, the significance for Wordsworth of these exotic 'analogues' in which a solitary consciousness encounters death—not so much their representation of sublime effects or momentous states of mind, as the fact that they guarantee the tale-teller's immortality or, at least, his continued empirical existence? Dramas involving risky survival may be especially liable to come to mind as a long poem reaches its end. We know, in fact, that Wordsworth had a change of plan and continued to expand *The Prelude* beyond this briefly glimpsed ending—as if he was unable to confront the cessation of his own tale ('the tale which I have left behind', l. 9), and with it, his extinction as an autobiographical figure within the poem. Park and Dampier become the sign of a continued life in writing and even beyond—surviving to travel on past the vividly anticipated endings to their stories. If Wordsworth himself briefly appears to us between the lines as a kind of Ancient Mariner, unable to arrest his own narrative and forced to retell his tale to

---

[21] W. Dampier, *A New Voyage Round the World* (2nd edn., London, 1697), 496; my italics.

[22] As Theresa M. Kelly points out, however, Park—like Dampier—was later to lose his life; see *Wordsworth's Revisionary Aesthetics* (Cambridge, 1988), 130.

whoever will listen, this is no more than to say that the compulsion to narrate always involves a compulsion to repeat, and that the compulsion to repeat simultaneously signifies and averts death. These narratives of averted endings offer signification itself as a token of survival in the face of the overwhelming dangers of textual exploration. The text becomes rainbow as well as sea, promising adamantine firmness as well as oceanic usurpation. Converted from a shifting sea of tropes to a fixed system of analogy, both nature and figuration lose their dangers and the writer can continue his voyage of exploration, buoyed up by the very signs which had earlier threatened to engulf him.

Anthropomorphism and Romantic Analogy

Writing of anthropomorphism and trope in the lyric, Paul de Man makes the distinction between trope (a figural mode of representation) and the foreclosure of figuration involved in anthropomorphism, defined as 'an identification on the level of substance' that 'takes one entity for another and thus implies the constitution of specific entities prior to their confusion, the *taking* of something for something else that can then be assumed to be a *given*'. Though close to metaphor (as in the case of an Ovidian metamorphosis, or 'the resemblance between a natural scene and a state of soul'), anthropomorphism characteristically works to arrest the play of figuration with a name or personification:

Anthropomorphism freezes the infinite chain of tropological transformations and propositions into one single assertion or essence which, as such, excludes all others. It is no longer a proposition but a proper name, as when the metamorphosis in Ovid's stories culminates and halts in the singleness of a proper name, Narcissus, or Daphne or whatever. Far from being the same, tropes such as metaphor (or metonymy) and anthropomorphism are mutually exclusive.[23]

The proper name that functions most obviously as an anthropomorphism in Wordsworth's poetry is 'Nature'; but by the same

[23] 'Anthropomorphism and Trope in the Lyric', *The Rhetoric of Romanticism*, pp. 240–1. De Man is commenting and elaborating on a sentence by Nietzsche which appears to elide metaphor, metonymy, and anthropomorphism. For a recent discussion of de Man's contribution to the critique of Romantic ideology, see C. Norris, *Paul de Man: Deconstruction and the Critique of Aesthetic Ideology* (New York and London, 1988), 218–64.

token, both 'Mind', 'Man', and 'Imagination' (and, for that matter, 'Soul') also function as naturalized proper names, or stand-ins for 'Wordsworth' himself. The *'taking* of something for something else' is in this case tantamount to saying that the natural is human—and that the human is natural, a given rather than (for instance) a linguistic or figural construct.[24] For de Man, the chief characteristic or tendency of lyric poetry is to render its tropes as anthropomorphisms, so that metaphor becomes a way to make the human into a naturalized essence or talisman against figurality.

De Man's focus on this moment when tropological transformations are frozen, or entities assumed to be givens, displays the habitually profound scepticism of his writing when questions of figurality arise. If privation is the condition of understanding, since understanding itself can only be figural, then 'Death is a displaced name for a linguistic predicament' (a predicament which autobiography and epitaphs inscribe with especial bleakness).[25] No wonder, then, that at the approaching end of Wordsworth's lyric autobiography—his self-authored epitaph—the question of death and the question of anthropomorphism should converge in the powerfully overdetermined manner of the 'Analogy' passage. It seems fair to gloss anthropomorphism with Wordsworth's own term. 'Oft tracing this analogy betwixt | The mind of man and Nature' (ll. 26–7), he finds in analogy itself a 'pleasing argument' capable of averting the ending of an empirical self threatened by both autobiography and figuration. Nature is simply a proper name for man, and the 'deep and gloomy breathing place' glimpsed from Mount Snowdon can become the natural counterpart of the human as a given entity. But there is more to be said about analogy. Kant's usage is especially provocative and illuminating in relation to Wordsworth's. 'The analogies of experience' which constitute a culminating section of *The Critique of Pure Reason* (1781) are famous for embodying Kant's argument that experience is only possible in the light of relational categories such as causality, space,

[24] As Cynthia Chase writes of de Man's reading of anthropomorphism, 'Taking the natural as human, it takes the human as given. This is to take the human as natural, to create a naturalness of man from which man and nature in effect disappear as the distinction between them is effaced': see *Decomposing Figures: Rhetorical Readings in the Romantic Tradition*, pp. 83–4, as well as the discussion of the ideology of lyric poetry in de Man's writing, ibid. 106–10.

[25] See *The Rhetoric of Romanticism*, p. 81.

and time.[26] But Kant's *Critique of Aesthetic Judgement* (1790) offers a discussion of analogy more relevant to Wordsworth's poem, as well as throwing light on his use, not so much of the term, as of the tropological system—the systematic denial of tropes—which it works to conceal.[27]

'*Rhetoric*', writes Kant, 'is the art of transacting a serious business of the understanding as if it were a free play of the imagination; *poetry* that of conducting a free play of the imagination as if it were a serious business of the understanding.'[28] Here Kant seems to pay tribute at once to the necessity of transacting 'a serious business of the understanding' (rhetorical argument) by way of tropes, and to the truth claims of poetry ('a free play of imagination') despite the dependence of poetry on tropological structures. Given this deconstructive mode, not to mention Kant's implicit founding of all acts of understanding on metaphor, it is hardly surprising that Derrida, in *La vérité en peinture* (1978) should allude to Kant's project in *The Critique of Aesthetic Judgement* as the attempt to 'fill a crack, a cleavage, an abyss (*Kluft*)' between what Kant calls 'the realm of the natural concept, as the sensible, and the realm of the concept of freedom, as the supersensible'—realms between which 'there is a great gulf fixed, so that it is not possible to pass from the former to the latter (by means of the theoretical employment of reason), just as if they were so many worlds, the first of which is powerless to exercise influence on the second'; even though the second is meant to exercise its influence on the first.[29] For Kant, these are the respective realms of

[26] For the place of the 'Analogies of Experience' in Kant's thought, see G. Buchdahl, *Metaphysics and the Philosophy of Science* (Cambridge, Mass., 1969), 641–71, and A. Melnick, *Kant's Analogies of Experience* (Chicago and London, 1973).

[27] For Kantian aesthetics and Kantian analogy as a point of reference for de Man's critique of Romantic ideology, see Norris, *Paul de Man: Deconstruction and the Critique of Aesthetic Ideology*, pp. 53–9. If Wordsworth himself knew Kant's third *Critique*—and there is no evidence that he did at this point—then it would have been via Coleridge, whose serious study of Kant's writings began in 1801 and who later singled out *The Critique of Aesthetic Judgement* as 'the most astonishing' of Kant's works; see G. N. G. Orsini, *Coleridge and German Idealism* (Carbondale and London, 1969), 47–8, 159. For a brief discussion of the relevance to Coleridge's thinking of Kant's third *Critique*, see also P. Hamilton, *Coleridge's Poetics* (Oxford, 1983), 47–54.

[28] *Kant's Critique of Aesthetic Judgement*, trans. J. C. Meredith (Oxford, 1911), 184.

[29] 'The Parergon', *La verité en peinture*, trans. C. Owens, *October*, 8 (1979), 4. The quotation is from *Kant's Critique of Aesthetic Judgement*, trans. Meredith, p. 14.

understanding and reason. What makes the risky passage from one to the other possible in Kant's writing is the insistence on 'a ground of the *unity* of the supersensible that lies at the basis of nature', or analogy. Kant's insistence that the same laws ultimately govern the supersensible and the sensible is the bridge over the abyss. As Derrida puts it, however, 'The abyss elicits analogy—the active recourse of the entire *Critique*—but analogy succumbs to the abyss as soon as a certain artfulness is required for the analogical description of the play of analogy.'[30] To become aware of the tropological status of analogy is to tumble into the abyss, losing one's footing as in Kant's classic formulation of the Sublime ('The point of excess for the imagination . . . is like an abyss in which it fears to lose itself').[31]

How might this illuminate the Snowdon passage in Book XIII? One answer lies in Kant's extensive use of analogy as a term to shore up the symbolic bridging of the abyss between nature and supernature (the 'sensible' and the 'supersensible')—not to mention his linguistic analysis of words so overdetermined in relation to his own argument as to represent an implicit demonstration of the rhetorical dependence on tropes of all acts of understanding:

In language we have many such indirect presentations modelled upon an analogy enabling the expression in question to contain, not the proper schema for the concept, but merely a symbol for reflection. Thus the words *ground* (support, basis), to *depend* (to be held up from above), to *flow* from (instead of to follow), *substance* (as Locke puts it: the support of accidents) and numberless others . . . express concepts without employing a direct intuition for the purpose, but only drawing upon an analogy with one, i.e. transferring the reflection upon an object of intuition to quite a new concept, and one with which perhaps no intuition could ever directly correspond.[32]

In such precariousness we see (as Derrida notes) analogy tumbling into the abyss, becoming metaphorical just when it should provide us with firm ground to depend on, or the basis—the 'substance'— from which stable meanings might flow. Because Kant's insistence on the indissoluble bridge between the 'supersensible' or symbolic realm and the realm of nature, or the 'sensible', finally eludes his own attempts at stabilization, *The Critique of Aesthetic Judgement*

[30] 'The Parergon', trans. Owens, p. 4.
[31] *Kant's Critique of Aesthetic Judgement*, trans. Meredith, p. 107.
[32] Ibid. 223.

provides an analogue (an analogy) both for Wordsworth's rhetorical strategy in *The Prelude* and for the rhetorical predicament
which we see at its clearest in the Snowdon episode.

The passage from *The Critique of Aesthetic Judgement* which has
the most direct bearing on Wordsworth's deployment of 'counterpart' and 'analogy' in Book XIII is the one in which Kant writes,
apropos of 'the animating principle in the mind' ('Soul' or *Geist*)
which is 'nothing less than the faculty of presenting *aesthetic ideas*',
that the imagination builds up a 'second nature' on the basis of
'actual nature':

The imagination (as a productive faculty of cognition) is a powerful agent
for creating, as it were, a second nature out of the material supplied to it by
actual nature . . . we even use it to remodel experience, always following,
no doubt, laws that are based on analogy, but still also following principles
which have a higher seat in reason (and which are every whit as natural to
us as those followed by the understanding in laying hold of empirical
nature). By this means we get a sense of our freedom from the law of
association (which attaches to the empirical employment of the imagination), with the result that the material can be borrowed by us from nature
in accordance with that law, but be worked up by us into something else—
namely, what surpasses nature.

Such representations of the imagination may be termed *ideas*. This is
partly because they at least strain after something lying out beyond the
confines of experience, and so seek to approximate to a presentation of
rational concepts (i.e., intellectual ideas), thus giving to these concepts the
semblance of an objective reality. But, on the other hand, there is this most
important reason, that no concept can be wholly adequate to them as
internal intuitions. The poet essays the task of interpreting to sense the
rational ideas of invisible beings, the kingdom of the blessed, hell, eternity,
creation, &c. Or again, as to things of which examples occur in experience,
e.g. death, envy, and all vices, as also love, fame and the like, transgressing
the limits of experience he attempts with the aid of an imagination which
emulates the display of reason in its attainment of a maximum, to body
them forth to sense with a completeness of which nature affords no
parallel; and it is in fact precisely in the poetic art that the faculty of
aesthetic ideas can show itself to full advantage.[33]

While Kant admits here that the imagination can create for itself a
second nature propped on nature, he is careful to add, parenthetic-
ally, that the principles at work are 'every whit as natural to us as
those followed by the understanding in laying hold of empirical

[33] *Kant's Critique of Aesthetic Judgement*, pp. 176–7.

nature'. The imagination may sense its freedom from nature, but. this freedom is by no means arbitrary. For Kant, as for Wordsworth, however, the analogy on which he insists amounts in the end to an argument for imaginative usurpation notwithstanding its material prop. Imagination, like Kant's reason, effectively triumphs over the laws of nature (the realm of the understanding), freeing us from the laws of association and transforming material borrowed from nature into 'something else—namely, what surpasses nature'. We are on the way to Wordsworth's final claim at the end of *The Prelude*, not that imagination and nature are counterparts, but that the mind becomes a thousand times more beautiful than the earth.

If we read the Snowdon episode in the light of this passage from *The Critique of Aesthetic Judgement*, the very idea of a counterpart —of analogy—becomes a sign of imminent usurpation, or the workings of an imagination paradoxically driven to exceed the confines of the nature on which it depends. Analogy, Derrida observes, is elicited by the emptiness of the abyss—by the cleft it attempts to bridge. The sea of mist (more oceanic than the ocean itself) or the 'fracture in the vapour' whose sublimity is that of an idea 'transgressing the limits of experience', give us naturalized analogy, or trope masquerading as essence. In the Snowdon episode, the aestheticizing language applied to the chasm could, however, be read as referring not so much to the 'fracture in the vapour', as to the poetic representation of ideas—in Kant's terms, the interpretation to sense of rational ideas about what is invisible. The emphasis on making visible is what matters here (compare Kristeva's definition of metaphoricity as a 'movement towards the discernible, a journey towards the visible').[34] 'What the moon saw' is a vision, or revelation—a metaphor—of the invisible powers of mind (and nature). When Wordsworth meditates on the Snowdon landscape, seeing in it 'The perfect image of a mighty mind', his insistence that nature has offered an analogy for the workings of the imagination thus tends, not so much to endow nature with the power of supernature, as to elevate the mind itself (his mind) as the proper object of aesthetic contemplation. In its capacity for metaphorical activity, the mind always usurps nature, even though nature can apparently envision something for itself (a sea of mist instead of a real sea). The aesthetic, in short, surfaces as a

---

[34] *The Kristeva Reader*, ed. Moi, p. 247.

retrospective defence against the threat to subjectivity implicit in
the Snowdon scene; thus conceived, the mind becomes adamantine,
like the unmutilated rainbow over Coniston. If figuration involves
mutilation, the aestheticized imagination involves the restitution of
an imaginary wholeness—'a completeness of which nature affords
no parallel'. Wordsworth first sketches the potential loss of
individual consciousness in the roar of waters, then celebrates its
restoration by way of the consoling fiction that in nature and in
man, analogously, is a super-subjectivity ('The perfect image of a
mighty mind') able to withstand extinction. In the last resort, he
posits the mind as his crowning anthropomorphism in order to halt
the tropological play of the poem and bring it to a close on the
promise of salvation.

   This is the function of anthropomorphism as de Man describes
it—to naturalize (and so to preserve) the human against figuration.
The closing site for this tropological arrest in *The Prelude* is its
singling out of the individual mind as the unique ground of
understanding. 'Such minds', Wordsworth insists, 'are truly from
the Deity'; their highest bliss is

                              the consciousness
         Of whom they are, habitually infused
         Through every image, and through every thought,
         And all impressions . . .

                         (*Prel.* xiii. 108–11)

If tumbling into the abyss involves no longer knowing who you are,
such habitual consciousness of self represents the apotheosis of
stable identity. This is the egotistical Sublime in action. What the
moon saw was itself, 'infused | Through every image'. To arrive at
such a moment of self-consciousness posited on aesthetic self-
mirroring might be viewed as the final goal of any autobiographical
work concerned to instate the mind of the writer as its ultimate
ground—its central and animating anthropomorphism. This is the
note on which Wordsworth ends his poem, with his insistence that
the lesson taught by *The Prelude* is 'how the mind of man becomes |
A thousand times more beautiful than the earth | On which he
dwells' (xiii. 446–8). Representing the mind of man as an aesthetic
object allows Wordsworth to save the mind, not by way of
Providence, but by way of the agency which functions as
providential in the poem, namely, 'Nature'. If nature is the

anthropomorphism that makes signs adamantine in the face of the dissolving movement of metaphor, the function of Wordsworth's Romantic analogy is to stem the tropological unravelling of the autobiographical figure. Romantic lyricism and Romantic auto-biography derive their confidence from this rhetorical and con-ceptual move—a move at once self-conscious, self-reflexive, and, in the last resort, always mined from beneath by the fracture in the vapour or abyss which both de Man and Derrida identify with figuration. For Kant, rhetoric transacts the business of the understanding as if it were the free play of imagination, and poetry conducts the free play of imagination as if it were the business of understanding. *The Prelude* (an extended Romantic analogy or lyric autobiography) is Wordsworth's rhetorical attempt to bridge the figurative and insubstantial abyss which is its ground, on which it depends, and from which its meanings flow. The hidden lesson in his teaching (how the mind of man becomes more beautiful than nature) is how to read his poem as Romantic analogy; as a naturalization of the Romantic and aesthetic ideology which it embodies. This is the instruction which installs *The Prelude* as the privileged aesthetic object of our critical attention, assuring its reception as both readable and Romantic by a succession of Romantic reader-critics, of whom Wordsworth himself was the first.

Appendix

'Even yet thou wilt vouchsafe an ear'
(The 'Analogy' passage from MS W of *The Prelude*)

Even yet thou wilt vouchsafe an ear, O friend,
And something too of a submissive mind,
As in thy mildness thou I know hast done,
While with a winding but no devious song
Through [   ] processes I make my way   5
By links of tender thought. My present aim
Is to contemplate for a needful while
(Passage which will conduct in season due
Back to the tale which I have left behind)
The diverse manner in which Nature works   10
Oft times upon the outward face of things,
I mean so moulds, exalts, endues, combines,
Impregnates, separates, adds, takes away,
And makes one object sway another so
By unhabitual influence or abrupt,   15
That even the grossest minds must see and hear
And cannot chuse but feel. The power which these
Are touched by, being so moved—which Nature thus
Puts forth upon the senses (not to speak
Of finer operations)—is in kind   20
A brother of the very faculty
Which higher minds bear with them as their own.
These from their native selves can deal about
Like transformation, to one life impart
The functions of another, shift, create,   25
Trafficking with immeasurable thoughts.
Oft tracing this analogy betwixt
The mind of man and Nature, doth the scene
Which from the side of Snowdon I beheld
Rise up before me, followed too in turn   30
By sundry others, whence I will select
A portion, living pictures, to embody
This pleasing argument.
                                It was a day
Upon the edge of autumn, fierce with storm;
The wind blew down the vale of Coniston   35

Compressed as in a tunnel; from the lake
Bodies of foam took flight, and every thing
Was wrought into commotion high and low,
A roaring wind, mist, and bewildered showers,
Ten thousand thousand waves, mountains and crags,   40
And darkness and the sun's tumultuous light.
Green leaves were rent in handfuls from the trees;
The mountains all seemed silent, din so near
Pealed in the traveller's ear, the clouds [? ?],
The horse and rider staggered in the blast,   45
And he who looked upon the stormy lake
Had fear for boat or vessel where none was.
Meanwhile, by what strange chance I cannot tell,
What combination of the wind and clouds,
A large unmutilated rainbow stood   50
Immoveable in heaven, [?] [? been] [?]
With stride colossal bridging the whole vale.
The substance thin as dreams, lovelier than day,
Amid the deafening uproar stood unmoved,
Sustained itself through many minutes space,   55
As if it were pinned down by adamant.

   One evening, walking in the public way,
A peasant of the valley where I dwelt
Being my chance companion, he stopped short
And point to an object full in view   60
At a small distance. 'Twas a horse, that stood
Alone upon a little breast of ground
With a clear silver moonlight sky behind.
With one leg from the ground the creature stood,
Insensible and still; breath, motion gone,   65
Hairs, colour, all but shape and substance gone,
Mane, ears, and tail, as lifeless as the trunk
That had no stir of breath. We paused awhile
In pleasure of the sight, and left him there,
With all his functions silently sealed up,   70
Like an amphibious work of Nature's hand,
A borderer dwelling betwixt life and death,
A living statue or a statued life.

   Add others still more obvious, those I mean
Which Nature forces on the sight when she   75
Takes man into the bosom of her works—
Man suffering or enjoying. Meanest minds
Want not these moments, if they would look

Back on the past, and books are full of them.
Such power to pass at once from daily life, 80
Such power was with Columbus and his crew
When first, far travelled into unknown seas,
They saw the needle faltering in its office,
Turn from the Pole. What chivalry was seen
With English heroes in thy golden times 85
Elizabeth—such perhaps to those behind
That followed closely in a second ship,
Tried comrades in his perils, did present
Sir Humphrey Gilbert, that bold voyager,
When they beheld him in the furious storm 90
Upon the deck of his small pinnace sitting
In calmness, with a book upon his knee—
The ship and he a moment afterwards
Engulphed and seen no more.
            Like spectacle
That traveller yet living doth appear 95
To the mind's eye, when from the Moors escaped,
Alone, and in the heart of Africa,
And overcome with weariness and pain
That he [?] at length the sense of life,
Sunk to the earth, did find when he awaked 100
His horse in quiet standing at his side,
His arm within the bridle, and the sun
Setting upon the desart. Kindred power
Was present for the suffering and distress
In those who read the story at their ease 105
When, flying in his Nicobar canoe
With three Malayan helpers, Dampier saw
Well in those portents of the broken wheel
Girding the sun, and afterwards the sea
Roaring and whitening at the night's approach, 110
And danger coming on, not in a shape
Which in the heat and mettle of the blood
He oft had welcomed, but deliberate,
With dread and leisurely solemnity.
Bitter repentance for his roving life 115
Seized then upon the vent'rous mariner,
Made calm at length by prayer and trust in God.
Meanwhile the bark went forward like an arrow,
For many hours abandoned to the wind,
Her steersman. But a slackening of the storm 120
Encouraged them at length to cast a look

Upon the compass, by a lighted match
Made visible, which they in their distress
Kept burning for the purpose. Thus they fared
Sitting all night upon the lap of death   125
In wet and starveling plight, wishing for dawn,
A dawn that came at length, with gloomy clouds
Blackening the horizon; the first glimpse
Far from the horizon's edge, high up in heaven—
High dawn, prognosticating winds as high.   130

(*Prel.* 496–9)

Select Bibliography

ABEL, E. (ed.), *Writing and Sexual Difference* (Chicago and London, 1982).

ABRAMS, M. H., *Natural Supernaturalism* (New York, 1971).

ALTER, R., and KERMODE, F. (eds.), *The Literary Guide to the Bible* (Cambridge, Mass., 1987).

ALTHUSSER, L., and BALIBAR, É., *Reading Capital*, trans. B. Brewster (London, 1970).

ARAC, J., *Critical Genealogies: Historical Situations for Postmodern Literary Studies* (New York, 1987).

—— GODZICH, W. and MARTIN, W. (eds.), *The Yale Critics: Deconstruction in America* (Minneapolis, 1983).

AUDEN, W. H., *The Enchafed Flood or the Romantic Iconography of the Sea* (New York, 1950).

AUSONIUS, *Ausonius*, trans. H. G. E. White (London and Cambridge, Mass., 1919).

BAGEHOT, W., *The English Constitution*, ed. Lord Balfour (London, 1949).

BALL, W. W. R., *A History of the Study of Mathematics at Cambridge* (Cambridge, 1889).

BARISH, J., *The Antitheatrical Prejudice* (Berkeley, 1981).

BARTHOLOMEUSZ, D., *Macbeth and the Players* (London, 1979).

BEATTIE, J., *The Minstrel* (London, 1771).

BERRY, F., *Poetry and the Physical Voice* (London, 1962).

BERSANI, L., *A Future for Astyanax: Character and Desire in Literature* (Boston, Mass., and Toronto, 1969).

BLACKBURN, R., *The Overthrow of Colonial Slavery, 1776–1848* (London, 1988).

BLAIR, H., *Lectures on Rhetoric and Belles Lettres* (1783), ed. H. F. Harding (2 vols.; Carbondale, 1965).

BLANSHARD, F., *Portraits of Wordsworth* (Ithaca, NY, 1959).

BLOOM, H., *The Ringers in the Tower* (Chicago, 1971).

—— (ed.), *Deconstruction and Criticism* (London, 1979).

BOULTON, J. T., *The Language of Politics in the Age of Wilkes and Burke* (London, 1963).

BROMWICH, D., *Hazlitt: The Mind of a Critic* (New York and Oxford, 1983).

BROWNE, Sir Thomas, *Religio Medici and Other Works*, ed. L. C. Martin (Oxford, 1964).

BUCHDAHL, G., *Metaphysics and the Philosophy of Science* (Cambridge, Mass., 1969).

BURKE, E., *The Correspondence of Edmund Burke*, ed. A. Cobban and R. A. Smith (9 vols.; Cambridge, 1967).

—— *Edmund Burke*, ed. I. Kramnick (Englewood Cliffs, 1974).

BURKE, E., *A Philosophical Enquiry into the Origin of Our Ideas of the Sublime and Beautiful*, ed. J. T. Boulton (London, 1958).
—— *Reflections on the Revolution in France*, ed. C. C. O'Brien (Harmondsworth, 1968).
—— *Speeches of the Right Honourable Edmund Burke* (4 vols.; London, 1816).
—— *The Works of Edmund Burke* (5 vols.; London, 1855–64).
BUTLER, J., *The Analogy of Religion, Natural and Revealed, to the Constitution and Course of Nature* (London, 1736).

CARLYLE, T., *Critical and Miscellaneous Essays* (5 vols.; London, 1905).
CHANDLER, J. K., *Wordsworth's Second Nature: A Study of the Poetry and Politics* (Chicago, 1984).
CHASE, C., *Decomposing Figures: Rhetorical Readings in the Romantic Tradition* (Baltimore, 1986).
CLARK, R. B., *William Gifford: Tory Satirist and Editor* (New York, 1930).
CLARKSON, T., *Essay on the Slavery and Commerce of the Human Species* (London, 1786).
—— *History of the Rise, Progress, and Accomplishment of the Abolition of the African Slave-Trade* (2 vols.; London, 1808).
COLERIDGE, S. T., *Biographia Literaria*, ed. J. Engell and W. J. Bate (2 vols.; Princeton and London, 1983).
—— *Coleridge's Shakespeare Criticism*, ed. T. M. Raysor (2 vols.; London, 1960).
—— *Collected Letters of Samuel Taylor Coleridge*, ed. E. L. Griggs (6 vols.; Oxford, 1956–71).
—— *The Collected Works of Samuel Taylor Coleridge: Essays on His Times*, ed. D. V. Erdman (3 vols.; Princeton and London, 1978).
—— *The Friend*, ed. B. Rooke (2 vols.; London, 1969).
—— *Lectures 1795 on Politics and Religion*, ed. L. Patton and P. Mann (Princeton, 1971).
—— *The Notebooks of Samuel Taylor Coleridge*, ed. K. Coburn (3 vols.; London, 1957–73).
—— *Seven Lectures on Shakespeare and Milton*, ed. J. Payne Collier (London, 1856).
—— *Specimens of the Table Talk of the Late Samuel Taylor Coleridge*, ed. H. N. Coleridge (London, 1835).
COLOMBO, F., *The Life of the Admiral Christopher Columbus by his Son Ferdinand*, trans. B. Keen (New Brunswick, 1959).
COWLEY, A., *The English Writings of Abraham Cowley*, ed. A. R. Waller (2 vols.; Cambridge, 1905).
CRANE, R. S. (ed.), *Critics and Criticism Ancient and Modern* (Chicago, 1952).

DAMPIER, W., *A New Voyage Round the World* (2nd edn., London, 1697).
DARWIN, E., *The Botanic Garden: Part II, The Loves of the Plants* (Lichfield, 1789).

DAVIS, D. B., *The Problem of Slavery in the Age of Revolution* (Ithaca, NY, 1975).

DE QUINCEY, T., *The Collected Writings of Thomas De Quincey*, ed. D. Masson (14 vols.; Edinburgh, 1889–90).

—— *Confessions of an English Opium-Eater and Other Writings*, ed. G. Lindop (Oxford and New York, 1985).

—— *De Quincey as Critic*, ed. J. E. Jordan (London and Boston, Mass., 1973).

—— *Recollections of the Lakes and the Lake Poets*, ed. D. Wright (Harmondsworth, 1970).

DERRIDA, J., *Speech and Phenomena*, trans. D. B. Allison (Evanston, 1973).

DONOGHUE, J., *Dramatic Character in the English Romantic Age* (Princeton, 1970).

DRESCHER, S., *Econocide: British Slavery in the Era of Abolition* (Pittsburgh, 1977).

—— *Capitalism and Antislavery: British Mobilization in Comparative Perspective* (Oxford, 1988).

EATON, H. A., *Thomas De Quincey* (New York, 1936).

ELTIS, D., *Economic Growth and the Ending of the Transatlantic Slave Trade* (Oxford, 1987).

—— and WALVIN, J. (eds.), *The Abolition of the Atlantic Slave Trade* (Madison, 1981).

EQUIANO, O., *The Interesting Narrative of the Life of Olaudah Equiano, or Gustavus Vassa the African, written by himself* (2nd edn., 2 vols.; London, 1789).

EUCLID, *Euclid's Elements*, trans. I. Barrow (2nd edn., London, 1686).

FARRELL, J. P., *Revolution as Tragedy: The Dilemma of the Moderate from Scott to Arnold* (Ithaca, NY, 1980).

FELMAN, S., *Writing and Madness*, trans. M. N. Evans and the author (Ithaca, NY, 1985).

FERGUSON, F., *Wordsworth: Language as Counter-Spirit* (New Haven and London, 1977).

FOWLER, A., *Kinds of Literature: An Introduction to the Theory of Genres and Modes* (Cambridge, Mass., 1982).

FREUD, S., *The Standard Edition of the Complete Psychological Works of Sigmund Freud*, trans. and ed. J. Strachey (24 vols.; London, 1953–74).

FRY, P. H., *The Poet's Calling in the English Ode* (New Haven and London, 1980).

FURNEAUX, R., *William Wilberforce* (London, 1974).

GARNER, S. N., KAHANE, C., and SPRENGNETHER, M. (eds.), *The (M)other Tongue: Essays in Feminist Psychoanalytic Interpretation* (Ithaca, NY, and London, 1985).

GEGGUS, D. P., *Slavery, War, and Revolution: The British Occupation of Saint Dominigue 1793–1798* (Oxford, 1982).

302 *Select Bibliography*

GITTINGS, R., and MANTON, J., *Dorothy Wordsworth* (Oxford, 1985).

HAKLUYT, R., *The Principall Navigations, Voyages, Traffiques, and Discoveries of the English Nation* (8 vols.; New York and London, 1907).
HAMILTON, P., *Coleridge's Poetics* (Oxford, 1983).
HARTMAN, G., *Beyond Formalism* (New Haven and London, 1970).
—— *The Fate of Reading and Other Essays* (Chicago and London, 1975).
—— (ed.), *New Perspectives on Coleridge and Wordsworth: Selected Papers from the English Institute* (New York and London, 1972).
—— *The Unremarkable Wordsworth* (Minneapolis, 1987).
—— *Wordsworth's Poetry 1787–1814* (New Haven, 1964).
HAZLITT, W., *The Complete Works of William Hazlitt*, ed. P. P. Howe (21 vols.; London, 1930–4).
HENRIQUES, F., *Prostitution and Society* (3 vols.; London, 1963).
HERTZ, N., *The End of the Line* (New York, 1985).
HOLLANDER, J., *The Figure of Echo: A Mode of Allusion in Milton and After* (Berkeley and London, 1981).
—— *Rhyme's Reason: A Guide to English Verse* (New Haven and London, 1981).
HOMANS, M., *Bearing the Word: Language and Female Experience in Nineteenth-Century Women's Writing* (Chicago and London, 1986).
HOSEK, C., and PARKER, P. (eds.), *Lyric Poetry: Beyond New Criticism* (Ithaca, NY, 1985).
HUME, D., *Of the Standard of Taste and Other Essays*, ed. J. W. Lenz (Indianapolis, 1965).

JACOBUS, M., *Reading Woman: Essays in Feminist Criticism* (New York and London, 1986).
JOHNSON, B., *A World of Difference* (Baltimore, 1987).
JOHNSON, S., *Lives of the English Poets*, ed. G. Birkbeck Hill (3 vols.; Oxford, 1905).
JOHNSTON, K. R., *Wordsworth and the Recluse* (New Haven and London, 1984).

KANT, I., *Kant's Critique of Aesthetic Judgement*, trans. J. C. Meredith (Oxford, 1911).
KATES, G., *The Cercle Social, the Girondins, and the French Revolution* (Princeton, 1985).
KEATS, J., *The Letters of John Keats*, ed. H. E. Rollins (2 vols.; Cambridge, Mass., 1958).
KELLY, T. M., *Wordsworth's Revisionary Aesthetics* (Cambridge, 1988).
KINNAIRD, J., *William Hazlitt: Critic of Power* (New York, 1978).
KNAPP, S., *Personification and the Sublime: Milton to Coleridge* (Cambridge, Mass., and London, 1985).
KRAMNICK, I., *The Rage of Edmund Burke: Portrait of an Ambivalent Conservative* (New York, 1977).

KRISTEVA, J., *Desire in Language: A Semiotic Approach to Literature and Art*, ed. L. S. Roudiez (New York, 1980).
—— *The Kristeva Reader*, ed. T. Moi (New York, 1986).
—— *Powers of Horror: An Essay on Abjection*, trans. L. S. Roudiez (New York, 1982).

LACAN, J., *Écrits*, trans. A. Sheridan (London, 1977).
—— *The Four Fundamental Concepts of Psycho-Analysis*, ed. J.-A. Miller, trans. A. Sheridan (New York, 1978).
LAMB, C. and M., *The Works of Charles and Mary Lamb*, ed. E. V. Lucas (5 vols.; London, 1903–4).
—— *The Letters of Charles and Mary Anne Lamb*, ed. E. W. Marrs, Jr. (3 vols.; Ithaca, NY, 1975–8).
LIPKING, L. (ed.), *High Romantic Argument: Essays for M. H. Abrams* (Ithaca, NY, and London, 1981).
LIU, A., *Wordsworth: The Sense of History* (Stanford, 1989).
LOUVET, J.-B., *Narrative of the Dangers to which I have been Exposed* (London, 1795).

McGANN, J. J., *The Romantic Ideology: A Critical Investigation* (Chicago and London, 1983).
McKENDRICK, N., BREWER, J., and PLUMB, J. H. (eds.), *The Birth of a Consumer Society: The Commercialization of Eighteenth-Century England* (Bloomington, 1982).
MACKINTOSH, Sir James, *Vindiciae Gallicae* (London, 1791).
DE MAN, P., *Allegories of Reading: Figural Language in Rousseau, Nietzsche, Rilke, and Proust* (New Haven, 1979).
—— *Blindness and Insight: Essays in the Rhetoric of Contemporary Criticism* (2nd edn., Minneapolis, 1983).
—— *The Rhetoric of Romanticism* (New York, 1984).
MARTIN, J. R., *Reclaiming a Conversation: The Ideal of the Educated Woman* (New Haven and London, 1985).
MAZZINI, J., *The Duties of Man and Other Essays* (London, 1907).
MELNICK, A., *Kant's Analogies of Experience* (Chicago and London, 1973).
MEYER, H., *The Poetics of Quotation* (Princeton, 1968).
MILTON, J., *The Poems of John Milton*, ed. J. Carey and A. Fowler (London, 1968).

NEWTON, Sir I., *Philosophiae Naturalis Principia Mathematica* (London, 1687).
NEWTON, J., *An Authentic Narrative of Some Remarkable and Interesting Particulars in the Life of . . .* (6th edn., London, 1786).
—— *Letters to a Wife* (Edinburgh, 1808).
—— *Thoughts upon the African Slave-trade* (London, 1788).
NORRIS, C., *Paul de Man: Deconstruction and the Critique of Aesthetic Ideology* (New York and London, 1988).

OLNEY, J. (ed.), *Autobiography* (Princeton, 1980).

ONORATO, R., *The Character of the Poet* (Princeton, 1971).

ORSINI, G. N. G., *Coleridge and German Idealism* (Carbondale and London, 1969).

OWEN, A. L., *The Famous Druids* (Oxford, 1962).

PAGE, H. A. [JAPP, A. H.,], *Thomas De Quincey: His Life and Writings* (2 vols.; London, 1877).

PAINE, T., *The Rights of Man*, ed. H. Collins (Harmondsworth, 1969).

PALEY, W., *The Principles of Moral and Political Philosophy* (London, 1785).

PARK, M., *Travels in the Interior Districts of Africa . . . in the Years 1795, 1796 and 1797* (2nd edn., London, 1799).

PARKER, P., *Inescapable Romance: Studies in the Poetics of a Mode* (Princeton, 1979).

—— *Literary Fat Ladies: Rhetoric, Gender, Property* (New York and London, 1987).

PARREAUX, A., *Daily Life in England in the Reign of George III* (London, 1966).

PAULSON, R., *Representations of Revolution 1789–1820* (New Haven, 1983).

PIGGOT, S., *The Druids* (London, 1968).

POPE, A., *The Poems of Alexander Pope*, ed. J. Butt *et al.* (9 vols.; New Haven and London, 1961–7).

POULET, G., *Mouvements premiers: Études critiques offertes à Georges Poulet* (Paris, 1972).

—— *Studies in Human Time*, trans. E. Coleman (Baltimore, 1956).

RAWLEY, J. A., *The Transatlantic Slave Trade: A History* (New York and London, 1981).

REED, A. (ed.), *Romanticism and Language* (Ithaca, NY, 1984).

REED, M. L., *Wordsworth: The Chronology of the Early Years, 1770–1799* (Cambridge, Mass., 1967).

REIMAN, D., JAYE, M., and BENNETT, B. (eds.), *The Evidence of the Imagination* (New York, 1978).

RICHARDSON, W., *Essays on Some of Shakespeare's Dramatic Characters* (5th edn., London, 1798).

RICOEUR, P., *Freud and Philosophy*, trans. D. Savage (New Haven, 1970).

ROE, N., *Wordsworth and Coleridge: The Radical Years* (Oxford, 1988).

ROSENMEYER, T. G., *The Green Cabinet: Theocritus and the European Pastoral Lyric* (Berkeley, 1969).

ROUSSEAU, J.-J., *Émile, or On Education*, trans. and ed. A. Bloom (New York, 1979).

—— *Œuvres complètes de Jean-Jacques Rousseau*, ed. B. Gagnebin and M. Raymond (4 vols.; Paris, 1959–69).

SAMMES, A., *Britannia Antiqua Illustrata: or, the Antiquities of Ancient Britain* (London, 1676).

SCHLEGEL, F., *Dialogue on Poetry and Literary Aphorisms*, trans. E. Behler and R. Struc (Philadelphia, 1968).
—— *Friedrich Schlegel's 'Lucinde' and the Fragments*, trans. P. Firchow (Minneapolis, 1971).
SCHNEIDER, B. R., *Wordsworth's Cambridge Education* (Cambridge, 1957).
SCHWARTZ, J., *The Sexual Politics of Jean-Jacques Rousseau* (Chicago and London, 1984).
SHELL, M., *The Economy of Literature* (Baltimore, 1978).
SMITH, N. K., *New Studies in the Philosophy of Descartes* (London, 1952).
SMITH, O., *The Politics of Language, 1791–1819* (Oxford, 1984).
SOLOW, B. L., and ENGERMAN, S. L. (eds.), *British Capitalism and Caribbean Slavery* (Cambridge, 1987).
SPENSER, E., *The Faerie Queene*, ed. A. Hamilton (London, 1977).
STEINER, G., *After Babel* (London, 1975).
STRONG, M., *An Essay on the Usefulness of Mathematical Learning* (2nd edn., Oxford, 1721).
SWIFT, J., *A Tale of a Tub*, ed. A. C. Guthkelch and D. N. Smith (2nd edn., Oxford, 1958).

TAYLOR, E. G. R., *The Mathematical Practitioners of Hanoverian England 1714–1840* (Cambridge, 1966).
TEMPLE, Sir William, *Five Miscellaneous Essays by Sir William Temple*, ed. S. H. Monk (Ann Arbor, 1963).
THEOCRITUS, I., *Greek Pastoral Poetry*, trans. A. Holden (Harmondsworth, 1974).
THOMPSON, T. W., *Wordsworth's Hawkshead*, ed. R. Woof (London, 1970).
TOBIN, J., *Cursory Remarks upon the Reverend Mr Ramsay's Essay on the Treatment and Conversion of African Slaves in the Sugar Colonies* (Bristol, 1785).
—— *A Short Rejoinder to the Reverend Mr Ramsay's Reply with a Word or Two on some other publications of the same tendency* (Bristol, 1787).
TODD, F. M., *Politics and the Poet* (London, 1957).

WALVIN, J., (ed.), *Slavery and British Society 1776–1846* (Baton Rouge, 1982).
WARDLE, R. M., *Hazlitt* (Lincoln, Nebr., 1971).
WATTS, I., *The Knowledge of the heavens and the earth made easy, or, the first principles of astronomy and geography explained by the use of globes and maps* (London, 1726).
WEEVER, J., *Ancient Funerall Monuments* (London, 1631).
WEISKEL, T., *The Romantic Sublime: Studies in the Structure and Psychology of Transcendence* (Baltimore and London, 1976).
WILLIAMS, E., *Capitalism and Slavery* (2nd pr., Chapel Hill, 1945).
WIMSATT, W. K., and POTTLE, F. A. (eds.), *Boswell for the Defense, 1769–1774* (New York, 1959).
WITTREICH, J. A., Jr., *The Romantics on Milton* (Cleveland, Ohio, 1970).

WOLLSTONECRAFT, M., *A Vindication of the Rights of Men* (2nd edn., London, 1790).

—— *A Vindication of the Rights of Woman*, ed. M. Kramnick (Harmondsworth, 1975).

WOOLF, V., *Collected Essays of Virginia Woolf*, ed. L. Woolf (4 vols.; London, 1966–7).

WORDSWORTH, C., *Memoirs of William Wordsworth* (2 vols.; London, 1851).

—— *Social Life at the English Universities in the Eighteenth Century* (Cambridge, 1874).

WORDSWORTH, J., *William Wordsworth: The Borders of Vision* (Oxford, 1982).

WORDSWORTH, W., *The Borderers*, ed. R. Osborn (Ithaca, NY, and London, 1982).

—— *Descriptive Sketches*, ed. E. Birdsall (Ithaca, NY, and London, 1984).

—— *The Letters of William and Dorothy Wordsworth*, ed. E. de Selincourt, 2nd edn., *The Early Years*, rev. C. L. Shaver (Oxford, 1967).

—— *The Poetical Works of William Wordsworth*, ed. E. de Selincourt and H. Darbishire (5 vols.; Oxford, 1940–9).

—— *The Prelude 1799, 1805, 1850*, ed. J. Wordsworth, M. H. Abrams, and S. Gill (New York and London, 1979).

—— *The Prelude*, ed. E. de Selincourt, rev. H. Darbishire (2nd edn., Oxford, 1959).

—— *The Prose Works of William Wordsworth*, ed. W. J. B. Owen and J. W. Smyser (3 vols.; Oxford, 1974).

—— *The Salisbury Plain Poems of William Wordsworth*, ed. S. Gill (Ithaca, NY, 1975).

YEAZELL, R. B. (ed.), *Sex, Politics, and Science in the Nineteenth-Century Novel. Selected Papers from the English Institute* (Baltimore and London, 1986).

Index